INTERNATIONAL BUSINESS

Roger Bennett
BA, MSc (Econ), DPhil
London Guildhall University

M&E
PITMAN
PUBLISHING

London • Hong Kong • Johannesburg • Melbourne • Singapore • Washington DC

PITMAN PUBLISHING
128 Long Acre, London WC2E 9AN

A Division of Pearson Professional Limited

First published in Great Britain 1996

© Pearson Professional Limited 1996

A CIP catalogue record for this book can be obtained from the British Library.

ISBN 0 7121 1058 5

10 9 8 7 6 5 4 3 2 1

Typeset by WestKey Limited, Falmouth, Cornwall
Printed and bound in Great Britain by Bell & Bain, Glasgow

The Publishers' policy is to use paper manufactured from sustainable forests.

CONTENTS

v

PREFACE

International business is a wide-ranging subject that incorporates, *inter alia*, exporting and importing; foreign assembly, manufacturing and sale of goods; the import to one foreign country of items from a second country for subsequent re-export or local sale; the setting-up of permanent establishments in other nations; and the licensing and franchising of a firm's technologies, know-how or production techniques. It is an important area of study that is increasingly prominent in the curricula and syllabuses of business degrees and diplomas and in the programmes of the major professional bodies that examine in the management field.

The problem with international business as an academic discipline from the student point of view is that it is so far-reaching that students frequently need to refer to source materials scattered across textbooks and journal articles in a broad variety of subjects: economics, organisational behaviour, business finance, international marketing, human resources management, and so on. Accordingly, my purpose in writing this book is to collect together into a single volume all the essential topics connected with international business and to present these clearly, concisely, and in an informative and readable way. The text attempts to summarise the extensive literature of international business, focusing on basic principles rather than esoteric techniques. It has, among other things, chapters on the nature of international business, economic and other key commercial environments, cultural influences, international marketing and human resources management, strategy and cross-border operations, and the finance of international trade. The implications for business of West European economic and political integration are also dealt with, together with the prospects and business problems of East European states.

My thanks are due to Rosalind Bailey who word-processed the manuscript, to Adrienne Crossley for research assistance, and to Pitman Publishing for efficiently expediting the production of the book.

1

THE NATURE OF INTERNATIONAL BUSINESS

INTRODUCTION TO INTERNATIONAL BUSINESS

1. Definition of international business

International business involves commercial activities that cross national frontiers. It concerns the international movement of goods, capital, services, employees and technology; importing and exporting; cross-border transactions in intellectual property (patents, trademarks, know-how, copyright materials, etc.) *via* licensing and franchising; investments in physical and financial assets in foreign countries; contract manufacture or assembly of goods abroad for local sale or for export to other nations; buying and selling in foreign countries; the establishment of foreign warehousing and distribution systems; and the import to one foreign country of goods from a second foreign country for subsequent local sale.

All the basic tools and concepts of domestic business management are relevant to international business (for information on these see the M & E text *Management*). However, special problems arise in international business not normally experienced when trading or manufacturing at home. In particular:

- Deals might have to be transacted in foreign languages and under foreign laws, customs and regulations.
- Information on foreign countries needed by a particular firm may be difficult (perhaps impossible) to obtain.
- Foreign currency transactions will be necessary. Exchange rate variations can be very wide and create many problems for international business.
- Numerous cultural differences may have to be taken into account when trading in other nations.
- Control and communication systems are normally more complex for foreign than for domestic operations.
- Risk levels might be higher in foreign markets. The risks of international business include political risks (of foreign governments expropriating the firm's local assets, of war or revolution interfering with trade, or of the imposition of restrictions on importers' abilities to pay for imports); commercial risks (market failure, products or advertisements not appealing to foreign customers, etc.); and financial risks – of adverse movements

in exchange rates, tax changes, high rates of inflation reducing the real value of a company's foreign working capital, and so on.

- International managers require a broader range of management skills than do managers who are only concerned with domestic problems.
- Large amounts of important work might have to be left to intermediaries, consultants and advisers.
- It is more difficult to observe and monitor trends and activities (including competitors' activities) in foreign countries.

Why study international business?

Nowadays the great majority of large enterprises operate internationally (as do an increasing number of small to medium sized firms), so that an awareness of the major issues in international business is a valuable asset for any manager in a company that deals with suppliers, customers, contractors, licensees, etc., in other countries. The study of international business helps the individual supplement his or her knowledge of general business functions (accounting and finance, personnel, marketing, etc.) through examining issues, practices, problems and solutions relating to these functions in foreign states. Also, it develops a person's sensitivity to foreign cultures, values and social norms, thus enabling the individual to adopt broader perspectives and hence improve his or her overall managerial efficiency. Note how firms involved in international business necessarily operate in multifaceted, multicultural environments.

2. Why firms engage in international business

Businesses undertake international operations in order to expand sales, acquire resources from foreign countries, or diversify their activities (Anderson 1993). Specific reasons for doing business abroad include the saturation of domestic markets; discovery of lucrative opportunities in other countries; the need to obtain materials, products or technologies not available in the home nation; increases in the flow of information about conditions in foreign states; desires to expand the volume of a firm's operations in order to obtain economies of scale; or the need to find an outlet for surplus stocks of output. Further motives for operating internationally are as follows:

(a) Commercial risk can be spread across several countries.

(b) Involvement in international business can facilitate the 'experience curve' effect, i.e. cost reductions and efficiency increases attained in consequence of a business acquiring experience of certain types of activity, function or project. These effects differ from economies of scale (see below) in that they result from longer experience of doing something rather than producing a greater volume of output. Moreover, the firm's management is exposed to fresh ideas and different approaches to solving problems. Individual executives develop their general management skills and personal effectiveness; become innovative and adopt broader horizons. All these factors can give a firm a competitive edge in its home country.

(c) Economies of scope (as opposed to economies of scale) might become available. Economies of scale are reductions in unit production costs resulting from large-scale operations. Common examples are discounts obtained on bulk purchases, benefits from the application of the division of labour, integration of processes, the ability to attract high calibre labour and the capacity to establish research and development facilities. Similar benefits might occur from 'economies of scope', i.e. unit cost reductions resulting from a firm undertaking a wide range of activities, and hence being able to provide common services and inputs useful for each activity. Note how economies of scale might not be available if the firm has to modify its products, promotional strategies and business methods substantially for each country in which it operates, and that the extra costs of foreign marketing, establishment of subsidiaries in other countries, market research, etc., could erode the benefits obtained from a higher volume of output.

(d) The costs of new product development could require so much expenditure that the firm is compelled to adopt an international perspective.

(e) There might be intense competition in the home market but little in certain foreign countries.

(f) A company's overall strategies and plans can be anchored against a wider range of (international) opportunities. Sudden collapses in market demand in some countries may be offset by expansions elsewhere.

(g) Cross-border trade is today much easier to organise than in the past. International telephone and fax facilities are much better than previously and facilities for international business travel are more extensive. Hence it is simpler to visit potential foreign customers, partners and/or suppliers, to select the best locations for operations, and thereafter to control international activities.

3. The process of internationalisation

A company's first experience of international business might be the receipt of an unsolicited order from abroad, or a foreign firm offering to supply material or other inputs. Demand for imports or exports might arise from the non-availability from local producers of products possessing certain desired features and/or quality levels from local producers; from price differentials between imported and locally supplied items; or from inefficiencies in local distribution systems that prevent local firms from providing goods. Accordingly, the establishment of an export or import department is for many firms the first step towards wider internationalisation of operations. This involves the recruitment of specialist staff competent in the techniques of foreign trade, in the financing of international transactions, and in shipping and other transport documentation. Staff within the export department must be knowledgeable about various world markets, and will probably be multilingual.

As the work of an import or export department expands, its inadequacy as a vehicle for doing foreign business might become progressively evident. The firm will (or should) have acquired detailed knowledge of business methods in relevant foreign countries and in export/import procedures, and thus might be capable of dispensing with export/import intermediaries. Hence the company may set up its own branches, subsidiaries, and possibly production operations in other countries. It might start conducting its own international marketing research (rather than relying on research agencies), place advertisements directly in foreign media, organise transport to or from foreign destinations (perhaps using its own vehicles), and raise finance from foreign sources. Then the company may license foreign companies to produce its brands, or engage in franchising or local manufacture. Thus it becomes a genuinely international business, although foreign markets are still being served predominantly from the company's home nation and, as yet, no large-scale direct foreign investments have occurred. Nevertheless, the firm is prepared to engage in foreign production, to invest in foreign businesses and to adopt regional perspectives that do not focus on particular nation states. Distinctions between international and domestic perspectives on company operations disappear: all the firm's corporate strategies now possess an international dimension.

The next stage in the internationalisation process might involve the firm undertaking joint ventures with foreign partners and/or establishing substantial permanent presences in other states – each operation having its own employees, premises, warehouse, delivery vehicles, etc., and operating *as if* it were a local firm. Setting up sizeable subsidiaries in other countries enables the firm to project local images in foreign nations, to acquire know-how and technical skills only available locally, reduce production costs (e.g. because of cheaper raw materials or labour), obtain investment grants from foreign governments, and perhaps minimise its worldwide tax liability. A permanent local presence is particularly useful in situations where there are long channels of distribution, where the product is technically complex and requires extensive after-sales support, or where large-scale ongoing advertising and/or sales promotions are required (Calof and Beamish 1995).

As more and more of its activities take place in foreign countries and as sales and profits become critically dependent on world markets, so the business moves towards becoming a genuinely multinational company (MNC), i.e. one that owns production, distribution, service and other units in many nations and (importantly) plans the utilisation of its resources on the global scale (Samiee and Roth 1992). An MNC will seek to maximise its revenues at the world rather than national level, locating its operations wherever conditions are most favourable and regardless of the country in which the company's head office is based. Trade liberalisation, growth in the world economy and easier trans-national transfer of technologies and human and financial resources have greatly stimulated the number and rates of expansion of MNCs over the last 40 years. Their activities are discussed in Chapter 9.

REGIONAL TRADING BLOCS

4. The Triad

Most international trade involves at least one member of the 'Triad' comprising the European Union, the signatories of the North American Free Trade

Agreement (NAFTA), and the Pacific Rim. Within each of these regions there is a concentration of economic activity, affluent consumer markets, and extensive manufacturing potential. The European element of the Triad, is based on the EU, the North American element on the USA, and the Asian element on Japan. Lucrative markets exist in all three pillars of the Triad and to ignore any one of them could sacrifice on enormous volume of potential sales. Increasingly, moreover, there are strata of relatively homogenous customer types in all three regions, so that the same products can be sold across the world in an essentially similar way. Other important similarities of the core nations of the Triad include aging populations, common tastes and buying habits among the young, high consumer incomes, and rapid rates of technological development within firms.

According to K. Ohmae, large and/or technologically advanced companies need to operate in certain 'lead markets', since new trends, product characterisitics and changes in consumer preference occur in these countries prior to their transfer abroad. Such firms need to be 'where the action is', if only to observe current developments at first hand and to monitor the activities of rival firms. Also, the cost advantage of producing goods in cheap-labour countries and exporting them to NAFTA, the EU or Japan is, Ohmae argues, gradually eroding. The advantages of a company becoming a 'Triad power', as Ohmae puts it, include:

- constant interaction with the world's most important markets
- the ability to develop a universal product attractive to customers throughout the Triad
- the capacity to penetrate very quickly new markets arising within the Triad
- the potential to respond rapidly to competitors' threatening behaviour.

5. Regional economic groupings

Triad domination and the general restructuring of the world economy makes it essential for businesses to look at potential markets in a regional context rather than country by country. Each nation has of course its own particular features, as determined by a specific mix of historical, cultural and behavioural factors. Increasingly, however, similar attitudes and perspectives are found within the same social strata in different countries in a regional group, facilitated by liberalisation of trade and large-scale cross-border movements of capital and labour. More and more, consumers within particular regional blocs are driven by comparable motives, needs and perspectives. Regional economic alliances among nations create huge markets, facilitate cross-border transactions, and enable companies based in the region to obtain economies of scale sufficient to make them competititve in the global market. It is hardly surprising, therefore, that the development of regional trade and economic groupings has been one of the outstanding phenomena of the post-Second World War period, with the European Union leading the way.

Types of economic grouping

The loosest form of economic grouping among nations is the regional co-operation group (RCG) whereby several governments participate in a scheme for developing certain industries across their national frontiers, usually in conjunction with private sector businesses. Each country contributes to the cost and undertakes to purchase a specific amount of the outputs of the industries concerned. More substantial is the 'free trade area', i.e. a grouping of nations which remove trade barriers against each other, but with each member country continuing to determine and apply its own unique set of barriers (tariffs, quotas, etc.) to the entry of imports from outside the free trade area.

'Customs unions' differ from free trade areas in that not only is there free trade within the union, there is also a common external tariff which is applied to imports from the rest of the world. Quotas and other non-tariff barriers are determined by and for the customs union as a whole, not by individual members. The next highest stage is the 'common market', wherein business methods, procedures, rules on competition, etc., are harmonised among member nations and there is free movement within the market of capital and labour as well as goods. Commercial laws drafted by the authorities of the common market override domestic national legislation.

Today there exist around 30 organisations of nation states intended to foster economic co-operation. NAFTA and the European Union are perhaps the best known. For South East Asia there is ASEAN (the Association of South East Asian Nations) which is a free trade area comprising Brunei, Indonesia, Malaysia, Philippines, Singapore and Thailand. South and Central America have three economic groupings: ANCOM, the Andean Common Market (Bolivia, Colombia, Ecuador, Venezuela and Peru); LAIA, the Latin American Integration Association (Argentina, Bolivia, Brazil, Chile, Colombia, Ecuador, Paraguay, Peru, Uruguay and Venezuela) which is a free trade area; and the Central American Common Market (CACM) which comprises Costa Rica, El Salvador, Guatemala, Honduras and Nicaragua. ANCOM is probably the world's most well-developed common market after the EU, although the enormous gap in the national wealth of the better off members (Venezuela, Colombia and Peru) and the other two has created many problems. Hence a two-tier tariff system operates, with the three 'richer' countries having one common external tariff, leaving Bolivia and Ecuador to offer tariff inducements to non-members in order to increase their trade. Within LAIA, Argentina, Brazil, Paraguay and Uruguay have formed a 'Southern Common Market' (known as 'Mercosur') which is seeking to achieve free internal circulation of goods and services, a common external tariff, plus the harmonisation of members' economic and exchange rate policies. Mercosur has a bilateral trade agreement with the USA.

Other important regional economic groupings include the Arab Common Market which comprises Jordan, Iraq, Libya, Kuwait, Syria and Egypt; the 'Gulf Co-operation Council', which operates a common external tariff and has free internal movement of goods, capital and labour within certain Arabian Gulf countries; and the Caribbean Community and Common Market (CARICOM) which was established in 1973 to eliminate customs duties and import restrictions among member nations and to co-ordinate economic policies and development within the area. Although a common market is developing in southern Africa (based on the Republic of South Africa), progress towards economic integration in the rest of non-Arabic Africa has been slow, essentially because:

- There are many conflicts of interest between richer and poorer African nations.
- Political conflicts between African states are common.
- National borders in Africa are often the consequence of agreements between former colonial powers and in no way relate to tribal and ethnic divisions, which exert powerful influences on patterns of trade between African states.
- The frequency of *coups d'états* in certain states has caused neighbours to be reluctant to enter long term-agreements with any one government.

Nevertheless, significant tariff reduction programmes have been implemented by French-speaking African countries via the *Communauté économique de l'Afrique de l'Ouest* (CEAO), which itself belongs to the broader Economic Community of West African States (ECOWAS). The latter has 15 members and the stated aim of full economic integration. It is dominated by Nigeria, which accounts for over 40 per cent of all ECOWAS exports.

6. Implications of the formation of regional economic groupings

International economic integration leads to mutual interdependence among participating nations, with the fortunes of each country depending on the performance of the body as a whole. The main consequence for international management of the formation of regional trading blocs is that business decisions increasingly need to relate to (at least) several countries as a whole and not just to individual nations. In particular, decisions concerning the extents and locations of the subsidiary activities of international businesses will be affected as much by the desires to (i) avoid high common external tariffs, (ii) obtain local investment grants and subsidies, and (iii) satisfy the requirements of regional (rather than national) consumer segments, as by any other consideration. The larger blocs now have the economic and political power to *force* trade liberalisation on previously protectionist countries. Tariffs and so on are likely to fall on a reciprocal basis, leading to *more* rather than less international competition. In the longer term, however, the overall pattern of international trade might shift towards a greater volume of transactions *within* regions rather than between individual nations and the triad of Europe, the USA and Japan, so that countries not belonging to a bloc will be driven towards joining one.

Consequences of the formation of a common market

The specific implications of the formation of a common market include:

(a) Creation of new trade within the bloc, possibly at the expense of trade with the rest of the world (although the latter might actually increase in consequence of economic growth stimulated by increased intra-bloc commerical transactions).

(b) Pressures on exporters to the bloc to reduce their prices as common external tariffs are imposed. Exporters may decide to cut their prices in order to remain competitive.

(c) Availability of economies of scale within the bloc because of the larger market.

(d) Increased inward direct investment from non-bloc companies seeking to avoid common external tariffs.

(e) Removal of many of the risks of exporting from one member state to another (impositions of trade barriers, exchange controls, etc.).

(f) More competition within national markets, leading to a levelling out of product prices in various countries.

(g) Increased levels of cross-border mergers, acquisitions and technology transfer.

Common markets are being formed in the poorer regions of the world for a number of reasons. Production of items within the bloc that would otherwise be imported is stimulated; foreign investment is encouraged; and 'infant industries' may be protected from competition from non-common market states.

INTERNATIONAL ORGANISATIONS

The work of a number of international organisations affects the conduct of international business. Organisations connected with the European Union are examined in Chapter 2. Other important international organisations are discussed below.

7. The Organisation for Economic Co-operation and Development (OECD)

Since 1961 the OECD has provided a forum for the government representatives of the world's industrialised democracies to discuss and attempt to co-ordinate their economic policies. OECD has over 200 specialised bodies that conduct research and prepare statistics on aspects of economic and social policy. Civil servants of member countries serve on these bodies. The Organisation's governing body (comprising Ministers from member states) meets about once a year. OECD seeks to expand international trade and to encourage member countries to give economic assistance to underdeveloped nations. It has huge statistical resources and, as well as publishing extensive statistical data on member states, uses these to prepare semi-annual short-term forecasts (i.e. of 12 to 18 months in the future) of members' economic prospects.

The group of ten (G-10)

This was established in 1962 by ten leading OECD countries which agreed to lend US $6 billion to the International Monetary Fund (see 9). G-10 acts as a forum for discussing international monetary arrangements and liaises with the Bank for International Settlements (see 11). A subset of the seven largest members of G-10 is known as G-7, the heads of state of which meet periodically to review world economic and political problems.

8. The World Trade Organisation (WTO)

Prior to 1994 the World Trade Organisation was known as the General Agreement on Tariffs and Trade (GATT). It is a Geneva-based institution founded in

1947 to encourage multilateral (as opposed to bilateral) trade and to minimise tariff levels and non-tariff trade barriers. Its 116 members include all the industrialised nations, over 70 developing countries, and a number of East European states. To date there have been eight rounds of negotiation (the eighth being referred to as the 'Uruguay round'), resulting in 180 treaties. WTO rules now cover 90 per cent of world trade, and are based on the following principles:

(1) *Non-discrimination*, meaning that each member country must apply the same rates of tariff to imports from all member nations, although customs unions and free-trade areas are permitted and special arrangements apply to underdeveloped countries (*see* **9**). This principle is sometimes referred to as the application of 'Most Favoured Nation' treatment to all WTO members.

(2) *Resolution of disputes via consulation*, though note that the 'dumping' of exports at less than their cost of production may be counteracted by retaliatory measures targeted at the offending country.

(3) *Non-legality of quantitative restrictions on imports*, unless a country is economically underdeveloped, is experiencing severe balance of payments difficulties, or if an agricultural or fisheries product is involved.

Countries in dispute first try to settle their problems bilaterally. If this fails, a working party is convened to investigate the matter and make a recommendation. Should the offending nation ignore the recommendation the aggrieved country is permitted to retaliate.

The Uruguay settlement

Conclusion of the Uruguay Round in December 1993 created the most significant trade agreement in GATT's history. Tariffs will fall by an average 40 per cent throughout the world by the year 2000. The USA and the EU each cut tariffs on the other's product by 50 per cent immediately, with more cuts to follow. GATT itself was restructured, renamed as the 'World Trade Organisation', and its powers extended. The deal included new measures relating to (i) the protection of intellectual property and the prohibition of trade in counterfeit goods, (ii) the reform of national agricultural subisidies, and (iii) trade in services.

In relation to intellectual property the Uruguay settlement provides for the following:

(a) Patent protection for 20 years regardless of where an item is invented or whether it is imported or locally produced.

(b) Limitations on the use of compulsory licensing (*see* **11:10**) for patented products (licences are easily obtained in some underdeveloped countries).

(c) Copyright protection for at least 50 years from the creator's death. This is to include computer software and compiled databases.

(d) All countries will have to introduce laws to prevent the unauthorised disclosure of trade secrets.

(e) Provision of equal treatment for domestic and foreign intellectual property holders.

Developed countries were given one year in which to introduce appropriate legislation, developing nations have five years, and the poorest countries ten years. However the latter were required to allow the filing of patents from 1995 and their implementation ten years following the date they were filed.

Benefits and problems of the WTO

Since 1947 GATT has reduced international tariff levels significantly across a wide range of products. It has encouraged 'good behaviour' in the conduct of international trade, and led to much useful dialogue and communication among nations. Fresh measures prejudicial to international trade (other than a number of hidden non-tariff barriers) have not been initiated since the first GATT negotiations. The European Union in particular will benefit enormously from the 1993 agreement in a number of areas, including:

(a) The extension of WTO rules to cover trade in services (notably banking, insurance and telecommunications), which today accounts for 20 per cent of all international trade by value. Note how private sector services now contribute just under 50 per cent of the EU's aggregate GDP and employ 42 per cent of all EU workers. Industry, conversely, provides just a third of total GDP and 32 per cent of employment.

(b) The opening up of world markets (especially in North America and Australia) to European exports of agricultural products, natural resources, and textiles originating in Italy, Greece and Portugal.

(c) Significant international tariff reductions for chemicals, pharmaceuticals, scientific equipment and spirits – all of which the EU exports in large quantity.

(d) The limits that will be placed on national governments' capacities to subsidise inefficient local industries.

Apart from the ongoing debate on the degree to which the principle of reciprocity should be applied, the main problems associated with the WTO are that:

(a) The wording of the original 1947 GATT agreement is vague and complicated, making it quite easy to circumvent commitments.

(b) The WTO cannot *itself* impose sanctions.

(c) Policing the use of hidden non-tariff barriers has proven difficult. As soon as one variety of hidden barrier is outlawed, another might be invented.

(d) An increasing number of governments outside the major trade blocs are currently advocating *bilateral* trade treaties as a means for counteracting the power of the regional trade groupings. To the extent that bilateral agreements are concluded they undermine WTO's position and international influence.

(e) Underdeveloped countries have been just as unwilling to renounce excessively protectionist import controls as have economically advanced nations been reluctant to accept more Third World imports.

(f) Rule changes require a two thirds majority of members. There is one vote one country regardless of the sizes of the voting nations.

9. The United Nations (UN)

Established in 1945, the UN aims to maintain international peace and security and to develop international co-operation on economic, social and cultural matters. In its economic role the UN operates through a number of funds and agencies, e.g. the International Monetary Fund, the World Bank and UNCITRAL (*see* below). UN headquarters are in New York, but some of the agencies are located in other countries.

The International Monetary Fund (IMF)

This United Nations body commenced operations in 1947 to facilitate an international system of fixed exchange rates. Each country deposited with the IMF a certain amount of its own domestic currency (known as its 'quota') so that the IMF accumulated a large pool of foreign exchange. Countries in balance of payments difficulties could then purchase from the IMF foreign currencies up to 200 per cent of the value of their quotas, using their own domestic currency in exchange. All currencies were fixed in value against the US dollar, which acted as the cornerstone of the system. By the early 1970s, however, the system of fixed exchange rates had collapsed due to exchange rate speculation, the regular devaluation of important currencies, and persistent balance of payments deficits on the part of some nations (matched by equally persistent surpluses run by others), and flexible exchange rates became the norm. Thereafter the IMF's role increasingly focused on Third World issues. Loan packages for underdeveloped countries have been organised and special foreign currency drawing facilities arranged. These packages have been criticised for the strings the IMF attached to them, requiring economically poor countries to impose draconian deflationary policies (which caused large-scale unemployment and falling living standards), to improve industrial productivity and reduce the rampant inflation common in recipient nations.

The United Nations Conference on Trade and Development (UNCTAD)

UNCTAD was formed in 1964 as a permanent body attached to the UN General Assembly. The essential reason for its creation was the dissatisfaction expressed by underdeveloped countries about the operation of GATT (*see* 8) and in particular GATT's application of the principle of reciprocity, i.e. that underdeveloped as well as economically advanced nations were required to reduce tariffs, even though this worsened the balance of payments positions and foreign exchange shortages of poorer states. UNCTAD's main role is to act as a pressure group representing Third World interests. Its successes have included:

- Implementation of the Generalised System of Preferences (GSP) whereby the export of most categories of manufactured industrial product from underdeveloped to developed countries receive duty-free treatment
- International action to create a fund to help stabilise the prices of exports of primary commodities from developing nations
- A significant reduction in shipping prices for exports from Third World countries.

The International Bank for Reconstruction and Development (IBRD)

Generally known as the 'World Bank', this offshoot of the United Nations began in 1946 and is the world's largest international lending institution. The Bank borrows in the international capital markets and lends to developing countries at fixed rates of interest. These loans have been criticised for the harsh domestic austerity programmes that the Bank insists be implemented by recipient countries.

10. The International Labour Organisation (ILO)

Industrially developed nations have for many years attempted to establish internationally agreed norms and standards of behaviour for the conduct of employee relations. The primary motive for this was to ensure that no one country would compete unfairly against its rivals through reducing labour conditions within its industries to unacceptably low levels. Standards themselves relate to minimum conditions for people at work and to social security for those who are unemployed. With the exception of EU Directives and Regulations, standards are voluntary unless formally incorporated into the laws of particular member countries. Often, governments prepare codes of practice based on the recommendations of international standards setting bodies.

The ILO was founded in 1919 and is the most important body concerned with setting labour standards. Its constitution requires the ILO to:

- encourage the improvement of the conditions of workers
- discourage particular countries from failing to adopt humane conditions of labour
- promote the principle that labour not be regarded as a mere 'commodity or article of commerce'
- support the view that the price of labour be determined by human need and that workers are entitled to a reasonable standard of living.

Each ILO member nation sends two government representatives, one employer representative and one trade union representative, to the ILO Conference which meets annually in Geneva. Conference debates and accepts or rejects recommendations put to it. Examples of recommendations accepted by the ILO Conference are that:

- there be freedom of association in all member countries
- workers have the right to strike
- specific health and safety measures be obligatory in certain industries
- recognised trade unions have the right to conduct activities on employers' premises
- employees be protected from dismissal for trade union membership.

The obvious problem facing the ILO is that national governments will only adopt an ILO recommendation if it corresponds with current government policy. Otherwise it will be ignored, or left to collective bargaining, or introduced in a greatly weakened form.

11. The Bank for International Settlements (BIS)

Founded in 1930 the BIS seeks to promote co-operation between the national central banks of the world's developed countries. The main role of the BIS is to help central banks manage and invest their monetary reserves. Each central bank deposits part of its foreign exchange reserves with the BIS, which lends or invests these funds on a short-term basis. The BIS conducts research and publishes statistics.

THEORIES OF INTERNATIONAL TRADE

Theoreticians seek general explanations of phenomena in order to 'see the wood from the trees' and to make sense of what otherwise would be a bewildering array of seemingly random items of information. Theories of international business attempt to answer two questions: why nations trade, and what determines the pattern of international investment. Trade theories are examined in **12** to **15**; possible explanations of direct foreign investment in **16**.

12. Comparative cost theory

In his famous book *The Wealth of Nations* (published in 1776) Adam Smith put forward the theory that international trade would occur in situations where nations had 'absolute advantages' over rival states, i.e. they could produce with a given amount of labour and capital larger outputs of certain items than any other country. The flaw in this argument is that it fails to explain why countries with an absolute disadvantage in all their products (i.e. countries which produce *less* of everything made within the country, using a given amount of labour and capital, than other nations) still engage in international trade. A possible resolution of this question was suggested by the eminent economist David Ricardo, who in 1817 alleged that trade among nations resulted from differences in the 'comparative' advantages of countries in the production of various items, not differences in absolute advantage. Ricardo assumed that the cost of producing any good depended *only* on the amount of labour used in its production, and that firms and workers could not move freely between nations (a reasonable assumption for the early 1800s).

The theory is illustrated by Table 1.1, which shows the time needed to produce two hypothetical items in two different countries. It takes more days of labour to produce both items in country 2 than in country 1, so that country 2 has an absolute disadvantage in the production of each item. Ricardo assumed

Table 1.1

	Item A	Item B
Country 1	3 days labour	4 days labour
Country 2	6 days labour	5 days labour

(importantly) that one unit of item A would be exchanged for one unit of item B, i.e. that a person in country 1 with a single unit of A could sell it to someone in country 2 in return for a single unit of B, and vice versa.

In this example trade will *still* benefit both countries because country A has a comparative advantage in the production of item 1 (it can produce a unit of item 1 in fewer days than it takes to produce item 2) while country B has a comparative advantage in item 2. If country 1 makes and exchanges a unit of A in return for a unit of B from country 2 then it obtains for an outlay of 3 days labour an item that would require 4 days labour if it were produced at home. Equally, country 2 benefits from the transaction as it receives for a cost of 5 days labour an item that would need 6 days if produced domestically. Hence trade is profitable for all concerned.

Although fascinating, Ricardo's solution rests on the severe assumptions that:

- Firms in country 2 cannot move their operations to country 1 where both items can be produced at lower cost.
- Only the amount of labour used in production determines the cost of an item. This ignores the impact of technical advances on the use of capital equipment.
- Items exchange for each other at a predetermined and constant ratio.

Also, the theory does not explain why certain goods are cheaper in certain countries. This issue was addressed by E. Heckscher and B. Ohlin in the 1930s.

13. The Heckscher–Ohlin theory of international trade

According to the Heckscher–Ohlin theory, goods prices differ because production costs differ, and production costs themselves depend on the amounts and costs of labour, capital and natural resources used when making various products. Each country possesses a specific mix of labour, capital and other 'factor endowments': some have abundant supplies of labour; others are rich in natural resources, etc. If an item embodies a large amount of labour, and if labour is cheap and plentiful in the producing country, then that product will be cheap by international comparison and thus likely to be exported to the rest of the world. In general, a country will export those items which incorporate relatively large amounts of its most abundant factor, and import those products which include relatively small amounts of the factor with which it is least endowed. In other words, differences in factor endowments determine differences in comparative advantage, which themselves shape the pattern of international trade.

14. Empirical performance of international trade theories

The comparative cost, Heckscher–Ohlin and other hypotheses relating to international trade have been tested extensively and, alas, no firm conclusions have emerged. Indeed, much empirical evidence flatly rejects the fundamental propositions of these theories. Extensions and modifications of conventional international trade theory have led to increasingly complex models, which themselves give rise to further problems and contradictory results.

Factors that might confound orthodox trade theories include:

(a) The rapid pace of technological development, which causes national advantage to shift frequently and in unpredictable ways.

(b) Skilful marketing that can increase foreign demand for relatively expensive exported goods.

(c) Governments regularly seeking to improve national balance of payments positions *via* the imposition of tariffs, import and exchange controls, etc.

(d) The fact that trade theories regard nation states as independent trading units. In reality large multinational companies shift goods, services and capital among their subsidiaries in various countries at prices quite different to those at which a firm in one country would sell to a customer in another. This matter is discussed in Chapter 9.

(e) Poorer countries often having national economic development plans which encourage the importation of capital goods that otherwise would not have a market in these nations.

(f) Multinational companies frequently shifting from exporting to particular countries to local production in those countries.

(g) Sparcity and inaccuracy of the information upon which firms base their international trading decisions.

15. The work of Michael Porter

Observing that traditional economic theories fail to explain why certain countries have succeeded in the post-Second World War era, M. E. Porter put forward a fresh hypothesis concerning the basic determinants of the national competitive advantages that lead to international trade. Porter's analysis begins from the following propositions:

(a) The capacity to automate complete production processes means that workforce costs and competencies are not as critically important to successful operations as they once were.

(b) Companies today are increasingly international in outlook and able to shift operations from country to country at will.

(c) The rise of the multinational corporation has broken the link between corporate efficiency and the quality and availability of resources (labour, capital, etc.) within the firm's own country. An MNC is not dependent on the resource base of just one nation; it operates wherever and whenever conditions are favourable.

(d) The workforces and capital market arrangements of many industrialised countries are today broadly comparable, so that companies have greater choice over where they can locate activities. Hence the pressures of supply and demand will tend in the long term to equalise the costs of skilled labour and capital in these countries. Today, automated equipment can easily be substituted for labour, and modern technology enables the creation of synthetic substitutes for expensive raw materials.

These new realities, Porter argues, mean that firms need constantly to seek new sources of competitive advantage. In particular they need to operate internationally in order to fine-tune their competitive strengths and to identify and then remove weaknesses. Selling to the most demanding consumers causes a firm to achieve quality and service levels it would not otherwise attain. The key determinant of contemporary national competitive advantage, Porter suggests, is product and process innovation – not cheap labour or an abundance of natural resources. Indeed, lack of the latter can actually spur a country to a high level of technological innovation.

According to Porter, six sets of variables determine a nation's ability to compete internationally, namely:

(1) Demand conditions: the strength and nature of domestic demand; consumer desires, perceptions and levels of sophistication.
(2) Factor conditions: skilled labour, road and rail infrastructure, natural resources, etc.
(3) Firm strategy, structure and rivalry: the organisation and management of companies and the extent of domestic competition.
(4) Related and supporting industries: extent of supply industries, ancillary business services, input component manufacturers and so on.
(5) Government policies, including rules on business competition, state intervention in industry, regional development, health and education and (importantly) vocational training.
(6) Luck and chance.

Porter analysed data on the world's major industrial and trading nations and arrived at the following conclusions:

(a) Lack of national resources (e.g. of oil, labour, minerals, etc.) can spur a country to a high level of innovation.

(b) To be successful nations must move from having factor-driven to having investment-driven economies, followed by a further move to an innovation-driven economy. The latter contrasts with the 'wealth-driven' economies of certain countries, which have complacent businesses and are in decline despite per capita GDP continuing to rise.

(c) The creation of domestic monopolies through mergers and takeovers creates moribund economic environments that are not conducive to innovation, even though domestic monopolies may have to compete fiercely on the international level.

(d) Nations with governments that have been heavily involved with industries have generally been the least successful.

THEORIES OF INTERNATIONAL INVESTMENT

16. The product life cycle theory of international investment

The product life cycle (PLC) hypothesis asserts that, like people, products are conceived and born, mature, decline and eventually die. Hence, a product has a 'life cycle' comprising a series of stages. The introductory phase is characterised by high expenditures (for market research, test marketing, launch costs, etc.) and possibly by financial losses. Early customers will be attracted by the novelty of the item. Typically, these customers are younger, better educated and more affluent than the rest of the population. No competition is experienced at this stage. There is extensive advertising during the introduction, the aim being to create product awareness and loyalty to the brand.

There should now follow a period of growth, during which conventional consumers begin to purchase the product. Competition appears at this stage. Then the product enters its *maturity* phase. Here the aim is to stabilise market share and make the product attractive (through improvements in design and presentation) to new market segments. Extra features might be added, quality improved, and distribution systems widened. Competition intensifies; appropriate strategies now include extra promotional activity, price cutting to improve market share, and finding new uses for the product. Eventually, the market is saturated and the product enters its phase of *decline*. Public tastes might have altered, or the product may be technically obsolete. Sales and profits fall. The product's life should now be terminated, otherwise increasing amounts of time, effort and resouces will be devoted to the maintenance of a failing product.

It could be, however that, a product that has reached the end of its life cycle in one country may have a fresh lease of life elsewhere. Indeed, L. T. Wells advanced the theory that product life cycles explain the pattern of direct foreign investment in developing countries by western MNCs. According to the argument, an item is introduced to a developing country and, at first, has little or no serious competition. Then the product is imitated by local suppliers so that several companies now sell the item. Hence, product differentiation *via* the addition of new features, provision of service facilities, etc., becomes necessary in order to secure a competitive edge. Local competitors might even improve upon the product and begin to export their versions of it to the originating firm's own country. Competition intensifies, and price cutting occurs until the product is no longer profitable for the foreign exporter to supply. Note how foreign imitators might enjoy lower labour and other local production costs, and spend nothing on new product development. The exporter conversely has to pay transport costs plus import duties. Thus the exporting company is likely to establish its own local manufacturing facilities in order to be able to compete on price with local firms. Also it must quickly create a strong brand image and effective communications with agents and distributors 'in the field'. Thus direct foreign investment (DFI) in less developed economies by firms from richer nations was the only way they could compete against locally based low cost imitating businesses.

Empirical evidence tended to support this theory during the 1950s and early 1960s, but not thereafter, possibly for the following reasons:

(a) New product innovation is today so rapid that product life cycles are too short for it to be worthwhile establishing foreign production facilities dedicated to a particular item.

(b) Although firms in less developed countries may be able to produce products cheaper than western rivals they cannot necessarily transport, market and distribute them efficiently.

(c) In practice, MNCs often launch new products in developed and under-developed countries simultaneously.

(d) MNCs frequently choose low-cost countries as production sites for the worldwide sale of a good, i.e. no production occurs in economically advanced nations.

(e) As alternatives to DFI, Western firms may engage in licensing or contract manufacturing in order to produce goods in less developed countries.

There are, moreover, a number of fundamental problems with the basic PLC hypothesis itself. The length of life of a new product cannot be reliably predicted in advance, and many products cannot be characterised in life cycle terms (basic foodstuffs, or industrial materials for instance). Importantly, variations in marketing effort will affect the durations of life cycle phases and determine the timing of transitions from one stage to the next. Products do not face inevitable death within predetermined periods: the termination of a product's life is very much a management decision. In many cases a product's lifespan may be extended by skilful marketing. Also, management can never be sure of the phase in its life cycle in which a product happens to be at a particular time. How, for instance, could management know that a product is near the start and not the end of its growth phase, or that a fall in sales is a temporary event rather than the start of a product's decline?

The expected demise of a product can become a self-fulfilling reality; management may assume wrongly that sales are about to decline and consequently withdraw resources from the marketing of that product. Hence, in the absence of advertising, merchandising, promotional activity, etc., sales do fall and the product is withdrawn! Yet another problem is the enormous number of (sometimes random) factors that can influence the durations of phases, turning points and levels of sales. Competitors' behaviour may be the primary determinant of the firm's sales, regardless of the age of the product.

17. Market imperfections and monopolistic advantage theories

These assert that large firms engage in international business in order to create near monopoly conditions for their operations. Thus, for example:

- Cross-border patent licensing agreements carve up foreign markets and prevent competition in relation to the patented item.
- Foreign production in countries with very low labour and other costs

followed by the export of the resulting output to the parent company's home nation enables the company to undercut its domestic competitors and drive them out of business.

- Acquisition of foreign sources of raw materials and/or other inputs or of foreign distribution outlets means that the firm 'internalises' the entire procurement, supply and distribution system within a single organisation, hence reducing uncertainties and risks and restricting competition (*see* **18**).

More generally, 'imperfections' in foreign market conditions are said to explain international investment by companies. Stephen Hymer, for example, has argued that firms only invest abroad if they have attributes not possessed by local foreign rivals and there are barriers ('market imperfections') that prevent these rivals from obtaining the attributes of the foreign company. Attributes could relate to economies of scale in production, marketing or organisational management skills; preferential access to finance or raw materials; or the use of a superior technology. These advantages must be of a magnitude sufficient to offset the costs of operating abroad (need to conduct research into the local market, foreign exchange risks, transport costs, etc.) and, subsequent writers have suggested, may be 'firm specific', 'ownership specific', or 'location specific'.

Ownership-specific factors relate to such matters as the extent of a company's share capital, receipt of government grants and subsidies, and proprietary rights over intellectual property. Location-specific advantages include low prices for locally purchased inputs, low transport costs, easy communications, availability of local business support services (advertising agencies, market research firms, etc.), a skilled and low-cost labour force, and the avoidance of trade restrictions imposed by the host country government in order to reduce imports. Other relevant factors are market size and rate of growth and the extent of local competition. Examples of firm-specific advantages are the ownership of well-known brands, special marketing skills, attractive product features, patents, economies of scale or access to capital markets.

18. Dunning's eclectic theory of international production

John Dunning's 'eclectic theory' of foreign investment asserts that the likelihood of a firm investing abroad depends essentially on firm-specific factors, location-specific factors that make it advantageous to invest in a particular country, and 'internalisation' advantages which cause the internal transfer of labour, capital and technical knowledge within the firm to be more cost-effective than using outsiders, such as licensees, import agents, distributors and so on.

Internalisation

Arguably, firms invest directly in other countries in order to cut out the use of (expensive) suppliers and distributors. Hence all stages in the supply process are brought under a common ownership so that the full benefits of research and development can be obtained (by avoiding the use of licensees – *see* 11:6), and working capital better utilised. Also foreign government import regulations might be avoided through producing in a local subsidiary rather than exporting direct. All aspects of marketing will be controlled by the supplying firm, and there are no intermediate sales or value added taxes. Knowledge can be transferred around the company at will. Note however that extra costs have to be incurred by a firm that does things for itself rather than using outsiders. Internal communication and administration costs increase and there are additional costs associated with having to operate in unfamiliar environments.

Problems with theoretical models of DFI

While interesting in themselves, none of the models previously outlined is sufficiently general to explain all aspects of the foreign investment behaviour of international companies. Each theory purports to give reasons for certain investment activities, but contradictory evidence can be advanced against all of them in certain circumstances. The theories are partial and incomplete and adopt different ideological perspectives. In particular, these theories tend to ignore the influences of the psycho-social and other human aspects of international managerial behaviour, and of the governments of nation states. Theories of international investment sometimes contradict each other, and should really be regarded as 'opinions' rather than as theories capable of empirical verification. Arguably, moreover, the field of international business is so complex and fast changing and covers so many disparate elements that no general theory can be valid for very long.

Progress test 1

1. What special problems arise in international business not normally experienced when conducting business at home?

2. How do economies of scope enable a company to obtain a competitive edge?

3. What is 'the Triad'?

4. What is an MNC?

5. Explain the difference between a free trade area and a common market.

6. What is the 'Group of Ten'?

7. What is UNCTAD and what is its role?

8. How does comparative cost trade theory differ from the Heckscher–Ohlin approach?

9. Explain the product life cycle theory of international investment.

10. Define 'internalisation' in the context of Dunning's eclectic theory of international trade.

2

THE EUROPEAN UNION

FUNDAMENTALS

1. Origins and development of the European Union

In 1951 six countries (Belgium, France, West Germany, Italy, Luxembourg and the Netherlands) signed the Treaty of Paris establishing the European Coal and Steel Community (ECSC); an arrangement involving the abolition of import duties on cross-border movements of Coal and Steel within the six countries, while imposing a common external tariff on supplies of these products from the rest of the World. Also, the six member states agreed to co-ordinate their national policies relating to the payment of government subsidies to domestic coal and steel industries, to remove restrictions on the free movement of coal and steel within the ECSC, and to outlaw discriminatory practices that impeded free competition in relation to these goods. The European Economic Community (EEC) was a common market of the same six countries set up in 1957 *via* the Treaty of Rome. A 'common market' is a trading group with tariff-free trade among member states in conjunction with the application of a common external tariff to imports from outside the group. In a common market, quotas and other non-tariff barriers are determined by and for the entire common market, not by individual members. Business laws, rules on competition, etc., are harmonised among member nations and there is free movement within the market of capital and labour as well as goods. Commercial laws drafted by the authorities of the common market override domestic national legislation. This differs from a 'free trade area', which is a grouping of nations which remove trade barriers against each other, but with each member country continuing to determine and apply its own unique set of barriers (tariffs, quotas, etc.) to the entry of imports from other nations that do not belong to the free trade area.

EURATOM (the European Atomic Energy Community) was also constituted in 1957 as a means for developing the peaceful use of nuclear and atomic energy within the six states. Initially, EURATOM, the EEC and ECSC were managed by separate administrative institutions. From 1967 onwards, however, these institutions were merged and the resulting bodies used to manage EURATOM, the ECSC and the EEC, which collectively became known as the 'European Community' (EC). Denmark, the UK and Ireland joined the EC in 1973, followed by Greece in 1981, Spain and Portugal in 1986, and Austria, Finland and Sweden in 1995. Other countries are scheduled to enter in the near future, and many nations have either applied for membership or expressed their wish to accede to the Community (now known as the 'European Union', see below).

The desire for European unification

At least 40 million Europeans (east and west) died in consequence of the two World Wars 1914–18 and 1939–45 (Hartmann 1983). Europe in 1945 was devastated. Mass bombing, occupation by foreign armies, the use of industrial capacity for armaments production rather than for the supply of civilian goods, destruction of the housing stock, disruption of international trade and the collapse of agriculture in many regions had impoverished European nations and left the continent disunited and heavily dependent on US foreign aid. It seemed, moreover, that no West European country had actually gained anything from the war. Much of Germany had been reduced to rubble; France, Benelux and Denmark experienced nearly five years of military occupation; while the United Kingdom (the dominant power of pre-War Western Europe) was in a perilous economic state. Food rationing applied throughout Western Europe until well into the 1950s.

It was obvious to many influential politicians and other important decision makers that the best long-term prospects for peace, economic development and political stability lay in West European integration. Foremost among the advocates of closer economic and political ties between European states was Jean Monnet, the Minister of Planning in the immediate post-Second World War French government of Charles De Gaulle. Monnet had been closely involved in the negotiations for a political union between Britain and France proposed following the invasion of France by Germany in 1940. This union would have entailed common defence and foreign policies as well as the harmonisation of financial and economic activities. The fall of France in June 1940 prevented the union from going ahead although Monnet was able to develop his ideas in subsequent years, culminating in his drafting of the 'Schuman Plan' (named after Robert Schuman, the French Foreign Minister) through which coal and steel production in France and West Germany were to be pooled. Hence neither France nor Germany could dominate the control of these (then) strategically important resources.

2. The Treaty of Paris and the Treaty of Rome

Under the Paris Treaty the production of coal and steel within the ECSC was to be supervised by a 'Council of Ministers' drawn from the six member nations and assisted by a secretariat based in Luxembourg. A Court of Justice to interpret and enforce the Treaty was also established. From the outset the ECSC had its own 'legal personality' to which member countries transferred some of their sovereign rights. The 'High Authority' of the ECSC (of which Monnet was appointed President) was empowered to adopt legally binding 'Decisions'. There was also a 'Common Assembly' to represent the peoples of member states, though it only had an advisory role.

The Treaty of Rome

The Treaty of Rome demanded the free movement of goods, labour, services and capital within the six founding countries; the establishment of common external tariffs on all imported products; the harmonisation of business laws in member countries; and common policies for agriculture, transport and business competition. It is important to note that the precise forms of the common policies were not specified, only that they be devised and implemented. Thus, for example, the way the common agricultural policy developed was not determined by the Treaty of Rome. As with the ECSC the Treaty gave the EEC a distinct legal personality and set up institutions to administer the system: an Assembly (subsequently renamed the European Parliament), a Council of Ministers with the power to legislate, a Court of Justice, and a 'European Commission' (akin to the High Authority of the ECSC). The EURATOM Treaty was signed in Paris on the same day (25 March 1957), EURATOM also had its own autonomous institutions prior to the 'Merger Treaty' effective from 1967. Thereafter the same institutions governed the ECSC, EEC and EURATOM, but derived their powers and functions from whichever Treaty they were acting under at a particular moment in time. Hence the European Commission was technically the 'Commission of the European Communities' (plural) rather than just the Commission of the EEC.

Other key events

A number of other events had a bearing on Europe's progress towards economic and political unification. The Benelux customs union of Belgium, Luxembourg and the Netherlands was formed in 1948, with tariff-free internal trade and a common external tariff. Lessons learned from the Benelux experiment proved invaluable when setting up the European common market. In 1952, Monnet suggested the formation of a 'European Defence Community' and a 'European Political Community', neither of which were implemented, although a wide-ranging Franco-German Co-operation Agreement was signed in 1963.

Dislike of the idea of European political integration was a major factor contributing to the formation in 1958 of the European Free Trade Area (EFTA) by Austria, Denmark, Norway, Portugal, Sweden, Switzerland and the UK. EFTA emerged as a response to the EEC from European countries which wanted free trade, but without further economic unification. All these states subsequently defected to the EU, except for Norway and Switzerland. EFTA now comprises the latter two nations plus Iceland and Liechtenstein (Finland was also a member for a time, prior to it joining the EU in 1995). In 1970 the central banks of the six EC countries agreed a monetary support mechanism, and in 1981 the European Currency Unit was introduced.

3. The Single European Act

All internal import tariffs within the EC had been abolished by 1968, but a number of non-tariff barriers to intra-Community trade persisted, notably national differences in technical standards, rules on public procurement, and the provision of work permits to foreign EC nationals. In 1985, therefore, EC heads of state agreed to accelerate the development of a single European market. This resulted in each EC country implementing in 1986/87 the 'Single European Act' (SEA) *via* their domestic legislatures. The SEA transformed the EC from being little more than a customs union into a genuine single market with complete freedom for Community businesses to set up anywhere in the EC and to engage in cross-border intra-Community trade *as if* they were doing business within a single country. Under the revised terms of operation of the Economic Community the following were to apply:

(a) Free movement of labour, with workers from member nations able (i) to obtain employment and live in any Community state, (ii) to receive unemployment benefit in their chosen country of residence, and (iii) to have equal access to public housing and to education for their children in the adopted nation. Individuals could then retire and continue to live in that country.

(b) Free movement of capital, so that firms and individuals could obtain finance and/or deposit funds anywhere in the Community. All intra-Community exchange controls have now been abolished.

(c) Freedom of establishment for businesses, enabling any EC resident to commence operations (or purchase an existing firm) in any Community state and to compete on equal terms with local enterprises.

(d) Open access to public sector contracts (i.e. supply contracts for national and local governments agencies and publicly owned organisations) for all EC firms.

The Single European Market was to be completed by January 1993. Accordingly, hundreds of measures were initiated in order to dismantle trade barriers between EC nations; remove obstacles to free competition; harmonise technical standards and business procedures; and generally promote European economic integration. Also a number of social initiatives (such as aid for regional development and/or for the retraining of unemployed workers) accompanied the programme with a view to improving living standards and stimulating growth. Qualified majority voting (*see* **16**) was introduced for matters relating to the harmonisation of technical standards and business practices; the free movement of goods, services and capital; freedom of establishment for firms; and the common recognition of the qualifications of workers.

4. The Maastricht Treaty, 1992

This agreement (formally known as the Treaty on European Union) concerned economic and political union. The majority of EC members committed themselves to the introduction of a single European currency by the end of the decade. Britain (and subsequently Denmark) negotiated the right not to adopt the common currency if they so wish, and the UK further refused to accept the European Social Charter (*see* **26**). The Maastricht Treaty also included agreements on common foreign policy and defence, and established a 'Cohesion Fund' to promote economic development in the EC's poorer regions. The EC changed its name to 'European Union' following ratification of the Treaty by member states in 1993.

The Maastricht Protocol

A version of the European Social Charter was included as a separate chapter of the proposed Maastricht Agreement. Britain used its veto to prevent acceptance of this 'Social Chapter', but the (then) other eleven countries wished to go ahead. Accordingly, all 12 countries agreed that the EU eleven excluding the UK could use EU procedures and institutions to implement the Social Chapter, with the UK 'dropping out' of deliberations and discussions on these matters and not being obliged to apply decisions arrived at by the other eleven states.

5. How the EU is financed

The annual budget of the European Union averages about one per cent of its aggregate gross domestic product and around three per cent of EU member countries' combined budgetary expenditure. Each year's budget has to be approved by the Council of Ministers (*see* 7) and the European Parliament (*see* 9). Collection of EU budget revenues is based on the 'principle of own resources', the money coming from:

- Customs duties collected by each member country from the common external tariff.
- Agricultural levies.
- Up to one per cent of a country's VAT receipts on certain goods and services.

The above funds are deemed to belong to the EU, not national governments – which in effect act as tax collectors for the Union.

Agricultural support and the common fisheries policy absorb the bulk of the EU budget. Otherwise the money is spent on regional development (accounting for about 12 per cent of total budgetary expenditure), the 'European Social Fund' (two per cent), the Social Cohesion Fund (two per cent), plus a variety of lesser Funds and support programmes (e.g. for research and technical development). The Social Fund is intended to help reduce youth unemployment and encourage vocational training; the Cohesion Fund was set up in 1992 to improve the economic and industrial infrastructures of less-developed EU nations, especially in relation to transport systems and the physical environment.

The budgetary process

The budgetary process is as follows:

(a) By May of each year the European Commission calculates the percentage rate by which 'compulsory' expenditure (*see* 10) needs to be increased.

(b) By July the main EU institutions (Parliament, the Commission, the ECJ, the Court of Auditors and ECOSOC – see below) submit estimates of their expenditures for the following year.

(c) In September the Commission prepares a preliminary draft budget and places this before the Council of Ministers, which has to adopt it (by qualified majority voting if appropriate) by early October.

(d) The draft budget must be handed over to the European Parliament within 45 days, and changes may be recommended. These suggestions have to be considered by the Council of Ministers within 15 days. The draft now returns to Parliament, where it is accepted or rejected. If the budget is thrown out a fresh draft needs to be submitted.

Criticisms of the EU budget

Critics of EU budgetary systems allege that far too much money is spent on the common agricultural policy (CAP) and not enough on regional and industrial development; that there is little budgetary discipline (spending seems constantly to expand); that costs will soar as poorer countries from Eastern Europe and the Mediterranean join the Union (all requiring big subsidies from the rest of the EU); and that the national distribution of contributions to the budget is grossly unfair. For example, the UK is one of the less well off members of the EU, yet is one of its largest financial contributors. This is because the country's agricultural sector is small and efficient and hence receives relatively little from the CAP, and because Britain is a major international trader so that it imports large amounts of goods from non-EU sources (a significant part of the duties on these imports have to be turned over to the EU). The counter-argument to complaints about the extent of the UK contribution is that such duties actually 'belong' to the EU and not the United Kingdom, i.e. that they are the EU's *own resources*.

EU INSTITUTIONS

The principal EU institutions are the European Commission, the Council of Ministers, the European Court of Justice, and the European Parliament. Additionally there are three major EU committees (the Economic and Social Committee, the Consumer Consultative Council, and the Committee of the Regions) plus two support organisations: the Court of Auditors and the European Investment Bank.

6. The European Commission

Located in Brussels the European Commission is effectively the civil service of the EU. There are 20 Commissioners. Germany, Spain, France, Italy and the United Kingdom each contribute two Commissioners; other countries contribute one. National governments select their countries' Commissioners, in 'common accord' with other member countries and with the approval of the European Parliament. Appointments are for (renewable) five-year terms. Most Commissioners are ex-politicians, although former trade union leaders and business people sometimes serve. The President of the Commission has to be agreed by the governments of all EU states. Once appointed, Commissioners are obliged to adopt pan-EU rather than nationalistic perspectives.

Each Commissioner has a specific area of responsibility and is advised and assisted by around half a dozen personal appointees. The distribution of responsibilities is determined by the Commission itself, by majority vote if necessary. Commissioners meet on a weekly basis in a 'College of Commissioners' at which important decisions are taken. Staff reporting to the Commission (of which there are nearly 14000) are organised into Directorates-General, which are then placed into groups for allocation to the responsibility of particular commissioners. Examples of Directorates-General are DG II (Economic and Financial Affairs), DG VI (Agriculture), DG XII (Science and Research and Development), and DG XVII (Energy).

The Commission's role is threefold:

(i) to plan policies arising from the Treaty of Rome, the Single European Act, the Maastricht Agreement and other relevant Treaties and hence to initiate proposals to the Council of Ministers (*see* 7) for new Directives and Regulations;

(ii) to implement decisions taken by the Council of Ministers; accordingly, the Commission drafts the annual EU budget (which it then places before the Council of Ministers and the European Parliament), administers the various funds established by the EU (the social and regional funds for example), and negotiates international agreements on behalf of the Union;

(iii) to act as the guardian of EU Treaties; in this capacity the Commission is empowered to take member states to the European Court of Justice (*see* 9) if they fail to comply with EU legislation, and will mediate disputes between member states' governments. The Commission has a limited power to legislate in its own right in the field of competition policy, and may impose fines on companies that violate EU competition regulations. Decisions within the Commission are taken via *simple* majority voting.

The Commission is advised by a network of committees, of which there are two sorts:

(i) *Expert committees* comprising specialists and technical experts nominated by national governments. Some of these committees meet on a periodic basis, others are essentially *ad hoc*. Examples of expert committees are the Advisory Committee on Restrictive Practices and Dominant Positions and the Advisory Committee on Action for the Elderly.

(ii) *Consultative committees* made up of representatives of interest groups. These are organised, chaired, and funded by the Commission itself without reference to national governments. UNICE and ETUC are examples of organisations that contribute members to consultative committees.

Criticisms of the Commission are that:

- It has too much power (possibly because other EU institutions have failed to provide firm leadership).
- Although nominally independent, Commissioners do in fact possess national and political allegiances which might influence their judgement.
- At the time they are appointed Commissioners are typically drawn from the ranks of the political parties that currently form the governments of member states. Governments change, however, so that the political complexion of the Commission at any given moment might not reflect political opinion in member nations.

7. The Council of Ministers

This is the major decision-making body of the European Union and consists of representatives of the governments of each EU country. Membership of the Council is constantly changing according to the subject being discussed. Thus, for example, the Council will comprise Ministers of Transport when transport matters are under consideration; Ministers of Agriculture when agricultural topics are being discussed, and so on. Ministers from Austria and Sweden have four votes each, the Finnish representative has three votes. Luxembourg has two votes; Denmark, Finland and Ireland three; Austria and Sweden four; Belgium, Greece, the Netherlands and Portugal five; Spain eight; and France, Germany, Italy and the UK ten. The Council has a rotating presidency with member nations taking turns, in alphabetical order, to assume this role for six-month periods.

Holding the Presidency is a serious matter, since it involves, *inter alia:*

- seeking consensus among member nations on recent EU initiatives
- arranging, setting agendas for and chairing all Council meetings
- proposing compromises when disputes arise
- representing the Council in dealings with non-member countries and non-EU institutions
- ensuring consistency in the development of EU policies; this is facilitated by a 'Troika' arrangement involving meetings between representatives of the current, preceding and immediately forthcoming Presidencies
- advancing the interests of the European Union.

Council meets normally between 90 and 100 times a year. It has its own Secretariat and a staff of around 2000 people.

Support and administrative work for the Council of Ministers is provided by COREPER (the Committee of Permanent Representatives) comprising the Ambassadors to the EU of the member countries, assisted by their advisers and national civil servants. The role of the Council of Ministers is to create Directives and Regulations (which are legally binding on all member states), according to the procedure outlined in **16**.

8. The European Council

This is not to be confused with the Council of Ministers, as the 'European Council' is in fact the name given to the summit meetings of EU heads of state that occur twice each year. The President of the European Commission and the Ministers for Foreign Affairs of all member states assist at these meetings, which aim to establish an overall strategic direction for the European Union.

The requirement for the European Council to meet at least twice-yearly is embodied within Article 2 of the Single European Act, although no specific powers or functions are mentioned. In practice, however, meetings of the European Council are *extremely* important for the determination of EU policy.

Council itself is chaired by the head of government of the state currently holding the Presidency of the Council of Ministers. Representatives of this country are responsible for preparing European Council meetings. Hence the chair can influence the composition of agendas and the degree of vigour with which certain items are discussed. Apart from matters raised by the chair, agenda items normally include:

- the current state of the European economy
- proposals put forward by the European Commission
- matters that the Council of Ministers has been unable to resolve
- urgent issues in the field of international relations, e.g. emergency famine relief, breakdowns in multilateral trade negotiations, military assistance to the United Nations, and so on.

Periodically, agenda items concerning the enlargement of the European Union and/or institutional and constitutional reform also require attention.

The advantage the European Council enjoys over the European Commission and the Council of Ministers is its ability to determine for itself what it will do and how it will develop. Decisions are taken at the highest possible level and, once finalised, they are sure to be implemented. Disadvantages include lack of formal procedures, and possible domination of meetings by political posturing more concerned with impressing national electorates than with advancing the interests of the EU. Arguably, moreover, the Council has undermined the European Commission's authority in relation to the initiation of policies, and is making it difficult for the European Parliament to extend its role.

9. The European Court of Justice (ECJ)

This comprises one judge from each member state. Additionally Germany, France, Italy, Spain and the UK each supply one Advocate-General: the other states collectively rotate three Advocates-General. As the European Union is enlarged, then whenever there is an even number of member countries the larger countries will participate in a system involving the rotation of an extra judge. Appointments are for (renewable) six-year terms, with partial replacement every three years. An important difference between the ECJ and English legal system is that whereas in the latter judges are selected from barristers, the ECJ contains judges from other countries who were appointed from a much wider field, including university academics.

Advocates-General have the same status as judges. Their role is specified by Article 166 of the Treaty of Rome as that of 'making impartially and independently reasoned submissions in open court on cases brought before the ECJ in order to assist the Court in the performance of its duties'. The post is derived from the French legal tradition and has no counterpart in English law. An Advocate-General will digest all the facts of a case as would a judge, and then states his or her opinion prior to the judges hearing the case reaching their decision. A single judgement is given by the ECJ, without any statement of dissenting views.

The working language of the ECJ is French, reflecting the heavy influence of the French legal system on the Court's administrative procedures. The Court sits in Luxembourg.

ECJ procedures

These are intended to be as informal and straightforward as possible. Much of the Court's work is conducted through written communications, rather than requiring the attendance of large numbers of people at the Court's premises. An action begins with an application by the plaintiff stating the subject matter of the dispute, the grounds of the action and the remedy sought. The Court's Registry translates this into appropriate languages and notifies the defendant and other interested parties. Defendants must lodge their defences within a month of the date of service of the application. Cases are conducted in the language chosen by the applicant. There are no Court fees.

One of the judges hearing the case is appointed the *Juge-Rapporteur*. This person prepares a preliminary report suggesting how the case should be handled. Expert witnesses may now offer opinions; documents relevant to the case are examined. The Juge-Rapporteur then presents to the Court a summary of the facts and of the parties' arguments. Next, each party presents its written pleadings, which are translated into French plus any other necessary language and distributed to Court members. There is a brief oral hearing, followed by a statement of opinion by an Advocate-General. The Court now deliberates on the case and delivers a judgement.

Prior to the enlargement of the European Union in 1995 full Court sittings required an odd number of judges, with a quorum of seven (or three for lesser cases heard in Chambers) although this is due to alter according to the number of countries actually joining the Union. Decisions are by majority vote, The Court's jurisdiction extends to disputes between member states; between the European Union and member states; between individuals and corporate bodies; appeals against decisions by the highest Courts of member countries, plus matters arising from the interpretation of EU Treaties. Much of the work of the ECJ concerns allegations of non-compliance with EU legislation, especially in the field of business competition. Since 1995 the Court has had the power to fine member nations for not respecting its judgements. There is no appeal against an ECJ ruling, which is legally binding in all member countries (possibly overriding national Court decisions or government legislation). Cases may be referred to the European Court by individuals, national Courts or governments, by the European Commission, or by the Council of Ministers. The Court is also willing to act as an independent arbitrator. Legal aid is available to persons or organisations wishing to use the Court, at the latter's discretion.

The Court of First Instance

So heavy was the workload of the ECJ that a 'Court of First Instance' was established in 1989 to hear cases mainly involving competition law, damages actions brought by individuals, and actions initiated by officials of the European Commission. Each member country contributes one member to the Court, the decisions of which are subject to appeal to the ECJ on (only) points of law.

Advantages and problems of the ECJ

The ECJ provides the individual with an extra possibility for appeal against potentially biased judgements in national legal systems. Its rulings are final and the Court has been generally effective in ensuring that EU Treaties and legislation are actually applied. Increasingly, however, litigants in test cases in national Courts assume they will have to go to the EJC for the ultimate decision on an issue. Arguably this undermines and makes irrelevant the work of national legal systems in relation to important matters of legal principle. The ECJ has been criticised, moreover, for the long periods that elapse prior to cases reaching Court, and for not having a sufficient range of sanctions.

10. The European Parliament

The original European Parliament (known as the 'European Assembly') was not democratically elected at all. Rather, its membership was nominated by the governments of EEC member countries with a remit of exercising an advisory and overall supervisory role. This was justified by the EEC's founding fathers on the grounds that during the Community's early years it was essential to have strong central control by the Council of Ministers; otherwise little would ever get done. Another argument for restricting the European Parliament's role is that democratic decision making already occurs through national Parliaments and hence through the Council of Ministers. Nevertheless, it was recognised that the EEC would eventually need a democratic governing body, so the powers of the European Parliament have been increased systematically over time.

Today the European Parliament is directly elected by the people of the European Union although it is not (at the time of writing) a law-making body as such. Rather, it acts as a forum for discussion and gives its opinions on proposals referred to it (compulsorily) by the European Commission. Also, Parliament has the powers:

- to dismiss the European Commission *via* a vote of censure that obtains at least a two-thirds majority of the votes cast (the larger EU countries have more members of the European Parliament than the smaller nations)
- to change or reject the annual draft budget of the EU. Note however that Parliament's ability to *change* the budget only applies to 'non-compulsory' expenditure, i.e. that which is not the consequence of EU legislation. This includes social, regional and industrial policies and covers about 40 per cent of the total EU budget. 'Compulsory' expenditure, conversely, is that committed under the Treaty of Rome or as a result of EU legislation, e.g. spending on the common agricultural policy. The Parliament may only propose alterations to this type of expenditure: final decisions are taken by the Council of Ministers. However the Parliament may reject the budget *outright* on a two-thirds majority vote. This has never happened: a 'conciliation committee' comprising representatives from the European Parliament and the Council of Ministers exists to try to resolve disagreements before they reach crisis proportions.
- to veto the appointments of new European Commissioners
- to put questions to the European Commission and Council of Ministers and have them answered (the answers are given by Ministers from the country currently holding the presidency of the Commission)
- to advise the European Council, although this advice may be ignored in most subject areas
- to reject major international agreements negotiated by the Commission.

31

There are 624 MEPs. Luxembourg contributes 6 members; Ireland 15; Denmark and Finland 16; Austria 20; Sweden 21; Belgium, Greece and Portugal 25; Netherlands 31; Spain 64; France, Italy and the UK 87; Germany 99. MEPs enjoy the (important) right to be informed about the European Commission's activities. In particular, the Commission is obliged to reply to Parliamentary questions within a specified period. Answers to questions may be written or oral, but all are published in the *Official Journal* of the EU. If a question is put orally then a supplementary question may be asked.

Parliament has numerous standing committees including, *inter alia*, committees on the environment, women's rights, political affairs and the reform of EU institutions. There are in addition temporary and special committees set up on an *ad hoc* basis. Members of the European Commission can be summoned to attend these committees to explain the Commission's position on particular issues. Reports of committees serve as the foundation for the majority of Parliamentary debates. Such reports may be initiated by individual MEPs or by the Council of Ministers.

Criticisms of the European Parliament are that:

(a) It is subject to intense lobbying by outside commercial interests, much of this being done in secret.

(b) As it is an advisory rather than law-making body, all its substantive recommendations have to be considered by other EU institutions. This imposes an enormous administrative strain on these other institutions. For example, the Council of Ministers will typically be considering around 450 EP opinions at any particular moment in time.

(c) Parliament does not have to be consulted by the Council of Ministers on all intended legislation (notably that involving external relations, including trade treaties [Nugent 1994]).

Petitions to the European Parliament

Every EU citizen has the right, individually or collectively, to file a petition with the European Parliament. This commonly occurs in relation to VAT matters, barriers to the free movement of capital, and questions relating to EU law. Parliament has a 'petitions committee' comprising representatives of member countries and political parties selected on a proportional basis. This committee decides whether a petition is admissable and, if so, whether an EU law has been violated. Admissable petitions are then heard by a Parliamentary committee, to which the European Commission may be invited to express an opinion. A Parlimentary 'Resolution' of the petition is then drafted. If the petitioner is not satisfied with the Resolution the matter may be referred to the European Court of Justice.

11. The Economic and Social Committee (ECOSOC)

Also known as 'The Other Assembly' (after its original formal title 'The Economic and Social Consultative Assembly'), ECOSOC is a Brussels-based advisory body comprising representatives of trade unions, professional bodies and other interest groups and which expresses opinions on Commission proposals. ECOSOC emerged from the negotiations preceding the Treaty of Rome. It was a logical development considering that five of the EEC's six founder members (West Germany being the odd country out) already had comparable organisations within their own national systems. Specific reasons for the formation of ECOSOC included:

- recognition of the need for an influential forum in which sectional interests could express their views
- fears that the European Assembly (subsequently the European Parliament) would not be adequate as a vehicle for discussing social issues
- acceptance of the fact that European economic integration implies social change.

Luxembourg contributes 6 members; Denmark, Ireland and Finland 9; Austria and Sweden 11; Belgium, Greece, Portugal and The Netherlands 12; Spain 21; and the remaining countries 24 each. Members are split into three groups representing employers, employees, and 'various other interests'. National governments nominate individuals to serve on ECOSOC, although the Council of Ministers makes the final selection. Members serve on a part-time basis for renewable four-year periods. The chair of ECOSOC rotates between the three groups for two years at a time.

According to the European Commission, ECOSOC exists to 'represent groups of persons active in economic and social life'. It scrutinises Commission proposals and suggests amendments. Members of ECOSOC are in close touch with officials of the Commission and with key people in their own countries. The Committee may issue 'Own-Initiative Opinions' on any subject of relevance to the European Union. As well as expressing opinions, ECOSOC publishes information and reports on issues of contemporary concern, liaises with various international bodies, and organises conferences.

ECOSOC is important because (i) it represents directly the interests of important business groups, (ii) *by statute* it must be consulted on any proposal made by the European Commission that has a social aspect, and (iii) its opinions have to be expressed before the proposal goes to the Council of Ministers. Many European Commission proposals have been amended, or even abandoned, in consequence of referral to ECOSOC.

The Committee meets in plenary session on a monthly basis. Its detailed work is completed by specialist committees. The organisation has eight sections, as shown in Figure 2.1. Sometimes, outside experts are engaged to comment on Commission proposals.

12. The Consumer Consultative Council and the Committee of the Regions

The Consumer Consultative Council has a membership made up of representatives from the EU's major consumer organisations. It serves as a forum for discussion, a medium for conducting research into consumer affairs, and a

Figure 2.1 ECOSOC

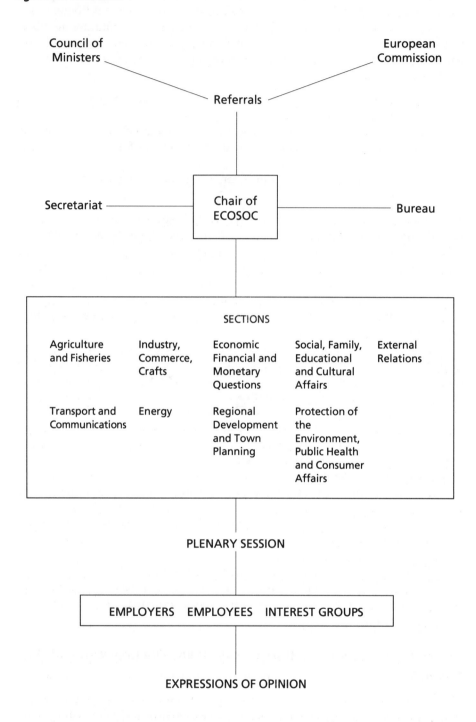

Source: Economic and Social Committee

vehicle for initiating new proposals concerning consumer interests for consideration by the European Commission. The Committee of the Regions is an advisory committee which first met in 1994 and aims to promote regional development and the representation of the interests of the EU's regions. (Prior to enlargement in 1995 the Union had 237 distinct regions.) The national composition of the membership of the Committee is the same as for ECOSOC (*see* 11), with which it shares administrative services.

A number of factors led to the formation of this Committee, in particular:

(a) The very large sums of money being paid to regions in the forms of investment grants, research and development incentives, etc., and hence the need to have regional representation within the organisations responsible for distributing these funds.

(b) The huge variations in wealth and income that occur between the regions of EU member countries. The Union's ten most prosperous regions have three times the level of per capita income of the ten poorest (all of which are in Greece and Portugal).

(c) The possibility of mutually destructive competition between regions as they attempt to attract new business investment.

(d) The reality that regional politicians already lobby EU institutions in a high-powered manner.

Members are appointed by national governments for four-year terms. Although the terms of reference of the Committee of Regions are still evolving, it has to date:

- advised the European Commission on how the EU's Cohesion Fund should be spent; the Cohesion Fund finances economic development in the Union's poorer countries
- expressed opinions on pan-European transport systems and on education and training programmes
- established links with the European Parliament and with industrial and employers' associations.

13. The Court of Auditors

Established in 1977, the Court of Auditors comprises one auditor from each member state and has the following functions:

(a) Examination of the accounts of the EU and all its organisations.

(b) Monitoring the EU's general budget and all EU borrowing and lending.

(c) Ensuring the legality and accuracy of EU financial transactions.

(d) Production of reports on financial misconduct and/or the waste of EU money.

Auditors are appointed by the Council of Ministers for renewable six-year periods.

Each auditor must be professionally qualified in the audit field, and promise to act in the EU's interest independent of national considerations. Members of the Court elect a President who holds the office for a (renewable) three-year term. The Court is situated in Luxembourg and has fewer than 450 employees – a small number considering the extent and importance of its role.

14. The European Investment Bank (EIB)

Based in Luxembourg, the EIB was set up in 1958 to finance capital investment projects intended to develop the economies of the (then) EEC member countries. Today it is one of the largest lending and borrowing institutions in the World. It borrows on the international capital markets and on-lends for projects mainly in the EU's less prosperous regions. The Bank does not seek to make a profit and thus can offer low rates of interest on loans. A maximum of half the cost of a project may be funded. Projects themselves usually involve infrastructure improvement (e.g. telecommunications systems, energy conservation, transport, or environmental protection). The Bank also finances projects in economically underdeveloped countries with which the EU has co-operation agreements, and lends money to East European nations to assist them in their transition to market economies. Its shareholders are the member states of the EU, and its board of governors comprises the Finance Ministers of the EU countries. Executive control lies with the Bank's President and six vice-Presidents, all appointed for renewable six-year terms by the board of governors on the recommendation of a separate part-time board of directors. The latter consists of 21 banking experts: 20 nominated by member states and one by the European Commission.

The Bank is managed according to commercial principles: it is not in the business of dispensing aid. However, because it is non-profit making and itself enjoys a very high credit rating (so that it is able to borrow cheaply) the EIB can lend at extremely attractive rates. Repayments may be deferred for the first couple of years; repayment periods vary from five to 20 years. Normally the Bank is only interested in lending sums of at least 10 million ECU. To qualify for funding, projects must:

- improve economic and social cohesion (typically by contributing to the economic development of underdeveloped regions); *or*
- facilitate the modernisation and hence increased competitiveness of EU industry; *or*
- provide benefits to several EU countries (in the fields of transport or telecommunications for example).

Projects must be technically sound and financially viable (evidenced by adequate security against EIB loans).

15. Criticisms of the European Union

Critics of West European economic and political integration (or the 'Eurosceptics' as they are sometimes called) allege that the EU is inadequate in some or all of the following respects:

(a) The EU is fundamentally undemocratic. Decisions are made and implemented without the debate and the checks and balances characteristic of national political systems.

(b) There is too much bureaucracy and red tape.

(c) National governments lose their sovereignty over basic issues affecting the lives of the citizens they were elected to represent.

(d) No pan-European policy can benefit every EU country to an equal extent. In reality there already exists a 'two-speed' Europe. Certain nations, regions and groups of citizens are bound to lose from the application of pan-European policies.

(e) Too much money is spent on the Common Agricultural Policy, which continues to absorb the bulk of EU expenditures. The CAP is allegedly unfair, inefficient, and encourages waste.

(f) EU Committees, it has been argued, are in reality toothless tigers. The Economic and Social Committee has been particularly criticised for being over-large, bureaucratic, ineffective, and concerned more with uttering patronising statements than with genuinely influencing EU affairs.

(g) Member states differ in relation to how vigorously they enforce EU Directives. Note that the European Commission only employs around 13,000 staff (a third of whom are concerned with translation and interpreting) compared with perhaps 20,000 civil servants employed by a single UK Ministry. Thus the Commission has to rely on national governments to implement and administer agreed EU policies. The Commission itself has been criticised for being excessively bureaucratic and too powerful (it exerts strong influence at all stages in the legislative procedure). Note the enormous complexity of the Commission's role, the need to integrate the activities of people from all the EU member countries, and having to work in (currently) nine different languages. Also the Commission depends heavily on national governments for the supply of information and for investigating allegations of infringements or non-implementation of EU law.

Advocates of greater European integration reply that, in reality, there can be no such thing as absolute national sovereignty in the modern world. International trade is extensive and affects the economic performances of all advanced nations. Every West European country is locked into defence treaties and depends heavily on partners for military assistance. Genuine democracy within the EU can be achieved immediately through giving the European Parliament proper legislative powers. The European Commission, moreover, is in fact the *servant* of the Union, not its master. Its role is simply to suggest, not to approve, new legislation. All major EU decisions require the consent of the Council of Ministers.

Reform of EU institutions

The main overall criticism of EU institutions is perhaps that (apart from the European Parliament) they have remained largely unchanged since they were set up in the 1950s; yet the size of the EU has grown, as have the levels of importance of the decisions taken by various institutions. A number of enquiries have been conducted into how the EU institutions could be reformed (Archer 1994), but few actions have been taken. This is due perhaps to:

- a general reluctance to interfere with systems and procedures that seem to be working reasonably effectively
- fears on the part of national governments that proposed reforms (which would have to be ratified by national Parliaments) might be turned down at the national level amid much political controversy
- resistance to change within the institutions themselves.

LAW-MAKING IN THE EUROPEAN UNION

16. Forms of EU legislation

There are three types of EU legislative measure:

(a) *Regulations*, i.e. laws that apply immediately and equally in all member states.

(b) *Directives*, which specify a necessary outcome (e.g. to achieve equal pay for work of equal value done by men and women) but then allow the government of each member country to introduce its own particular legislation to achieve the desired objective. Every Directive states a time period (usually two years but sometimes longer) within which member states must attain the result required by the Directive. If this does not occur within the designated period an individual may seek to enforce the Directive through his or her national Courts.

(c) *Decisions* of the European Court of Justice, which have the same effect as Regulations.

Additionally, the European Commission issues 'Recommendations' which are not legally binding, but express the Commission's considered opinions about how certain matters should be dealt with. Commission 'Notices' are also important, especially in relation to competition law. These are pronouncements of the European Commission on various matters, such as:

- the legality or otherwise of exclusive dealing contracts with commercial agents
- co-operative joint ventures
- the activities of motor vehicle intermediaries
- exclusive purchasing and distribution agreements.

Although a notice can be withdrawn, and despite the fact that the Commission is not legally bound by the terms of a Notice it has issued, it is unlikely that the Commission could fine a company in relation to a restrictive agreement covered by a Notice.

Today, EU Directives, Regulations, etc., affect most aspects of European business. There are Directives on consumer protection, advertising and cross-border broadcasting, company administration, intellectual property, agency and distribution arrangements, business mergers and acquisitions, working conditions, health and safety, gender equal opportunities in employment, and on numerous other facets of personnel and general business management.

Voting procedures

Unanimity is required for decisions concerning taxation, employment and social protection, social security, employee participation in management decision making, the employment conditions of third country nationals legally working in the EU, and financial measures for job creation. Otherwise, 'qualified majority voting' applies, i.e. each nation casts a number of votes according to the size of its population but, in order to ensure that small countries do not have to surrender vital national interests, a certain threshold number of votes must be exceeded before a proposal can be accepted (this was 54 out of 76 before the enlargement of the Union in 1995).

17. The legislative process

The procedure whereby Directives and Regulations become legally binding on member countries is as follows:

Stage 1 Staff of the European Commission originate a proposal. The idea might have come from a national government, a national or EU level interest group, or from a particular member of the European Commission. The Commission organises a study of the issue, in consultation with national governments and relevant interest groups. ECOSOC and specialist committees of the European Parliament might also be approached on an informal basis. A draft proposal is then put before the Council of Ministers and published in the *Official Journal* (OJ) of the European Union.

Stage 2 The Council of Ministers initiates the 'consultation procedure', i.e. it formally requests the opinions of ECOSOC and the European Parliament. Comments received are published in the OJ, and suggested amendments are referred back to the Commission. A revised proposal may emerge which again goes to ECOSOC and the European Parliament. National governments and interest groups will express opinions on the proposal. COREPER (*see* 7) will arrange a working party to discuss the text of the proposal and make appropriate comments, liaising with the Commission where necessary.

Stage 3 The Council of Ministers adopts a common position on the proposal. This might mean rejection of the proposal, unanimous approval or approval by qualified majority voting if this is permitted for the issue concerned. The proposal now goes before the European Parliament and the 'co-operation procedure' is implemented, as shown in Figure 2.2. Final legislation is published in the OJ. If the Council of Ministers fails to act (see Figure 2.2) the proposal lapses, is dropped, or started again from the beginning.

The procedure has been criticised for being slow and cumbersome. It takes years before proposals become law, and the need to appease so many disparate

Figure 2.2 The co-operation procedure

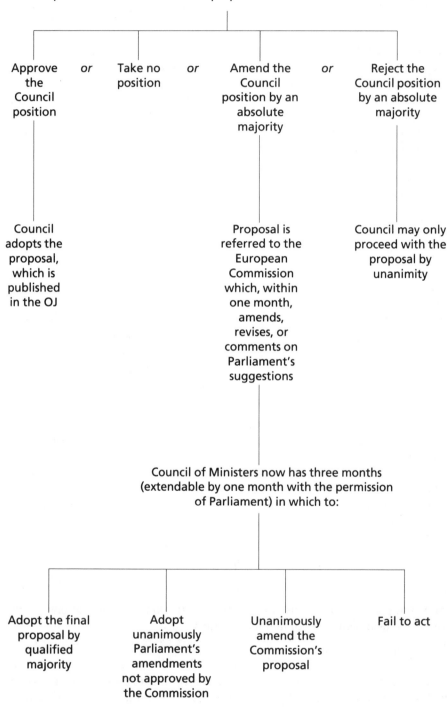

European Parliament receives the proposal and within three months must:

Approve the Council position   *or*   Take no position   *or*   Amend the Council position by an absolute majority   *or*   Reject the Council position by an absolute majority

Council adopts the proposal, which is published in the OJ

Proposal is referred to the European Commission which, within one month, amends, revises, or comments on Parliament's suggestions

Council may only proceed with the proposal by unanimity

Council of Ministers now has three months (extendable by one month with the permission of Parliament) in which to:

Adopt the final proposal by qualified majority

Adopt unanimously Parliament's amendments not approved by the Commission

Unanimously amend the Commission's proposal

Fail to act

national interests arguably results in compromises that satisfy no specific member country.

Subsidiarity

In 1992 the (then) 12 member countries of the EU agreed that the 'principle of subsidiarity' should be applied to EU legislation, i.e. action should not be taken at the Union level if the desired objective could be better achieved through separate government policies implemented by each member state. Thus, the Commission should only initiate proposals for EU legislation where trans-national considerations have to be taken into account, where EU Treaties de-mand pan-Union legislation, where the scale of pan-EU action would facilitate the solution of a problem, or where the harmonization of national laws or practices is essential to achieve agreed EU objectives. It was further decided in 1992 that:

(a) Local difficulties should be resolved by local action, not by EU legislation.

(b) Laws should not be imposed if voluntary co-operation among member countries could achieve similar outcomes.

(c) The actions required by EU laws should be as simple as possible.

(d) Only minimum standards should be set at EU level, leaving each nation to apply more stringent requirements if it so wishes.

(e) The benefits of intended EU laws should be measured against the costs they are likely to impose on EU citizens and local and national governments.

18. Problems with EU legislation

A number of difficulties have been encountered when attempting to devise and implement pan-European Union laws, as follows:

(a) Most Union level laws will be detrimental to at least one EU member, either because it conflicts with national policy or represents such a break with existing practice that it will be more expensive to apply than in nations where it is already embodied (wholly or in part) in domestic legislation. For example, a law com-pelling employers to grant full holiday pay to part-time workers would be expensive to implement in a country where there is no requirement to pay part timers during holidays, yet costless in a nation in which this is compulsory.

(b) The need to negotiate compromises results in long delays (lasting many years in certain cases) in the law-making process.

(c) Unanimity is still required for legislation concerning certain matters.

(d) Some proposed EU legislation has domestic political implications for the governments of a number of member nations.

(e) In general, penalties for breaking EU laws are determined by member states rather than at the Union level. Thus the fine or term of imprisonment for violating a law resulting from an EU Directive (on equal opportunities or insider dealing for example) might vary substantially from country to country.

19. Harmonisation of technical standards

The need to produce several different versions of an item in order to satisfy the disparate technical product standards of various countries has greatly impeded European industry's ability to secure economies of scale in production. Common technical standards across the EU greatly enlarge a supplying company's market size, and stimulate new product development through ensuring that new products which conform to pan-EU technical standards can sell in all EU nations.

There are two Community-level standards-making bodies: CEN (Comité Européen de Normalisation) and CENELEC (Comité Européen de Normalisation Electro-technique). CEN and CENELEC are based in Brussels and represent, in effect, federations of all the national standards-making institutions of the EU. New European standards are adopted through weighted majority voting by the national bodies. Eventually these new standards will replace all existing national specifications. CEN and CENELEC are told by the European Commission which particular standards are to be processed through the system. Then the various national standards authorities (DIN in Germany, AFNOR in France, the UK's BSI, etc.) discuss the matter and agree a joint position. Typically, an existing national standard is used to begin a debate; otherwise an entirely new standard has to be drafted – either by a national standards body, by a small committee of representatives from several national standards bodies, or by an expert outside consultant. In the overwhelming majority of cases however an existing standard will form the initial basis for the fresh specification. Note how the national standards organisations with most pre-existing standards are necessarily the most influential when pan-European standards are being produced. Of all the EU countries, Germany's DIN system has the greatest number of standards on its files, and is the biggest producer of new standards (about 1,400 per year, more than double the annual output of BSI). This makes German DIN standards enormously important within Europe.

Problems experienced when setting standards

The sheer volume of the work that needs to be undertaken, its complexity, and competing national interests have meant that the development and introduction of pan-EU standards have been extremely difficult. Hence the European Commission attempted to improve the situation through (i) the Information Directive of 1983, and (ii) the so called 'New Approach' to technical harmonisation and standards launched in 1985. Under the Information Directive, national standards-making bodies are legally obliged to advise other EU countries prior to their introducing fresh national standards. The standards bodies of the other nations may then study the proposals, comment on them and make recommendations. Obviously, the standards authority of the initiating country has a large incentive to accept these recommendations since their incorporation into the technical specifications of the resulting products will enhance their saleability in other markets. A major consequence of the Directive was to encourage still further the concentration of standards setting into the the hands of just a few national bodies, notably the German DIN, France's AFNOR, and Britain's BSI. Increasingly, national standards produced by these bodies act as pan-European standards, quite apart from European Union considerations.

The New Approach of the EU to technical standards is for the Commission to specify the overall level of safety and other 'essential requirements' that a product must satisfy, and describe (a) how these requirements can be met, and (b) the evidence ('Attestation') needed to prove that requirements have been satisfied for a particular item. Any product that complies is then legally entitled to be sold throughout the EU. However, the actual function of devising detailed standards is undertaken by national standards-making bodies.

Criticisms of the general philosophy of setting technical standards are that (i) excessive harmonisation of standards reduces customer choice and can inhibit the development of new products, and (ii) the creation of pan-European standards might serve merely to strengthen the positions of US, Japanese and other Pacific Rim suppliers through enabling them to increase their competitive strength and facilitate their assault on the European market (non-EU firms benefit from being able to sell an unmodified product right across Europe just as much as EU companies).

20. Lobbying

In view of the enormous importance of EU activities and decisions it is hardly surprising that numerous organisations wish to exert influence on EU affairs. The major lobbyists are businesses (especially multinational companies); political representatives of the EU's poorer regions; and environmental, consumer protection and other interest groups. Of particular importance has been the rise of the 'Euro-group', i.e. a group with members sharing a common interest in several EU countries. The majority of Euro-groups represent various industrial and agricultural sectors (Greenwood 1992). Lobbying can be highly effective. Note that apart from the bundle of measures necessary to implement the Single European Market, less than half the proposals put forward by the European Commission have actually passed into law. Lobbying can occur *via*:

- Members of the European Parliament (MEPs). An MEP will sit on various Parliamentary committees and have many contacts with Commission staff. Committees of the EP hear about proposed legislation at a very early stage. Parliament has an information office that will advise which MEPs have interests in particular areas. MEPs may be seen in their constituencies, in Brussels or in Strasbourg.
- Trade associations, interest groups or MPs in national Parliaments.
- Representations to members of ECOSOC.
- Civil servants in appropriate national Ministries.
- COREPER (at the time that working parties are being formed).
- Professional lobbyists (a sizeable lobbying industry has arisen in Brussels).
- The European Commission itself. Industry associations sometimes arrange meetings between groups of heads of large businesses and European Commissioners and their staff (Mazey and Richardson 1993).

The Commission does not object to lobbying *per se*, because the Commission itself can benefit from the process. Lobbyists might be able to provide useful information which the Commission would otherwise have to gather, possibly at very high cost. Also the Commission needs to 'keep its finger on the pulse' of current events in particular areas, and generally wishes to gain the support of powerful pressure groups when formulating proposals. If the Commission drafts proposals opposed by influential groups then the process of gaining their acceptance by the Council of Ministers could be difficult.

Disadvantages to lobbying are that the better organised and more powerful pressure groups (especially those financed by big business) are bound to exert greater influence than poorly co-ordinated (but equally worthy) lobbyists, that the process is undemocratic, and that it is open to corruption.

UNICE and ETUC

Founded in 1973, ETUC is a confederation of 35 trade union organisations of 20 West European (not just EU) countries. It seeks to influence EU policies on work and employment matters, and has direct representation on the Consumer Consultative Council (see 12). UNICE is a confederation of employers' associations in 22 West European nations. It co-ordinates the views of its members on business and employment issues and lobbies the Commission and other EU institutions. UNICE has a number of policy committees and working groups, a substantial permanent staff, and has been quite successful in influencing EU legislation.

Meetings between ETUC and UNICE have occurred since 1985, promoted by the European Commission *via* the so called *Val Duchesse* dialogue. To date however no tangible outcomes have emerged from these discussions. UNICE has refused to allow itself to become a *de facto* bargaining body responsible in part for determining the direction of EU social policy. ETUC similarly has no desire (or constitutional authority) to negotiate agreements. Hence the social dialogue initiated by the *Val Duchesse* talks have remained purely consultative, and arguably inconsequential (Rhodes 1992).

BUSINESS IMPLICATIONS OF WEST EUROPEAN INTEGRATION

21. Economic factors

As competition within the EU intensifies firms are compelled to use their resources more efficiently, leading inevitably to unemployment in some industries and regions. EU nations have become much more dependent on other member countries for imports and exports than before, and their businesses have a greatly enlarged market. Increased competition should eliminate incompetent managements, reduce consumer prices and stimulate cross-border trade (with consequent improvements in rates of economic growth). Business rationalisations should help European firms compete more effectively in the rest of the world. The pursuit of competitive advantage may lead to more research and technical development and hence to product innovation. A wider choice of products is now available to West European consumers, who may purchase items supplied tariff-free from other EU countries.

Benefits and problems for the individual business

Benefits of European integration for the individual firm include larger markets leading to economies of scale and hence the possibility of developing a business capable of competing with US and Pacific Rim rivals; lower input costs; faster cross-border transmission of new business practices and ideas; and easier access to joint venture partners in other EU countries. No foreign trade documentation is needed for intra-EU transactions, and the cross-border EU transport infrastructure is improving year by year.

Threats to the individual business arising from European economic integration include:

- Reduced market shares for many companies
- A higher level of uncertainty making it difficult to take long-term investment decisions
- Increased possibilities for hostile takeover attempts as competing firms seek to position themselves in the most advantageous market locations
- Entry to existing markets of powerful Japanese and US companies which manufacture locally in order to avoid paying the EU common external tariff
- Potential for price wars, especially as large firms enter new markets previously served only by smaller companies.

22. Further implications for business of West European economic integration

Completion of the European Single Market has numerous implications for EU businesses, including the following:

(a) The need to monitor EU legislation in order to assess whether, and if so to what extent, new Directives or Regulations will affect the firm.

(b) Increased competition in consequence of any EU firm being able to sell its products freely in all EU states.

(c) Access to tariff-free inputs from other EU countries.

(d) Opportunities for the sale of a standardised product across Europe following the introduction of a harmonised technical standard.

(e) The need to conduct market research to establish the nature of consumer tastes and preferences in other EU nations.

(f) The ability to tender for public sector contracts anywhere in the EU.

(g) Mergers and takeovers as firms sell and buy over a wider area and thus seek local subsidiaries to handle their foreign EU activities.

(h) Possibly the need to redesign products to make them suitable for foreign EU markets

(i) Increases in employee benefits and remunerations as the European Social Charter is implemented.

(j) The need to adopt pan-European perspectives when formulating business strategies (*see* **22**).

(k) Fresh training requrements, especially in languages and the business conditions and practices of other EU nations.

(l) The ability to commence or expand operations at will in the lowest cost and most profitable locations in the Union.

(m) Opportunities for the cross-border recruitment of skilled workers.

(n) The need to translate and perhaps redraft sales and purchasing contracts and promotional literature to make them suitable for foreign EU countries.

23. Strategic aspects

European business is dynamic, sophisticated, complex, and altering faster and more extensively than in any other international trading area. Markets are fragmenting into many more sub-units than in the past and there is intense rivalry for domination of markets from efficient low price and aggressive foreign European firms. To succeed in this environment a business must be adaptable, immediately aware of fresh opportunities, able to manage change and, importantly, able to learn from and quickly rectify its mistake. Volatility and the numerous uncertainties connected with the current situation establishes the need for strategies, management styles and organisational systems that are flexible and easily altered to suit the needs of changing conditions. Examples of flexibility include the following:

(a) Alignment of internal business systems (organisational, procurement, staffing, budgeting, marketing, quality control, etc.) to satisfy pan-European operational requirements (Jacquemin and Wright 1993).

(b) Action-oriented strategies rather than fixed quantitative objectives. Strategies should be seen as a sort of route map for guiding the enterprise towards the attainment of its mission, not as a collection of rigid rules. For further information on strategic management see *Corporate Strategy and Business Planning*, published in this series.

(c) Linking strategy with operational management (Brown 1994).

(d) Ensuring that the company's core businesses can cope with environmental turbulence.

(e) Installation of effective management information systems capable of identifying the threats and opportunities arising from the firm's involvement with pan-European trade.

(f) Adoption of genuinely holistic approaches to business operations. Strategies for conducting pan-European business affect the firm in its entirety, cutting across functional and departmental divisions and thus needing to be implemented as a whole.

Among the many strategic decisions that need to be taken by companies engaged in cross-border European trade, the following are especially important:

(a) Market entry strategies: whether to sell direct to foreign EU customers rather than using intermediaries; choices between having branches instead of subsidiaries in various countries (*see* 16:5); licensing, franchising and the protection of intellectual property.

(b) Formation of cross-border joint ventures.

(c) Determination of the depth of market penetration desired, product characteristics and development and (importantly) whether to adopt a differentiated or undifferentiated approach (*see* 17:3).

(d) Financial strategies concerning debt versus equity financing (*see* 15:9), levels of reserves to be held, choice of the countries in which to raise funds, etc. There is an old adage that whereas British companies are in business merely to make profits, German companies exist to produce goods – irrespective of short-term fluctuations in levels of profits or trade. And it is indeed the case that significant differences in perceptions of appropriate company missions and business strategies occur among firms in various European nations.

(e) Organisational design and development strategies involving the selection and implementation of the administrative arrangements best suited to obtain maximum benefit from an enterprise engaged in pan-European trade.

(f) Human resources strategies, incorporating decisions on such matters as:

- The types of managerial recruit best equipped to handle the demands imposed by open pan-European competition, and where to find the best people
- Training expenditures on the management skills required for doing business in European markets. Examples of relevant competencies include language skills; export marketing; logistics and documentation; trading in foreign currencies; familiarity with EU advertising media; knowledge of the contents and implications of relevant EU Directives; and familiarity with EU market structures and business methods.

A combination of offensive and defensive strategies is required. The former for assaulting new markets; for improving, altering and developing products; obtaining EU public sector contracts; entering strategic alliances with foreign European firms; and so on. Defensive measures might be necessary in order to retain domestic market share, cut costs and maintain the keenest local prices, and avoid being taken over by a foreign EU company. Mergers and/or collaborative ventures with other domestic businesses may be essential to develop a critical mass sufficient to fight off increased competition from EU rivals or to operate joint procurement, research or distribution services.

24. Nature of the West European market

The West European market is dominated by a 'golden triangle' (roughly within the area enclosed by Liverpool, Cologne and Paris) that contains more than half the entire EU population, but with a land mass smaller than the UK. The Union itself represents one of the largest and most affluent integrated trading groups in the developed world. It has four really large markets: Germany, France, Italy and the UK. Germany has West Europe's highest population, and is the dominant economic power. Other West European nations have smaller populations but many are, nevertheless, extremely affluent and represent lucrative markets for foreign firms, and even the poorer EU members are experiencing steady long-run economic growth. The outstanding demographic fact pertaining to Western Europe is the low (or zero) rates of growth of population in most nations. This has caused a significant increase in the average age of the West European population and (in consequence) changing attitudes and spending patterns among European consumers. At the same time, younger Europeans are increasingly well educated, with nearly a quarter of the West European population now in some kind of full-time education. Virtually all EU households possess a television set and telephone, and nearly 95 per cent have a refrigerator. Rates of ownership and other key consumer durables are high. An important consequence of West European prosperity is the low number of people per average household in EU countries compared to other states. Typical household size varies between 2.1 and three for all member nations except Ireland, where the average is 3.8. There are 60 United Nations member countries with average household sizes of five or more.

Even before the accession of Sweden, Austria and Finland in 1995, the combined national income of the then 12 EU countries exceeded that of the United States by more than ten per cent and was more than double that of Japan. Germany has Western Europe's highest level of industrial production, followed by France, Italy and the UK. Spain's industrial production is 42 per cent that of France. The Netherlands and Belgium have industrial outputs of 26 per cent and 16 per cent respectively of the French figure. Today Germany accounts for nearly 20 per cent of all European consumer spending (including non-EU and Eastern block countries). France accounts for 13 per cent, and Italy and Britain for 12 per cent each. The European Union is the largest single international trader in the world, accounting for more than a fifth of global imports and exports (compared with about 15 per cent for the USA and ten per cent for Japan).

Post Second World War Western Europe has seen the emergence of comparable fashions, music, television programmes, and (importantly) a broadly similar youth culture in all industrially developed nations. The fact that more Europeans visit other countries than at any time in history has greatly contributed to this trend, as have the activities of large multinational corporations that offer near identical products in all European states. Note however that European economic integration does not mean that Germans will cease to be German, that the Dutch will no longer be Dutch, or the French will not be French. The Single Market has not created 'grey uniformity' among national consumer populations; indeed, regional cultures appear if anything to have been reinforced, with the consequence that small but significant niche markets are flourishing throughout the EU.

THE SOCIAL DIMENSION OF THE EUROPEAN UNION

25. Social aspects of the Single Market

A major requisite of the Treaty of Rome is that EU countries actively seek to raise the living standards of their citizens (Rhodes 1992; Gold 1993). Measures adopted to achieve this aim are collectively known as the 'social dimension' policies of the EU. Such policies include:

- job creation and training schemes
- equal opportunities programmes
- provision of information on opportunities for employment and training
- legislation on industrial health and safety.

26. The European Social Charter

In December 1989 the European Council voted by eleven to one (the UK being the dissenting member) for the adoption of a Community Charter of fundamental social rights. The effect of this 'Social Charter' would be to establish uniform employment conditions throughout the Community, including matters relating to remuneration, training, living and working conditions, access to company information, consultation, and participation in management decision making. The philosophy underlying the Charter is the belief that the Single Market will only succeed if both sides of industry (employers and labour) are fully involved in creating a new united Europe.

It is important to note that under the Single European Act 1987, any proposal regarding employee rights and interests, and/or the free movement of people, requires unanimous agreement among member nations before it becomes legally binding. Accordingly, acceptance of the Social Charter is *voluntary*, and may not be imposed on any EU state against its wishes. The Charter itself would guarantee individual rights to the following:

(a) Fair remuneration. This would involve the specification of rules for establishing a fair wage.

(b) Health, protection and safety at the workplace.

(c) Access to vocational training throughout a person's working life, including the right to retraining.

(d) Freedom of association and collective bargaining, i.e. to belong or not belong to a trade union and for unions to have the right to bargain with employing firms.

(e) Integration into working life of disabled people. The provision of training for the disabled, accessibility to work premises, availability of special transport, and explicit consideration of disabled people during the ergonomic design of equipment.

(f) Information, consultation and worker participation in company decision making, especially in enterprises that operate in more than one EU country.

(g) Freedom of occupation, residence and movement of workers, including equal treatment *vis-à-vis* local taxes and social security entitlements.

(h) Improvement in living and working conditions. This embraces equality of treatment for part-time and temporary workers, controls on night working, and requirements for weekly rest periods and paid holidays.

(i) Social protection, including adequate unemployment and other social security benefits.

(j) Equal treatment of men and women.

(k) Protection of young people, with a minimum working age of 15 years (16 for full-time employment) and a ban on night work for those under 18.

(l) Reasonable living standards for senior citizens, with a specified minimum income underwritten by the state.

27. Advantages and problems of the Social Charter

Implementation of the Charter will create a social partnership between the two sides of industry and will improve social cohesion within the European Union, hence raising living standards and the skill levels of workers and greatly contributing to increased productivity.

Some of the subjects dealt with in the Charter are already covered by existing EU Directives, but the Charter will pull together into a unified whole a variety of currently fragmented employment and social policies (Wise and Gibb 1993).

If adopted, the Charter will be more than a statement of intentions; it will become legally binding in all EU states – which will have to legislate to ensure that the rights it embodies are guaranteed within their frontiers. Also, the draft Charter insists that member countries commit themselves to 'mobilise all the resources necessary' to implement its provisions.

Objections to the Social Charter have included the following:

(a) Some its requirements violate the 'principle of subsidiarity', i.e. the EU's agreed position that laws be imposed at the EU level *only* if social policy objectives *cannot* be achieved *via* government action within each member state.

(b) Matters pertaining to consultation, employee representation, etc. are perhaps best resolved through *voluntary* collective bargaining between employers and trade unions.

(c) The operating costs of certain businesses could increase dramatically following the Charter's implementation, making EU companies uncompetitive compared to companies in Pacific Rim countries and the USA.

(d) Application of some of the Charter's provisions would necessitate the creation of large bureaucracies within government departments and much administrative inconvenience within firms.

(e) Intervention and control go against the spirit of free enterprise that supposedly underlies the decision to create a Single European Market.

(f) Currently, social protection is greatest in the more affluent EU states. As laws on social protection are harmonised there could be a tendency to 'harmonise upwards' towards higher (and more expensive) common standards, thus imposing unbearable additional costs on poorer EU countries.

Social dumping

The European Trade Union Confederation (ETUC) has alleged that without the pan-European application of minimum social and employment conditions, 'social dumping' will occur, i.e. that there will be unfair undercutting of the price of labour by certain countries. Absence of a minimum wage, lack of employment protection for part-time and casual labour, no minimum working week, and the general denial of Social Charter benefits enables employers to pay low wages, reduce other employment costs and hence charge lower prices for their outputs. This is seen as a violation of Single Market principles. The counter-argument to the proposition that social dumping leads to the countries involved having a competitive advantage is that a low-wage low-productivity labour-intensive economy is only suitable for the production of certain types of item. In the long term it could lack the high technology skills, education and training systems, and the dynamics needed for sustainable growth. Also, industrial relations problems may be more severe in low-wage countries.

Progress test 2

1. List the member countries of the EU.

2. Explain the difference between a common market and a free trade area.

3. What was the purpose of the Treaty of Paris?

4. Why was the Single European Act considered necessary?

5. What is the Maastricht Protocol?

6. How is the European Union financed?

7. Explain the role of the European Commission.

8. List the main functions of the President of the Council of Ministers.

9. What is the role of the Court of First Instance?

10. State three criticisms of the European Parliament.

11. Why is ECOSOC sometimes referred to as 'the Other Assembly'?

12. Outline the reasons behind the formation of the Committee of the Regions.

13. Explain the difference between an EU Directive and an EU Regulation.

14. What is CENELEC?

15. State the main objections to the European Social Charter.

16. Define 'social dumping'.

3

EAST EUROPE

FUNDAMENTALS

1. Introduction

Business in East Europe is characterised by enormous commercial energy, high aspirations and escalating demands for imported goods, but also by economic disruption, extremely low living standards in many regions, acute shortages of foreign exchange, managerial inefficiency, mass unemployment and inability to pay for imports. The area has a population of 400 million (including the former USSR) and there is excess demand for nearly every type of product. Consumers are well educated and as such are responsive to advertising and other promotional campaigns. Literacy levels are among the highest in the world, and many workers possess top class industrial skills. At least 85 per cent of all workers in Poland and Hungary have completed some form of industrial training; a higher percentage than for any European Union country.

Most East European nations have extensive engineering industries capable of manufacturing virtually all categories of item (over a quarter of all output in Hungary, Poland, Russia and the Czech and Slovak Republics consists of manufactured goods), and the local availability of such items greatly enhances the possibilities for barter trade. Note how the combination of low wages with highly skilled industrial workforces could lead to Western manufacturers locating just inside the Western borders of East European nations, in order to serve West European markets. Also, the existence of well-educated and highly trained workforces raises the possibility of technological leapfrogging by East European states, provided their commercial infrastructures are satisfactory.

2. Nature of the East European market

Important consumer import markets have arisen for food items (consequent to the removal of price controls and hence the uncompetitiveness of certain locally produced items); house and home improvement goods (resulting from the pressing need to make good dilapidated housing); clothing and footwear; and computer hardware and software of all kinds. Other areas of increasing demand include automotive products, electronic equipment (especially videos), toys and health care items. Equipment for business and industrial modernisation is in particularly heavy demand. Opportunities for industrial exports to East Europe focus on building materials, office equipment, textile and food processing equipment, medical supplies, machinery of all kinds, items connected with environmental improvement, telecommunications, distribution and transport equipment, and computers. Openings have arisen for the export from West to East Europe of agricultural equipment (as former state-run and inefficient collective farms are modernised), white goods and pharmaceuticals. The sale of automotive products is sure to increase sharply as road systems improve.

The majority of East Europeans live in cities and have lifestyles essentially similar to urban dwellers in the West, although rates of ownership of consumer goods and other household items are well below those for advanced Western States. East European consumers are familiar with Western products, advertisements and selling methods and wish to purchase Western exports. However, wages are low (on average barely ten per cent of West European and US levels) so that consumers do not have the cash to satisfy their demands. The populations of East European nations are generally younger than in the west. A crucial feature of East Europe is its ethnic diversity. There are substantial numbers of people of German descent living in Poland, Romania and Russia. Bulgaria has a large Turkish minority; there are Russians and Hungarians in Romania, Croats in Hungary, Poles in Russia, Ukrainians in the Slovak Republic, and so on. Often, diverse local cultures and languages co-exist within the same national frontiers. This gives rise to the need for extensive research into national markets. Unfortunately, market research data and facilities are extremely limited in these countries.

LIBERALISATION AND PRIVATISATION

3. Economic liberalisation

Transition to a market economy has several dimensions: privatisation, removal of price controls, abolition of state subsidies to industry, the opening up of foreign trade and investment, making the local currency internally and externally convertible, and the establishment of business services and institutions (banks, insurance companies, stock exchanges, etc.). Each of these requires an enormous amount of effort, and progress has varied from nation to nation. Some East European countries (notably Poland, Hungary and the Czech Republic) adopted 'big bang' approaches to liberalisation. Others have proceeded more cautiously. In Russia the transition to a Western style economy was supposed to occur via the Shatalin Plan of 1989, although not all of its objectives have been achieved. The plan itself involved a 500-day programme for installing capitalism in the Russian Republic, requiring the:

- removal of all price controls
- elimination of state subsidies on food and rents
- establishment of a stock exchange
- recognition of trade unions
- offer for sale of state-owned factories to their employees through share issues

- sale of collective farms to peasants
- privatisation of 40 per cent of all Russian industry (60 per cent of the food industry and 50 per cent of construction) by the 400th day
- reduction of the size of the state budget deficit to five per cent of its initial figure within 100 days.

It is important to note that the economic and political situations of many East European countries are in a state of turmoil and liable to sudden and unexpected change. All remain nominally committed to market reforms, though the pace, pattern and detail of reform frequently alters in consequence of political factors.

4. Privatisation of enterprises

Privatisation of industry lies at the heart of the liberalisation process, but is proving extremely difficult. Many of the firms offered for sale are simply unviable (Frydman and Ropaczynski 1993). They are overmanned, technically backward, burdened with debt, and not worth buying at any price. Others require drastic reorganisation and labour redundancies to bring them up to international standards. And even when an enterprise is profitable there are few local residents with sufficient cash to finance the purchase.

East European governments have privatised state-run enterprises in order to improve their efficiency, to enable market forces to determine which should succeed and which fail, and in consequence of pressures exerted by the World Bank, International Monetary Fund and other financial institutions which have lent money to these nations (Schwartz and Lopes 1993). Other hoped-for benefits of privatisation include a reduction in the state bureaucracy needed to administer industrial affairs, cuts in budget deficits, lower taxes, and the creation of an internationally competitive economy capable of sustaining long-run growth. It is important to realise, moreover, that the word 'privatisation' in East Europe has a different meaning to how it is used in the West. In a technical sense, an East European enterprise is privatised when at least 51 per cent of its ownership is transferred into private hands. However, East European governments continue to give direct and indirect assistance to private firms. In particular, labour costs to enterprises are far lower than in the West because of the extensive social welfare and income support mechanisms that apply in East European states. Enterprises frequently receive cheap loans from state-owned banks, and market their outputs through collective distribution systems. Arguably, therefore, East European privatisation is as much a *political* as an economic phenomenon: intended to underscore a government's commitment to individualistic values and the encouragement of personal initiative in the accumulation of private wealth.

5. Privatisation methods

Various approaches to privatisation have been adopted, including mass sales, sector-by-sector disposals, and conversion of individual operations into private companies. For example, in 1991 the former Czechoslovakia denationalised many state-run enterprises via a voucher system intended to convert a mass of state firms into private businesses very quickly and at minimal cost. Importantly, the government did not attempt to restructure firms and/or industries prior to their privatisation.

Residents were able to purchase books of vouchers at a very low price, these vouchers then being exchangeable for shares in companies of their choice as they were put up for auction. If people were not prepared to take shares in certain enterprises, the firms involved simply went into liquidation. Foreigners were not allowed to purchase vouchers, but 100 per cent ownership of enterprises was allowed. The currency became internally convertible at the same time. A Stock Exchange was established to create a marketplace for shares. Around eight million people participated in the scheme. Privatisation has been severely hindered by disputes over the ownership of land and property nationalised in 1948.

Russia too initiated a voucher system. Book of vouchers were issued free of charge to any resident over 18 years of age wishing to participate. Around 100 million people took vouchers. Poland, Hungary and Bulgaria privatised a number of particular industrial sectors, one at a time. The idea was to retain key sectors intact and prevent investors taking only the very best companies within them. Privatisation of individual enterprises occurred concurrently in these (and all other East European) states. The Hungarian authorities, for example, converted a number of state firms into private companies which were then offered to the highest bidder. Private shareholding has been encouraged *via* the provision of interest-free five-year loans to finance share purchases. As in other East European nations, numerous disputes are arising over who exactly owns the land on which shops, factories and offices are built. In Poland management buy-outs have been a common device for shifting enterprise ownership into private hands. Otherwise businesses were handed over to local authorities and National Investment Funds which then became responsible for their privatisation. A Stock Exchange has been established, which will offer for sale shares in particular enterprises. Bulgaria and Romania have been more cautious in privatising their economies than most other East European states, preferring to encourage new start-ups of private businesses rather than the wholesale selling off of state-owned firms. Romania is privatising many of its industries by transferring their ownership to five investment trusts, which in turn will administer enterprises as joint stock companies. The remainder are available to international investors.

The case for rapid privatisation is that if privatisation is slow then existing inefficiencies are preserved. Fast privatisation means however that very many enterprises will not survive competition, leading to high unemployment (Aylen 1987; Asah 1990). Further difficulties are that:

(a) Many enterprises are sure to fail immediately following their entry to free markets, leaving shareholders with worthless investments.

(b) The price reductions and special inducements needed to unload certain firms may be so costly to the national authorities as to make the programme uneconomic.

(c) The administrative systems established to organise privatisations are themselves bureaucratic and frequently inefficient.

(d) The task involved is so enormous that there may be little prospect of success. Arguably a much longer-term perspective should be adopted.

(e) The financial infrastructure needed to facilitate privatisation did not exist at the time enterprises were put up for sale. There were no merchant banking, underwriting or pre-existing share transfer systems; no accounting standards, financial information or credit rating companies, investor relations consultants to assist with the preparation of prospectuses, etc. Privatisation has proven problematic even in countries that have extensive financial services industries (the UK and France for example).

(f) The speed at which privatisation proceeded gave it a high profile and perhaps generated unrealistic expectations among the population, which was encouraged to believe that privatisation would, at a stroke, solve all a country's economic problems.

(g) Although much East European industry is worthless, parts of it have great potential and it is arguable that these sectors have been sold off far too cheaply.

6. Economic problems in East Europe

Privatisation only makes sense in the context of an economy in which prices are determined by the forces of supply and demand, otherwise there are no fundamental criteria against which to assess a newly privatised business' capacity to survive. Yet allowing prices to rise has caused great hardship for the populations of East European states. It is likely to be the case, however, that prices will only stabilise once they are determined entirely by market forces. Also the price system itself might not direct resources in the most profitable ways. Even the most optimistic forecasts suggest that only a minority of East European enterprises can compete internationally, and that many have no hope of survival in the long term. Others might continue but only after drastic restructuring. The situation is made worse by the fact that in the past central planners encouraged the creation of very large production units, as they were easier to control and their outputs could be dovetailed into national and regional planning frameworks. As they collapse these huge combines are creating mass unemployment in particular areas. High rates of inflation have occurred as cheap sources of raw materials disappeared.

Conversion of East European economies from centrally planned to private enterprise systems has been traumatic. National incomes tumbled, although the few figures that are currently available suggest that Hungary, Poland and the Czech (but not the Slovak) Republic have experienced positive growth since 1993. Other East European economies continue to experience acute difficulties, though note that published information relates primarily to the (rapidly declining) public sectors of these countries and that their expanding private sectors may in practice partially offset the observed reductions in official national incomes. Economic austerity measures imposed in attempts to curb inflation and increase earnings of foreign exchange have had an enormous social cost. Income distributions within East European states are increasingly uneven, and the unemployed face grave poverty.

Foreign trade

An important feature of East European economies is their relative lack of involvement with international trade, resulting from decades of government policies aimed at economic self-sufficiency and Eastern bloc political isolation. East European import tariffs are generally high, and many East European nations apply protectionist foreign trade policies. However, tariffs are beginning to fall in consequence of the conclusion in December 1993 of the Uruguay Round of GATT and through bilateral trade agreements between individual countries and the US, Japan, and (in particular) the European Union. Tariff rates vary enormously between East European nations and among product groups, and rates themselves are subject to sudden and unpredictable alteration. Quota and import licensing systems are common. Free ports and free trade zones (*see* 12:7) now exist in Bulgaria, Hungary, the Czech Republic, Russia, Romania, Belarus, Estonia and the Ukraine.

Exports to Western markets are relatively low, leading to chronic shortages of foreign exchange. Currency devaluations are common, leading to increased import prices, including imports of much needed capital goods.

7. Operational difficulties

Among the many operational problems confronting foreign companies wishing to do business in East Europe the following are worthy of particular mention:

(a) The impossibility of preparing accurate business forecasts in fast changing and uncertain economic, political and legal environments.

(b) Foreign firms having to compete against state-owned local enterprises that continue to receive government subsidies.

(c) Having to rely on payment by cheque or post office transfers for consumer purchases (in consequence of the underdevelopment of commercial banking systems).

(d) Sparcity of market information.

(e) Delays and frustrations arising from having to deal with numerous (well-meaning) state officials who do not possess the authority to take significant decisions.

(f) Labour problems for firms wishing to establish a permanent presence resulting from employees not being culturally attuned to the cut and thrust of free labour markets. In Russia, for example, school leavers prior to liberalisation were assigned to jobs for three-year periods during which they could not be dismissed. Working methods in many industries are so out-of-date that employees' attitudes may have been adversely affected, leading perhaps to an unwillingness to accept the latest technologies. In Poland and Romania, foreign companies may dismiss workers in manners analogous to those used in the West. Elsewhere however local rules on labour lay-offs apply, and can make dismissal procedures extremely problematic and protracted.

(g) Lack of formal business procedures. These countries have yet to develop proper legal frameworks for consumer and employee protection, contract, business insolvency, etc., within a private enterprise system.

All East European countries now have internally convertible currencies, meaning that local currency (roubles for example) can be freely exchanged into foreign currencies (such as US dollars) at a local market price set by supply and demand. However, not all East European states allow the unfettered transmission of hard foreign currencies (i.e. those which are internationally acceptable as a means for financing transactions) to other countries. Hence, although domestic currency can be exchanged for foreign currency and the latter used to purchase items *within* the country concerned, the export of hard currency might be restricted. A common condition is that foreign firms can only repatriate locally earned profits in the form of hard currency to the extent that these companies *earn* foreign exchange through selling their outputs to third party nations. Note however that such limitations are systematically being removed.

Foreign investment

Foreign ownership of local enterprises is permitted in all East European nations, although some states impose restrictions on foreigners' abilities to purchase land. The latter results from the fact that in most East European countries the state at some time or other confiscated all land and buildings so that, on privatisation of these assets, there is much confusion regarding who owns specific properties: the families from whom they were initially confiscated; past or present occupants; or recent purchasers. There are no local content requirements in any East European country. All East European nations now have laws guaranteeing foreigners that their investments will not be expropriated, or that full (hard currency) compensation at current market value will be paid if expropriation occurs. In most East European countries the taxes on the profits earned by foreign enterprises are low relative to international standards (and lower than for domestic firms), and all East European states provide extensive grants and subsidies for new job creation, location in depressed areas, inward technology transfer, and for research and technical development.

MANAGEMENT, PROSPECTS AND THE EU

8. Management of East European enterprises

Prior to economic reform, enterprise management in East European countries was regarded as a technical resource whose role was to plan, organise and deploy resources to achieve targets set by central state administrators who, in effect, held a government monopoly over business affairs. This had the following consequences:

(a) Managers' performances were appraised not in terms of their ability to improve profitability, but rather of their contributions to national, local and industry economic plans.

(b) Decisions did not have to be based on the comparative prices of inputs and final products. Instead, decisions related to general economic, political and/or technical considerations.

(c) Managers did not need to concern themselves with marketing, or even with making goods appear attractive to consumers.

(d) Firms were instructed where to obtain supplies and where to deliver final outputs.

(e) Arguably, lack of commercial accountability meant that managers could take reckless decisions without fear of consequences.

For decades managements were told who would supply their inputs and how they were to price their outputs. Goods were distributed by the state, which also determined how labour was to be treated and how much the individual worker was to be paid. Output levels were decided centrally according to the requirements of national and regional economic plans. Foreign trade was conducted (with the exception of Hungary) through foreign trade organisations (FTOs) operated on product lines. FTOs would buy and sell on their own accounts, find foreign customers for specific deals, research international price levels for various products and determine foreign technical standards requirements.

These circumstances led to an acute lack of commercial management skills among enterprise managers. The absence of managerial know-how is particularly severe in the following areas:

(a) Quality management and quality assurance standards (ISO 9000 for instance).

(b) Cost and management accounting. Concepts of profit, loss, overheads absorption, marginal cost pricing, etc., had little meaning in a centrally planned Socialist economic system. Not knowing how much it costs to produce a particular item results in arbitrary pricing decisions with consequent detrimental effects on profits.

(c) All aspects of marketing.

(d) Organisation design and development.

Managements need to learn how to structure their internal organisations in manners that will equip them for international competition, with new departments to deal with advertising and marketing, personnel management, information technology, and so on.

9. Long-term prospects for East Europe

Once their transition to well-organised mixed economies is complete the East European states will constitute one of the world's most attractive environments for international business. Communications between East European and other nations are straightforward, and it is easy to investigate East European markets first hand. Business laws, rules and practices in East European countries will soon be identical with those of the West, while improvements in industrial infrastructures will themselves increase employment, output and hence consumer demand.

East European consumers may be characterised as having the capacity to become sophisticated and discerning buyers, but at present lacking the cash to satisfy their requirements. They are familiar with Western products, advertisements and selling methods and, critically, they want to purchase imported goods. Entrepreneurs in East Europe are desperately anxious to establish contacts with Western partners, and fresh possibilities for profitable business constantly emerge. The region is a seller's market: everything is in demand, the only missing factor is the hard currency needed to pay for imports.

It is not generally feasible to do business in East Europe opportunistically and without taking a long-term view. Many years will elapse before these countries are able fully to transform their legal, accounting and business education systems to Western standards and have stable economies with modern industrial infrastructures and convertible currencies. Accordingly, firms must be prepared to wait for a number of years prior to obtaining a significant return, and have to accept a high level of risk in the interim period. The pace of economic progress in East European nations will depend substantially on the nature of their relations with the EU. Several East European countries have stated their desire to join the Union, although a number of factors militate against this eventuality in the short to medium term. Disruptions in the East led to large-scale immigration from East European countries into France, Italy, Benelux and (especially) Germany. This in turn caused political problems for West European governments and, it seems, disinterest in the prospect of opening the Single Market's borders to workers from East European states (as would happen automatically if these countries joined the EU). Another difficulty is that since many East European nations are heavily dependent on agriculture they would immediately qualify for huge amounts of EU agricultural subsidies and support. The Common Agricultural Policy in its present form could not cope with the resulting drain on its resources. Also the fact that East European countries are poor by Western Standards means that they would absorb most of the EU's regional development budget.

The low wage costs of East European enterprises could give them a competitive advantage against EU firms. Average per capita income of Bulgaria, Hungary, Poland, Romania and the Czech and Slovak Republics is about 12 percent of the average for the European Union, and just 60 per cent of the per capita GDP of Portugal – the poorest member state.

10. The Visegrad group and EU Association Agreements

In 1995 Hungary, Poland and the Czech and Slovak Republics decided to begin dismantling tariffs against each other (aiming to create a free trade area within a decade) and to co-ordinate their effects to join the European Union. Advantages enjoyed by these countries (which came to be known as the 'Visegrad group') include their geographical nearness to affluent West European markets, their trained and generally well-educated workforces, low labour costs, and reasonable industrial infrastructures. The Visegrad nations were the first to establish 'Association Agreements' (also known as 'Europe Agreements' in order to distinguish them from similar agreements between the EU and certain other non-East European nations) with the European Union, providing for reciprocal trade concessions between the EU and these states plus the setting up of a legal framework for political dialogue among the parties. EU Association Agreements with other East European nations followed. The main provisions of Association Agreements were as follows:

(a) All quotas on entry to EU markets of products other than those listed in **(c)** below have been abolished, and EU import tariffs are being reduced systematic-ally. The East European countries will themselves remove quotas and tariffs by the year 2002. Only goods with at least 60 per cent East European local content will qualify for duty-free EU entry.

(b) Workers from these countries who already live in the EU may continue to reside in the Union and (importantly) will receive social security benefits equal to those available to EU residents. However, further labour migration to the EU will to be permitted.

(c) The Union has committed itself to allow open entry to East European food, coal, steel and textiles, but only in the long run.

(d) Association Agreement countries can continue giving state aid to backward industries. However they had to begin applying EU rules on business competition from 1995.

Consequent to the signing of Association Agreements about 60 per cent of EU imports from these countries now enter the Union free of duty, and the intro-duction of new trade restrictions on exports to and from signatory countries is prohibited. In 1992 the EU concluded ten-year 'Trade and Co-operation Agreements' with Albania, Latvia, Estonia and Lithuania. These are bilateral trade agreements offering improved (but not preferential) access to EU markets.

Problems with Association and Trade and Co-operation Agreements

Critics of Association and Trade and Co-operation Agreements allege that they are too partial and are to be implemented over too long a period to be effective. What is really needed, they argue, is a 'big bang' to link East and West Europe immediately and inextricably and genuinely boost economic development in Eastern nations. In principle, Association and Trade and Co-operation Agree-ments provide beneficiaries with lower tariffs and more favourable export opportunities than other states, plus an assortment of financial credits and direct assistance schemes. In reality, however, the hoped-for benefits have not been fully realised. Fears of cheap agricultural and other products from East Europe have led to the imposition of *de facto* protective measures in several EU countries, and the European Commission has not intervened to outlaw violations of the original agreements. The Agreements themselves leave many opportunities for the imposition of restrictions on their implementation. Recession in Western Europe, moreover, has depressed West European firms' sales within EU nations hence increasing the latter's reluctance to allow low-cost East European products free access to their markets. The fact that so many East European enterprises continue to enjoy state subsidy is another reason advanced for not opening up West European markets to Eastern businesses. Trade between East and West Europe has grown rapidly since the collapse of communism, although it still represents only a small percentage of total EU external transactions. Imports to the EU from the Visegrad countries, for example, never accounted for more than six per cent of aggregate EU imports prior to 1995.

11. The European Bank for Reconstruction and Development (EBRD)

Established in 1991 the London-based EBRD has 53 member countries plus the European Union and the European Investment Bank. Its purpose is to facilitate the transition to market economies of East European nations through fostering private enterprise and entrepreneurial initiative. This it does by providing loans, direct financial investments and technical assistance to East European states that have demonstrated their commitment to multiparty democracy and the maintenance of human rights. Under the Bank's internal rules at least 60 per cent of its funding must go to existing private companies or state-owned enterprises undergoing privatisation or to the creation of new companies (including joint ventures with foreign investors). The remaining 40 per cent is directed towards infrastructure and other public sector projects. Further EBRD activities include the analysis of specific industry sectors and particular issues relating to privatisation and economic restructuring, and the publication of research studies.

The Bank receives its money from Western governments, supplemented by borrowing on the international money markets, and uses its resources to fund projects intended to:

- implement privatisation
- encourage direct foreign investment
- restructure industries and develop industrial infrastructures
- create and strengthen financial institutions
- improve the physical environment.

Typically the Bank will contribute up to 35 per cent of the cost of a project, the rest coming from local banks and project sponsors. The criteria applied when evaluating proposals submitted by private companies or enterprises about to be privatised include commercial viability (evidenced by the clear existence of sound market prospects), significant contributions of permanent risk capital by sponsors, the extent to which the enterprise's competitiveness will be improved, the quality of management and the dependability of the technology involved. Loans are denominated in convertible currencies and must be repaid in those currencies. Normally the projects to be funded must have a value of ECU 5 million or above. The bank does not *itself* provide technical assistance, financial advice or training to funded projects, relying instead on member governments and/or consulting firms to supply these services. Fees for such purposes are regarded as a permissible use of EBRD funding.

COUNTERTRADE

Although countertrade is used throughout the world as a device for settling cross-border transactions it is particularly common for trade between East European and Western countries. The following discussion applies to countertrade activities in all other regions.

12. Nature of countertrade

Countertrade encompasses barter, compensation trading (see below), and other forms of direct or indirect exchange of goods for goods across national frontiers. Typically it occurs in situations where one or more of the parties is unable to pay for imports using foreign currency, either because its central bank has insufficient stocks of foreign exchange or in consequence of government restrictions on the availability of foreign exchange imposed for political reasons (Kotabe 1989). According to the OECD, countertrade may account for anything up to five per cent of total world trade; ten per cent for trade involving developing nations, and 35 per cent for trade between the latter and East European states.

13. Advantages and disadvantages of countertrade

Countertrade enables international trade to take place without the need to exchange hard currency. Developing countries are able to import high-technology products and pay for them using items they might not otherwise have been able to market internationally. Exporters can sell their outputs in a wider range of countries, including many large and fast-growing markets. Countertrade can assist technology transfer from advanced to developing countries and facilitate economic growth in the latter. Importantly, it can be used to circumvent protectionist government policies in certain nations (Jacobs and Palia 1986). Note how the individual exporter can use countertrade to offer what is in effect an extremely favourable price to a potential customer in a country where there is fierce local competition. It may even be more convenient for a customer to pay in goods rather than in cash, as a countertrade deal can provide an immediate market for a firm's output, without any need for advertising or other forms of promotion.

Problems with countertrade

Critics of countertrade allege that it distorts the normal competitive process whereby prices are determined by the interplay of supply and demand in free markets. Only a minority of companies have the knowledge or capacity to engage in countertrade (so the number of firms competing within certain countries is diminished), and there is little empirical evidence that countertrade actually improves the foreign exchange positions of the countries in which it is common. A problem confronting the national tax authorities of a country involved in extensive countertrade is that the dumping of a foreign product at below its cost of production may be occurring without the fact being evident (because the price at which the item is imported is not stated in monetary units).

Accordingly, national tax authorities which suspect that countertrade deals are in reality a form of disguised dumping might impose *ad hoc* import duties on the transaction. To avoid such accusations and to ensure that all local anti-dumping rules are complied with, the exporter might record all details of the intended deal in a separate document (known as an evidence account) which is formally deposited with the appropriate government department of the importer's country. Specific difficulties faced by the individual firm involved in a countertrade deal are:

(a) Its administrative cost and complexity.

(b) The possibility of a sudden collapse in the world market price of the goods received as payment, and the scarcity of potential third party buyers for certain types of item.

(c) That foreign customers might be more interested in having their suppliers act as unpaid distributors for their outputs in foreign markets than in the imported goods themselves.

(d) The possibility of disputes arising over the acceptability of the level of quality of the barter goods actually delivered, especially if no precise quality specification for the goods has been agreed. An exporter could be landed with poor quality goods which are difficult to sell. This imposes warehousing costs on the firm receiving them and causes a deterioration in its liquidity position.

(e) Delays in the delivery of barter items, due perhaps to production hold-ups, transportation or documentation difficulties, the need to obtain an export licence, etc.

(f) Absence of clear-cut procedures for resolving disputes (in contrast with deals involving the exchange of goods for money).

14. Techniques of countertrade

Firms engaging in countertrade involving product categories with which they are already familiar might decide to organise and administer their own countertrade transactions. If the company has little knowledge of the items it will receive in payment for exports, however, then the services of an expert intermediary will probably be necessary (Vergariv 1985; Welt 1990). Countertrade intermediaries will store and process goods and advertise and otherwise promote the items on offer. The intermediary will act either as an agent or a principal and normally charge between three and 15 per cent commission for its services.

Barter, i.e. the straightforward exchange of item for item (so many barrels of oil for so many units of machinery for example), is the simplest form of countertrade. Deals are usually transacted at the prevailing world market prices of the products involved. Barter arrangements are also known as 'contra-trading' or 'reciprocal trading'. Barter transactions are easy to set up, and unavoidable in situations where hard currency to pay for imports is unobtainable. In risky situations the exporter might insist on receiving the barter goods before despatching the export consignment. The exporter sells these goods, the money received being paid to an independent third party (usually a bank) which holds it 'in escrow' (meaning that the money is held in trust until certain conditions have been fulfilled). As soon as sales revenues are sufficient to finance the deal the exporter sends off the goods and the third party releases the money.

Switch deals occur where the exporter (or an intermediary) arranges for the disposal of the barter goods to a third party, which receives the goods direct from the importer and assumes responsibility for selling them – often in foreign countries. Switch trading *via* intermediaries originally developed in Austria, where banks have traditionally been prepared to advance cash to exporters prior to finding third party customers for the goods. Many Austrian banks have subsidiaries which directly engage in international trade, and so may actually buy the products offered by importers (enabling importers to make cash payments to suppliers).

Compensation dealing, as opposed to straight barter, is where the exporting firm receives part payment in its own currency and the remainder in goods. *Buyback* occurs when a firm supplies plant and equipment to a foreign importer under a contract requiring the exporter to accept output produced by the plant and equipment supplied as whole or part payment for the transaction. If wages and other non-capital production costs are lower in the importing country then the plant and equipment supplier can obtain finished output at highly competitive prices. The problem is finding buyers for the output received. Note how this could lead to the exporter entering into competition with its own domestic customers (to whom the firm might have supplied similar plant and equipment to produce the same type of item). Buyback contracts need to specify very carefully the quality level and delivery schedule of the buyback product. It is sometimes the case that a government will sanction the import of major capital goods only on condition that they contain a specified proportion of local inputs or that the exporter agrees to purchase locally produced items of at least a certain value. This is known as an 'offset' arrangement, and might include a buyback element.

The term *counterpurchase* is sometimes used to denote the situation whereby the exporting firm receives part payment in its own currency or a hard foreign currency and the balance in the currency of the importer's country. The exporter then uses the latter currency to purchase whatever products in the importer's country happen to be available.

Progress test 3

1. What are Association Agreements? Which countries have Association Agreements with the EU?

2. Which countries belong to the Visegrad group?

3. List the main elements of the Shatalin Plan of 1989.

4. What benefits did East European countries hope to obtain from the privatisation of state-owned enterprises?

5. Explain the voucher method of privatisation.

6. List five operational difficulties confronting Western companies wishing to do business in East Europe.

7. Why do many East European nations impose constraints on foreign companies' abilities to purchase land?

8. Why is it necessary to take a long-term view when doing business in Eastern Europe?

9. What is a Trade and Co-operation Agreement?

10. Outline the role and functions of the EBRD.

11. What is a buyback agreement?

12. List the main advantages to countertrade.

4

BEYOND EUROPE

This chapter examines the problems and benefits that an international business might experience when operating in regions outside West and East Europe. The areas considered are North America, Japan and the Pacific Rim, China, Southern Asia, Africa, South America and the Middle East.

NORTH AMERICA

1. The North American Free Trade Agreement (NAFTA)

Effective from 1994, NAFTA created a free trade area (*see* 1:5) between Canada and the USA (two of the world's richest countries) and Mexico (a poor and economically underdeveloped country). The aim was to eliminate all tariffs and trade obstacles between member countries by the year 2009; internal tariffs on a large number of product categories were removed at once.

NAFTA has a population of 363 million, making it one of the most important economic trading areas in the world. Common technical product standards are being introduced, so that standards applied by any one NAFTA country will be acceptable throughout the area. Thus an international business needs only to meet one set of standards for the entire NAFTA market. There are stringent 'local content' rules to prevent non-NAFTA firms assembling goods in Mexico and hence avoiding US and Canadian tariffs and quotas. Third country products imported into one country cannot be re-exported to other members as if they were domestically produced goods *unless* certain minimum percentages of their manufacturing costs have been incurred in the importing nation. For Canada and the US the figure is 50 per cent; for Mexico the local content requirement can be as high as 80 per cent. Formation of NAFTA has created the need for additional documentation when moving goods imported from outside NAFTA from one member country to another. An extra certificate of origin is required; rebates of import duty are available to importers who re-export items to other NAFTA states. NAFTA's wider objectives are to:

- improve and consolidate political relationships among member nations
- help Mexico earn additional foreign exchange to meet its foreign debt burden
- decrease the flow of emigration from Mexico to the US by providing job opportunities 'south of the border'

- create a stable and predictable environment for investors
- increase employment throughout the region
- reduce consumer prices through extending competition
- enhance the competitive advantage of NAFTA-based firms operating in wider international markets
- create fresh business opportunities in expanding national markets (especially Mexico, which is developing rapidly).

Citizens of any NAFTA country may freely invest in any NAFTA nation. Rules on the protection of intellectual property are being harmonised across the area, as are regulations on pollution control (at present Mexico has less stringent laws on environment protection than Canada or the USA).

2. The United States of America

The USA is the world's largest import market, although consumer characteristics and preferences vary substantially from state to state. Three quarters of the USA's 260 million residents live in cities. Population is growing fastest in southern and western states, and slowest in the northeast. It is important to realise that each US region has its own distinct climate, industrial structure and pattern of consumer tastes. The US population can be roughly categorised as 20 per cent poor and 20 per cent affluent, with the rest between the two extremes.

The majority of Americans can trace their origins to a specific foreign country within the last half dozen generations. About 23 per cent of all Americans claim their ancestry to be German, 16 per cent Irish, 13 per cent English, 10 per cent African and 6 per cent Italian. Twelve per cent of US residents are black and nearly ten per cent Hispanic. In California about ten per cent of the population are of Asian extraction, and 25 per cent Hispanic. In total there are around 20 million Hispanic US citizens (originally from Latin America) and their numbers are growing. Hispanics could be the biggest US minority group by the end of the decade.

Doing business in the USA

Each of the USA's 50 states, plus the District of Colombia, has its own set of commercial laws. Additionally there are Federal laws that apply throughout the country. This results in great complexity and the need to take full account of legal factors when marketing products. The country is perhaps the most litigious in the world. It has more lawyers per 100,000 head of population than any other nation and resort to the law to settle commercial disputes is commonplace. Note that US lawyers work on a no-win no-fee basis thus creating incentives for aggrieved parties to seek legal redress (each side normally bears its own costs regardless of the outcome of the case). State *and* federal laws extend to product safety and quality requirements, competition, advertising and sales promotions, and banking and finance.

Distributors are jointly liable with importers and original manufacturers for damages resulting from defective products, but they typically include clauses in their contracts with suppliers that explicitly pass back liability. Misleading advertising is illegal under Federal law. This means making 'false representations' (express or implied) and/or failing to disclose misleading facts. Trade marks can but need not be registered in order to enjoy legal protection. All that is required is positive proof of first use. A registered trade mark that is dormant for two years can be challenged by a competing business. It is unlawful to import into the USA articles bearing a brand name or other trade mark already owned by a US firm, unless the trade mark owner has given permission. US Customs will deny entry to such items provided the US owner has registered the brand name or trade mark with the Commissioner of Customs.

The USA is a very large country, so most foreign firms doing business in the US find that they need to engage local rather than national agents. It is most unlikely that a single representative will have the expertise and/or capability to handle a product throughout the entire US market. Agency agreements are governed by the general law of contract; there is no Federal legislation on the subject although many states have particular rules on agency termination and compensation. Great care is needed when drafting agency (or distribution) agreements, since any contract to fix resale prices, impose territorial restrictions, or handle competing products has the potential to violate US anti-trust legislation. Aggrieved parties are permitted to sue for three times the level of actual damages incurred.

JAPAN AND THE PACIFIC RIM

3. Japan

Japan is one of the most affluent countries in the world, with a population of around 125 million. The rate of growth of the population is modest, so that the average age of Japanese people is rising. Japan has an unusual demographic structure in that it has large proportions in both the young *and* old age brackets relative to other countries. The nation has one of the highest life expectancies in the world, due perhaps to the Japanese lifestyle and diet. There are nearly 35 million people aged over 55, representing a large and lucrative 'silver market'. Older Japanese people are relatively free spending compared to the rest of the population, due substantially to savings habits and the widespread operation of occupational pension schemes – resulting in very few Japanese senior citizens having to rely on their children for financial support, although over half of them share premises with their children. Senior citizens are big spenders on travel and leisure goods. Population and economic activity are concentrated on the eastern coast, particularly in the conurbations around Osaka and Tokyo (population 12 million). A 900 km coastal region running south west from Tokyo contains half Japan's total population and 80 per cent of its manufacturing capacity.

Japan is often criticised for unfairly blocking the importation of foreign goods. Examples of complaints made against Japanese import procedures include:

- Extensive and complicated product safety testing requirements, with the need to test excessively large samples under excessively arduous conditions. Pre-shipment testing has not been allowed for certain products so that testing has had to be completed in Japan, with the shortage of qualified inspectors leading to long delays in the testing process.

- Unexpected modifications to mandatory technical product standards imposed at very short notice, with the issue of guidelines on product standards to Japanese firms but not to foreigners.
- Refusal of customs officers to give reasons for rejecting the import of specific consignments.
- Allocation of product safety acceptance certificates to local Japanese agents rather than to foreign manufacturers so that if the latter change their agents the entire testing process has to be repeated.

A further problem is the relatively small number of independent buying firms. There exist in Japan numerous collaborative agreements among Japanese firms that create problems for foreign companies wishing to enter the Japanese market and which would be illegal under the monopoly and competition laws of many other nations. Groupings of firms occur *via* financial links, sharing common suppliers, or through joint control of distribution outlets. These groups of Japanese businesses ('Keiretsu' as they are called) exert powerful influences on the Japanese economy.

In response to these criticisms the Japanese government has introduced a package of measures intended to boost the import of manufactured goods, including the abolition of tariffs on imported machinery and several hundred other types of product, plus Corporation Tax rebates for firms increasing the value of their imports of manufacturers by more than ten per cent per year. An official Trade Ombudsman has been appointed to investigate complaints of unfair discrimination against imported products. 'Buy foreign' campaigns have been initiated among both industrial buyers and final consumers, and import missions and trade fairs have been organised to help foreigners enter the market. Also the government has encouraged local agents to handle imports and requested exporters to purchase more foreign items.

Doing business in Japan

Domestic distribution systems are complex, costly and bureaucratic. There are several levels in the distribution chain; each link in the chain taking a substantial margin. Also a relatively high proportion of distribution outlets are partially or wholly owned by suppliers in comparison with other developed countries. Long and complicated distribution channels result in the prices of imports rising by three to five times their FOB level (*see* 12:6) prior to their reaching the end consumer.

Many international businesses selling in Japan do so *via* one or more of the giant Japanese trading houses (*sogo shoshas*), which have offices throughout the world and which deal in a huge variety of products. Sogo shoshas will lend money to importing customers. They developed in the early years of the post-Second World War period when Japanese businesses needed to export but possessed little knowledge of foreign markets or export procedures, gradually extending their role from that of simple intermediary to one of direct involvement with exporting companies. Retailing within Japan is complex. Japan's estimated one million retail outlets range from large supermarkets and department stores to a multitude of one-person businesses. There are twice as many retailers per 1000 population in Japan as in the USA. There is obvious consumer demand for a large number of small retail stores, and the layout and architecture of Japanese cities frequently prevents the construction of large integrated retail units.

Brand names or other trade marks need to be registered. Simply being the first firm to use a particular trade mark does not confer ownership of it, as is the situation in many other countries: formal registration with the state authorities is required. Registration confers protection for ten years in the first instance, and may be renewed indefinitely thereafter. However, if a brand name or other trade mark is not used in Japan for three consecutive years then another firm can apply to a Japanese Court to have the registration cancelled.

Advertising in Japan must not 'impede competition or treat consumers unjustly'. Misleading advertisements must be withdrawn on the orders of the country's Fair Trade Commission. The latter also approves industry Codes of Practice on the advertising of various categories of products.

In Japan, business is conducted predominately on the basis of trust rather than litigation, and contract law is far less strict than in the West. There is less than one tenth the number of lawyers per 1000 population in Japan than in several other advanced industrial countries. The country has a Civil Code, but this has little to say about business relationships other than when home selling or credit transactions are involved. Contracts are governed essentially by provisions agreed between the parties, and disputes are normally resolved without legal action. (This 'custom and practice' approach to the regulation of commerce can lead to imprecision regarding the rights and duties of buyer and seller.) Rules on agency are vague. Agents are regarded as long-term partners of the principal's business rather than as people engaged to supply *ad hoc* services. Contracts can be terminated without indemnity provided a provision to this effect is written into the initial agreement. A common device for arranging local representation in Japan is to open a 'Representative Office', which is a legally recognised form of business in this country but which does not have to register with the local District Legal Affairs Bureau, as is the case when setting up a branch. However, Representative Offices cannot engage directly in manufacturing or other operational functions; rather they are restricted to supplying auxiliary services such as advertising, market research, information gathering and so on.

4. The 'four dragons' and the newly industrialised countries of the Pacific Rim

Hong Kong, Singapore, South Korea and Taiwan are sometimes referred to as the 'four dragons' of the Pacific Rim. The first pair are essentially trading nations; the other two are important manufacturing countries in their own right. Most of Hong Kong's trade is with the Chinese mainland, which takes a third of the Territory's exports and provides nearly 40 per cent of its imports. Note moreover that about 80 per cent of Hong Kong's exported goods are in reality re-exports from China, and that much foreign investment in China is channelled through Hong Kong.

Singapore has the second highest per capita GDP in Asia after Japan. Its population is predominately Chinese (76 per cent) with 15 per cent Malay and 7 per cent Indian. The country is a self-contained business centre with state-of-the-art facilities and ancillary business services; many joint venture and distributorship arrangements in neighbouring countries are organised from the territory. Business is conducted in the English language. A big problem for Singapore is its heavy dependence on external trade, especially with the USA which takes 60 per cent of the country's exports and provides 40 per cent of all inward foreign investment.

South Korea is one of the economically strongest newly industrialised countries in the Pacific Rim, with an average growth rate exceeding 6 per cent per annum since 1965. The country's economy is one of the most open in the world, with a 75 per cent ratio of trade to national income. Taiwan is the twentieth largest GDP in the world. The country is populated predominantly by overseas Chinese, and despite the fact that Taiwan and China have no *official* relations, trade between the two is enormous (albeit passing through Hong Kong) and there is much Taiwanese investment in mainland China.

The highest rates of economic growth in the Pacific Rim are currently occurring in Indonesia, Malaysia, the Philippines and Thailand, although per capita national incomes are much lower than in the Four Dragons. Problems that might be experienced when doing business in some of these countries include:

- the difficultly of protecting intellectual property (counterfeiting is common)
- high import duties
- ethnic diversity and political tensions between various ethnic groups
- poor industrial and commercial infrastructures
- frequent imposition of exchange controls.

CHINA AND SOUTHERN ASIA

5. China

Commercial business systems and practices were introduced to China in the late 1970s, but were (and remain) subject to tight central government control. The country comprises 23 provinces, five autonomous regions and three municipalities. There is a single official language (Mandarin), although large numbers of southern Chinese people speak Cantonese, and there are six other widely spoken local languages. China is home to numerous religions. There are at least 100 million Buddhists, 20 million Muslims, at least 5 million Protestants (various denominations) and the same number of Roman Catholics. Confucianism and Taoism are the other main religions. Barely 75 per cent of the population is literate.

China's economy is developing rapidly, especially in the private sector (currently restricted to retailing, provision of personal services, food outlets, and firms with no more than seven employees) and in the country's Special Economic

Zones (SEZs). The first of these was set up in 1979 in Shenzen in Guangdong Province, which borders Hong Kong. Guangdong itself has achieved levels of economic growth and development comparable to those of South Korea and Taiwan. Several more large SEZs were set up in the 1980s, including the entire island of Hainan. In 1984, the SEZs were supplemented by 14 Economic and Technical Development Zones (ETDZs) in towns and cities along China's coast. SEZs and ETDZs are essentially freezones (*see* 12:7), have very low tax rates for local businesses, and may accept any amount of foreign investment.

A number of difficulties apply to foreign companies wishing to operate in China, as follows:

(a) Foreign investors are still required to obtain approval for their intended projects from the Chinese government authorities and to deal with the state bureaucracy.

(b) There are shortages of people with business skills.

(c) Consumer incomes are very low.

(d) Although legal protection of intellectual property was introduced in 1988, counterfeiting is commonplace.

(e) Imports into China are subject to tight quota and licensing agreements, and usually have to go through the state Foreign Trade Corporation (which takes care of all customs formalities). Chinese currency is generally inconvertible, and there is an endemic shortage of foreign exchange.

(f) There are few ancillary business services (advertising agencies, market research firms, etc.).

(g) Distribution systems are poor.

(h) Commercial laws were only drafted in the 1980s, and are frequently imprecise.

(i) There is little information on consumer tastes and preferences.

6. Southern Asia

The Indian sub-continent is one of the poorest areas of the world, with a huge population but extremely low per capita incomes and slow rates of economic growth. Import tariffs are high; currencies are not generally convertible; industrial infrastructures are inefficient and there is an extensive government bureaucracy that interferes with business operations. In certain areas a handful of firms dominate key distribution systems. Pakistan is the richest country in the region, with a per capita GDP about 20 per cent higher than in India. Ninety-seven per cent of the population of Pakistan are Muslims, and the Islamic religion is highly influential in all aspects of life. Nearly half the population are under 15 years of age and only 2.5 per cent over 65. Sixty per cent of all Pakistanis are illiterate (compared with 45 per cent in India).

Bangladesh is an extremely poor nation, depending substantially on foreign aid which provides half the country's foreign exchange and contributes 10 per cent of Gross National Product. Sri Lanka has much potential for economic development, but is regularly disrupted by conflicts between the country's Buddhist Sinhalese (who account for 70 per cent of the population) and Hindu Tamils (who comprise about 18 per cent). Muslims, Christians, ethnic Malays and Eurasians also live in this nation. Superimposed on religious and ethnic divisions are factional political rivalries that frequently erupt into fighting. India's population is characterised by ethnic divisions (ranging from the Aryan peoples in the north to the Dravidians of the south) and by linguistic diversity. Eighty per cent of the population live in villages. There are about 120 million affluent Indians, with living standards at least comparable with those of Western Europe, and around 400 million people officially classified as unable to afford the basic necessities of life.

AFRICA

7. Doing business in Africa

Africa consists of a mixture of very different economies, including some that are quite well off (oil-rich Libya for instance) and others, like Ethiopia, which rank among the poorest nations in the world. International businesses operating in Africa face a maze of regulations, which are subject to regular and unanticipated alteration. Hence supplying firms need to monitor import and foreign currency regulations on a *continuous* basis (controls and prohibitions can be introduced with less than 24 hours notice) and to take great care where African sales are concerned. Special problems connected with doing business in Africa include:

- Extensive trade barriers including measures to protect local industries, to correct balance of payments deficits and to improve the incomes of particular interest groups. As well as tariffs and quotas there are occasional bans on imports of all forms of 'non-essential' goods to certain countries for prescribed periods (normally in consequence of balance of payments crises). Eighty per cent of all products imported to Africa south of the Sahara excluding South Africa are subject to non-tariff import barriers of some kind, notably discretionary licensing and restrictive foreign exchange controls.
- Large fluctuation in currency exchange rates.
- Prohibitions on hard currency leaving specific countries for anything up to several years at a time.
- The need to obtain a licence for the import of many items to poorer African nations.
- Absence of proper links between urban centres and rural areas, resulting in the fragmentation of markets.

Selling to Africa's 13 landlocked countries can be especially difficult. Overland transport routes are often sub-standard and air links can be poor. Consignments may be held up for long periods at two or three points in the transport system, and goods have to be warehoused during the delays at considerable expense.

The sea journey from Western Europe to (say) Dar-es-Salaam or Mombasa in East Africa normally takes less than four weeks (depending on the number of calls at other ports en-route), but it can take up to five further months for a cargo to reach its final inland destination. Firms need to complete and despatch export documentation long in advance of the transportation of the consignment. Translations of documents may be required as shipments cross national borders. Missing documents or even slight errors within them can cause long hold-ups. Note how communications between African towns might be poor even though communications between those same towns and cities in Europe, Japan or America may be first-class.

The major economic problem facing Africa south of the Sahara is that, in aggregate, population increases are negating the consequences of economic growth, essentially because of the uneven distribution of income within the continent (meaning that the extra people are predominantly destitute poor without the means or possibilities to obtain the incomes needed to purchase significant amounts of goods). According to the United Nations, 4 out of 10 black African pre-school children were suffering from acute protein deficiency in 1990. Foreign aid has risen, but there is little direct foreign investment (less than $US20 billion per annum for the whole of Africa in the early 1990s). Trade between these countries and the outside world is about the same today as in the early 1980s. UN figures suggest that more than half of all sub-Sahara African nations except South Africa depend on just one or two commodities for more than 70 per cent of their export incomes, making them extremely vulnerable to downturns in external demand. Several African countries depend totally on foreign aid; many more are heavily reliant on aid payments. Aid donors, however, are increasingly reluctant to transfer resources to undemocratic nations in view of the political instability (and hence regular civil wars, insurrections, guerrilla fighting and subsequent waste of the aid money donated) that the absence of democracy frequently involves.

8. South Africa

South Africa is the dominant economic power of the southern part of the African continent. The nation is a hotchpotch of races, cultures, distribution and purchasing systems, lifestyles and consumption patterns. Important differences exist between consumers in urban and rural areas, in townships and hostel neighbourhoods, between people in the north and south of the nation, among whites of disparate European origins, blacks in various tribal districts, and between the emerging black middle class and the financially better off sections of the mixed race community. The country has First, Second and Third World consumers, and a huge range of product requirements. Among whites, living standards vary from levels comparable to those of the most affluent residents of Western Europe and the USA, through to modest incomes (which nevertheless are substantial relative to those of most black Africans) for the increasing numbers of white unemployed. Many black South Africans live in dire poverty, especially in rural areas which in effect are agrarian economies operating quite independently of the country as a whole. There is little industrial infrastructure within black rural areas, low rates of economic growth, low life expectancy and high infant mortality.

South Africa has a diversified economy with a strong manufacturing base and extensive natural resources, well developed financial services and a large business community. The problem confronting international business is, of course, the need to penetrate multi-racial, multi-cultural, multi-lingual markets (each differentiated by income, lifestyle and area of residence as well as race) and to appeal to widely disparate customer categories. A new *racially integrated* market is emerging which obliges suppliers to devise cross-cultural non-racial campaigns attractive to all ethnic groups. Analysis of the consumer behaviour of black South Africans is especially complicated. There are, for example, no obvious correlations between illiteracy and level of income or between educational background and consumer preferences, as is the case in developed Western countries. And market research is extremely difficult and expensive on account of the nation's geographical size. Postal and telephone research methods are not available to researchers in many areas: the former because of unevenly distributed postal services and widespread illiteracy among the population, the latter because few households in rural or black urban areas own a telephone. Hence, the face-to-face interview is the commonest research technique. Note the need for research firms to engage separate teams of interviewers to conduct investigations.

Vernacular radio is at present the only medium capable of reaching the entire South African population in their home language. It is crucially important for communicating with black consumers, especially in remote rural areas where there are acute shortages of electricity. The electricity problem has greatly impaired the spread of television to many parts of the country, leaving radio and outdoor as the dominant media for advertising. Frequently the two are used in combination, with posters providing visual support to promotional messages broadcast on radio.

Consequent to the ethnic diversity of the country and its numerous niche markets, most foreign firms doing business in South Africa rely heavily on specialist intermediaries and advisors when marketing their products. South Africa's advertising industry has an infrastructure equal in sophistication to that of any developed country. Virtually all the multinational advertising agencies now operate in South Africa, pursuing the lucrative business flowing from multinational clients currently re-establishing themselves in the South African market. Also there are numerous local agencies. Not surprisingly, South African agencies are well-versed in the art of multi-cultural advertising, and adept at tracking the 'likeability' of clients' advertising messages within the various ethnic communities. A high proportion of the white, Asian and mixed race communities can be reached through a few city stores; conversely, a huge distribution effort is needed to reach a comparable percentage of the black population. As target market segments are broadened to encompass all ethnic groups and, in particular, lower income consumers, distribution has to be extended to include village outlets as well as city supermarkets and major chains. There are in the black townships numerous 'shops' consisting simply of a converted portion of a private house stocking and selling a few essential products needed by the immediate neighbourhood. These outlets are open 24 hours a day and carry only the most popular brands. Hence it can be *extremely* difficult for new brands to enter this important system. Also supplying firms lose all control over presentation and final selling prices.

SOUTH AMERICA

9. Doing business in Latin America

In the past Latin America was a difficult region in which to do business in view of its political instability, bureaucratic state control over companies, trade barriers and currency inconvertibility, and the regular expropriation of foreign firms. Much has improved however in consequence of the general democratisation of the region, liberalisation of trade policies and the removal of exchange controls. Nevertheless, per capita incomes are low, and political risk remains – not least because economic growth has yet to benefit large numbers of people. Expectations of improved living standards have risen in all sections of society, but the uneven distribution of income and wealth in Latin America means that mass poverty persists even while economies are expanding. It is important to note that large proportions of Latin America's middle and upper income groups (which account for a large proportion of total wealth) are concentrated in a handful of cities, creating geographically small local markets possessing tremendous purchasing power – ideal targets for high-priced consumer products. Other positive characteristics of the Latin American scene are that most of the region's major debtor countries have reached agreements with lenders to reduce and reschedule national debts (thus giving Central and South American governments room to manoeuvre when liberalising and expanding their economies) and that protectionism is being abandoned throughout the area. Foreign investment is rising rapidly and substantially. The International Monetary Fund predicts an average annual growth rate of about 3 per cent for Latin America to the year 2000, and it is not impossible that Latin America could take off and become the 'new Pacific Rim'.

THE MIDDLE EAST

10. The Arab world

The Arab world comprises 20 countries containing 155 million people linked by a common heritage, culture and language but with extreme differences in political orientation. Living standards vary enormously, ranging from affluence in the oil-rich Gulf to dire poverty elsewhere. Some Arab states are politically radical; others are extremely conservative in the political and social spheres. Political risk in the Middle East frequently involves religious factors, since the opposition to the governments of several Middle Eastern countries have a fundamentalist religious base. Further risks include the possibilities of a long-term decline in the price of oil and a deterioration in relations between local nationals and the large numbers of foreign workers in many Middle Eastern countries. A factor encouraging political uncertainty is perhaps the absence of democratic government throughout the region.

Apart from the Arabic language, the major factor unifying the Arabic World is the Islamic religion, which affects all aspects of life in Arab countries. It is a basic driving force behind contemporary Arab culture and society, affecting all aspects of behaviour, attitudes, beliefs and morals. Advantages to doing business in the Arabic Middle East include the linguistic and cultural homogeneity of the region (cultural traits within one Arab state are likely to be replicated in others so that promotional messages appropriate for one Arab country will probably be suitable elsewhere); the responsiveness of Arab consumers to Western promotional methods (a Western image is a powerful selling point in many Arab nations); and easy access to markets. Tariff rates are generally low and access to markets is easy. Trading systems are well-developed, and there is a big demand for imported consumer durables. There are vibrant public sectors in oil-rich Arab nations, based on development projects financed by oil revenues. Note moreover how the oil-rich Arab countries have large (predominately male) immigrant populations, comprising professionally qualified westerners plus industrial labourers from poorer Middle East and Asian states. These immigrant groups represent substantial markets in their own right.

Problems confronting businesses wishing to operate in the Arab Middle East are as follows:

(a) Low rates of market growth in a number of nations. The richer Arab countries have chosen to invest their wealth predominantly in non-Arab states outside the Middle East.

(b) The wide geographical area of the pan-Arab market.

(c) Paucity of ancillary business services, especially in the market research and advertising fields.

(d) Long distribution chains, frequently accompanied by family ownership of distribution channels. Family control can result in business decisions being taken on a highly personal basis.

Progress test 4

1. What is NAFTA? Which countries belong to NAFTA?

2. Why is the US legal system so complex?

3. What is the Japanese 'silver market'?

4. What is a *sogo shosha*?

5. Name the 'Four Dragons' of the Pacific Rim.

6. Which Pacific Rim countries are currently experiencing the highest rates of economic growth?

7. What is a Chinese Special Economic Zone?

8. List five problems likely to be encountered by Western firms doing business in China.

9. Name the richest country of the Indian sub-continent and the poorest country of that region.

10. List five problems attached to doing business in central African states.

5

CULTURAL INFLUENCES

1. Importance of culture

International managers need to know about cultural differences among nations in order to be able:

- to communicate effectively with customers, suppliers, business associates and partners in other countries, and with foreign employees (Subhash and Tucker 1995)
- to conduct negotiations and understand the nuances of the bargaining postures of the other parties to a negotiation
- to predict trends in social behaviour likely to affect the firm's foreign operations
- to understand ethical standards and concepts of social responsibility in various countries (Ferraro 1990)
- to predict how cultural differences will affect consumer reactions to advertisements and other promotional forms.

Some of the more important cultural influences on business and society can be grouped under the following headings.

(a) Business environments

Relationships between trade union confederations and employers' associations. Role of government in business affairs. Employment conditions. Extent of employee participation in management decisions. How meetings are conducted. Degree of formality of personal relationships.

(b) Marketing

What people buy (taboos, local tastes, historical traditions, etc.). When people buy (e.g. the spending boom around Christmas in Christian countries). Who does the purchasing (men or women) and the overall pattern of consumer buying behaviour. Which consumer needs are felt more intensely. Which family members take which purchasing decisions. Attitudes towards foreign-supplied products. How the female form may be used in advertising. The acceptability of nudity and/or what parts of the human body may be shown in advertisements. The extent of an advertisement's display of physical contact between people (of the same or of differing sexes). The degree of elegance, quality, urbanity, etc., expected of advertisements. The nature of the national media that carry advertisements, e.g. whether the country has a tabloid press, the editorial content of magazines, newspapers, and radio and television programmes, and the attitudes expressed by the media towards national issues (manifest in non-coverage of 'taboo' subjects, adoption of ideological 'lines', etc.).

(c) Social attitudes

Attitudes towards work and material possessions, entrepreneurship, politics, religion, the role of women in society, wealth accumulation, willingness to accept risk, morality, social class, respect for the law and social institutions, etc.

A firm needs to become progressively more aware of foreign cultures as the nature and extent of its foreign operations alter. Exporters, for example, need only consider those cultural factors likely to affect the foreign marketing of their products. A company that engages in licensing or franchising will need to know something about the general business cultures of the nations in which licenses will be issued. Firms with foreign subsidiaries have to manage local labour and thus require a knowledge of local norms concerning employee relations, attitudes towards work, and so on.

2. Nature of culture

A national culture is the set of beliefs, perspectives, motivations, values and norms shared by the majority of the inhabitants of a particular country. It is reflected in the laws of the country and in its institutions and social standards, though note how laws and institutions may themselves help to form a national culture. Within a nation there might exist a number of sub-groups, each with its own subculture. These subcultures can be very important in shaping a country's destiny, and conflict violently with the national culture as a whole.

Culture is easier to recognise than to define, involving as it does a complex set of interrelating beliefs and ways of living (Leeds *et al* 1994). A nation's culture represents a collective frame of reference through which a wide range of issues and problems are interpreted. It determines how symbols, sounds, pictures and behaviour are perceived by individuals and affects socialisation, friendship patterns, social institutions, aesthetics and language (Usunier 1993). Culture has three primary characteristics: it is *shared* by a group; it is something that people *learn*; and it depends on *environmental* circumstances. A crucially important function of culture is that it helps the individual define *concepts*. A 'concept' is a conscious linking together of images, objects, stimuli or events. Individuals receive huge numbers of messages, so the brain needs a system for classifying them into groups, which can then be dealt with efficiently. For instance, apples, oranges and bananas are all separate and unique items, but the brain will categorise them into a single concept of 'fruit'. Conceptualisation helps the individual to manage data, identify relations among events and objects, and to discover similarities and differences which enable the comparison of items of information. This is vitally important for the design of advertising images because culturally based conceptualisations can determine how a message is interpreted (as good or bad, conservative or risqué, etc.) and *how* the message recipient responds to its contents.

Convergence of cultures

A number of factors have encouraged the convergence of certain aspects of culture among nations, notably:

- improvements in transport and communications and a huge increase in the number of people who visit foreign countries
- globalisation of media, with similar television programmes, newspaper and magazine articles, etc., appearing in all nations
- similarities in the tastes and consumption patterns of young people
- the operations of MNCs across the world, supplying standardised products and frequently using undifferentiated marketing strategies
- a seemingly worldwide increase in consumers' willingness to accept fresh ideas and to try new products
- adoption of similar technologies in numerous countries, creating common work experiences and working methods.

3. Culture and language

The world has about 3,000 distinct languages and around 10,000 dialects. A number of countries have more than one language. Canada for example recognises English and French; Belgium has Flemish in the north, French in the south, and German in the south east. India has 15 main languages and around 800 dialects; around 200 dialects were spoken in the former USSR. Some ex-colonies of Western nations have an 'official' language used for public administration, government communications and the administration of justice, and which is taught in schools alongside the local language or dialect. Typically the official language is English or French (according to the former occupying power) and is used to maintain the unity of the country in the face of numerous regional languages, dialects and (often) ethnic groups. An interesting development has been the adoption of English as the official 'corporate language' of a number of multinational firms that are not based in English-speaking nations (Philips in the Netherlands for instance). Hence intra-firm communications between branches, subsidiaries, etc., in various parts of the world are conducted in English, with company executives being expected to be able to communicate in English as a matter of course.

Translation difficulties

Languages and culture are intimately intertwined, as language is the vehicle through which ideas and perceptions are expressed. Many aspects of a community's culture are reflected in the language it uses, and a detailed knowledge of that language provides illuminative insights into the relevant culture. Equally, ignorance of the nuances of a particular language creates boundless opportunities for the misinterpretation of messages. This creates many difficulties for translation between languages because the cultural concepts underlying particular words and phrases need to be matched as well as (or rather than) the words themselves. Examples of absurd (and commercially damaging) translations abound. For example, Ford's Pinto car sold poorly in certain parts of Latin America, where the word 'pinto' is slang for 'small male sexual organ'. A translation into German of the slogan 'Come alive with Pepsi' turned out as 'Rise from the grave with Pepsi'. Schweppes tonic water became Schweppes bathroom water when translated into Italian. 'Chrysler for power' translated into 'chrysler is an aphrodisiac' in Spanish.

Non-linguistic influences

The meaning of body language also differs from nation to nation. For example, disagreement is indicated by shaking the head from side to side in some countries (the UK for example), or by nodding the head or perhaps by waving a hand in front of the face in certain parts of the world. Showing the soles of the feet to another person (as when putting feet on a desk or placing a foot on the knee) is considered a grave insult in some regions. Further examples of culturally sensitive body language are joining together the thumb and index finger, the 'thumbs up' sign, folding the arms, and sitting cross-legged (as is the case in some Middle Eastern countries). An important cultural difference affecting the conduct of international business relates to the ways in which individuals express (or conceal) their disagreement with other people's statements. Openness and plain speaking is the norm in Western Europe and North America, but not in the Far East – where it may be considered extremely impolite to disagree with a stranger. Many misunderstandings arise from this situation, with Westerners believing that they have successfully negotiated a deal whereas in fact the other side has no intention of confirming the bargain.

Culture affects how people think, quite independently of what they do or the words they utter. Examples are whether people approach issues analytically rather than intuitively, and whether individuals inwardly feel they should be organised and methodical, rather than 'taking life as it comes'. Attitudes towards space and time also differ between nations. Turning up late for an appointment is regarded as a great insult in some countries, as normal in others, or as acceptable only for high ranking social groups. Multinational firms operating in some parts of the world experience great difficulty in getting locally recruited workers to attend work punctually and for pre-set periods. Similarly, different cultures have different norms regarding the physical distance that one person should stand away from another in various circumstances. Physical nearness to other people is regarded as correct in some cultures but rude (representing a violation of 'personal space') in others. Handholding and other forms of physical contact have different meanings in disparate societies.

4. Cultural analysis

In 1945 G. P. Murdock published a highly influential study of what he referred to as 'cultural universals', i.e. aspects of culture supposedly found in all societies. To the extent that cultural universals exist, societies can be regarded as essentially the same and cultural differences between them relatively unimportant. Examples of cultural universals are interest in sport, bodily adornment, courtship, household hygiene, sexual taboos, gift giving, status differentiation, etc. Subsequent approaches to the analysis of culture and the consequences of cultural analysis have focused on lifestyle and, in particular, the taxonomy of cultures into 'high context' or 'low context' categories. The former relates to that which is internalised and/or embedded within the person and not expressed in an explicit manner (Hofstede 1980). Individuals who share the same high-context culture do not feel any need to explain their thoughts or behaviour to each other. Hence high-context culture relies heavily on non-verbal communication. Japan is frequently cited as an example of a country with a high-context culture. Communication within a high-context culture is fast and efficient, but can break down in relation to outsiders who may not be able to comprehend what the high-context group believes or is talking about. Behaviour within a high-context culture is stable and predictable. A problem is that the nature of a particular high-context culture might be misunderstood by outsiders in consequence of the latter's stereotyping of the former's members. In a low-context culture, conversely, communications need to be explicit: words, signs, symbols, rituals, etc., are used to rationalise, communicate and explain cultural norms and social activities. Low-context cultures emphasise individualism rather than collectivism. Communications are clear and precise, and it is necessary to argue and persuade when presenting propositions. Members' values, attitudes, perceptions and patterns of behaviour are diverse and liable to change quickly. It is sometimes suggested that the USA is a good example of a low-context culture.

These issues are important for international businesses, which need to understand the nuances of specific foreign culturally high-context or low-context groups in order to design marketing campaigns and promotional messages that will appeal to them.

Norms and values

A major part of cultural analysis is the identification and characterisation of group norms within various societies. Group norms are shared perceptions of how things should be done or common attitudes feelings or beliefs. As norms emerge, individuals begin behaving according to how they feel other group members expect them to behave. Entrants to an existing society will feel isolated and insecure and hence will actively seek out established norms that will act as a guide to how that person ought to behave. Norms, therefore, facilitate the integration of an individual into a social group, and thus will be eagerly accepted by new members.

Social values are moral principles or standards against which the desirability of certain modes of behaviour may be assessed. Values help determine what an individual considers important, personal priorities, and how he or she assesses other people's worth. Values change over time; some may disappear entirely as environmental circumstances alter. Also, values may vary across industries and from state to state. Nevertheless social values contribute greatly to 'national temperament', a concept easier to recognise than to define, encompassing as it does such matters as tolerance of opposing viewpoints, display of emotion, self-discipline, degree of formality of relationships, etc. National values affect the acceptability of specific messages and symbols, and make important contributions to national culture. For example, 'masculine' values help determine the influence of advertisements that contain assertive messages, that emphasise toughness and vigour, and appeal to the competitive instinct. 'Individualistic' values within consumers imply a preference for advertisements with nonconformist, egocentric themes that focus on the pursuit of self-interest, self-control, etc. Other core values might relate to honesty, social responsibility, ambition and so on. The aim is to discover the existence of similar values within groups of consumers in different countries and hence present a common value-specific theme when promoting a product in disparate states.

5. Evaluating cultural differences

Managers of multinational companies need to assess the importance of the cultural factors likely to be encountered when doing business in various foreign markets. A thorough understanding of another country's culture can only be obtained by learning its language (and becoming aware of the significance of differences in regional dialects); knowing its history; mixing with host nationals socially as well as in working situations; and living in the country for several years. These are obviously impossible tasks for the great majority of managers of international businesses. But it is feasible to identify those cultural influences most likely to cause problems for the firm. One approach to this task is to take an overall view of the cultures of particular nations; another is to focus on just a handful of key variables. The problem with the former method is the enormous number of cultural influences that could be considered. In practice therefore it is more common to seek to identify a handful of key variables believed critically relevant to the firm's operations in each of the countries in which it does business and to examine their implications in great depth. The variables involved might relate to material culture (attitudes towards the possession of objects, accumulation of wealth, etc.), motivation to work, social institutions and social structure, and so on, according to the nature of the enterprise's work. Examples of the methods that might be adopted when applying partial approach are:

- Conducting research in order to describe a typical day in the life of a local consumer of a certain type of product
- An in-depth analysis of the employee relations system of a certain nation, with a view to exposing the underlying attitudes of workers towards employment and their employers
- Studies of the factors that cause local customers to be attracted to a specific category of good.

The difficulty with partial cultural assessment is that although it might identify critical variables relevant to an issue at a particular moment, these variables might change very quickly (see below). Culture, moreover, depends in large part on the *interrelations* between such variables as well as on the elements themselves. And it is easy to assume (wrongly) that a difference between nations is 'cultural', whereas in fact the difference relates to a mundane matter such as firm size, nature of the technology used in production, form of ownership of the enterprise, etc. Note also that in a number of nations there exist regional and social class distinctions within the country that outweigh the effects of dissimilarities between the culture of that particular nation and others. People undertaking the same occupation in disparate nations may share more in common with each other in terms of attitude, lifestyle, housing conditions and so on than they share with fellow nationals. Indeed, some analysts have suggested that the influence of culture on customer preferences is over exaggerated. Theodore Levitt, for example, contended that provided a company supplies reliable high quality products at attractive prices then customers throughout the world will be happy to purchase them in a standardised form (Levitt 1983). He suggested moreover that to the extent that international firms do modify their outputs for local markets, this results more from managerial preassumptions that differences in local preferences exist than from actual variations in national preferences! Culture represents just one of several environments within which a company operates. Political considerations and/or economic laws of supply and demand frequently outweigh cultural effects.

Predicting cultural change

National cultures change over time, possibly in consequence of the following forces:

(a) Immigration and emigration, especially if the people coming in have a different religion and lifestyle than members of the existing population.

(b) Rising (or in some cases falling) living standards.

(c) Improvements in education systems, with consequent increases in the proportions of the population that is literate.

(d) Economic destabilisation (as occurred in East Europe in the early 1990s for example).

(e) Opening up of foreign trade and the influx of new ideas from other countries.

(f) Increased opportunities for consumption (a wider range of products, shorter working hours, longer holidays, etc.)

(g) Urbanisation of populations.

(h) Changes in the extent of government control of an economy.

(i) Improvements in state welfare provision: old age pensions, child support, national health services and so on.

(j) Introduction of new technologies which necessarily change working practices and relationships.

Examination of trends in these and similar variables can help a firm predict cultural changes likely to affect its operations in a particular country.

6. Stereotyping and self-referencing

An international manager's awareness of national differences should not be clouded by stereotyping, i.e. the attribution to an individual by other people of a number of characteristics assumed typical of the group to which the person belongs. Self-stereotyping can also be important, and create problems. Thus for example managers from countries generally regarded as superefficient may regard *themselves* as superefficient, regardless of whether this is actually the case. Equally serious is the problem of cultural 'self-referencing, i.e. the (unconscious) preassumption by an individual that the culture of his or her own country is the appropriate one against which other cultures should be assessed. Rather it is necessary to look at problems and issues from *foreign* as well as home country norms and perspectives and identify clearly the difference between the two. Local nationals should be consulted, as they will be sensitive to local cultural influences and will understand the 'inner logic' of the local way of life.

Ethnocentrism can cost an international business dear. Ethnocentrism is the tendency to regard one's own nation, group or culture as superior and to compare the standards of other nations, groups or cultures against this belief. It can lead to fundamental misunderstandings of foreign consumer attitudes and business practices, to inefficiency, and bad relations with host country governments. Ethnocentrism contrasts with polycentrism, which regards other nations, groups and cultures as different but of equal value, and with *geocentrism*, that sees some but not all nations, groups and cultures as being of equal status. (The term geocentric is also used by some writers to describe the management approach adopted by companies which co-ordinate all their activities on the global scale, planning and resourcing without regard for national considerations.) A possible disadvantage with polycentrism is that it can cause a firm (inappropriately) to avoid transferring excellent home country practices intact to other nations. Also, delegation of duties to local subsidiaries may be excessive, leading to problems of control and co-ordination.

To overcome potential biases when evaluating foreign cultures, the following procedure might be adopted:

(a) Define the issue or problem to be studied in terms of the cultural norms, traits and perspectives of the home country.

(b) Repeat this exercise, without applying value judgements, using the cultural norms, traits and perspectives of residents of the foreign country.

(c) Compare the results of (a) and (b) and identify cultural differences that emerge from the analysis.

(d) Consider how these cultural differences might influence the interpretation of the original issue or problem.

(e) Redefine the issue or problem having removed cultural bias.

7. Culture and the multinational company

Multinational companies (perhaps unwittingly) are important agents for transplanting foreign cultures into nations. Normally a firm will seek to work within existing local culture patterns, although this may not always be possible. Accordingly, MNCs establishing fresh subsidiaries in foreign countries and which need to introduce working methods that might conflict with local cultures should try to build upon rather than destroy traditional values and practices; implement controversial measures only when there is a definite need for them; try to protect employees from the adverse consequences of unfamiliar methods;

and communicate with employees as much as possible. Special problems apply when existing foreign firms are taken over in their entirety as going concerns, as certain culturally related management practices and policies will apply within the acquired businesses. The following are particularly likely to have been influenced by the national culture of the host country:

(a) Extent of individual loyalty and commitment to an employing company. Managers identify with their employing organisations very closely in some countries. Elsewhere they may feel more committed to an occupation, profession or specific functional role.

(b) Whether decision making is centralised or decentralised. Cultural factors might cause the senior managers of organisations in certain nations to take all important decisions themselves. In other countries employee participation in management decision making and extensive delegation are common.

(c) Authority systems within firms: whether they are hierarchical and bureaucratic, or democratic, flexible, and free and easy. This will relate to organisation structure, especially the number of levels of management within the enterprise.

(d) The extent of nepotism within organisations.

(e) Attitudes towards bribery (*see* **9**).

Culture and motivation

Many aspects of motivation have a cultural dimension. The factors that motivate people in one society might only have a limited effect in others, and it would be mistaken for MNC managers to assume that personnel in foreign branches and subsidiaries can be motivated using the same approaches as in the head office country. What is clear, however, is that the same basic motivational process applies to people in all nations, namely the existence of an unsatisfied need, followed by attempts to satisfy the need and (hopefully) eventual need gratification. Individuals pursue goals that they value, but the particular goals that they work towards may well be heavily influenced by national culture. In other words the specific 'needs' felt by individuals can have a cultural foundation. The problem is that in many countries there are numerous subcultures, each generating its own unique set of need perceptions. Hence the task of identifying the cultural factors underlying motivation in a particular country becomes extremely complex.

8. Lifestyles

Culture is a major determinant of lifestyle. Other important influences on lifestyle are income, upbringing, personal experiences, and relationships with the community at large. Lifestyle involves a pattern of living habits, leisure pursuits, types of entertainment purchased, degree of involvement with the community and so on. It seems, moreover, that consumers often buy goods they feel they ought to purchase in order to pursue a particular lifestyle rather than products they objectively need! 'Vicarious participation' in a certain desired way of life (e.g. healthy, sophisticated, outdoor, 'man-about-town', etc.) is sometimes possible *via* consuming goods mentally associated with the lifestyle to which the individual aspires.

Lifestyles have been analysed and classified into a number of categories. The aim is to identify in consumers certain common characteristics, such as:

- attitudes towards home, family, security and the propriety of the *status quo*
- whether they are 'inner directed' (i.e. concerned with personal growth individual freedom and human relations) or 'outer directed' materialists who gain greater satisfaction from physical consumption of goods
- the degree of logic and rationality they apply to purchasing decisions
- whether their outlooks are 'conservative and traditional' or whether they are 'innovative and adventurous'
- the extent to which their main concern is merely to exist and survive rather than engage in luxury and/or conspicuous consumption
- whether they are motivated by materialistic or non-materialistic drives.

For each of these dimensions a number of sub-categories may be discerned (e.g. ambitious achievers; the near-destitute struggling poor; the materialistic young, etc.) within various countries. Then the particular characteristics of each group in each market can be described and the geographical whereabouts of these consumers pinpointed. Accordingly, it becomes possible to redraw the map of the world, not according to national frontiers, but rather in terms of the locations of specific types of consumer.

Within economically advanced nations the basic distinction that emerges from lifestyle studies is between haves and have-nots. Among the haves there appear to be three groups: idealists involved in the higher realms of human affairs (art, music, ecology and so on); materialists with high profile spending habits; and a comfortably off suburban middle class exhibiting 'traditional' attitudes and consumer behaviour. Have nots, it seems, divide into two categories: those who (while poor) have skills, jobs (albeit with occasional bouts of unemployment) and some prospects; and a disaffected underclass without cultural or economic roots, and which is prone to long-term unemployment.

9. Bribery

Bribery is deeply embedded in the cultures of many nations. It is said to distort market mechanisms, create unfair competitive advantage for certain firms, and hence lead to an inefficient allocation of national resources. Yet although bribery is officially frowned on throughout the world (including those countries in which it is extensively practised), it is not illegal in a number of countries. Indeed it might even be tax deductible as a business expense! Inducements paid to public servants are subject to particular criticism, as in this case it is the innocent taxpayer (rather than private shareholders) who ultimately foots the bill. Acceptance of bribes by government officials results in many countries from the historical tradition of 'prebendalism', i.e. the charging of fees by holders of public positions that receive only a nominal stipend. Governments overlook petty corruption on the part of minor officials because otherwise they would have to increase the latter's wages to levels sufficient to induce them to remain in their jobs. Nations with poorly developed tax systems do not have the wherewithal to finance an extensive civil service and thus implicitly rely on public officials supplementing their meagre salaries by taking unofficial gratuities.

Large-scale bribery in advanced industrial countries results perhaps not from pernicious intent on the part of the bribers, but rather from the fact that so many Western markets are dominated by a small handful of firms in uncompetitive environments, i.e. it is lack of genuine competition within a sector that is the root cause of corruption. Bribery on this view is little more than a natural business response to a particular situation. In many of the less developed nations bribery is accepted as a normal part of business life. Bribes are not considered to be 'corrupt' payments, but rather as fees for commissioning a service – just like any other service fee or personal commission. Equally, low value payments might be seen as the equivalent of the 'tips' conventionally given to waiters, waitresses or taxi drivers in developed countries. It may not be possible to conclude deals quickly and efficiently without the payment of bribes in certain nations (Boatright 1993).

The case for adopting a liberal approach to bribery can be based on the following arguments:

(a) Distinguishing between a 'bribe' and a 'gift' is problematic. Note how the giving of small gifts is very common in Western countries. But what constitutes a 'small' gift; and where should the line be drawn between low and high value items? An expensive gift to a managing director with a million pound annual salary might be considered reasonable; yet the same gift to a lower ranking employee could be deemed as corruption!

(b) There is in reality no reliable means for ensuring that all gifts are reported, so why bother attempting to control the practice?

(c) Firms *not* engaging in bribery in some countries stand to lose money, resulting in job losses and other detrimental economic effects for the host countries concerned.

(d) Consultancy and agency fees remitted to third parties might in fact be bribes, yet be virtually undetectable as improper payments.

(e) Arguably, bribes should be seen as an integral part of the market system. If firms find it worthwhile to offer bribes they will do so, and a 'market price' for bribes will emerge in any given situation depending on the supply and demand for favours. Note that because bribes are 'unofficial' in nature, there is no guarantee that the recipient will in fact fulfil his or her part of the bargain.

Anti-corruption laws are to be found in a number of countries. Domestic law always applies to this matter, because there is at present no international agreement regarding the control of corrupt practices. Significant differences exist in the details of the laws on corruption in countries which have them, since governments and societies apply disparate definitions and interpretations of what a 'corrupt practice' actually entails. The USA has particularly stringent laws on these matters. Its Foreign Corrupt Practices Act 1977 was the consequence of the bad publicity that accompanied a number of bribery cases involving US-based multinationals which, under the Act, are now forbidden from giving bribes or any other questionable payments *anywhere in the world*. Heavy fines can be imposed on any US resident who knowingly accepts a bribe or authorises the payment of a bribe.

Progress test 5

1. Why do managers of international enterprises need to know about cultural influences?

2. How might national culture affect the marketing function?

3. Define culture.

4. List the three primary characteristics of culture.

5. What factors have encouraged the convergence of national cultures?

6. Why are language and culture closely related?

7. What is a cultural universal?

8. What is a group norm?

9. How can national cultural differences be evaluated?

10. List some of the main factors that can cause a national culture to change over time.

11. What is meant by 'self-referencing'?

12. Define ethnocentrism.

13. What is 'lifestyle'?

14. Discuss the case for adopting a liberal approach towards bribery.

6

THE INTERNATIONAL ECONOMIC ENVIRONMENT

1. Importance of the economic environment

Businesses exist and trade within national economic systems that possess unique characteristics, prospects and difficulties; and within a global environment with features that transcend national frontiers (notably the international monetary environment, Chapter 14). International managers need to take an interest in both the economic structures of the countries in which they wish to do business and in the international economy as a whole, in order to:

- establish the sizes and characteristics of various markets
- assess the degree of risk attached to operating in specific nations
- identify high growth sectors
- make investment decisions
- deploy company resources in the most effective way.

Typically an international firm's foreign subsidiaries will collect information on national economies; headquarters staff then interpret it (possibly in liaison with local subsidiary managers) and make cross-national comparisons using standard criteria. Head office might issue to subsidiaries *pro forma* questionnaires concerning local economic conditions, to be filled-in on (say) a semi-annual basis.

ECONOMIC SYSTEMS

2. National economic policies

All governments would claim to aspire to the attainment of four major economic objectives:

- full employment
- a high rate of economic growth
- a low rate of inflation
- absence of a deficit in the country's balance of payments.

Certain governments would also include additional targets such as equality in the distribution of the nation's wealth, an even pattern of regional economic development, making the country attractive to foreign investors – or other objectives congruent with the political complexion of the government concerned. In relation to the four primary objectives, however, the basic problem is that economic policies which help achieve the first pair of aims (full employment and a high rate of growth) are usually damaging for the second pair. Expansionary measures such as low interest rates, tax cuts and increases in public spending stimulate the economy and create jobs, but also encourage (a) firms to raise their prices and (b) workers to demand higher wages (using the threat of industrial action in a labour shortage situation). Also, increased consumer expenditure leads to higher imports and a worsening of the country's balance of trade!

The policy-making problem, therefore, is how best to balance the effects of the policies needed to achieve the four objectives. Of course, the difficulty would be overcome if it were possible to have a separate and *independent* policy to deal with each *objective* in isolation. For example, interest rates could be varied to control inflation; public spending and/or tax rates could be altered to secure economic growth; tariffs, quotas and import controls could be applied to improve the balance of payments; and government make-work programmes and perhaps military conscription could be used to secure full employment. In the real world, however, democracies cannot impose draconian legislative controls (and it is by no means certain that the laws would be obeyed if they did), and international agreements (plus the threat of foreign retaliation) prohibit interference with the flow of foreign trade.

3. Foreign economic policy

This comprises all the government's policies and decisions concerning the magnitude, composition, direction and nature of the country's international trade and investment. It includes, *inter alia*, tariff policy, exchange rate policy (e.g. decisions on whether to intervene on foreign exchange markets in order to stabilise the price of a nation's currency and, if so, to what extent); grants and subsidies offered to foreign investors; and macroeconomic fiscal and monetary policies (tax and interest rate changes for example) intended to influence the balance of payments. Specific targets of foreign economic policy might include the following.

(a) Reduction of a country's dependence on international trade. This 'isolationist' stance is very rare nowadays but is still pursued by a few national governments which justify it on the grounds that extensive foreign trade:

- creates economic instability (especially in consequence of exchange rate changes and their effects on import prices and hence domestic rates of inflation) and interferes with national economic plans
- discourages national self-sufficiency, hence making the country vulnerable during times of war
- damages domestic industries the outputs of which are displaced by foreign imports
- makes the country's economic welfare dependent on foreign markets and/or sources of supply.

(b) The direct opposite of the above, i.e. expansion of foreign trade and the encouragement of direct foreign investment in order to (i) maximise the benefits of international specialisation, (ii) increase the choice of goods available to domestic consumers, and (iii) enable domestic companies to obtain economies of scale.

(c) Maintenance of domestic employment. A government might seek to create jobs for its own residents through (i) controlling imports of items that compete with home-produced goods in labour-intensive industries, and (ii) offering large inducements to foreign firms to set up operations within the home country.

(d) Creation of equilibrium in the balance of payments (*see* **10**). Persistent balance of payments deficits inevitably lead to currency depreciation and hence to higher import prices. To prevent fluctuations in the domestic economy caused by balance of payments problems a government might intervene the moment difficulties begin to appear and impose trade restrictions designed to remove the payments deficit very quickly.

(e) Stimulation of domestic economic development, e.g. by protecting 'infant industries' (*see* **12**).

Governments may adopt *laissez-faire* or interventionist economic policies. Each approach has advantages and disadvantages for domestic residents, and many implications for the operations of international businesses.

4. Advantages and disadvantages of free market economies

Advocates of free markets argue that *laissez-faire* government policies will in normal circumstances guarantee the attainment of a just and equitable society. Business people, they argue, are in business to maximise their profits, not to make moral judgement about others. Thus, through constantly seeking to improve profitability, firms – according to this argument – increase not only their own returns, but also the wealth of the wider society. In a market economy prices determine which goods firms want to produce; production costs and the availability of resources determine how they are produced (and the incomes that factor inputs shall receive); while consumer spending determines the market prices which themselves generate production. Goods that are most wanted by consumers command the highest prices. Hence, firms will consciously seek to satisfy consumer demands and will demand the quantity and types of labour needed to meet this requirement.

Concerns for the environment, social justice, etc., are treated in much the same way as demands for particular products. For example, it is assumed that if people want the environment to possess certain characteristics, they will be prepared to pay for them, and organisations will naturally spring up that (in return for payment) will seek to manipulate the environment to satisfy the public's desires. Social considerations need not concern individual firms. Managers are not trained or competent in social work, and business is not part of the social security system.

The case against free markets

The opposing view asserts that state intervention is essential for ensuring that firms do not behave in irresponsible and socially damaging ways. Large businesses possess enormous economic and – by implication – social power. They can manipulate communities and appropriate for themselves revenues far in excess of those justified by their contributions to society. Firms are able to initiate social change, and it is reasonable therefore that society, through its elected representatives, determines the direction that change should take. Businesses, moreover, are components of a wider economic, social and legal system. As social organisations, they must necessarily be concerned with social issues – education and training, occupational health and safety, incomes and employment, labour relations, equal opportunities and so on. Thus, some managerial prerogatives must be surrendered for the common good.

5. Interventionism

The advantages claimed for interventionist approaches are as follows:

(a) With intervention, production and employment levels are not dependent on the whims of the market (which can behave in a highly erratic fashion) but rather on a systematic national economic plan that takes into account the needs of *all* sections of society. Economic growth can be stimulated, leading to low rates of unemployment in the long run.

(b) The dignity of labour is recognised. Workers are regarded at the national level as genuine social partners and not merely as another means for producing output.

(c) Environmentally damaging and other anti-social consequences of free-market activities can be prevented.

(d) The state can promote equality of income distribution among the population.

(e) National resources may be directed towards social ends, with social justice and fair living standards for all.

Problems with extensive government intervention include the possibilities that it might:

- put important economic decisions affecting the wealth of millions of people into the hands of a small number of incompetent bureaucrats
- create inefficiencies and overmanning throughout the economy
- cause industries to be inflexible and highly resistant to change (since the profit motive which frequently impels the introduction of new technologies and methods is artificially constrained)
- distort the pattern of competition and give unfair advantages to certain enterprises, industries and employee groups
- restrict personal freedom
- make a country internationally uncompetitive.

Note, moreover, that when governments commit errors the errors they commit are on a grand scale; large numbers of people are likely to suffer following the implementation of an ill-considered policy.

ECONOMIC STRUCTURE

6. Key economic variables

Managers of international businesses need to understand and assess the economic forces at work in a large number of nations. Key variables that have to be examined include gross domestic product (GDP) in total and per head of population, the regional distribution of GDP, levels of capital investment, consumer expenditures, labour costs, inflation rates and levels of unemployment. Comparison of the economic conditions prevailing in many disparate countries is a formidable task. There are problems of data comparability, unreliability of information on certain economies, differences in data collection periods, and so on. Each firm will of course be interested in a particular set of economic variables specifically relevant to its operations, and will concentrate on these at the expense of other information. Thus, a business that processes large amounts of raw materials will want to know about the availability of these resources in various parts of the world; the costs of extracting them in different countries; local transport systems, etc. It will not be bothered about per capita income levels and other data relevant to consumer analysis. A consumer goods manufacturer, on the other hand, needs to gather information on rates of growth of GDP, consumer expenditure, household incomes and other consumer-related economic statistics, but will not be concerned whether potential targets for market entry do or do not possess natural resources.

Variables frequently examined when assessing national economic environments include the following:

(a) *Economic structure*. The structure of a country's economy is determined by the size and rate of growth of its population, income levels and the distribution of income, natural resources, agricultural and manufacturing activities, and the magnitude of its services sector. Economic *infrastructure* is the totality of all the external facilities and services that support the work of firms, including (i) communication and transportation systems, (ii) electricity supply, and (iii) 'commercial infrastructure' that encompasses banking and financial services, distribution networks, advertising agencies, market research and public relations firms, etc. Lack of economic infrastructure is a major impediment to the improvement of living standards in the world's poorer nations.

(b) *Industry structure*. The structure of a specific industry is determined by such factors as:

- Barriers to entry and to exit. An example of the latter is the need to abandon expensive specialist capital equipment following withdrawal from an industry sector.

- Number of competing firms.
- Distribution of market shares among businesses, e.g. whether all firms have roughly equal market shares, rather than a handful of companies dominating the market.
- Average size of competing units.

(c) *Market growth*. This is usually measured in real local currency terms. A 'real' monetary value is one that has been adjusted for the effects of inflation (if all prices double then the nominal value of total consumption within a country will also double, even though only the same quantity of goods is being purchased). Local currency valuations need to be used because translations into other currencies (US dollars for example) are affected by (sometimes very large) exchange rate fluctuations, creating false impressions of changes in market demand.

(d) *Income levels* (normally proxied by gross domestic product per head of population) and rates of economic growth. A country might have high per capita GDP yet experience stagnant rates of growth. 'Disposable' (or 'net') income is another important variable. This nets out tax payments from individuals' gross incomes.

(e) *Sectoral trends*. Growth and economic activity within a country might vary significantly among specific industry sectors.

(f) *Openness of the economy*. The ratio of a country's imports and exports to its gross national product indicates its vulnerability to fluctuations in international trade. A nation with a high foreign trade/GNP ratio depends heavily on the economic well-being of the countries to which it is exporting. Closed economies, conversely, have a high degree of control over their economic futures.

(g) *International indebtedness*. The comparison of a nation's obligations to service and repay foreign debt with its foreign exchange earnings shows its capacity to remain solvent in the face of a balance of payments crisis. Note however that a high foreign debt servicing requirement could be a positive economic indicator, possibly suggesting that a country has borrowed heavily in order to invest in modern plant and equipment in order to secure a brighter economic future.

(h) *Degree of urbanisation*. This is an important factor because in most countries there are many important differences in incomes and lifestyle between urban and rural areas. Major dissimilarities are likely to apply in relation to:

- Shopping patterns: the frequency with which consumers visit shops; size and type of retail outlet; average value of purchase (city dwellers typically go shopping more often than people in the countryside), etc.
- The natures of goods purchased
- Expectations in relation to the quality and technical sophistication of products
- Education levels, since cities usually offer more possibilities for formal eduction. This in turn affects literacy rates and hence local residents' perspectives on a whole range of issues.
- The ease with which goods can be distributed.

7. Gross domestic product (GDP)

GDP is the total value of all final goods and services produced in the economy over a 12 month period. Gross *national* product (GNP) is GDP plus net property income from abroad (i.e. net profits, dividends, rent and interest). *Net* national product (also known as 'national income') is GNP minus depreciation of the country's capital stock. Cross-national comparisons of GDP are extremely problematic. The reliability of information varies from state to state, and a number of conceptual problems are involved, as follows:

(a) Only monetary exchanges are included. Thus 'do-it-yourself' activities are not counted; nor is voluntary charity work or 'self-service' production such as food items produced by agricultural workers and consumed by themselves and their families. Such activities are very important in some nations.

(b) It is assumed that goods prices represent the true worth of the items purchased. This might not be true, because monopolies may be supplying certain goods and monopolies can charge prices far higher than their natural levels.

(c) Environmental pollution and deteriorations in the quality of life caused by higher levels of production are ignored.

(d) In developing countries, observed increases in GDP can be meaningless as it could simply be the case that more people in remote areas are beginning to use money as a means of exchange (rather than barter) and that money transactions are recorded: actual production levels might not have altered at all.

(e) State-owned industries might deliberately underprice their outputs.

(f) Income from illegal activities (smuggling, prostitution or the sale of narcotics for example) is not counted, even though these activities are big earners in certain countries.

(g) The quality of output could rise dramatically, but if its price remains stable GDP will not be seen to rise.

(h) GDP only includes physical investment. Improvements in human capital (the skills of the workforce, health of the population, etc.) are not considered.

THE BALANCE OF PAYMENTS

8. Importance of the balance of payments

The principal source of information on a country's external trading relations is the statement of its balance of payments, which is a summary record of all the transactions that occur between residents of that country and foreigners over a specified period of time. Most nations publish their balance of payments figures monthly, quarterly and annually. The accounts themselves show the structure of a nation's external trade, its net position as an international lender or borrower, and trends in the direction of its economic relationships with the rest of the world.

The state of a country's balance of payments is a good overall indicator of its economic health; the likelihood of the country's government imposing foreign exchange controls, import restrictions and deflationary economic policies such as tax increases and interest rate rises; and whether a devaluation might occur. Examination of a country's balance of payments account can also indicate the extent of competition likely to be encountered from other imported products.

9. The balance of payments account

The account itself is constructed on the principle of double-entry book-keeping, meaning that each receipt and payment is recorded twice, once in each of two columns (debit and credit), so that when the two columns are totalled they must in theory add up to the same amount. In practice, however, measurement errors and delays in the reporting of transactions prevent this, so that a 'balancing item' has to be inserted in order to reconcile the two sides of the account. Receipts resulting from exports or inflows of capital are recorded as credit items; payments for imports and capital outflows appear as debits. Balance of payments accounts attempt to identify the reasons behind various categories of international receipts and payments. Hopefully, therefore, it becomes possible to establish the values of total payments by domestic residents to foreigners (and vice versa) for such purposes as the purchase of imports, the use of services (shipping for example), short and long-term lending, or direct foreign investment. Hence the account is divided into categories for long-term and short-term financial transactions; transactions initiated by the national monetary authorities and all other monetary movements; and transactions involving goods and services. A further division contains information on the value of 'unilateral transfers' such as gifts or wages sent by workers in one country to their relatives in other states. There is a standard United Nations recommended layout that all countries apply in order to make possible the international comparison of the balance of payments positions of various nations.

10. Deficits and surpluses

Newspaper and television reports regularly refer to 'deficits' and 'surpluses' in a country's balance of payments account. But the balance of payments always balances (by definition) so how is it possible to define shortfalls or excesses in this regard? In fact, reported 'deficits' or 'surpluses' actually refer to particular groupings of transactions *within* the body of the accounts. The most widely discussed grouping is perhaps the 'current account' of the balance of payments, which records physical imports and exports plus international transactions in 'invisibles', i.e. non-physical items such as residents' receipts of pensions, interest and royalties from abroad (and payments of such items to foreign countries), domestic firms' fees for arranging the transportation of goods belonging to firms in other countries, private gifts (foreign workers sending parts of their wages to families in other countries for example), and so on. The 'balance of trade' within the current account is the balance on visible (physical) imports and exports.

The other major grouping frequently identified is the 'capital account' which shows the balance on transactions in financial assets, including direct portfolio investments in foreign shares and debentures (and foreigners' purchases of these assets within the country concerned), movements in short-term financial assets such as Treasury bills and other short-dated stock, intergovernmental loans, and changes in the country's official gold and foreign exchange reserves.

Clearly, reserves will decline if, for example, there is a current account deficit but no offsetting inflow of capital account funds, because residents' demands for foreign exchange to pay for imports will exceed foreigners' demands for the deficit country's currency, so that the deficit country's currency exchange rate will fall *via* the forces of supply and demand for foreign exchange. Hence in order to prevent the exchange rate dropping too far (consequently increasing import prices and thus the domestic rate of inflation) the deficit country's government will sell part of its stock of foreign exchange reserves on the open market in order to satisfy the excess demand for foreign currency. Note, however, that this can only be a temporary measure because the country only has a limited amount of reserves. Therefore, in the face of a continuing deficit it must either be prepared to allow the exchange rate to fall to a very low level, or implement deflationary economic policies (tax rises, higher interest rates, cutbacks in public spending, etc.) and/or import and exchange controls designed to remove the current account deficit.

11. Interpreting balance of payments statements

Many difficulties are associated with the interpretation of balance of payments statements. For example, smuggling is a significant activity in some countries – but not one that is officially recognised or recorded in their balances of payments. Also there might be innocent non-recording or under-recording of some consignments of imported or exported items: agents might conduct business on behalf of foreigners but not be aware that this is the case, companies often engage in transfer pricing (*see* 17:**13**), and so on. Note, moreover, that a country's balance of payments account represents a statement of its external trade position over a particular period. It does not indicate the *causes* of the underlying forces that led to the results.

Accounts for the same period can change radically over time as more data becomes available. For example, the current account for the first quarter of a certain year might show a deficit when first published, but a surplus when subsequently revised in about 12 months' time. Yet media attention (and stock exchange reaction) focuses on the preliminary figures as they appear. And the groupings of transactions within the accounts themselves are to some extent arbitrary. A 'deficit' becomes a surplus if certain items are removed and others inserted in a particular category. The magnitude of the balancing item can be enormous compared to other elements of the accounts. Indeed it sometimes exceeds the total value of a country's current account deficit or surplus! Current account deficits themselves only become problematic if there is no corresponding inflow of capital account deficit, this being offset by capital account transactions.

FREE TRADE VERSUS PROTECTION

The case for free trade rests on the proposition that it enables firms and countries to specialise in the activities they perform best; leading to greater efficiency, more production and higher standards of living throughout the world. Jobs are created, consumers enjoy a wider choice of goods, firms have wider markets, and there is extensive communication between people in different nations (thus facilitating world peace and international understanding). Governments increasingly recognise the benefits of free trade, and there has been widespread liberalisation of international trade practices and procedures during the post-Second World War era. Yet despite their nominal support for free trade, many nations continue to use restrictive measures in order to improve their balance of payments. All countries have import tariffs; some have exchange controls and non-tariff restrictions (import quotas for example); a few operate a variety of hidden import barriers.

12. Reasons for protection

Tariffs are imposed to reduce the level of imports (hence improving the balance of payments) and to raise revenue for the state (Giles 1986). In order to achieve the latter objective a tariff needs to apply to an 'essential' good in the sense that importers will continue to buy it despite the higher tariff-inclusive 'domestic price'. Other reasons for restricting imports include the following:

(a) Saving domestic jobs. This is often advocated when foreign competitors are paying their workforces extremely low wages. The difficulty with the argument for restricting imports from low wage countries is the fact that wage rates are just one of several determinants of unit labour costs: productivity differences can more than offset the effects of low wages, so that goods made in high wage nations may actually be cheaper than in low wage regions.

(b) Developing 'infant industries', i.e. enabling recently established industries to secure a sound domestic base before they have to face international competition. Thus, restrictions imposed to achieve this objective are intended to be short term, designed to facilitate a rapid change in a country's economic structure, and possibly accompanied by generous tax and other incentives for companies investing in the relevant sector. The justification for protecting infant industries is that certain types of business require economies of scale in production, marketing, research and technical development, finance and general management in order to be able to compete on the world stage. Hence firms need to attain a certain minimum volume of output very quickly, or they will not survive. Foreign competition would prevent this from happening, so that government needs to protect domestic markets for local firms until they have developed the critical mass necessary for them to be able to fend for themselves. Local consumers face higher prices and restricted product choice in the short term, but should benefit from living in a stronger economy in the longer period. Objections to the infant industry argument are that:

- If the industry concerned really does have a bright future then local and international capital markets should be willing to finance short run losses in anticipation of expected long-term gains. Hence there ought not to be any need for government support.
- To the extent that economies of scale exist they can soon be realised through mergers of domestic firms and/or by entering joint ventures with foreign businesses.
- Government officials have to decide which particular industries to support. They must 'pick winners' from a range of candidates vying for government help. Politicians and civil servants often do not possess the skills and business experience necessary to make such decisions, and generally have a poor track record in making successful choices. Also 'infant industries' might never grow up: the absence of foreign competition encourages inefficiency and lack of investment. Note moreover that infant industries can be encouraged through direct government subsidy rather than import restrictions, and in this case consumers will not have to pay a higher price.

(c) Protecting old and inefficient industries while they are modernising. The counter-argument here is that unprofitable firms should be allowed to go to the wall, and that any business with reasonable prospects ought to be able to attract private backers to finance its rationalisation.

(d) Preserving national heritage and culture. Certain agricultural and craft industries have been protected on this justification.

(e) Facilitating the implementation of an overall industrial strategy through encouraging the development of some activities while discouraging others.

(f) Strengthening the country's bargaining position in international trade negotiations.

(g) Diversifying the domestic economy, especially if the country depends on the export of just one or a few items of its earnings of foreign exchange.

(h) Stimulating production in industrial sectors which supply goods that compete with imports. Retaliation by other countries is the obvious problem with this approach.

(i) Defending 'strategic industries'. Armaments and defence-related industries are sometimes protected in order to guarantee the availability of these items in the event of war. The counter-arguments here are that (i) direct government subsidies would enable these industries to survive without having to resort to tariffs and other protective devices, and (ii) foreign firms can always be taken over during a war (provided local residents are competent to manage these enterprises). Also it is usually far cheaper to stockpile strategic items than the price of preventing their importation.

Some countries also protect 'basic' industries such as agriculture or certain types of manufacture on the grounds of national security, arguing that the government cannot allow these sectors to be driven out of business through competition with imports because they are essential in the event of a national emergency.

(j) Attracting foreign investment. Exporters to a nation with high tariffs may decide to set up their own producing units inside the country in order to avoid paying tariffs on shipments to the markets or having to confront other protective measures. (This is said to have occurred on a large scale following the formation of the European Common Market.) Such foreign investment supplements domestic capital and raises the technological profile of the nation concerned. The counter-argument is that inward investment could equally be attracted through the provision of government grants and subsidies, although these have to be financed by local taxpayers, and the higher taxes involved might be politically unpopular. Tariffs encourage domestic production at no monetary cost to the government, whereas subsidies, tax relief, investment grants and other handouts to domestic firms all have to be paid for.

(k) Retaliating against unfair trade practices on the part of foreign suppliers, e.g. to prevent the dumping of items in a country at a price lower than their cost of production (Matsumoto and Finlayson 1990). Dumping can wipe out domestic competition, but does allow consumers to obtain goods at a very low price – at least in the short term. This is a complex matter which is considered further below.

13. Dumping

It can be extremely difficult to assess whether selling prices are in fact below production cost. The World Trade Organisation (*see* 1:8) defines dumping as any sale in an export market at a price below the price charged in the supplying firm's own country (plus transport and foreign distribution costs), whatever the motivation (disposal of surplus stock, penetration of markets, etc.). It is an 'unfair trading practice' under WTO regulations, so that the governments of affected countries are permitted to impose special import taxes on offending products.

Firms engage in dumping to undercut foreign competitors and drive them out of business, to use existing spare capacity in order to develop foreign markets, and/or to shift end-of-range stock. The customs authorities of individual countries decide whether an item has been 'dumped', although European Union nations apply a uniform calculation to the issue. Under the EU rules the price considered is that which the exporting firm charges to non-related local distributors, *not* the price paid by final consumers. A non-related local distributor is one that is not tied to the supplying firm *via* an agency agreement or exclusive dealership. If all distributors are in fact 'related' to the supplying foreign firm then the price charged to end consumers is used. Problems arise in assessing reasonable values for mark-ups attributable to transport, distribution, and other costs involved in foreign selling, and from the common situation whereby firms supply a market with units of the same item produced by subsidiaries in *several* different countries (so that there is no single 'domestic' price for the purpose of comparison).

Because dumping is universally regarded as an unfair business practice, governments are allowed to seek to prevent it (under Article 6 of the GATT agreement) wherever it occurs persistently and is clearly intended to damage local competition (although firms can dispose of [genuinely] surplus stock at very low prices on an *ad hoc* basis). However WTO rules require that anti-dumping taxes (known as 'countervailing duties') may only be applied when there is 'material injury' to domestic industry and the dumping is the 'principal cause' of injury to local firms producing 'like products', and not some other factor.

14. Arguments against protection

Trade restrictions may benefit some parts of a country's economy, but will damage others because potential importers are denied access to foreign products and the overall pattern of domestic economic activity is distorted. Further problems with trade restrictions are that they:

(a) Invariably provoke retaliation by other countries.

(b) Reduce the overall volume of world trade, thereby lowering global income and employment. Note that importing countries rely on other nations for markets for their exports, so that import controls which damage foreign countries must, by definition, adversely affect the export potentials of the nations that impose controls in the first instance. Foreign countries need to earn from exports the foreign exchange necessary to pay for imports.

(c) Create unemployment among those concerned with the handling, storage, transportation and distribution of imported goods.

(d) Might encourage domestic price inflation through removing competition from foreign suppliers. Consumers have to pay higher prices not only for imports that are subject to tariff and non-tariff barriers, but also for domestically produced substitutes the prices of which will be bid up as consumers switch from imports. Domestic producers might expand their outputs in response to these higher prices, yet the nation as a whole loses out because the goods are costing more than the price at which they could have been imported.

(e) Foster complacency and inefficiency within domestic firms, which might not bother to introduce the latest working methods or invest in new equipment

(f) Reduce the variety of products available to domestic consumers.

Arguably, the only way to reduce unemployment and improve a country's balance of payments in the long term is to restructure its economy and introduce fiscal and monetary policies appropriate for remedying the country's *underlying* economic problems. Protectionist measures do not address the economic fundamentals that cause poor economic performance in the first place.

TECHNIQUES OF PROTECTION

15. Tariffs

Restrictions can apply to imported goods themselves or to the importer's ability to pay for them. The commonest form of protection is the import tariff, i.e. a tax or customs duty imposed on goods crossing international frontiers. A tariff could be calculated as a specific amount of money per item imported or as a percentage of the value of the imported goods. The latter form is known as an *ad valorem* tariff. A combination of specific and *ad valorem* duties applied to an import is called a 'compound' tariff. Specific duties discourage lower period imports of a class of item. For example, a specific duty of £5 per pair of shoes will be felt more keenly on bottom end of the market shoes imported at, say, £15 per pair than on luxury shoes imported at £60 a pair. Percentage tariffs, conversely, make higher priced imports relatively more expensive.

Common markets such as the European Union have common external tariffs, so that all member countries apply exactly the same levels of tariff on all goods from all nations outside the common market. This means that it can be expensive and troublesome to enter a common market but that once entry has been effected the imported goods face no further tariffs and minimal control over cross-border movement within the area.

Tariff systems in general may be 'single column' or 'double column'. The former apply the same duty to imports of a particular product no matter where the goods come from; the latter allow for the imposition of different tariff rates on imports of the same item from different countries. Sometimes goods are imported, pay a tariff, and are then re-exported to other countries with all or part of the initial tariff payment being refunded by the government of the importing country. Such reimbursements are known as 'drawbacks' and frequently arise when imports are used as inputs into other goods destined for export to foreign nations.

16. Quantitative restrictions

Import 'quotas' impose definite limits on the number or total value of a certain item imported into a country. A quota system might operate on a 'first-come first-serve' basis whereby any goods arriving after the quota limit is exceeded are simply refused entry, or through the issue of licences to certain companies and only allowing these businesses to import relevant products up to a specified amount. The latter policy could generate mergers and takeovers in the importing country, with firms acquiring others merely in order to obtain their import licences.

Quota restrictions might be avoided by modifying imported items in order to redefine them into non-quota categories, or by routing consignments through countries with which the importing nation has special trading arrangements. Sometimes, exporters can enter joint ventures with local manufacturers and hence gain exemption from quota restrictions. Other non-tariff devices include 'import deposits' whereby importers have to deposit with their country's central bank a significant proportion (e.g. 50 per cent) of the price of the goods imported, the money being repaid only after a lengthy period (hence tying up the firm's working capital); and 'import surcharges', i.e. *ad hoc* levies on particular imported goods.

17. Other non-tariff barriers (NTBs)

These might include the imposition of arbitrary short periods in which buyers may apply for import licences; complex customs procedures and deliberate delays in processing documentation caused by customs officers; or customs authorities deliberately classifying products into inappropriate high-tariff categories so that the exporter has to initiate a time-consuming and expensive appeal. Goods might have to be imported into a country *via* ports a long distance from final destinations; separate customs, importation and other documentation procedures may have to be applied to imports of the same product of the same company but which enter the country from different subsidiaries of the supplying firm. Other 'hidden' barriers to the importation of goods have included the following:

(a) Insistence by the customs authorities that imported products undergo several safety checks, each one having to be conducted by an official from a different government department.

(b) Complex rules on packing and labelling. A country's customs authorities might require that imported products bear a brand name, country of origin, the importer's tax identity number, etc.

(c) Restrictive specification of technical product standards. Much politics is involved in the determination of technical standards, since the introduction of *mandatory* rules for all suppliers means that firms already satisfying the new standard have an initial advantage over their rivals. Note how the European Union is helping many developing and underdeveloped countries establish their own international standards based on EU norms. As these standards become compulsory, EU firms will be able to satisfy them ahead of US or Pacific Rim companies.

(d) Local content rules, i.e. requirements that in order to avoid import duty certain proportions of a product's inputs have to be sourced locally rather than being imported. The supposed objective is to prevent the establishment of 'screwdriver' plants that exist merely to assemble imported components and hence circumvent anti-dumping taxes and tariffs imposed on the importation of final products. Disputes frequently arise concerning the measurement of domestically sourced inputs (numbers, monetary values, etc.) and the accuracy of the firm's declarations of the extents of their use of locally supplied items.

(e) State subsidies to domestic companies to help them compete with imported products.

18. Exchange controls

Exchange controls seek to restrict importers' abilities to obtain the foreign currency needed to pay for imports. Hence the government might allocate foreign exchange directly to selected importing firms, issue foreign exchange licences, or impose queues and waiting lists for foreign currency distributions. Alternatively the authorities might artificially increase the exchange rate price of certain foreign currencies by limiting the supply of these currencies available for importers to purchase. Countries operating exchange controls typically require exporting firms to hand over to the national central bank all the foreign exchange they acquire. Other techniques of exchange control are:

- Restricting the availability of foreign exchange to the import of certain specified products.
- Only allowing foreign exchange to importers who enter into joint venture domestic manufacturing arrangements with exporting companies.
- The application of different exchange rates to different types of trans-action (although this is extremely rare under a long-standing interna-tional agreement that prohibits the use of multiple exchange rates for normal import/export activity).

TRADE IN SERVICES

19. Extent and nature of international trade in services

Cross-border trade in services such as advertising, banking, consultancy, com-munications, transportation, insurance, etc., has been the major growth area of world trade in recent decades. Data on the extent of international trade in services is harder to come by than for merchandise trade, although it is known to account for nearly 30 per cent of all cross-border transactions. This is hardly surprising considering how important the service sector has become in all developed countries. Services might be exported *via* direct sale in foreign markets, or through licensing (*see* 12:**6**), franchising or joint ventures with local companies. The big money earners in the international services field are:

- Entertainment, especially television programmes. In the late 1980s enter-tainment constituted the USA's *second largest* category of exporters (after aerospace).
- Shipping and the international airline industry
- Professional services such as advertising, accounting, legal services, public relations, etc.
- Retailing
- Hotels and tourism services
- Financial services (*see* **21**).

It is important to note that prior to the Uruguay Round of the GATT negotiations (see Chapter 1), non-tariff barriers that interfered with international trade in services were not prohibited under GATT regulations. Examples of discrimin-atory practices in the services have included:

- National and local governments only purchasing services from domestic suppliers.
- Laws requiring that exporters only take out cargo insurance with local insurance companies.
- Restrictions on the right of establishment of foreign service-providing firms (especially financial services businesses such as banks and insurance companies, and television and radio stations).
- Complex certification procedures that foreign companies must follow before offering a service within a particular nation.

- Governments not taking action against local counterfeiting of services provided by foreign firms.
- Requirements that the personnel involved in service provision possess highly specific qualifications that can only be obtained within the country concerned.
- State grants and subsidies paid only to local firms.

The settlement of the Uruguay GATT negotiations required that all WTO member nations agree to co-operate in order to end their differences over such matters as restrictions on foreign direct investment in services, discrimination against foreign firms, protection of the intellectual property embodied in computer software (especially databases), limitations on licensing practices, etc. (Nicolaides 1989).

20. International marketing of services

Comparative advantage (see Chapter 1) in the supply of international services could derive from professional expertise, use of computer technology, experience, organisational skill, or the firm's global reputation. Services differ from physical goods in that they are intangible; cannot be stored; may not (normally) be experienced prior to purchase; are heterogeneous (because the service provided to each customer may have to be unique), and often are produced and consumed at the same moment.

Such considerations create the following problems for the international sale of services:

(a) Pricing decisions are more complex than for national products.

(b) It is difficult to standardise the service offered across disparate national markets, especially when the personnel providing the service must exercise a high degree of judgement. Quality control becomes problematic.

(c) Because they cannot be stored, service offers need to be matched to demand very precisely, in several different national markets. Hence, sales forecasting becomes a highly important activity. Unlike the situation for physical items, production cannot be easily switched from one country to another.

(d) Typically, services cannot be 'exported' in the sense of sending them physically across national borders. The service must normally be performed *within* the market. Hence licensing, franchising or direct foreign investments are necessary.

(e) Customers in various nations may have entirely different expectations of the quality of service that should be offered.

(f) The skills needed to provide a particular service may be country-specific, so that extensive training of foreign employees might be required.

Heterogeneity of service provision and the need (usually) to customise service products for each national market means that decentralised organisation structures (*see* 20:**14**) are frequently found in firms that sell services across national frontiers.

21. International financial services

This is perhaps the fastest growing area of international services, especially in the European Union. Reasons for the expansion include:

(a) Financial services providers following their clients into foreign countries. As world trade has expanded so too has the demand for expert help with banking, insurance, currency dealing, etc.

(b) The formation around the world of numerous customs unions and free trade areas (*see* 1:5) that permit the unfettered movement of capital between member nations.

(c) Lucrative opportunities arising in countries where the existing financial services infrastructure is weak but with economies that are rapidly expanding.

(d) Ever-increasing consumer demands for credit, insurance, and other services that accompany rising living standards.

Special problems attached to the international (as opposed to domestic) marketing of financial services are as follows:

(a) Because financial services cannot normally be seen or handled, supplying institutions typically attempt to create images of trust, respectability, reliability and immaculate professional integrity. Note how the quality of a financial service is inextricably linked with the providing firm (rather than with physical materials used in construction or assembly). For example, a life assurance policy purchased from a well established company is usually regarded as of higher quality than one purchased from an unknown and newly established firm. The problem for the international sale of financial services is that different promotional messages and corporate identities may be needed to create appropriate perceptions of the supplying institution in the minds of consumers in disparate countries.

(b) Differences in economic and social environments in various nations means that the potential benefits of a financial service (security in old age, higher incomes in the future, the convenience of a bank account or credit card, etc.) that are emphasised in promotional literature need to differ among nations.

(c) Sales promotions for financial services frequently illustrate how *individual* consumer needs will be satisfied by the offer of a particular supplying firm. But these needs might differ markedly in consequence of cultural factors in various states.

(d) Suppliers have to be familiar with the financial services regulatory regimes of many nations. Most governments control the marketing of financial services, e.g. by insisting that annual percentage interest charges be prominently displayed, or that customers signing credit agreements have a statutory period in which to withdraw.

22. Financial services in the European Union

Residents of any EU country may purchase financial services from any EU provider regardless of where the latter is based. Firms and individuals can borrow money anywhere in the Union, while savers may deposit funds in any EU bank or other financial institution. People living in any member state are able to buy and sell shares in any European company no matter where it is situated.

Benefits to consumers of this situation include the availability of a wider range of financial products, and lower prices resulting from intense cross-border competition. Problems relate mainly to consumer protection and the practical difficulties of harmonising the (extensive) government regulations that control banks, insurance companies and other financial service institutions in various member countries. Accordingly, the European Commission has laid down minimum standards for 'financial security' and for the management procedures to be adopted by financial service providers. Financial security relates to (i) basic rules for the protection of insurance policy holders, investors, and other interested parties, and (ii) the extent of the information to be included in providers' publicity materials, prospectuses, brochures, and so on. Supervision of institutions remains the responsibility of the government of the country where the provider is *based*, rather than where the services are offered. Further key EU Directives concerning financial services are as follows:

(a) All banks and building societies must maintain a prespecified minimum proportion of their assets in reserve.

(b) The insolvency law of an EU credit institution's *home country* shall apply if it is wound up.

(c) Directors of investment companies must be 'of sufficiently good repute and standing'.

(d) Prospectuses for share issues that meet the legal requirements of one member country shall be legally acceptable in others, subject to certain minimum conditions.

(e) The accounts of banks, credit institutions and insurance companies must follow a standard format.

Additionally, the Commission has published recommendations regarding the nature of the contractual relation between credit card holders and card-issuing institutions. These recommendations concern the extent of a card holder's liability for a lost or stolen card and the burden of proof in disputed transactions.

RICH AND POOR NATIONS

Countries may be classified under various headings: the industrialised and economically developed market economies of West Europe, the USA and Japan; East European nations that have moved from central planning to market-based systems; high growth and rapidly industrialising countries (notably in the Pacific Rim); and the poorer 'underdeveloped' economies. Three quarters of all the world's exports are supplied by the industrialised nations of Western

Europe, North America, Australasia, South Africa, Japan and the Pacific Rim. These nations also take the same proportion of all the world's imports. Underdeveloped countries, conversely, have relatively little involvement with international trade – relying instead on large domestic agricultural and other domestic goods sectors to provide the bulk of their needs. The least well-off of the underdeveloped countries are sometimes referred to collectively as the 'Third World'.

23. Developing and underdeveloped countries

The United Nations Organisation defines 'developing' countries as those which have a quarter to a third of their population engaged in agriculture, but which also possess highly developed industrial sectors. There exist substantial industrial and consumer markets in these nations, with certain consumer groups enjoying high incomes and exhibiting all the characteristics of consumers in the more prosperous regions of the world. Developing countries can themselves be classified into two categories: richer and poorer. The former includes the oil-rich and newly industrialised nations plus some of the (relatively) wealthier Caribbean states. Poorer developing countries tend to be those with economies that depend on the export of a limited number of raw materials, causing them to be constantly short of the foreign exchange needed to import the capital equipment needed for diversification.

Underdeveloped countries, according to the UN classification, range from poor nations that possess domestic industries which produce significant outputs of industrial and consumer goods, to subsistence economies with hardly any industries. Countries in the former category have an urban middle class, a national education system and an essentially literate population; average incomes are low but rising, and there is a growing demand for consumer goods. Subsistence economies, conversely, have populations that are predominantly engaged in agriculture, consuming most of their own production and exchanging any surplus for other goods. Literacy is low and unemployment in urban areas extremely high. Both categories of underdeveloped nation face severe economic problems. They are trapped in a cycle of poverty. Their industries are not capable of producing large amounts of goods, hence there are low living standards, low levels of exports, shortages of foreign exchange for purchasing imported industrial equipment, lack of consumer purchasing power, and hence the absence of incentives for firms to invest in new industries. The economic infrastructure is inadequate, distribution systems are poor, and wages are very low so that consumers do not have the incomes necessary to purchase goods in substantial quantity. Thus firms do not have a market that justifies large-scale production, and so the cycle repeats itself.

Export problems of Third World countries

Third World countries face a number of serious problems in relation to international trade. Their share of world markets has fallen steadily for the last 40 years and, crucially, their rates of growth of exports have not been sufficient to support the extra imports needed for domestic economic expansion. They have not altered the composition of their exports to fit the requirements of sectors in which world demand is growing fastest. Exporters of primary products such as food, tobacco and raw materials have fared worse, for several reasons:

(a) Over the years technology has greatly improved the efficiency of primary product production, especially in agriculture, leading to price reductions. Hence the amount of a country's primary product that has to be exported in order to pay for a given amount of imports has increased (e.g. more tonnes of bananas have to be sold in other countries in order to pay for the import of one motor vehicle of a particular make than previously was the case). This is known as a deterioration in a country's 'terms of trade', meaning that more exports have to be sacrificed to obtain a fixed level of imports.

(b) The income elasticity of demand for primary products is low in the economically advanced countries that import these goods in large quantity. This means that a big rise in incomes in these nations will *not* lead to a significant rise in demand for primary products. Consumers tend to purchase a relatively constant amount of such items, regardless of whether their incomes rise or fall. Hence growth and prosperity in the developed world has not generated higher sales for the primary products supplied by poorer nations.

(c) Many primary products now face competition from synthetic manufactured materials.

(d) Industrialised countries' tariffs and other barriers against imported primary products have tended to be high. Also, both the European Union and NAFTA subsidise domestic agriculture very heavily.

(e) World market prices of primary products are subject to frequent, large and unpredictable variation, resulting in uneven export earnings for producing countries.

24. Characteristics of Third World countries

Low per capita Gross Domestic Product is the dominant feature of Third World nations. Typically they have low to moderate rates of economic growth; rapid rates of increase in population; poor industrial infrastructure; low life expectancy and high infant mortality. There is high unemployment combined with skills shortages and low rates of industrial productivity. Linguistic diversity is another factor in the make-up of many of the world's poorest states – with isolated regions speaking a unique version of the national language.

On the positive side, the governments of Third World nations invariably express a desire to increase their rates of economic growth, evidenced by large-scale public investment programmes (frequently financed by foreign aid from the rest of the world). This generates numerous opportunities for the export of these countries of industrial and agricultural equipment and other capital goods. (Note how the release of foreign exchange to pay for imports is more likely the more closely the technology of the imported products complements the objectives of the government's economic development programmes as a whole.) And all Third World countries have at least one urban area with a small

113

but prosperous middle class. The number of middle income families in these nations is increasing annually.

Trade versus aid

The question arises as to whether the rich developed countries should give more aid to the Third World, rather than seeking to increase the volume of trade between poor and prosperous nations. Advantages to expanding the amount of aid are that it:

- can help deal with short-term emergencies
- has an immediate impact (benefits resulting from trade can take many years before their consequences become apparent)
- may be targeted on specific projects and/or social problems
- supplements the scarce resources of poor countries
- presents no threat whatsoever to the jobs of workers in doner nations
- does not encourage the emergence of poor working conditions, long hours, low wages, etc., in firms making goods for export from Third World countries (Grilli 1993).

The advantages to additional trade are that it should:

- result in *permanent* improvements in living standards in underdeveloped nations
- enable firms in underdeveloped countries to obtain the efficiency benefits that result from exporting (*see* 16:1)
- increase tax revenues (from import duties and taxes on the profits of domestic companies) for the governments of Third World nations. This money can be used to improve the social infrastructure of these countries.
- break the 'dependency' culture and on-going lack of self-reliance that (arguably) results from continuous aid donations
- stimulate those sectors of the economy that have genuine prospects for economic development (aid might be used to subsidise 'no-hope' industries)
- generate benefits that are immune from government interference. Aid programmes can be terminated arbitrarily by donor nations. Recipient governments might not use the incoming money for its intended purpose.

25. Doing business in Third World nations

Firms from the developed world sell to and invest directly within Third World nations for a number of reasons, including the following:

(a) There might be little competition in the local market.

(b) Exclusive agency and distribution agreements and other restrictive business practices that would be unlawful in economically advanced nations may be permitted in underdeveloped countries.

(c) Firms prepared to make long-term investments in the Third World will be well placed to serve expanding markets as economic development accelerates.

(d) The modest stage of economic development of the Third World generates a large market for specific types of product in poor countries across the globe.

(e) Customers are generally less demanding than in developed countries, and might expect very little in the way of product promotion or development.

To succeed in the Third World, international businesses may need to adapt their products and/or methods of promotion to make them appeal to poorer and less literate consumers. Items might have to be simplified; instructions for use presented *via* pictures and symbols rather than words. Prices can be reduced through lowering the level of the quality of non-essential input components. The problem of long geographical distances of customers from product repair and maintenance facilities typical in many Third World countries can sometimes be dealt with by making products more robust and reliable, and by including spare parts for do-it-yourself repairs as an integral part of the product. Advertising may need to be more informative in poorer countries than in the developed world. Note how shopping (rather than advertising) is the primary source of information about goods in Third World states, with consumers typically seeking advice from peers prior to buying expensive consumer durables. Accordingly, conventional advertising activities can often be relegated to a subsidiary role.

26. The problems involved

Distribution can be a major problem when doing business in Third World countries. Channels of distribution are long and transport and warehousing systems frequently inadequate. An important consequence of long distribution channels is that exporters have to relinquish all control over final selling prices. Intermediaries' mark-ups fluctuate according to supply and demand and can be extremely high. Deficiencies in distribution systems can result in consumers not being aware of the alternative products available, so that they are unable to evaluate the value for money of certain items. This could make consumers unwilling to purchase products the quality of which they cannot appraise. Note the tendency of poorer Third World consumers to purchase non-food items less frequently than in other countries.

Further problems confronting firms wishing to do business in the Third World are that:

(a) Because customer purchases are severely constrained by low incomes, only a small range of low-cost items are purchased and customers are not able to demonstrate their preferences for product characteristics, styles, shapes, sizes and other selling points. In other words, consumers generate insufficient market information to enable suppliers to adapt their products to meet local requirements.

(b) There is little published information (government statistics, data books, market surveys, etc.) on market characteristics. Reliable data is sparse because governments do not regard the establishment of national statistical services intended to collect and collate information useful for market analysis as a major

115

priority, faced as they are with pressing problems in other areas. It may be that there is no electoral register. High birth rates and population shifts from villages to towns can quickly make census data obsolete.

(c) Pricing decisions are difficult in circumstances where high levels of demand are not matched by customers' ability to pay.

(d) Disparities in income, education and lifestyle found in the urban areas of Third World countries create many difficulties for firms wishing to use standardised promotional campaigns (*see* 17:4) in urban markets.

(e) Rural consumers are often illiterate and live in villages possessing minimal civic services (electricity, telecommunications, etc).

Numerous problems attach to conducting market research in Third World countries. Data collection difficulties arise from the poor mail and tele-communications systems characteristic of these nations, from low literacy rates (inhibiting the use of questionnaires), and the unwillingness of consumers in some areas to answer questions. There are few local research companies able to gather accurate information, and there is no pool of trained and experienced marketing research interviewers. Yet another difficulty is the absence of a common language in many Third World countries.

Progress test 6

1. List the four basic objectives of national economic policy. Why is it difficult for a country to attain all four objectives simultaneously?

2. What are the major components of foreign economic policy?

3. Explain the theoretical arguments for and against *laissez-faire* economic policies.

4. List the main variables that need to be examined when evaluating national economic environments.

5. A number of conceptual problems apply to the cross-national comparison of countries' Gross Domestic Products. What are these problems?

6. By definition, the balance of payments must always balance. How then is it possible to identify deficits and surpluses in balance of payments accounts?

7. Why do governments impose tariffs on imports?

8. What is an 'infant industry'?

9. Define 'dumping'. What are the problems involved in determining whether an item has been dumped?

10. Explain the difference between 'single column' and 'double column' tariff systems.

11. What are 'non-tariff barriers' to international trade? Give six examples of non-tariff barriers.

12. Why do countries impose exchange controls? Give examples of techniques of exchange control.

13. How do services differ from physical goods and what are the implications of these difference for the international marketing of services?

14. What is meant by the term 'Third Word'? List the characteristics of Third World countries.

15. List the advantages and disadvantages of (i) increasing the volume of trade with, and (ii) giving more aid to Third World countries.

7

COMPETITION, PRIVATISATION AND DEREGULATION

OWNERSHIP OF INDUSTRY

1. State involvement in industry

Recent decades have seen a major shift in government attitudes towards state involvement in economic affairs in the great majority of the world's nations. In the nineteenth century the proper functions of government were regarded as the maintenance of internal order, defence of the state against external attack, and the regulation of the domestic currency, and little more. Economic matters were left to the interplay of market forces within and between industrial countries, while most of what is today termed as the developing and/or Third World was colonised by Western nations. The imperial powers (notably Britain) extracted raw materials and agricultural produce from dependent territories (which were ruled directly by the governments of foreign imperial countries); imported these materials and foodstuffs very cheaply (prices being determined by the colonial ruler); and then manufactured goods which were exported to the colonies or to other industrialised nations – among which there was essentially free trade. This system became discredited in consequence of the dire social consequences of unfettered capitalism within industrialised countries (poor living conditions, unsafe working practices, environmental pollution, declining health of the population, etc.) and the adverse effects on colonies of the exploitation of their resources and labour. Western governments began to intervene in economic affairs in order to ameliorate social conditions, to assist declining industries, and to obviate the consequences for domestic employment of cheap free-trade imports. State involvement in the economic life of industrialised countries increased substantially during and between the two World Wars, and there was a growing confidence in the efficacy of national economic planning. Colonies demanded and won political independence, and regarded state regulation of industry as essential for achieving their newly established economic goals. By the 1960s the overwhelming majority of the world's nations controlled domestic business activity to some extent, directly or indirectly, often through public ownership of key industries. Accordingly, the circumstances in which international businesses could operate in other countries were substantially regulated and constrained.

2. Public ownership of industry

Nationalisation of industry has played a key role in governmental attempts to control economic development, typically in sectors regarded as crucial for economic progress and social welfare. Examples of such sectors were transport (including the provision of roads and bridges), water, gas and electricity supply, telephone and other communication systems, and health and medical services. There are three reasons why a government might nationalise a firm or industry:

1. The desire to control aggregate economic activity and hence rates of inflation, unemployment, growth, and the balance of payments.
2. Feelings that welfare-related services (medical services for example) should not be in private hands but instead freely available to all citizens regardless of income.
3. Perceptions by state officials that private enterprise is incompetent or inadequate in certain areas. As for example when a government steps in to rescue a failed private business.

Private firms can benefit from public ownership of basic industries (electricity, coal, steel, gas, etc.) through lower input prices made possible by zero or negative profits on public sector output. Also the public sector might be prepared to employ people during recessions in circumstances where private firms would not be able to afford to keep them on. This could stimulate aggregate purchasing power, providing firms with markets for their goods. A major advantage of state undertakings is that they are usually large. Thus opportunities exist for economies of scale, rationalisation and the standardisation of output.

3. Privatisation

Disillusion with nationalisation led in the 1980s and 1990s to the privatisation of publicly owned enterprises throughout the world, especially in South America, Eastern Europe and parts of Africa (Aylen 1987; Ash 1990). Specific reasons for privatisation have included the following:

(a) Dissatisfaction with the economic performances of state-owned industries and firms.

(b) Possible overstaffing in public concerns.

(c) Lack of incentives to maximise profits and productivity within public sector organisations.

(d) The damaging effects of political interference in the managerial decisions of nationalised industries.

(e) The fact that state-owned firms have not normally been allowed to diversify, since unfair competition with the private sector would then have occurred. Nationalised industries had unlimited access to finance for expansion *via* government (taxpayers') funds. Hence they could have used their vast resources to knock out competitors in any new industry they chose to enter. Accordingly, governments were obliged to impose precise limits on the activities of state-owned firms, thus depriving them of profitable expansion opportunities (Schwartz and Lopes 1993).

(f) Poor industrial relations in the public sector compared to private firms.

(g) Expected improvements in efficiency. Firms operating without state subsidy have to be efficient in order to survive. They are required to respond quickly to changes in consumer demand and to supply high quality products.

Privatised enterprises must approach national and international capital markets for the funds needed to finance their operations, rather than relying on the taxpayer for support. Arguably, this creates incentives for better management and compels organisations to establish commercial yardsticks against which performance may be assessed. Governments, conversely, allegedly gave state-run industries vague and conflicting objectives, interfered with management decisions (especially where pricing and employment were concerned), and encouraged bureaucracy and waste. Note moreover that governments can exploit consumers just as easily as private monopolies, and that large-scale production is not necessarily efficient. Indeed, complex administrative structures can cause big increases in production costs.

4. Consequences and problems of privatisation

Consequences of widespread privatisation of state-owned enterprises have included:

- An increase in the intensity of international competition (note that many of the organisations privatised were huge MNCs in their own right)
- Fresh opportunities for the supply of inputs to these firms
- The creation of private rather than public monopolies in certain fields
- More cross-border investment as privatised enterprises acquired foreign subsidiaries.

A number of problems have emerged as privatisation has proceeded. To the extent that industries previously run by the state are broken up into small competing units some duplication of effort inevitably occurs. Also the management of privatised units might not be any more competent than state officials! Other problems are as follows:

(a) Possible difficulties in raising from private investors the extremely large amounts of capital needed to re-equip major industries.

(b) Low returns on activities with a 'social' dimension, which might cause the new management to jettison socially beneficial operations.

(c) Possible higher input costs for the users of the outputs of privatised industries.

(d) Lack of accountability of the management of these industries (most of which provide essential services) to anyone other than private shareholders.

Simply transferring assets from the public to the private sector does not *guarantee* improved performance (Frydman and Ropaczynski 1993).

5. Privatisation in underdeveloped countries

The World Bank in conjunction with the International Monetary Fund has organised and supervised 'Structural Adjustment Programmes' (SAPs) in certain underdeveloped countries (Nigeria, Ghana and Kenya for example). SAPs provide extensive foreign aid via loans and grants for new investment, but require recipient nations to liberalise internal and external trade, to privatise state-owned industries and reduce government deficits. Immediate consequences have included high unemployment (as deflationary measures were imposed in attempts to reduce inflation) and reduced living standards. A key element in an SAP is the Structural Adjustment Loan (SAL), provided to help a country overcome serious balance of payments difficulties. SALs provide emergency short-term finance intended to prevent national insolvency. Money is made available to a national government on the strict condition that it reforms its national economy. SALs cannot be used for certain purposes specified in the loan agreement. This causes SALs to be politically controversial as they may require unpopular government actions such as currency devaluation, removal of price controls and the abolition of subsidies. Project loans will be held back until the macroeconomic readjustment phase has been completed.

SAPs have been a major factor encouraging privatisation of industry in the countries in which they have been implemented. Whether SAPs will generate genuine long-lasting benefits remains open to question.

REGULATION

6. Regulation of business activities

Business within a particular nation is controlled by domestic laws, voluntary restrictions imposed by self-regulatory organisations (stock exchanges or advertising standards authorities for example) and, in the European Union, by EU Directives and Regulations (for information on these see the M & E title *European Business*). The case for imposing strict laws on business activities rests mainly on the proposition that, left to its own devices, the business community is not capable of self-regulation because market forces and the quest for profit will *inevitably* cause at least some firms to break the rules. Businesses exist to make money, and not (so critics allege) to voice moral or ethical judgements concerning how goods should be promoted. Managers cannot reasonably be expected to determine what is or is not socially desirable. Hence, clear and binding laws – equally applicable to all firms – are necessary to protect the public good. Further arguments in favour of legal control include the following:

(a) As well as firms and consumers, the general public has an interest in how business behaves. Companies influence the environments in which *everyone* lives. The only way the public can affect the decision making of the large firms is through its elected representatives, who are empowered to impose legislative control.

(b) Large corporations with huge budgets might be able to distort consumer demand via dubious promotional claims. Therefore, laws are needed to ensure that big business does not exploit the consumer in this way.

(c) Legally binding rules and procedures define *precisely* what is allowed. This removes ambiguities and uncertainties, and creates a 'level playing field' for all firms.

(d) Individual rights (e.g. to privacy) can be safeguarded where these might conflict with the objectives of a large and powerful company.

(e) Consumers have an *absolute* right not to be misled by false claims, and not to be offended by unwanted intrusions upon them. Equally, businesses should be entitled to legal protection against false or misleading allegations made by competitors.

7. Self-regulation

Industries in many countries have self-regulatory bodies that issue advice and Codes of Practice to member companies. A Code of Practice is a document issued by a government agency, professional body, trade association or other relevant authority outlining model procedures for good practice in a particular field. Codes give examples of excellent and bad behaviour, and recommendations regarding how things should be done. Normally Codes are not legally binding, but may be looked at by Courts when determining the modes of behaviour that should have been adopted. See Chapter 9 for details of Codes of Practice pertaining to multinational companies.

Multinational and other businesses have reputations to consider, and are acutely sensitive to how the general public regards their actions. Individual managers are not immune from social and cultural influences; and the over-whelming majority of business executives would agree that certain fundamental principles of honesty, integrity, truthfulness, concern for the quality of life and involvement with the wider community should govern the conduct of business affairs. Thus it is not unreasonable to suppose that managers and organisations can be trusted to regulate their activities voluntarily and to promote public welfare. Self-regulation, its advocates argue, stabilises relationships between business and society, and is mutually beneficial in the long run. Firms will normally abstain from sharp practice because they recognise the ultimately destructive consequences it involves. Other arguments in favour of all self-regulation are as follows:

(a) Few laws can be drafted so accurately that they apply to all situations at all times. Business situations are dynamic; circumstances change; legal disputes may be settled long after they have ceased to be relevant to the situations from which they arose.

(b) Much uncertainty surrounds all litigation, even when the law is seemingly straightforward and precise. Note, moreover, that although strict interpretations of the law may be judicially correct, they can be disastrous for businesses and, ultimately, for the customers they serve.

(c) Voluntary controls may have greater force and a higher probability of implementation because those who must operate them have been actively involved in their initial formulation.

(d) To the extent that businesses abuse their position, public disenchantment with unregulated business activities will increase – leading to demands for legislation to curb excesses. Thus, companies have a built-in incentive to moderate their behaviour.

Opponents of self-regulation point out that firms are not *compelled* to adhere to voluntary guidelines, which they may interpret in a variety of (possibly bizarre) ways. And why should an industry self-regulatory body be any better at deciding what should and should not be permitted than state legislators? Government law makers are objective, and have the wider community interest to take into account. Other problems with self-regulation are that:

(a) Self-regulatory rules could be drafted in such a manner that they restrict competition among existing firms and inhibit the entry of new businesses to the relevant industry.

(b) Aggrieved consumers have no right of judicial appeal against the decisions of a self-regulatory body.

(c) Rules devised by organisations with a vested interest in the expansion of the advertising industry are likely to be heavily biased towards that industry.

COMPETITION

8. Competition policy

Countries have laws intended to prevent anti-competitive practices because their governments believe that competition increases business efficiency, extends consumer choice, expands employment and enhances the public good. Thus, most of the world's nations legally prohibit restrictions on entry to specific industries or markets; price-fixing agreements; 'concerted practices' whereby firms rig markets through their behaviour but without entering explicit agreements; exclusive distribution arrangements; and mergers and acquisitions that give rise to monopoly power. Further examples of measures that countries sometimes use to prevent anti-competitive practices include:

(a) Insistence on the complete transparency of cartel operations. In Denmark, for instance, any agreement or tacit concerted practice likely to exert a dominant effect on a market must be notified to the country's Competition Council within 14 days of its conclusion. Failure to register can result in daily fines. Also the Council is empowered to limit a firm's price and profit levels for up to twelve months.

(b) Giving a country's anti-trust authorities the power to dismember quasi-monopoly groupings retrospectively.

(c) Establishment of quantitative limits on business activity. French law, for example, prohibits any 'concentration' of businesses that controls more than 25 per cent of the sales, purchases or other transactions of a given market. A concentration is defined as any situation in which a company or group can directly or indirectly exercise a decisive influence on another company.

(d) Automatic investigation of any company or group with a market share exceeding a certain threshold.

(e) Requirements that all large-scale distribution agreements be filed and approved by the authorities.

9. Basic concepts of fair competition

Laws on competition need to define precisely what is meant by market power, market dominance, and abuse of a dominant market position. 'Market power' means the ability of businesses to increase significantly the prices of their outputs without losing sales. This differs from the idea of 'abuse of a dominant position', which occurs when a firm *actually* raises its prices to unjustifiably high levels. It is important to note that market power does not necessarily damage economic welfare especially if it offsets other distortions in the economic structure of a country, e.g. if a monopoly invests its excessive profits in a nation with inadequate capital markets which are not capable of providing the funds necessary for major new ventures.

Definition of the market

Assessment of market power requires the definition of a 'relevant market', since a given level of sales will represent a larger proportion of a narrowly demarcated market than of one that is liberally defined. Different countries apply disparate approaches to this question. United States, for example, describes a relevant market as 'the narrowest combination of a set of products and a geographic area such that if all the production capacity in that product set were owned by a single firm, that firm could profitably raise price by (usually) at least five per cent above a benchmark price for a significant non-transitory period'(US Department of Justice, Merger Guidelines, 1992). The benchmark price might be for the price prevailing before the merger of two companies, or some other pre-existing situation. In contrast the European Commission defines the relevant market very broadly, as the market for 'those products which are regarded as interchangeable or substitutable by the consumer, by reason of the products' characteristics and their intended use' (CEC 1992). This characterisation is deliberately imprecise so as to enable the Commission to be as flexible as possible in its interpretations.

Practical problems with the actual measurement of a relevant market include the following.

(a) Defining 'substitutable products' (or the product set of the US definition). Note how changes in consumer taste can alter consumer perceptions of what does or does not represent a viable substitute for a given item.

(b) Disentangling price movements attributable to market power rather than to the effects of general inflation within an industry or region.

(c) Uncertainties whether fresh supplying firms will enter the market (hence altering competitive conditions and the aggregate supply of a product set).

Measuring dominance

Intuitively the number of firms within a specific industry sector and the market shares of each of these companies would seemingly indicate whether there is a situation of market dominance. Note however that although the existence of a large number of competing firms in conjunction with an even distribution of market shares among them gives *prima facie* evidence of the absence of a dominant position by one or just a handful of companies, a small number of competing firms with some of these possessing high market shares does not *necessarily* mean that certain companies are actually dominant. High market share firms may have arrived at these positions unintentionally, with competitors having the *potential* to increase their (initially low) market shares at little cost or effort. Both the USA and the European Commission rely on observed market share to assess the degree of dominance.

10. Competition law in the European Union

The European Commission has a somewhat ambivalent attitude towards competition between firms and the growth of business organisations. On the one hand, the Treaty of Rome expressly forbids restrictive trade practices and/or monopolies likely to interfere with trade within or between countries. Simultaneously however the Commission recognises the need for Europe to possess large economic units able to achieve economies of scale and compete effectively in world markets. Thus, in recent years new regulations have been introduced which allow cross-frontier amalgamations and for large firms to organise themselves on a Europe-wide basis. Taxes which discriminate against cross-frontier mergers (compared to mergers within a single country) have been largely abolished, and many legal barriers to international amalgamations of EU firms have been removed. In general, the Commission now seems to favour larger European firms (Jacquemin 1993). Nevertheless, EU regulation of competitive practice is wide, covering horizontal and vertical integration, market sharing agreements, retailing arrangements (exclusive dealerships are not allowed), joint ventures, patents and trademarks, and franchise agreements. And the community regulations apply to services as well as goods.

Articles 85 and 86 of the Treaty of Rome

Article 85 of the Treaty of Rome prohibits trade practices which prevent, restrict or distort competition. Agreements by firms to carve up the European market among themselves are void and thus unenforceable in the Courts of member states. Article 86 prohibits firms which already occupy a dominant position in an EU market from abusing that position. A dominant position is defined as a position of economic strength which enables an enterprise to prevent effective competition by being able to operate independently of its competitors and customers. There have been cases in the European Court where abuse has occurred through firms increasing their market shares by taking over competitors, or through gaining control over the supply of raw materials and then cutting off supplies to competing firms. Additionally, the Treaty of Rome defines the following business practices as abuses of a dominant position:

- Imposition of unfair prices for purchase of raw materials or sale of final goods.
- Restrictions on production.
- Restrictions on distribution.
- Holding back technological development.
- Charging different prices to different consumers.

Articles 85 and 86 are directly enforceable in each country. Anyone who suffers is entitled to sue for compensation. At the EU level, the Commission will investigate a complaint registered under either of these Articles and, if proven, will ask the firm involved to alter its behaviour. If it refuses, the Commission will issue a formal warning – accompanied by reasons for its decision – and if this fails to achieve the desired change the Commission will approach the European Court for a ruling. Note however that in the end, firms cannot be physically dismembered, only fined heavily. Nevertheless, the Commission still remains anxious to encourage co-operation among smaller firms, to enable them to compete with bigger units. Accordingly, the Commission does not regard the following agreements as violating Articles 85 and 86; namely, agreements on:

Exchanges of opinion or experience
Joint market research
Joint collection of trade and market statistics
Co-operation on the preparation of accounts, or on matters relating to tax
Provision of trade credit
Joint debt collecting.

11. Exemptions for small firms

A wide range of practices common among small firms could be caught by EU competition law, notably:

(a) Exclusive dealership arrangements

(b) Joint ventures with other businesses

(c) Licensing of intellectual property rights

(d) Franchising.

EU law extends, moreover, to any concerted practice that prevents, restricts or distorts competition. A concerted practice is defined by the European Commission as a situation where businesses do not enter a formal agreement but where their collective actions imply collusion. In recognition of the fact that co-operation between small firms will not distort competition appreciably, the Commission has issued a 'Notice on Minor Agreements' exempting from Articles 85 and 86 all situations where:

- The goods or services covered by an agreement represent less than five per cent of the total market for these goods or services and *(additionally)*
- The aggregate turnover of the parties to the agreement is less than a certain threshold (currently ECU 200 million).

An agreement that breaks EU competition rules is regarded in law as null and void and thus unenforceable.

12. Block exemptions

Even if the criteria outlined in **10** and **11** are not satisfied the Commission may exempt agreements that:

- contribute to improving the methods of producing or distributing goods or to the promotion of technical or economic progress; *and*
- give consumers a fair share of resulting benefits; *and*
- will not significantly reduce competition across the entire Single European Market.

Applications for exemption must be submitted to the Commission unless the following are involved in which case an automatic 'block exemption' applies and no formal application is needed (provided of course that the above mentioned points are met):

(a) Exclusive distribution or purchasing agreements.

(b) Patent and (unpatented) know-how licensing.

(c) Research and development agreements.

(d) Motor vehicle agreements.

(e) Franchising.

INDUSTRIAL POLICY

13. Nature of industrial policy

Industrial policy is far more than government intervention in industry and/or the payment of subsidies to certain firms. Rather it concerns the entire macroeconomic and cultural environment surrounding business and trade in a particular country (Geroski 1989). It encompasses:

- Deliberate stimulation of certain industrial sectors through the award of public procurement contracts (especially by defence industries)
- Promotion of tripartite links between business, trade unions and government
- Development of national infrastructures (training, transport and communications systems, etc.)
- Grants for research and development
- Attempts to create an 'enterprise culture' within an economy through

giving special tax allowances to small firms and/or by relaxing bureaucratic administrative controls

- Government interest rate policy
- State provision of advice and information services (CEC 1990b)
- Competition law
- Statutory controls over collective bargaining and other aspects of industrial relations
- Encouragement of venture capital financing (*via* the creation of special allowances for instance).

Indeed, a nation could have an industrial policy without actually realising that this is the case. *Laissez-faire*, for example, is in itself an industrial policy.

The industrial policies of the nations within which they operate are of vital concern to multinational companies because:

- Industrial policy determines the framework within which government decisions on economic development are taken.
- The government grants and subsidies emerging from the industrial policies of various nations are today a crucial factor in MNC investment and operational decisions.
- National industrial policies can constrain MNC activities.

14. Purposes of industrial policy

Government concerns with industrial policy normally focus on:

- maintaining employment (often via regional subsidies for economic development)
- encouraging research and technical development (Peterson 1992; Sharp and Praoitt 1993)
- providing incentives for the creation of new businesses
- establishing technical standards for industries so that individual firms have substantial markets for their outputs
- facilitating improvements in social welfare
- forecasting trends in industrial structure (in order to help companies cope with structural economic change)
- identifying those industries with the greatest potential and those which need to be run down
- minimisation of excess industrial capacity at the national level.

Examples of specific governmental industrial policies intended to achieve these objectives include:

- subsidising technology transfer in key industry sectors
- helping firms export to high-growth foreign markets
- selective government purchasing
- providing technical assistance to companies (especially with research and development)
- assisting the settlement of labour/management disputes
- tariff protection for infant industries
- encouraging the setting up of joint ventures with foreign firms

- monitoring merger and acquisition activities, allowing some mergers while prohibiting others
- giving tax reliefs for the employment of additional workers
- promoting labour mobility *via* relocation grants and allowances.

15. Problems with industrial policy

Critics of national industrial policy allege that it:

- generates government bureaucracy and red tape
- wastes taxpayers' money on 'no-hope' projects
- stifles initiative and entrepreneurial activity
- impedes the necessary reallocation of resources away from inefficient industries towards profitable new ventures
- creates among firms a (debilitating) climate of dependency on state handouts, rather than stimulating genuine competitive advantage and awareness of customer needs
- causes countries to compete against each other in the provision of lucrative packages of state assistance intended to attract foreign investment
- requires civil servants without industrial experience to take critical decisions concerning the futures of major businesses
- encourages firms to develop lobbying skills and expertise in preparing grant applications, at the expense of getting on with the job
- can lead to the existence of large but unprofitable conglomerations capable of distorting competition and taking too high a market share.

Industrial policies invariably involve government intervention in industry and hence decisions by the state regarding which projects should be supported. This creates gainers and, of course, losers among competing industries and firms. The practice of 'picking winners' is extremely difficult, and politicians and civil servants have proven just as inept and unreliable when attempting this as any market system. It is easy for public servants (especially elected politicians) to confuse economic objectives with broader social aims, and government decisions on the allocation of state assistance are likely to be influenced by party political factors (such as the timing of elections).

Even if there is an incontrovertible case for public subsidy, determining the correct level of assistance for a specific project is extremely problematic. Note moreover that state financed R & D and related activities could simply reduce privately funded research that would have occurred in any event, and that all government assistance has to be paid for via higher taxes, which themselves might depress the national economy.

GRANTS AND SUBSIDIES FOR BUSINESS

National government grants and subsidies play a crucial role in MNC investment decisions. Allowances are payable to companies that locate in certain regions (*see* **16**), for research and technical development, and for special designated purposes (training of workers for example). Grant availability and values differ between nations, and are often the key factor when choosing where to situate new plant and equipment.

16. Regional assistance

Industrial infrastructures are weaker in underdeveloped regions, making the firms within them uncompetitive and extremely susceptible to the effects of downturns in national and international trade. It is hardly surprising, therefore, that governments give extensive assistance for regional development. In most countries the majority of grants and subsidies are directed towards specific industry sectors, though regional aid and industry-specific subsidies frequently overlap.

There are two approaches to the question of how regional aid should be allocated. The first relies on the theory that each region within a country possesses a particular set of resources (including human resources), industrial skills, and historical traditions which enable it to specialise in certain goods or services more efficiently than other regions. Hence, the argument goes, the government of the country should help regions develop these assets in order to establish healthy local economic infrastructures. Adoption of this approach in practice requires a government to pick winners and selectively subsidise specific enterprises, projects or types of activity. The problem of course is that the predicted winners frequently lose; their failure (arguably) being encouraged by the featherbedding created by public support. Also, discretionary awards require public servants to take important commercial decisions and are administratively complex, expensive and troublesome both for the applicant firm and the grant-awarding authorities. The other approach is to subsidise industrial development measures that benefit all firms and workers, regardless of lines of work or location. General tax allowances and employee training programmes are examples of this type of policy. Hence, some businesses will receive subsidies they do not need; while others might obtain them in forms that are not appropriate for their requirements (e.g. tax reliefs are useless for firms that earn negligible profits). Inefficient businesses might be subsidised, and the authorities cannot monitor the effectiveness of the grants awarded to particular companies. Advantages to automatic grants and subsidies include:

- Certainty, so that firms know in advance the value of the assistance they will receive for authorised projects, thus facilitating their financial planning.
- Transparency and equality of application. Civil servants and/or politicians do not have to decide which investments shall receive government funding.
- Administrative convenience. The government simply determines eligibility criteria for the subsidy. It is not required to select specific enterprises for subsidy.

17. Grants and subsidies for research and development

Most national governments are extremely anxious to encourage resident firms to undertake technical research and development, in order to improve their technological infrastructures and hence increase their long-term competitive situations. Research can be basic and intended to increase scientific and technical knowledge, or applied and meant to develop know-how and/or to generate short-term commercial advantage. R & D may be completed in-house, externally contracted, or performed in collaboration with other businesses. Collaborative research enables research costs and risks to be spread over several participants; firms can exchange know-how and expertise; there is no duplication of effort and the results of the project can be exploited simultaneously in several markets.

MNCs with subsidiaries in several nations and which intend initiating research activities might well find it worthwhile shopping around for the best package of national R & D benefits. The latter could include cash grants, tax rebates, help with exploiting outcomes and the free or low-cost use of national research facilities. Cross-border research consortia, moreover, should consider carefully whether they might be able to maximise grant income by undertaking particular aspects of a project in certain (high subsidy) countries.

18. Grants and loans from international financial institutions

A quarter of all the foreign aid flowing into underdeveloped countries is channelled through international financial institutions (IFIs) comprising United Nations agencies (notably the World Bank, the World Food and Health programs and the UN Environmental Program); the Multinational Development Banks (other than the World Bank) such as the African Development Bank and Asian Development Bank; and various Arab/OPEC financing institutions. Additionally there are various multinational and bilateral aid programmes. Annual multinational and bilateral aid flows now exceed US $100 billion, a quarter coming from OECD countries. The World Bank is the largest single provider of assistance. It offers loans for specific long-term projects ('project' loans), and loans to help underdeveloped countries overcome immediate short-term problems for which project grants are too slow and rigid to make any impact ('policy' loans). Project loans account for about half of all World Bank lending, and consist of:

(a) *Specific investment loans* to finance identifiable projects that are readily timetabled and costed

(b) *Sector loans* which provide 'umbrella' financing for a range of projects in an industry sector or geographic region

(c) *Technical assistance loans* to purchase technical expertise for project development and the training of project employees

(d) *Emergency reconstruction loans* to help countries respond to natural disasters

(e) *Sector adjustment loans,* i.e. loans aimed at a particular sector but not tied to specific projects. The Bank will supply a list of the sorts of project for which the money may be utilised.

(f) *Structural adjustment loans* (*see* 5).

Progress test 7

1. Why did governments frequently nationalise key industries during the early/mid twentieth century?

2. List the main reasons for the privatisation of state-owned industry.

3. Explain the difference between World Bank project loans and policy loans.

4. There are two approaches to the question of how regional assistance should be allocated. What are these approaches?

5. List six problems that might be experienced when implementing national industrial policy.

6. What are the main purposes of industrial policy?

7. What is a 'block exemption'?

8. Outline the essential contents of Article 85 of the Treaty of Rome.

9. What is meant by the term 'dominant position' in the context of competition law?

10. State the difficulties likely to be experienced when defining the extent of a 'relevant market'.

11. List four examples of measures that governments sometimes apply to prevent anti-competitive practices.

12. What are the main arguments against the self-regulation of industry?

13. What is a Structural Adjustment Programme?

14. List four problems associated with the privatisation of state-owned industry.

8

THE INTERNATIONAL POLITICAL AND LEGAL ENVIRONMENTS

POLITICAL FACTORS

1. Importance of the international political environment

Political factors determine the overall legal environment in which business operates, particularly with respect to the law of contract and rules on advertising and consumer protection. Political considerations also affect the business practices of a country, restrictions on entry to the market (tariff levels and controls over the foreign ownership of enterprises for example), the prices a firm can charge its customers, and its ability to repatriate profits. Other areas in which political factors play a crucial role include:

- The nature of regulatory frameworks
- The degree of governmental control over MNC activities
- The relative importance of various pressure groups within a nation
- The likelihood of trade embargoes (i.e. prohibitions on trade with particular nations)
- The extent to which it is necessary to take out insurance against possible losses resulting from political risk (Desta 1985)
- The tax regimes pertaining within specific countries
- The incidence of strikes and labour unrest accompanying political turbulence.

Economic and political environments inter-relate: political factors affect the economy, while economic hardship may trigger political upheaval. Note in particular how the election within a country of a government perceived by investors, financiers and bankers as 'anti-business' may lead to withdrawals of capital from the country resulting in a fall in the currency exchange rate, lower savings and domestic investment, and hence in higher interest rates and reduced economic growth.

2. Nature of politics

National politics are concerned with (i) the direction and administration of states, (ii) government, and (iii) the control of aggregate social relationships. 'Government' involves making and implementing laws, representing the state, and routine public administration. A 'state' is an association of people formed for specific common purposes, with a clearly defined territory, a system of laws, and an organised government. It is important to realise that a 'state' is not necessarily the same as a 'nation', i.e. a group of people who feel they have certain things in common such as a common ancestry, history or traditions, language, culture or religion. A nation does not necessarily have an independent state in which to live.

The government of a state has exclusive jurisdiction over its territory and its government is the only legal representative of the state in relation to other states. The government can enter into or abrogate any agreements with foreign states or with its own citizens. And it may use physical force to attain its ends. All the land surface of the earth is controlled by states (apart from the Arctic and Antarctic regions) so that, *ipso facto*, international businesses have to deal with nation states and are subject to their authority.

Sovereignty

Sovereignty means the ultimate absolute power of the state to coerce and control its citizens. Two problems immediately arise:

(a) In the modern world few (if any) states can claim the ability to make genuinely independent decisions. Countries rely on each other for goods, markets, mutual economic assistance, and defence. Capital is internationally mobile and no one nation can afford to lose foreign investment, whether physical or financial.

(b) It is unclear as to exactly *where* national sovereignty is located. Does it exist in the head of state, or in parliament, the prime minister, collectively within the cabinet, or in 'the people' and/or various interest groups?

In practice, debates on national sovereignty tend to revolve around such matters as:

- Who shall represent a particular state. Should this be a national government or a wider body such as the European Union?
- Whether the national parliament is solely entitled (i) to levy taxes of whatever amount and whenever it wishes, and (ii) to spend tax revenues on its own volition.
- Whether decisions of the national parliament can be overruled.
- Whether parliament can legislate on any matter it chooses.

National interest

A government's concept of 'the national interest' will depend on the cultures, backgrounds, perceptions and learned experiences of the decision makers involved, and will change over time and according to circumstances. An interest considered vital today (and over which the state is not prepared to make any concessions) might be relegated to secondary status (for which compromises are possible) tomorrow. Each country has a potentially huge list of national interests, and cannot possibly realise them all. Hence it is necessary to choose carefully which national interests actually to pursue. Note in this connection the 'about faces' of one country after another that initially attempted to control inward (or outward) foreign investment but then had to confront the reality that multinational companies can easily shift huge amounts of resources across national frontiers, and in some respects are often more powerful than nation states. Restrictions imposed by specific countries simply led to the diversion of economic activity to other regions.

A country's ability to achieve its national interests depends on its power, which could relate to its control over raw materials; scientific and technological know-how; the size, structure, health and education of its population; political stability and social cohesiveness.

3. Political instability and risk

'Political instability' can arise from internal revolution and insurgency, involvement in foreign wars, frequent changes in government (resulting in loss of confidence by investors, withdrawals of foreign exchange from the country, etc.), resignations of key government ministers, bad international relations, falling national income and living standards, high inflation and rising foreign debt. Political instability can result in the physical destruction of a firm's assets or their confiscation (with or without compensation) by a foreign government, extra taxes, imposition of import controls, and/or prohibitions on money leaving the country. The welfare (even the lives) of employees of foreign companies operating in politically unstable regions may be threatened, making it difficult thereafter to recruit either local or expatriate staff to work in subsidiaries in affected areas.

Political risk

Political risk can emerge from social unrest consequent to low and/or unevenly distributed incomes among a country's population, from competing political ideologies or ethnic groups within a nation, the rise or fall of individual political leaders, or from international relations (involvement in foreign wars for instance). Note however that political turbulence does not *necessarily* lead to adverse consequences for an international firm. In the modern world a country's economic prospects depend so obviously and heavily on inward foreign investment and the goodwill of the business community that persons and organisations activating domestic political upheaval may choose not to involve or alienate the companies on which the nation's future prosperity depends.

A distinction is sometimes drawn between 'macro' and 'micro' political risk. The former affects *all* foreign firms operating in the country to an equal extent. Examples include the imposition of exchange controls, special taxes on foreign firms, 'local-content' rules, etc. Micro risk, conversely, applies to a particular company, industry or project, e.g. import restrictions on a specific category of product, the compulsory breaking up of a very large firm into smaller units, cancellation of contracts, etc. Micro variables are further considered in **4** below.

4. Assessment of political risk

The need for political risk assessment arises from the damaging consequences of political instability for business operations; from the high cost of insurance in some nations (so that the advisability of foregoing insurance cover needs to be considered); and the fact that it is simply impossible to insure goods, plant and equipment, or against the risk of non-payment by customers in certain states. Political risk needs to be assessed systematically and monitored on a continuous basis: there are many examples of previously stable countries collapsing into anarchy with foreign firms losing all their investments (de la Torre and Neckar 1988).

In assessing the degree of risk attached to doing business in particular countries it is useful to examine the following sets of variables.

Political factors

Power base of the existing government. Is the country democratic or un-democratic, and if the latter then how does political opposition become manifest? How long has the government been in office. Whether there is a peaceful mechanism for transferring political leadership. The extent to which the population shares common values. Relations with other countries. Ethnic divisions within the country and whether ethnic minorities are properly represented in government. Incidence and severity of terrorism and/or violent political demonstrations. Whether fundamental political issues are openly debated. Responsiveness of the government to changes in public opinion and/or to pressure group influences. Extent of bribery and corruption among government officials. Legality or otherwise of strikes and trade unions. The past, current and stated future intended policies of the country's present government and of opposition groups. External military relations (involvement in wars, international alliances and so on).

The economic system

How closely are industries monitored and controlled by the state? What attitudes towards state control are held by the government and opposition groups? The distributions of wealth and income. Labour relations, the incidence of strikes and whether there exist orderly procedures for resolving industrial relations disputes. The effectiveness of public administration. Rates of economic growth and inflation. The level of unemployment. Balance of payments situation. Ratio of foreign debt to national income. The extent to which a country's export earnings depend on a handful of product categories (oil or sugar for example). Movements in the currency exchange rate. Domestic interest rates and credit expansion. Negative attitudes towards the nation held by international organisations such as the World Bank or the IMF.

Micro variables

Relations between the firm and the host country government and the local community. How many domestic residents hold key managerial/technical positions within the local subsidiary. Whether local people have an equity stake in the operation. Extent of interactions with local businesses (especially suppliers). Whether the firm has a technology that will not be available within the host country if the local operation is expropriated. The extent to which the firm is 'visible' in the local environment. Whether the business is competing with influential local companies. Dependence on inputs from local sources. How much of its profits the firm wishes to repatriate to the home base.

There are fundamental differences of approach to the identification of political risks in industrially advanced and democratic countries compared with totalitarian and economically underdeveloped nations in the Third World. In the latter countries political turmoil can lead to revolution, the widespread physical destruction of property, expropriation of foreign firms and the murder of company employees. Political upheaval in democratic economically developed countries is more likely to result in changes in taxes, business laws and regulations, the roles and activities of trade unions, investment, rules on competition, and general attitudes towards business.

Information for the evaluation of political risk

Information for political risk assessment may be obtained:

- from press reports, personal visits to foreign markets for consultations with Embassy officials and local business contacts, or from banks or international credit control agencies
- by engaging persons with expert knowledge of a country to prepare a report on its current and likely future situations
- from stated opinions by host country government ministers, officials, and opposition leaders on the industry to which the firm belongs, the type of product it is selling, and business generally
- by subscribing to the business risk monitoring services offered by consultancies specialising in this field; these firms employ panels of country experts to comment on various factors believed likely to affect the degree of risk attached to undertaking business in particular nations
- from trade associations or Chambers of Commerce.

Problems with information for political risk assessment are that it is likely to be biased, based on hearsay, out-of-date and unreliable, incomplete, quantitatively unmeasurable, contradictory and difficult to verify. Choice of the factors upon which an analysis should be based is necessarily subjective, and a huge range of variables may be relevant to the country concerned. The interpretation of information is also subjective. It is of course much easier to evaluate political risk in a democratic country wherein the views of government and opposition may be monitored via the press, parliamentary debates, party manifestos and similar documents. Much censorship occurs in undemocratic nations, and it can be extremely difficult (perhaps impossible) to establish the true situation.

5. Handling political risk

Confronted with high levels of political risk in countries in which they wish to do business, international firms might adopt the following tactics:

(a) Extensive use of agents and distributors and joint venture partners to handle sales to the market from outside nations, rather than direct investment in subsidiaries and/or owned distribution systems within the country. This occurred in South Africa during and immediately following the apartheid years. Foreign companies conducted business with South Africa 'at arms length', fearing the political disintegration of the nation.

(b) Shared ownership of subsidiaries, projects or operations with the government of the country concerned or with large, locally respected and well-established local firms.

(c) Involving government officials in the overall supervision of a subsidiary's affairs.

(d) Disguising the foreign identity and ownership of the subsidiary through third party holding of its shares, adoption of a local image, exclusive use of locally recruited managers and operatives, etc.

(e) Making the effort visibly to contribute to economic and social development within a host country: provision of training to local workers, widespread purchase of locally produced inputs, donations to community welfare programmes, and so on.

(f) Ensuring that total control over know-how and key technologies and processes remains in the hands of managers from the parent company. Hence the only option available to a government that confiscates the operation is to close it down. The situation is more favourable to the company if new 'inputs' of technology which only that particular firm can provide are periodically required.

THE INTERNATIONAL LEGAL ENVIRONMENT

International businesses confront different sets of laws in the various countries in which they operate. And not only must they abide by the domestic laws of each nation; they are also subject to supranational laws (those of the European Union for instance) which impose obligations beyond those of national legal systems. A country's legal system derives from its political and socio-economic systems, as government and society determine the nation's laws. Nevertheless, countries with very similar political systems and socio-economic characteristics sometimes have quite different laws. Major disparities in national law affecting international business occur in relation to:

- protection of intellectual property
- consumer protection and product liability
- competition among businesses
- the payment of bribes and other 'corrupt practices'
- advertising and sales promotions
- the formation and termination of contracts

- marketing practices *vis-á-vis* product characteristics (safety, physical contents, dimensions, etc.), packaging and labelling, brand names, length of guarantees, pricing, advertising and other forms of promotion
- the carriage of goods.

6. Domestic, international and supranational law

The domestic law of every nation deals with aspects of international business. Foreigners – whether individuals or firms – are normally regarded as if they were citizens of the country in question and are treated and protected on the same terms as native inhabitants. Special laws might be passed to guarantee the safety of foreign investments, but in general the ordinary law of the relevant country is applied whenever conflicts arise and disputes have to be settled. International law (or the 'law of nations' as it is sometimes called) applies to sovereign states (rather than individual citizens) and imposes rights and duties on nations in their dealings *with each other*. It derives from international conventions which establish rules agreed by contesting states; from international custom accepted as law within all nations; and from internationally recognised legal principles (Likta 1991; August 1993). Until the signing of the Treaty of Rome in 1957 (i.e. the treaty that set up the European Common Market) it was the case that a business could not of itself resort to 'international law' in the event of a conflict of interests across national borders. Businesses were subject entirely to the national laws of the countries in which they operated, although some of these laws might themselves be based on international agreements. In other words, an international business embroiled in a legal dispute had to seek redress from the national courts of the country in which the action was heard and could not obtain relief from any 'international legal system.'

The Treaty of Rome changed the situation by creating a new type of law that provided individual persons and businesses with the right to bring cases – on their own accounts – to a supranational legal body (Wyatt and Dashwood 1993). Equally, individuals and businesses assumed obligations extending beyond those imposed by the national legal systems of the countries in which they functioned. Thus, for example, EU companies are subject to laws on competition established at the pan-European level, while employees can (and frequently do) appeal to the European Court of Justice (which can override the national courts of any EU member country) on equal opportunities matters. Other regional treaties of economic and/or political co-operation followed the (then) European Economic Community in creating supranational judicial frameworks.

7. National legal systems

The legal systems of some countries are much better developed than others, particularly the mechanisms for the administration of justice and the enforcement of Court rulings. Most nations have legal systems based on one of the following:

(a) Common law

Common law approaches apply throughout the English-speaking world, including most countries of the former British Empire (English common law being imposed on those countries by the British during the period of colonial rule). These systems rely on historical precedent, on judgements in specific cases, and on *ad hoc* legislation to create and interpret statutes.

(b) Code law

Countries with Code law systems have all their laws written down in Criminal, Civil and/or Commercial Codes which are used to determine all legal matters. Hence, 'the law' on a particular issue can be looked up in the appropriate Article of the relevant Code. Most continental European countries (and hence their former colonies) have Code law systems. Note moreover that there are many similarities among these Continental systems due in part to the 1804 French Code Napoleon, which was subsequently imposed on Belgium, Italy, Luxembourg, the Netherlands, Spain, Greece, Portugal, and regions of Germany (Westphalia, Baden, and the Rhineland) occupied by France during the Napoleon Wars. Code laws also apply in Russia and Japan.

Although they are quite different in principle, common law and Code law systems do have similarities in practice. A large part of the law of common law countries in fact derives from statutes and legally binding government regulations, while Code law systems rely heavily on judicial interpretations of the meanings of the words embodied in legislative codes.

(c) Islamic law

Islamic law derives directly from the Koran and typically is mixed-in with the pre-existing common law or civil code provisions of the country concerned (many nations implementing Islamic law are ex-colonial territories which inherited foreign-imposed legal systems on independence). There are no fundamental differences between Islamic and other legal systems where international trade is concerned, although certain important practical rules apply to the conduct of business in Islamic countries, including the following:

(a) The payment of interest on financial dealings is forbidden, since it is regarded as improper to reward those with excess funds while penalising others (especially the poor) who need to borrow. This applies even to loans between businesses, since it is perceived as unjust to levy interest on organisations that assume risk in order to produce (socially useful) goods and services, yet at the same time provide a return for people who simply lend money.

(b) The principle of profit sharing is extensively applied. Islamic banks, for example, do not pay interest on deposits but instead distribute to investors 'profit shares' (the values of which are not known in advance) that result from the utilisation of the funds deposited.

(c) Instead of consumer credit being offered to customers *via* interest-bearing loan agreements or hire purchase, it is assumed that finance suppliers (the equivalent of finance houses or hire purchase companies in the non-Islamic world) themselves buy goods on behalf of clients and then resell them to clients at a higher price, with clients paying by instalments. The finance supplier's profit mark-up is the Islamic equivalent of interest on consumer credit.

(d) Written agreements witnessed by two independent outside parties are preferred to informal agreements reached by word of mouth.

RESOLUTION OF DISPUTES

Disputes arising from international transactions have to be resolved through negotiation, arbitration or litigation.

8. The conflict of laws

Different laws, interpretations and legal methods apply to commercial litigation within each nation, and conflicts between the legal systems of specific countries frequently occur.

Important disparities among the business laws of various countries include the following:

(a) Laws concerning the circumstances in which an offer may be withdrawn without penalty vary in detail between nations. Normally the law of the country in which obligations arising from a contract were intended to be *performed* will apply to this matter, although many disputes arise over the question of where exactly the performance was supposed to take place.

(b) Some countries (especially in Continental Europe) draw important distinctions between 'commercial' and 'non-commercial' contracts, with a lower burden of proof being necessary to establish the existence of the former, and disputes arising from commercial contracts being heard in special commercial courts.

(c) The intervals beyond which cases become 'statute barred' (so that no one can sue for compensation) differs among countries. In Britain, for example, the period for most classes of contract is six years; in France it can be up to 30 years, while in Germany it depends on whether the case concerns a commercial transaction and, if so, whether both the parties to the contract are traders.

(d) Consideration does not *necessarily* have to be proven prior to suing for breach of contract in certain nations. Examples of 'consideration' are the price paid for goods, the wages of employees (as consideration for providing labour), the hire fee paid for a lease of equipment, etc. Under English law a contract *cannot exist* without consideration.

(e) National differences occur *vis-à-vis* the legality of exemption clauses and penalty clauses included in contracts.

(f) In certain countries it is necessary to 'protest' unpaid debts prior to suing for payment. This means getting a notary public (i.e. a local person legally qualified to attest and certify documents) to ask the customer for payment or for reasons for non-payment. The latter are put into a formal deed of protest which is then placed before a local court as evidence of refusal to pay.

Nationalisation of foreign assets

Although the domestic laws of many countries guarantee that foreign businesses will not be taken over, there is no *international* law on this matter. Indeed, Article 2 of the United Nations Charter of Economic Rights and Duties of States adopted by the UN General Assembly in 1974 asserts that 'every state has and shall freely exercise full permanent sovereignty, including possession, use and disposal, over all its wealth, natural resources and economic activities'. In other words the UN supports the absolute right of member nations to nationalise or exercise partial control over businesses operating within their frontiers. This was not a unanimous decision: 120 countries voted for the Article, six against (five West European countries plus the USA), with ten abstentions (including Japan, Canada and several other West European states). Hence the vote represented a conflict between underdeveloped and economically advanced nations. The latter insist that expropriation should not take place or, if it does, that compensation be adequate and paid swiftly. A number of the world's poorer countries do not agree with this view, although virtually all nations today welcome foreign investment and specify precise rules regarding the payment of compensation to foreign companies whose assets are nationalised.

9. Where cases are heard

Each party to a contract is likely to want any dispute arising from it to be settled in that party's own country according to that nation's laws. But this is obviously not possible when businesses from different countries are involved. Often, therefore, contracts include 'jurisdictional clauses' which specify that the law of a particular country will apply, as agreed by the parties to the contract. This ensures that both sides know for certain their legal rights and obligations. Often the law of England is specified even though neither party resides in the UK. The reason for this is that English law has dealt with questions of international trade for many centuries, is well-documented, and has ready-made answers for most questions arising from international transactions. This may of course lead to Courts outside the UK having to interpret English law.

If a contract has no jurisdictional clause then the law of the country in which the case is heard (normally the defendant's nation, because the defendant cannot be compelled to attend a Court outside his or her own country) will apply. Jurisdictional issues within the European Union are covered by the Brussels Convention of 1982 and the Rome Convention of 1990, which establish the (sometimes complex) circumstances in which cases will be heard in particular EU nations. Either the contract of sale will name a country, or the country with 'the closest connection' with the contract must be chosen.

The concept of residence

Although an MNC operates on the global scale it cannot become an international legal entity as such. Its headquarters must be incorporated under the laws of a particular state, while its subsidiaries have to be set up through the laws of different nations. Questions arise regarding the definition of the nationality of a multinational enterprise (bearing in mind that its 'head office' might be little more than a nominal presence in a tax haven). This is important because the laws of the MNC's 'home' country will govern many of its core activities plus such matters as the responsibilities and liabilities of shareholders, taxation, availability of government grants and subsidies, and the degree of employment protection to be given to personnel. Countries apply differing legal tests when determining a company's nationality, for example:

- where the company was first incorporated (this is the view adopted by the US authorities)
- the country intended to be the home nation by the people forming the company, regardless of where it is actually incorporated
- where decisions are taken concerning most of the firm's worldwide business. This is to prevent a company pretending that what in reality is its head office is little more than a branch. Germany in particular has strict rules on this matter. The German authorities are empowered to assume that a branch of a 'foreign' business is in fact the decision-making centre of its worldwide operations, and will tax the 'branch' as if it were the company's HQ and in receipt of all monies resulting from international activities.

10. Arbitration

Arbitration means the settlement of disputes through the appointment of independent referees who hear and adjudicate cases. The referees must be agreed by each party to the dispute. This differs from 'conciliation', which is the use of an independent and fair minded intermediary to help resolve a dispute, with the conciliator acting as an 'honest broker' between the disputants – advising each side of the other's views and feelings and suggesting compromises (rather than reaching an independent decision, as happens with arbitration).

Arbitration versus litigation

Litigation has the advantage that the rights and duties of the parties are determined by known and definite laws, and that aggrieved parties can obtain redress that is legally enforceable. There are however a number of problems associated with litigation as a means for settling disputes, including:

- lengthy delays
- high costs
- possible bad publicity arising from the case
- fears that Courts will unfairly discriminate against foreigners
- the fact that certain business activities might have to be suspended while a case is being heard
- the lack of business experience of judges who determine cases.

An important practical problem is that of the proper translation of documents into a foreign language for consideration by a Court. The meanings of words can change during translation and the intentions of the contracting parties may become unclear. Matching words across languages is difficult enough; accurately translating legal concepts can be near impossible.

Arbitration is usually faster and cheaper than litigation. Cases are heard in secret so that neither party loses public goodwill through adverse media coverage. Arbitrators are themselves business people (advised by legal experts) with practical experience of the commercial world. No problems need arise from the conflict of national laws, because 'common sense' approaches can be applied to problems. Cases are heard on neutral ground, not in the national courts of one of the parties. However arbitration lacks legal precision, and still costs time and money. And one of the parties will not be happy with the outcome.

Arbitration bodies

A common procedure for resolving disputes between businesses is to insert an arbitration clause into the contract under which a certain international body will resolve the issue. The main arbitration bodies are the International Chamber of Commerce (ICC), the American Arbitration Association, the London Court of Arbitration and the International Centre for Settlement of Investment Disputes (ICSID). In practice the ICC is the most frequently used arbitration organisation. It is based in Paris and offers arbitration facilities both to members and to non-member companies. ICC proceedings begin with an attempt at conciliation by a panel of three persons nominated by the President of the ICC, followed by the appointment of an arbitration tribunal whose members are nationals of countries not involved in the dispute.

The ICSID was founded in 1967 and is sponsored by the World Bank. It arbitrates disagreements between national governments and foreign investors. Note how some nations adhere to the doctrine that simply by entering a country a foreigner implicitly consents to being treated in exactly the same way as a national of that country, and thus revokes any right to protection by the foreigner's home nation in the event of an investment dispute! ICSID has not itself lain down any rules on suggested rights and obligations of investing companies and host nations, but instead provides conciliation and arbitration services in cases where both parties agree to the Centre's involvement. However, ICSID decisions are binding and legally enforceable in all countries that signed the ICSID Convention (including all the industrialised nations). In general, if the parties to a contract agree to arbitration then the arbitrator's decision becomes legally binding under their domestic laws *via* the 1958 New York convention on the Recognition and Enforcement of Foreign Arbitratral Awards, the rules of which have been accepted by the overwhelming majority of the world's nations.

The International Court of Justice (ICJ)

This is a United Nations organisation, based at The Hague in The Netherlands, which adjudicates disputes between states. Only states that have agreed to accept the Court's jurisdiction need participate in cases. Private persons or businesses have no direct access to the ICJ, although private issues can be adjudicated if they are referred to the Court by national governments. And even if a private matter reaches the ICJ and is resolved, enforcement of the judgement is problematic as there is no international body to take action against a losing side that refuses to pay the compensation the Court has awarded.

11. International Conventions

A number of international agreements govern the legal frameworks to be applied to particular aspects of cross-border trade. Laws concerning the carriage of goods at sea follow the 'Hague-Visby Rules' in the majority of the world's trading nations. And notwithstanding this fact, nearly all bills of lading include clauses explicitly stating that at least some of the Hague-Visby rules will apply. The 'Hague Rules' were drafted in 1921 and subsequently extended (to become the Hague-Visby Rules) *via* the 1968 Brussels Protocol. Hague-Visby rules formally determine the legal status of the bill of lading and specify upper limits and a formula for calculating the carrier's liability for damage to cargoes. Claims must be lodged within one year of delivery or the date a cargo was lost.

Air transport is covered by the Warsaw Convention 1929 (subsequently amended) which sets maximum limits on liability for negligence and regulates the legal carrier relationships between air carriers and consignees. Conditions and performance of contracts for rail transport are governed by the 1985 *Convention Relative aux Transports Internationaux Ferroviaries* (COTIF). European road haulage is governed by the 1956 *Convention de Marchandises par Route* (CMR Convention) which lays down standard international contractual conditions for road transport, covering liability for loss or damage to goods and the maximum value for insurance claims against the haulier. Under the Convention the carrier is fully responsible for the acts and omissions of employees and agents, and specific documentation must be used. The Convention extends to contracts involving 'successive carriers,' e.g. road, rail, sea and air.

Two international Conventions have sought to harmonise the legal rules concerning the international sale of goods. The Hague Convention of 1964 drafted 'Uniform Laws' for (i) the sale of goods across national frontiers, and (ii) the formation of contracts for international sales. These Uniform Laws were reconsidered, extended and developed by the United Nations Commission on International Trade Law (UNCITRAL), which organised a 'Vienna Convention' to draft a commercial code for use in all international transactions. The resulting code included a clearly defined procedure for arbitration. UNCITRAL does not *itself* provide arbitration facilities; rather it lays down a model set of rules and procedures which other bodies can follow (Dore 1993).

The intention of the Hague and Vienna Conventions was that agreed Uniform Laws be incorporated into the domestic law of all United Nations countries. This has indeed occurred in many states, including the USA, France, Italy, the Netherlands, and in Scandinavia. In countries that have not acceded to the Convention (Britain for example) the Uniform Laws only apply if both parties agree to this happening (*see* **12**).

12. Uniform Laws

UNCITRAL Uniform Laws (see above) are extremely valuable for dealing with national differences in the law of contract. The basic requirements for the existence of a contract are that there be an offer and an acceptance, an intention to create legal relations and consent to the terms of the agreement. Also the contract must be legal and technically capable of being completed and in some countries (including the UK) there has to be consideration. National laws on these matters are similar in most respects, but with notable exceptions. Specific UNCITRAL rules on contract (which apply automatically in some states, elsewhere if the contracting parties agree that this shall happen) are as follows:

(a) Consideration is *not* necessary for the existence of a contract.

(b) An offer that is accepted is deemed to have been accepted at the moment of receipt and not the moment the offer was transmitted (as is the case under English law).

(c) An offer must be addressed to one or more particular people or organisations. Otherwise proposals not addressed to specific persons are not 'offers' but merely invitations to members of the public themselves to make offers to buy the goods. Examples of offers not addressed to specific persons include catalogues, circularised price lists, advertisements, etc. This does not contradict English law, but does reverse the rules on these matters of certain nations.

(d) If the party making an offer says it will remain open for a period, then it cannot be withdrawn during that period once the offer has been received by the other side (a reversal of English law, which states that an offer may be withdrawn at any time *before acceptance*).

Progress test 8

1. What is the difference between a state and a nation?

2. Define 'sovereignty'.

3. List the main variables that need to be considered when assessing political risk.

4. What is meant by the term 'International Law'?

5. Explain the difference between Code Law and Common Law.

6. What is the 'conflict of laws'?

7. List the advantages of arbitration as a means for settling international business disputes.

8. Outline the work of the ICSID.

9. List the UNCITRAL recommendations regarding the law of contract.

10. Political factors play an important role in many areas of international business; what are these areas?

9

THE MULTINATIONAL COMPANY

THE PROS AND CONS OF MULTINATIONALS

1. Nature of the multinational company

Section 3 of Chapter 1 characterised the multinational company (MNC) as a business with significant investments in several foreign nations, which derives a substantial part of its income from foreign operations, and which maximises its profits on the global rather than national level. There is, however, no single universally agreed definition of the meaning of the term 'multinational company', as the concept of multinationality has a number of dimensions. For some writers *ownership* is the key criterion. These commentators argue that a business only becomes truly international when it has a substantial number of shareholders in more than one country. Few businesses would be classed as 'multinational' on this basis. Another approach emphasises the nationalities of a company's senior management. According to this view, a firm only becomes multinational when headquarters management is recruited from several different countries. Again, not many businesses would satisfy such a yardstick (at least not at the senior management level). Many analysts define the MNC in terms of its multi-country organisation structure and operations. Hence, a firm that controls subsidiaries in a large number of nations is regarded as 'multinational'. An extension of this view is that firms with multinational operations *and* business strategies that treat the entire world as if it were one market are the only real MNCs. Among the various other benchmarks sometimes used to define 'multinationality' are that the company in question must:

- produce (rather than just distribute) abroad as well as in the headquarters country
- operate in a certain minimum number of nations (six for example)
- derive some minimum percentage of its income from foreign operations (e.g. 25 per cent)
- have a certain minimum ratio of foreign to total number of employees, or of foreign total value of assets
- possess a management team with geocentric orientations
- directly control foreign investments (as opposed simply to holding shares in foreign companies).

Some would argue that all the above criteria are irrelevant because, in reality, there can be no such thing as a truly multinational company since:

(a) All firms in fact have a nationality. This might be defined in terms of the nationality of the majority of a company's senior management team rather than the nominal location of its headquarters (which might be an offshore tax haven), but nevertheless a nationality exists. Hence it is naive to suggest that firms operating in multiple markets do not have national allegiances. There are 'US multinationals', 'Japanese multinationals', 'French multinationals', and so on.

(b) In practice firms that conduct business in many nations always seek, at the end of the day, to repatriate their profits to a particular country.

(c) Management style and behaviour reflects the social and cultural norms of a company's senior executives, which are largely determined by their national culture.

The approach to be adopted

This book adopts the view that the essence of multinationality in a company's operations lies in the globalisation of its management systems, perspectives and approaches to strategic decisions. An MNC's profits are maximised across the world as a whole, regardless of the particular locations of various activities (procurement, manufacture, etc.), the whereabouts of head office, or the nationality of its senior management. Resources are allocated to the areas that yield the highest return; there is no presumption that investments have to be restricted to certain countries. Worldwide operations are integrated *via* a global strategic plan drafted according to global criteria, and intended to appease interest groups in many different countries. An MNC's success or failure depends on global conditions and decisions, not those relating to a particular state. Decisions themselves are taken on the basis of global alternatives. It is not always possible to quantify such global approaches, and they need not relate to particular values of the above-mentioned variables. Also a genuinely multinational business does *not* have to be a giant enterprise: smaller firms can operate and maximise their returns globally just as very large companies.

2. Operating characteristics of MNCs

MNCs can reduce their sourcing and distribution costs compared to national businesses, can avoid tariffs, quotas and other trade barriers faced by exporters, and are able periodically to shift operations from high-cost to low-cost countries. They can penetrate markets throughout the world from supply points in several different countries, supplemented perhaps by exports from the parent firm plus *ad hoc* licensing and contract manufacture agreements. Their managements plan, organise and control company operations on a worldwide scale, with national markets being regarded as little more than segments of a broader regional customer base. A number of top jobs in a multinational company will be allocated to the nationals of various foreign countries, there will be joint strategic decision-making by headquarters staff and managers of foreign subsidiary units, and everyone concerned with the management of international operations will regard these as being at least as important as the management of activities in the headquarters country. Note how there exists within a large MNC an extensive 'internal market' involving the movement of finished goods, raw materials, component parts, know-how (and sometimes people) between various locations, flows of information, utilisation of inputs and the allocations of resources to their most profitable applications. Internal integration of business functions at the multinational level creates many possibilities for economies of scale and the spreading of costs over multiple markets. Operations are located wherever is appropriate to enable goods to be sold in the company's most important markets: technologies are developed in whichever countries have the necessary skills, research infrastructures and facilities.

3. The case for the multinational company

Advocates of the multinational company argue that MNCs are agents of change and progress, helping to create a worldwide economic order based on rationality, efficiency, and the optimal use of resources. Host countries acquire plant and equipment that otherwise would not be available, accompanied by the skills and know-how necessary for its operation. Local recruitment of junior managers creates a pool of managerial talent in the local community that can transfer its abilities across a wide range of industries. Prices are lower in consequence of economies of scale: domestic employment is stimulated. MNCs have contributed enormously to technology transfer between rich and poor countries. Technology transfer benefits the host country through introducing fresh ideas and practices and by improving the research and development infrastructure of the nation. MNCs facilitate economic development in the Third World and are catalysts for change and progress. The latest management techniques and business methods are diffused internationally.

An MNC's impact on a host country's exports (and hence its capacity to earn foreign exchange) can be dramatic. A number of large MNCs (especially Japanese companies) have established 'export platforms' in low-wage Third World nations in order to assemble components for the MNC's operations in other countries and also to sell these goods to other customers all over the world. This greatly increases the host nation's level of exports, thus generating hard currency that can be used to finance capital imports needed for economic development.

Although MNCs sometimes shift jobs from high-wage to low-wage countries, it may still be the case that total employment in the nations losing these jobs will expand in consequence of increased international trade between richer and poorer countries. Efficient allocation of the world's resources benefits everyone in the long run.

4. Criticisms of multinational companies

The view that MNCs allocate resources across the globe in an optimal manner rests on the proposition that the world's resources are best utilised through the interplay of unfettered market forces. The problem is that open and competitive markets exist in some parts of the world, but not in others, so that distortions in free market mechanisms will arise in some areas – generating side effects that upset the entire worldwide resource allocation process. Criticisms of MNC activities in host countries may be collected under the following headings.

(a) Political

MNCs have been accused on occasion of:

- supporting repressive regimes
- paying bribes to secure political influence
- not respecting human rights
- paying protection money to terrorist groups
- destabilising national governments of which they do not approve.

MNCs in reality are owned and controlled by the nationals of just a handful of Triad countries so that MNC domination of world markets effectively represents 'economic imperialism' on the part of these states. Subsidiaries of MNCs take their orders from company headquarters in another country staffed by managers who owe their allegiance to a foreign nation. Hence an MNC's subsidiaries might act as *de facto* instruments of the foreign economic policy of another state. The vast resources of large multinational companies enable them actually to challenge the sovereignty of smaller nation states. In particular their ability to transfer economic activity around the world can undermine underdeveloped countries' abilities to pursue national economic objectives.

In fact, fears that multinational companies would destroy nation-states in the developing world receded during the 1980s, due to a number of factors, including:

(a) Increasingly ferocious international competition among MNCs, which made them keen to establish good relations with host country governments.

(b) Development of better negotiating skills by host government representatives. Ministers and senior civil servants became adept at securing the best possible deals when bargaining with MNC managements.

(c) A wider dispersion of the home countries in which MNCs were based. Japanese, Korean and other Asian MNCs brought different approaches to host country relations compared to firms from Western Europe and (especially) the US.

(d) The emergence of large home-grown international businesses in a number of underdeveloped states.

(e) An increase in the number of small firms operating on the global scale.

(f) Greater cultural sensitivity on the part of MNC managers resulting from their longer experience of doing business abroad.

(b) Sales and marketing

Allegations in this category of criticism are that MNCs have

- undermined ancient cultures and traditions through the use of ubiquitous advertising and marketing methods
- engaged in misleading and deceiptful advertising in Third World countries
- promoted goods that waste valuable resources in poorer nations
- supplied products that are inappropriate to local needs
- not accepted responsibility for unsafe products.

(c) Environmental management

Environmentalists have attacked MNCs for:

- depleting natural resources too quickly (and not looking for artificial substitutes)
- polluting the environment
- not paying compensation for environmental damage
- causing harmful changes in local living conditions
- paying little regard to the risks of accidents causing major environmental catastrophes
- shifting environmentally 'dirty' activities to underdeveloped countries.

(d) Technology

The general issue of technology transfer is discussed in Chapter 11. Specifically MNCs have been accused of :

- using technologies that are inappropriate for the needs of the local economy. Typically MNCs do not develop technologies specifically relevant to the needs of host nations, as it is usually cheaper for an MNC to transfer an existing technique to a foreign country than to devise a new one appropriate for local conditions. This matter is discussed further in Chapter 11.
- charging license fees that are prohibitively expensive
- not engaging in research and development in host countries
- encouraging a 'brain drain' from poorer countries
- making host countries technolgoically dependent on the West
- not allowing local employees access to or information about key technologies
- not training local nationals in the operation of imported technologies.

Arguably the use by MNCs of capital-intensive production methods in less-developed countries undermines local businesses making similar items but with labour-intensive technologies, hence creating much unemployment. Also it might destroy the spirit of entrepreneurship within the local community, which becomes increasingly dependent on large foreign-owned companies for local employment. The counter-argument here is that typically MNCs enter foreign countries in order to supply new products not previously available to local consumers, and that often an MNC will pay its local employees higher wages than local companies. Note however that the latter practice might cause workers and managers to leave local businesses, further eroding the latter's competitive positions.

(e) Economic

Critics allege that MNCs have impeded rather than facilitated the overall economic development of many poorer countries, through concentrating economic activity in a handful of urban centres rather than promoting evenly balanced economic advancement across a nation as a whole. Arguably, MNC activities in underdeveloped countries have led to 'dual' economic structures with foreign-owned capital-intensive high-technology high-productivity industry sectors operating in parallel with labour-intensive low-productivity industries. The foreign-owned sectors might export most of their outputs (typically to economically advanced nations) and are managed primarily for the benefits of the MNCs concerned and the (rich) countries to which their products are sent – often at low prices. Thus, technical progress results not in higher incomes for local residents, but rather in lower prices which favour consumers in developed nations. These lower import prices for advanced countries further stimulate their economic development, enabling them to dominate the world! According to this line of reasoning it would be better for host countries to develop domestic industries serving local consumers rather than export sectors, in order to provide growth points for manufacturing, local dissemination of technical knowledge, urban education and infrastructure improvement programmes, and so on.

Other economic objections to MNC activities in underdeveloped countries are as follows:

(a) MNCs sometimes choose to import raw materials and input components for their foreign subsidiaries rather than procure them locally. Scarce foreign exchange is used to pay for the imports, and the host country's balance of payments suffers.

(b) Repatriations of MNC profits can put a strain on a country's balance of payments.

(c) MNCs might come to dominate key technically advanced sectors of an economy, causing the host country government to lose control over the nation's economic destiny in these critical areas.

(d) MNCs contribute to inequality in the distribution of income within a country. (The counter-argument here is that although local residents who work for an MNC might be rewarded generously compared to other citizens, it is the responsibility of the state rather than the MNC to ensure that national income is distributed fairly, *via* domestic taxes and subsidies.)

(e) Foreign firms periodically raise large amounts of capital on domestic money markets, hence 'starving' local companies of funds. The counter-argument to this accusation is that investors are not fools, and the fact that they choose to buy shares in foreign rather than local businesses is but a reflection of market mechanisms properly allocating financial resources to their most profitable uses.

(f) Personnel management and industrial relations

It has been alleged that certain MNCs:

- refuse to recognise trade unions or engage in collective bargaining
- do not apply equal opportunities policies that would be legally required in economically advanced nations
- use expatrate staff for all significant managerial positions, do not promote excellent locally recruited workers, and do not pass on managerial competencies to local employees
- ignore the occupational health and safety needs of local workers
- exploit host country labour
- do not involve local employees in management decision making.

Trade unions in some Western countries have criticised MNCs for:

- 'exporting jobs' through investment in foreign production
- exploiting low-paid foreign workers in countries where there is negligible employment protection
- transferring skills to other nations, thus enabling the latter to compete more fiercely in the home country market
- taking advantage of the tax advantages, investment grants and subsidies offered by foreign governments
- circumventing home country laws on business competition, labour relations, etc., through shifting production among countries.

CONTROL OF MNC ACTIVITIES

5. The case for control

Whereas the economic power and political influence of MNCs has expanded enormously over recent decades, the sociopolitical conditions of many of the countries in which MNCs operate have altered radically – often towards greater democracy and openness of government affairs. Democratic social institutions (such as elected parliaments) increasingly question existing arrangements between MNCs and their hosts, and are determined to ensure that the benefits of MNC operations are felt *within* national frontiers. Also governments sometimes fear a loss of political sovereignty as key sectors of their national economies are taken over by foreign enterprises, with possible adverse effects on local sociocultural environments. A government might believe that the state (as opposed to individuals and interest groups) has a responsibility to preserve the nation's sociocultural heritage, as well as seeking economic growth and development. Note moreover that MNC investment or disinvestment decisions can be of such a high value that they have the potential to disrupt the long-term economic plans of smaller nations, which have no control over these decisions. Further reasons why governments may seek to control MNC activities include:

(a) Wanting to ensure that MNCs behave in a socially responsible manner. This motive presupposes that because they are driven by the profit motive, MNCs cannot be relied upon to exercise social responsibility. It is assumed that they will inevitably resort to bribery and corrupt practices, surreptitiously attempt to exert political influence, seek to monopolise markets, etc.

(b) An ideological belief that the host country can attain national socio-economic goals more effectively through controlling MNC activities.

(c) National 'economic pride', reflected in dislike of foreigners being able to influence the domestic economy and/or in a particular political party advocating the control of foreign companies in order to gain political advantage. A government may want to be seen to be strong and independent.

(d) The desire to co-ordinate MNC activities with national economic plans.

Advocates of controls on foreign businesses allege that in reality the free market does not generate maximum efficiency and that it is essential for governments to intervene to prevent large international companies from abusing their power (Fagre and Wells 1982; Julius 1990). Opponents of controls argue that market forces will indeed ensure that multinational companies are managed efficiently, and to the benefit of host countries as well as the companies themselves. Also it is virtually impossible to police intricate controls effectively, and the costs of administration will probably outweigh the benefits.

6. MNC conflicts with national governments

Because MNCs seek to maximise their profits on a worldwide rather than a national basis, the policies they adopt may bring them into conflict with national governments, which want reasonable tax revenues from foreign businesses operating within their borders. Also governments might pressurise an MNC to create and maintain jobs in their own particular countries rather than in other nations, to train local labour and to engage in research and technical development. Conflicts can also arise over MNC transfer pricing policies which might deprive a country of much needed foreign exchange, over output levels (which have an impact on local employment), and an MNC's level of concern for the welfare of the local population (e.g. if a foreign company pollutes the local environment). Other potential sources of conflict include:

- differences in the core objectives of national governments and MNCs
- wage rates paid to local labour
- an MNC's competitive practices *vis-à-vis* domestic businesses
- the nature of the technologies transferred to underdeveloped countries.

Arguably conflict between MNCs and nation states is inevitable, and bound to increase in the future as cross-border movement of funds becomes easier and as competition for the world's diminishing stock of natural resources intensifies. Conflicts can arise between an MNC and host countries (see below) and with a company's home nation (*see* **8**).

7. Conflicts with host countries

Conflicts between MNCs and host countries are more common than conflicts involving home country governments. Disputes typically arise in two areas: those concerning MNC control and utilisation of host country resources, and disagreements about the division of the profits arising from MNCs' local operations. Tensions frequently result from the fact that companies invariably attempt to use the lowest-cost resources in the most productively efficient manner, whereas politicians often wish to encourage an economy to develop in a certain direction (high employment for example) regardless of efficiency considerations. It is important to recognise that although MNCs bring capital, technology, employment, etc., to host countries, the latter *themselves* give MNCs markets for their products, provide labour and raw materials for production, and may supply natural resources. Host country governments argue that since an MNC's local profits accrue from the use of local resources (raw materials, labour, capital and access to markets) then a large part of those profits should be paid over to the state. Equally, MNCs often allege that since their surpluses are generated by their highly efficient production and management methods then the contributions they make to the development of a nation's technological infrastructure and the extra local jobs they create should exempt them from having to pay high levels of tax.

In past decades governments in some parts of the world have viewed MNCs with mistrust and suspicion, accusing them of exploitation and of being the cause of numerous national economic ills. Today however the overwhelming majority of countries adopt a more pragmatic position, seeking to co-operate with MNCs in order to maximise the domestic employment, technical advance and improvements in local living standards that they create. This is a worldwide phenomenon and is true of all industry sectors, including mining and agriculture (in the 1970s and early 1980s more than half of all MNC/host country disputes that resulted in government takeovers of MNC assets involved the resource extraction industries, predominantly in Africa and Latin America). Democratisation of Latin America, liberalisation programmes and the privatisation of nationalised industries in Latin America, parts of Africa and indeed throughout the world (frequently as side conditions to aid packages from the World Bank) have lessened national goverments' desires to control MNCs, preferring instead to co-operate with them in order to attain higher rates of national economic growth. Nevertheless, ferocious bargaining between MNC and host country representatives frequently occurs prior to the establishment of major foreign capital investments. Negotiations will encompass the extent of the grants and subsidies to be paid for new start-ups, tax rates and the length of the 'tax holiday' before tax becomes payable, foreign currency repatriation matters, minimum output and enterprise employment levels, and whether government representatives are to contribute to the management of the local operation (e.g. through holding a seat on the board of the MNC's local subsidiary).

Factors facilitating an MNC's ability to negotiate effectively with a host government include the benefits it can bring to the host nation, its financial and human resources, expertise, international image, access to local media, and its previous experience of dealing with government officials. A host country's bargaining power will be greater the more it possesses natural resources, skilled labour or other factors needed by the MNC concerned. The time and effort involved in discussions can be very costly to a multinational company. Valuable markets might be lost while the firm is negotiating with government officials, and heavy legal costs could be incurred. Large amounts of management time might have to be devoted to MNC/government discussions, and the morale and motivation of the managers involved may deteriorate. An MNC's bargaining power *vis-à-vis* a host country government is typically at its peak prior to the start of local operations, and declines thereafter as local firms observe and imitate the MNC's imported technologies. Hence the MNC might systematically increase its contributions to the local economy and community over time in order to convince the host government of the continuing benefits deriving from the MNC's local operations.

8. Techniques of host country control

Techniques of host country regulation are legion, and include special taxes, minimum wage requirements, exchange controls, and possibly regulations requiring that:

- a certain number of host country nationals be employed in managerial positions (including seats on the subsidiary's board of directors)
- a subsidiary's exports attain a prespecified annual value
- some proportion of a subsidiary's inputs be supplied locally rather then imported (see below)
- imports by the subsidiary be restricted to some maximum value
- the very latest technologies be used in production
- the subsidiary not take more than a predetermined share of the local market
- a predetermined minimum number of new jobs be created
- the local subsidiary of an MNC to have local joint venture partners
- MNC subsidiaries obtain export/import licences
- restrictions apply to a foreign firm's abilities to acquire local businesses, fix export prices, select directors, independently choose where to locate plant, or to use expatriate staff.

Also a government might insist that the foreign firm train a certain number of locally recruited workers and engage in local technical research. The rate of expansion of an MNC's local activities could be limited, and restrictions imposed on its ability to repatriate profits.

Today, nations are generally loathe to impose too many controls on MNC operations, for fear of losing valuable foreign investment. However, all host countries take a keen interest in MNC affairs. Arguably, constant and thorough host government surveillance of an MNC's activities serves to keep the company 'on its toes': management is compelled to formulate its strategies extremely carefully, objectives are clarified, and concern for customers and local interest groups is enhanced.

Equity participation

Host country governments have on occasion imposed the requirement that some minimum percentage of the share capital of an MNC's local establishment be owned by host country citizens. This has been justified on the following grounds:

(a) Local shareholders will receive dividends resulting from the MNC's local operations, hence ensuring that some of the profits accruing to a foreign-owned establishment are actually distributed to local people.

(b) Host country citizens might use their influence as voting shareholders to encourage the MNC's local operation to work in the best interests of the host nation.

(c) The firm will be legally obliged to provide information to its local share-holders, preventing it from concealing the nature and extent of its activites.

Note moreover that host country governments which apply this rule are seen to be taking a 'tough stance' on the question of inward foreign investment, perhaps enhancing their political standing among the local population.

In some countries MNCs have been required to increase the proportions of their foreign subsidiaries' equity held by local residents systematically over time. In certain cases local tax incentives and investment grants were only available to subsidiaries with significant numbers of local shareholders. On occasion, countries have imposed local equity participation rules *after* foreign investments have taken place, much to the annoyance of the companies concerned, which complained bitterly of being the victim of 'backdoor expropriation'. Losses may have been incurred during a subsidiary's set-up and early operating periods and, MNCs complained, it was unfair to deprive them of parts of their well-earned rewards as soon as operations moved into profit, especially if the host government required that shares be sold to local residents at artificially low prices.

Local content requirements

These are rules insisting that certain proportions of locally supplied inputs be used in local production or that local labour account for some minimum per-centage of the total value of final output. Local content requirements are in practice extremely difficult to police and enforce. The host country government must either rely on the MNC to use the appropriate level of locally produced inputs, or must collect, verify and analyse large amounts of detailed data to ensure that the MNC is meeting its obligations. Also an MNC might itself purchase the local firms that supply inputs to the MNC's subsidiary, or set up its own local input manufacturing plants. Indeed a section of the MNC's existing operation could be hived off and used to furnish inputs. It then becomes questionable whether local content rules have actually been satisfied. Another possibility is for the MNC to continue supplying imported inputs to its subsid-iary, but at very low transfer prices, so that the proportion of the subsidiary's total costs represented by these imported inputs falls dramatically.

Expropriation

Nationalisation of MNC subsidiaries has proven extremely problematic in prac-tice, because national governments have not been able to market the outputs of these plants internationally, and have experienced great difficulty in recruiting and retaining technicians and managers with the requisite know-how and experience.

Evidence suggests that foreign firms are more vulnerable to expropriation the more they:

- operate within defence-related industry sectors
- are easier to manage without the involvement of foreign nationals
- extract and export a country's natural resources
- are poorly integrated into the local economy
- use mature and widely-diffused technologies
- are wholly owned subsidiaries of foreign enterprises rather than members of joint ventures with local firms.

MNC responses to control by host governments

MNC reactions to host country attempts to control their operations could include threats of complete withdrawal, reductions in the level of investment, changes in the organisation of the business in order to protect the confidentiality of key functions, and reductions in technology transfer. Also MNC managements might argue that they will not be able to meet host country demands unless they are given help with infrastructure facilities and/or the government reduces bureaucratic controls and implements business legislation favourable to multi-national companies (laws that make it easy to dismiss labour or laws enabling MNCs to circumvent regulations on business competition for example). Another tactic is for the MNC to launch a public relations campaign intended to create a strong image for local operations. High visibility can result from the MNC's local subsidiary:

- using a novel technology
- paying very high wages relative to local standards
- employing large numbers of local workers
- becoming involved with local communities
- providing a product that is completely new to the local market.

This approach may have positive or negative consequences. Some of these factors might impel a host country government to support the MNC's local activities. On the other hand they might encourage the government to control the local subsidiary still further.

9. Conflicts with the home country

MNCs emerge from enterprises based in particular countries and, as a firm's international operations expand, so too does its contributions to its home nation. Companies undertaking international operations achieve economies of scale and are thus able to supply low price outputs to the domestic market; they engage in R & D, earn foreign currency, introduce new products, pay large amounts of tax to the home country government, and employ increasing numbers of workers. Headquarters functions will naturally tend to be undertaken in the home country, further contributing to the overall economic development of that state. Eventually, however, competitive pressures and the drive for increased efficiency might cause an enterprise to allocate resources outside its home nation, a move possibly resented by citizens and the government of the home country. Workers in the home nation might lose their jobs; investment spending falls; and there is an outflow of financial capital.

Note how conflicts can also arise between an MNC's host countries and its headquarters' nation. The latter's government may seek to prevent the MNC from exporting large amounts of capital (and jobs) during recesssionary periods, while host countries might simultaneously be offering generous financial inducements to the MNC to invest in foreign nations.

Home country techniques for controlling MNC operations

The home country government has a number of advantages when attempting to prevent firms shifting operations to other countries:

(a) As the largest proportion of an MNC's assets is usually located in its home country the home country government can adopt a threatening posture towards these assets. Outright withdrawal of the totality of an MNC's home country operations is rarely feasible.

(b) Senior executives of MNCs are usually citizens of the home nation and will be conscious that, as individuals, they are subject to the laws and regulations of the home country. Also they share the same cultural norms and perspectives of the government officials, trade union representatives, community leaders, etc., with whom they discuss issues so that communications with these people are likely to be fast and efficient.

(c) MNC executives and home country shareholders will probably support the home country's basic economic objectives.

(d) It is possible for the home country government to exert strong indirect influence on MNC activities via informal contacts and advice given in private conversations.

Examples of direct home country controls and restrictions (many of which were pioneered by the government of the United States) on MNC's foreign operations include:

(a) Prohibitions on the transfer of technology to certain nations (e.g. the ban imposed by the US and other Western countries on the licensing of the latest computer technologies to firms in Eastern bloc countries prior to their economic and political liberalisation.

(b) Preventing firms from using money raised in the home country for foreign investment, as happened in the USA in the 1960s.

(c) Increasing the cost of the foreign currency that has to be obtained in order to invest abroad.

(d) Creation of tax regimes not conducive to DFI.

(e) Imposition of extra-territoriality provisions enabling the home country government to dictate the behaviour of an MNC's foreign subsidiaries.

(f) Requiring all significant foreign investments to obtain government approval prior to contracts being signed (as happened in Japan).

(g) Using domestic anti-trust law to restrict an MNC's ability to serve foreign markets, e.g. by regarding an MNC's acquisition of a foreign firm as the removal of the latter's ability independently to sell to the home country, and as such a threat to open competition in the home country. International joint ventures and cross-licensing agreements could also fall foul of domestic competition law.

10. Who should control MNC activities?

To the extent that MNC activities need to be regulated, who or what should exercise control? Two approaches to this question may be discerned. The first relies on the proposition that MNCs are no different from any other business so that any MNC operation within a country's national frontiers must conform to the laws and customs of that country. Hence the government of the nation concerned should be the controlling authority. The second approach asserts that since MNCs are supranational organisations, some of which have revenues considerably higher than those of many nations states, then control should be exercised by international bodies such as regional trading groups (the European Union for instance) or the United Nations.

Control by national governments

The domination of world trade by multinational companies obviously presents a challenge to national sovereignty over MNC activities. Yet a number of factors suggest that countries will continue in their ability to control MNCs for the foreseeable future, as follows:

(a) The formation of common markets and regional trading blocs throughout the world greatly strengthens nations' *collective* capacities to harness MNC activities for their own advantage. Threats of regulation might cause an MNC to withdraw from a particular country; but withdrawal from (say) the European Union, NAFTA or some other major trading group would damage an MNC very badly.

(b) Diminishing global stocks of natural resources will give countries that possess extensive natural resources enormous bargaining power *vis-à-vis* foreign companies.

(c) More countries than ever now have research and technical development infrastructures capable of at least imitating foreign technologies.

(d) Competition between MNCs has never been more ferocious, making it difficult for any one of them to 'take on' a national government.

(e) The end of the Cold War, the dismantling of apartheid in South Africa, the opening up of the Chinese market, and the economic liberalisation of countries all over the world have led to a big increase in international co-operation among nations. This new willingness to enter international agreements could result in international coalitions against multinational companies.

11. Supranational Codes of Practice

Concern over the possible emergence of destructive conflicts between nation states and multinational companies caused the international community (as represented by the United Nations, the OECD, UNCTAD and the International Labour Organisation [ILO]) to draft Codes of Practice intended to govern MNC operations. The reasoning behind this was that since smaller and poorer countries were finding it difficult to control MNCs' behaviour individually, then international action was required (Francis 1991; Frederick 1991). Hence, guidelines and standards of conduct for MNCs were laid down, not as binding laws but as 'rules of the game' to be followed voluntarily. The resulting Codes were not legally enforceable, and carried only a moral obligation to abide by their contents. Their objectives were to ensure the compatibility of MNC activities with host country development programmes, to encourage international investment, protect the interests of workers and consumers, and facilitate the resolution of disagreements between governments arising from MNC operations. A number of factors encouraged the development of these international Codes, including the following:

(a) Conflicts of national laws. An MNC operates in many countries and is subject to numerous legal systems. Each subsidiary has to abide by a unique set of local laws, and conflicts of national laws may occur. And what happens if an MNC's host country government prohibits its companies from trading with a certain foreign nation, does the prohibition extend to affiliates of the MNC in another country?

(b) The fact that different nations impose disparate demands on MNCs operating within their frontiers.

(c) Development of international regulatory mechanisms for monetary relations (via the IMF), and the conduct of trade (through GATT), leaving an obvious gap *vis-à-vis* direct foreign investment.

(d) A number of highly publicised cases of misbehaviour by MNCs in the 1970s and early 1980s; including the bribing of politicians, attempts to destabilise national governments, and neglect of health and public safety matters.

The Codes themselves were drafted by teams representing the underdeveloped countries, the economically advanced Western nations, and what was then the communist Eastern bloc. Many disagreements arose over the wordings of the documents, although all were based on the same basic premises, namely that:

- MNCs should contribute to economic and social progress in the countries in which they operate, should be sensitive to the needs of the populations of poor nations and accept that workers and consumers have rights
- governments must treat MNCs fairly and create proper legal frameworks for their activities.

12. The United Nations Code of Conduct for Transnational Corporations 1983

This is comprehensive set of recommendations concerning the behaviour of MNCs and their treatment by national governments. Its origins date back to a

1948 UN meeting in Havana, Cuba, which called for host countries to provide security for foreign investments, place restraints on ownership, and impose other reasonable constraints. The 'Havana Declaration' was never adopted by the UN General Assembly, although it served as a starting point for subsequent developments, notably:

- The 1952 UN Resolution on permanent sovereignty over natural resources
- The 1971 statement of the 'Group of 77' (i.e. developing countries that belong to the United Nations) that private foreign investment in poorer nations should generate inflows and avoid outflows of foreign exchange, enhance national investment, and incorporate 'adequate technology'
- The 'Georgetown Declaration' of the 1972 Conference of Non-Aligned Countries that private foreign investment should 'subserve national development objectives'.

In 1974 the UN's Economic and Social Council set up a Commission on Transnational Corporations comprising representatives from 48 countries and advised by trade unions, business and public interest groups from both the economically advanced and developing nations. At the same time the UN Secretariat was mandated to undertake research into political, legal, economic and social issues relating to multinational corporations in order to assist the Commission to prepare a Code of Conduct for MNCs.

The final version of the UN Code required MNCs, *inter alia*, to:

- respect the national sovereignty of host countries and observe their domestic laws, regulations and administrative practices
- adhere to host nations' economic goals, development objectives and sociocultural values
- respect human rights
- not interfere in internal political affairs or in intergovernmental relations
- not engage in corrupt practices
- apply good practice in relation to payment of taxes, abstention from involvement in anti-competitive practices, consumer and environmental protection and the treatment of employees
- disclose relevant information to host country governments.

Host countries themselves should, the Code insists, possess the absolute right to nationalise foreign-owned assets within their frontiers, but must pay proper compensation.

Demands by developing countries that the Code become legally binding were rejected by the UN General Assembly, at the behest of economically advanced countries. Many other disagreements between developed and developing nations emerged during the drafting of the Code, especially the following:

(a) Whereas underdeveloped countries wanted MNCs to be subject to the national laws and regulations of the nations in which they operate, economically advanced countries wished to see the application of internationally agreed rules on MNC behaviour in conjunction with the use of arbitrators who would be independent of host country governments to resolve disputes.

(b) Developing countries demanded that MNCs be required to pursue the economic development objectives of host countries. Industrially developed nations, conversely, insisted that MNCs be free to follow their own commercial interests and not be expected to undertake duties beyond their commercial resources and capabilities.

(c) Economically advanced nations wished to incorporate within the Code explicit requirements for host country governments to treat MNCs equitably and not discriminate against companies from any particular country. Moreover, an MNC's home country government should be empowered to represent the company's interests if negotiations with the host nation collapsed. Under-developed countries regarded these demands as challenges to their national sovereignty.

13. UNCTAD Codes

UNCTAD has issued two Codes of Practice: one on technology transfer, the other on restrictive business practices.

The UNCTAD Code on the Control of Restrictive Business Practices 1980

This has provisions on the prevention and elimination of restrictive business agreements and behaviour, the concentration of economic power, pricing, and conditions of sale. In drafting the Code, UNCTAD's experts sought to identify (i) restrictive business practices likely to hinder international trade (especially that of underdeveloped countries), (ii) measures needed to counteract such practices, and (iii) the information that would need to be gathered and exchanged between nations in order to monitor restrictive business agreements. They also wished to formulate model laws on business competition for use by developing countries. This was considered necessary because of the disparate approaches to anti-trust legislation adopted by developed and underdeveloped nations. The former emphasise free competition, free trade and freedom of investment (albeit to varying degrees), whereas developing countries' laws on these matters usually focused on the protection of local industry from the abusive practices (actual or perceived) of foreign enterprises. According to the Code, a restrictive business practice is 'any act or behaviour of an enterprise which, through abuse of a dominant position of market power, limits access to markets or otherwise unduly restrains competition and has or is likely to have adverse effects on international trade', especially the trade of developing countries and/or their economic progress. The term 'dominant position' is defined as a situation wherein one or a few enterprises can control a particular market. Major principles enunciated by the Code are as follows:

(a) Actions aimed at eliminating restrictive business practices should be taken at the regional, national and international levels. International action should include:

- Negotiations to achieve common approaches to the control of restrictive business practices

- Notification to the UN of exemptions to domestic competition law granted by national governments
- International dissemination of information on restrictive business practices, plus the regular exchange of views between national governments on anti-trust matters.

(b) Developing countries should have the flexibility to relax their rules on competition in order to encourage the establishment of new industries.

(c) MNCs should conform to the laws on restrictive business practices of the countries in which they operate, and in any event not engage in any of a list of cartel and other abusive practices specified within the Code.

(d) Nations should enforce their competition laws effectively, and treat enterprises in a fair, equitable and non-discriminatory manner. All states should take measures to prevent restrictive business practices that damage the trade and economic development of poorer countries.

The UNCTAD Code on Technology Transfer

Adopted in 1983 this Code advocated the 'unpackaged' transfer of technology between nations, access to technology for developing countries at reasonable cost, and the improvement of the technological capabilities of recipient nations. These recommendations are somewhat bland, in consequence of disagreements between developed and underdeveloped countries during the negotiations that preceded the drafting of the text. Poorer countries wanted the Code to apply to parent/subsidiary relationships, and to define certain business practices as 'restrictive' even though these practices were considered acceptable in most of the developed world. The economically advanced nations were adamant that existing rules on the protection of intellectual property not be undermined. Rather they wished to discourage business practices that hampered the transfer of technology (*via* licensing) across national frontiers. Developing countries, conversely, were not interested in any measure that would constrain their abilities to strengthen their domestic technological infrastructures.

14. The OECD Code of Practice on MNC operations

This 1976 declaration sought to encourage MNCs to contribute positively to economic and social progress within host nations. Its main provisions were that MNCs should:

- contribute to host countries' science and technology objectives by permitting the rapid diffusion of technologies
- not behave in manners likely to restrict competition by abusing dominant positions or market power
- provide full information for tax purposes
- consult with employee representatives regarding major changes in operations, avoid unfair discrimination in employment and provide reasonable working conditions

- consider the host nation's balance of payments objectives when taking decisions
- regularly make public significant information on financial and operational matters.

The Code recognised explicitly the importance of MNCs in the international economy and, in particular, their role in providing investment. However it stressed the need for MNCs to be sensitive to the needs and concerns of developing countries, and declared that 'every state has the right to prescribe the conditions under which multinational enterprises operate within its national jurisdiction, subject to international law and the international agreements to which it has subscribed. The entities of a multinational enterprise located in various countries are subject to the laws of those countries'.

15. The ILO Declaration on Multinational Enterprises and Social Policy

Adopted by the ILO in 1977 this Code addressed issues relating to employment, vocational training, working conditions, and industrial relations. The Code itself was drafted by a tripartite body comprising representatives of national governments, trade union and employers' organisations. It encourages consultation between MNC managements and their workers, but falls short of calling for global consultations between managers and employee representatives of all affiliates of a multinational company. Managements are requested to provide workers' representatives with whatever information is necessary for meaningful negotiations. Governments are asked to pursue active policies designed to promote full employment.

16. Benefits and problems of supranational Codes of Practice

Benefits anticipated from the promulgation of these Codes (especially the UN Code) included:

- a more co-operative attitude on the part of MNCs towards poorer host countries
- the incorporation of key elements of the Codes into MNC policies
- less uncertainty in the political and legal environments surrounding MNC operations, and greater stability in MNC relationships with national governments
- avoidance of the conflict of national laws *vis-à-vis* MNC activities.

An important benefit to MNCs that openly adhere to international Codes is their immunity from accusations of improper behaviour. Attacks on MNCs following these Codes by particular governments should lead to general condemnation of these countries by the international community. Note that although these Codes of Practice are not 'treaties' between nations and thus do not have the force of law (treaties normally become part of the national legislation of the signatories and as such are legally binding within those states) they do have a moral force, as they represent the view of the majority of the world's nations. Hence bad publicity is likely to attach to companies that wilfully contravene them. Moreover, Codes of Practice can act as models for specific countries that do in fact choose to legislate on MNC issues. Another possibility is for governments to insist that MNCs setting up major operations within their borders sign contracts whereby they agree to adhere to the provisions of a particular Code.

MNC responses to supranational Codes

MNC reactions to these voluntary Codes of Practice have been generally negative, ranging from indifference to open hostility. Representatives of a number of major MNCs have asserted that regulation of their activities is unjustified and unnecessary. The Codes imply misbehaviour by MNCs which, they allege, does not happen in practice. Arguably, moreover, attempts to regulate MNC activities distort the natural pattern of competition, hence leading to inefficiency in the allocation of national resources. MNC representatives have also insisted that since economic environments constantly change, the detailed provisions of any Code agreed today might be totally irrelevant to the needs of future situations.

Critics of international Codes of Practice refute the proposition that they should be made legally binding on the grounds that:

(a) Different nation states have disparate economic and social objectives and philosophies, so that forms of MNC control acceptable to some countries might be unwelcome in others.

(b) At present there is no supranational organisation capable of enforcing agreed regulations in all countries.

(c) Information gathering, administration and policing of controls would be extremely expensive.

(d) Law cases arising from supranational regulations would be highly complex, take years to resolve, and have uncertain outcomes.

Progress test 9

1. What is a multinational company?

2. List six benefits to the world economy allegedly created by the existence of MNCs.

3. State five examples of the political grounds on which MNCs have been criticised.

4. MNCs have been accused of using technologies that are inappropriate for the needs of local economies. Why?

5. Why do Western trade unions sometimes criticise MNCs?

6. State four reasons why national governments may wish to control MNC activities.

7. List the main potential sources of conflict between MNC and host country governments.

8. What are the factors that facilitate an MNC's ability to negotiate effectively with a host country government?

9. Give six examples of how governments can control MNC activities.

10. What are the justifications for the existence of local equity participation rules in relation to MNC subsidiaries?

11. In what circumstances are MNCs most vulnerable to the expropriation of their assets?

12. How can home countries control MNC operations?

13. List the main contents of the UN Code for Transnational Corporations.

14. What are the major sources of disagreement between developed and developing countries in relation to the drafting of the UN Code for Transnational Corporations?

15. List the main problems associated with the implementation of supranational Codes of Practice for MNCs.

10

DIRECT FOREIGN INVESTMENT

THE MOTIVATION FOR DFI

1. Trends in direct foreign investment (DFI)

Although international business has been a prominent feature of the economic development of a number of countries for the past 150 years (or longer in some cases), academic interest in the activities of MNCs really began following the wave of direct foreign investment by US companies in Western Europe that occurred between 1946 and the mid-1960s. Reasons for this upsurge in international investment probably included the formation of the European Economic Community (and hence the establishment of common external tariffs against imported goods); higher tariffs in non-EEC West European states; and the advantages to firms of being able to control foreign operations directly, cut out intermediaries, co-ordinate activity on an international basis, use internal resources to finance operations, and procure/manufacture their own inputs and move them around subsidiaries in foreign countries. (These advantages are known as 'internalisation' factors.) Another reason for US direct investment in Western Europe during the post-Second World War years appears to have been the difficulty of protecting the intellectual property embodied in licensing agreements, with numerous patent violations taking place within this period.

Thereafter, US companies invested abroad in order to break their dependence on the well-being of just the American economy. Hence they expanded into developed markets outside Western Europe, and to the developing countries of Latin America and the Far East. Growth rates were high in all these regions, and international business cycles were (conveniently) out of synchronisation in various parts of the world: when the US was in recession at least one of the other regions would be experiencing a boom. It followed that a spread of international investments would even out the firm's worldwide revenues and enhance overall performance in the longer term. The oil crises of 1973 and 1979 destroyed this pattern of expansion and contraction at alternating times in different countries, and *all* industrial countries faced similar economic problems at one and the same time. Subsidiaries of US multinationals in Europe, Latin America and Asia simultaneously began losing money, while home-based US operations generated losses in the same years. This led in the 1980s to the widespread rationalisation of US MNC activities. In the 1980s, moreover, large-scale West European direct foreign investment began in the USA, with European firms buying up

American companies at a bargain price. European businesses also started to invest heavily in the Pacific Rim. The 1990s saw further DFI by US and West European companies; plus a big upswing in Japanese, Korean and other Asian countries' investments in Europe (including East Europe), China and the US, as well as in Asia itself.

Political factors

In past decades a number of countries (notably Britain and the USA) have either banned or actively discouraged outward direct foreign investment. Dislike of DFI was based on the allegations that it:

- 'exported jobs'
- assisted the economic development of rival nations at the expense of the home country
- reduced domestic investment. (Note the preassumption here that the money that would have been sent abroad will automatically be invested in the home nation in consequence of restrictions.)

The counter-argument to these criticisms is that although the capital exporting country will experience an initial outflow of funds to finance foreign investment, this will normally be followed by substantial money inflows as the investing companies begin to repatriate their profits. Also the host nation will normally import more goods from the capital exporting country in consequence of the foreign investment.

Today the overwhelming majority of nations receiving direct foreign investment actively welcome it, and sometimes compete against each other in order to attract foreign firms. Often DFI brings capital into a country that itself cannot generate the funds needed for major investment projects. Further alleged benefits resulting from DFI include local job creation, improved managerial standards, introduction of new products, and a healthier balance of payments position for the host nation following the local production of goods that otherwise would have to be imported.

2. Reasons for DFI

Overall macroeconomic factors encouraging DFI have included:

- The increase in world trade and the opening up of new markets that have occurred in recent decades
- The development of new technologies that can be transplanted between countries
- Liberalisation of the economies of nations throughout the globe, including removal of exchange controls and controls on the repatriation of profits
- Establishment of common markets and other regional trading blocs with common external tariffs.

For the individual firm, specific motives for investing directly in foreign countries might involve communication difficulties with local representatives, lack of commitment on the part of commission agents, costly margins taken by independent distributors, and escalating administrative costs connected with organising foreign operations from the home base. A permanent local investment enables the investing company to do business just as any other local firm, which might be necessary or desirable in order to exercise close control over local marketing, or where a regional identity is necessary to create a credible image for the company. A local image can be useful in a number of respects:

(a) Host country governments might turn a blind eye to low-price strategies intended to dominate local markets if the firm involved is perceived as a domestic company; whereas allegations of and legal actions against import 'dumping' could follow from similar pricing policies pursued in the same country by a foreign firm.

(b) Local competitors may be considerably more sensitive to and react more vigorously against the actions of foreign rivals than against domestic businesses.

(c) Customers and dealers might be attracted to a local firm they come to regard as being fully committed to a permanent presence in the country concerned.

Further motives for commencing foreign production include:

- High transport costs associated with exporting
- Problems with licensees and the need to protect intellectual property
- Availability of investment grants from foreign governments
- Lower operating costs
- Faster access to the local market
- Undercapacity at home
- A desire to protect supplies of new materials and components only available from foreign countries
- Local content requirements (*see* 9:8)
- Especially favourable economic conditions in particular countries: buoyant markets, rising consumer incomes, easy access to finance, low interest rates, etc.
- Wanting to spread the risk of downturns in particular markets
- Acquisition of know-how and technical skills only available locally
- Desires to minimise worldwide tax burdens
- The need to engage in local assembly or part-manufacture.

Total ownership of a foreign subsidiary means there is no scope for arguments with partner firms; there is complete and immediate control over operations; and subsidiary operations can be fitted into the parent company's overall corporate strategies. Also, local restrictions on imports are circumvented, the local delivery of output might be greatly improved and better after-sales service provided. The close link between local production and local marketing might enable more rapid product modification in response to changing local demand. An obvious advantage to having production units in many disparate countries is the ability to hedge against political or other disturbances disrupting output at particular sites.

The essential problem with DFI is, of course, the substantial capital investment it requires. This cannot be sacrificed easily, whereas cancellation of (say) a contract manufacture agreement is (subject to the details of the contract) a cheap and straightforward matter. Apart from the local availability of manufacturing resources (labour, materials, etc.) the decision whether to invest in foreign manufacturing capacity will normally depend on such factors as the political stability of the country being considered, the extent of government investment grants and subsidies, legal matters such as the ease of patent protection, wage and other costs, restrictions on the repatriation of profits, and taxation.

3. Strategies for direct foreign investment

Strategies for DFI may be product-driven, market-driven, or technology-driven. Product-driven strategies arise when a firm's welfare depends critically on the properties, capabilities or composition of a specific product. For example, an international oil company cannot survive unless it continually explores for fresh reserves of crude oil and arranges for its processing and distribution. Hence it needs to invest in oil refineries, pipeline networks and so on in order to serve chosen markets. Many natural resource related industries pursue product-driven investment strategies, as do pharmaceutical companies, ceramics manufacturers and other businesses that are locked into a specific type of product. Market-driven strategies relate to the quest for new markets, served by foreign-owned local manufacturing plants and distribution systems. This type of DFI typically arises when a firm's existing markets cannot absorb its potential output. Technology-driven strategies are found among enterprises that rely on the application of state-of-the-art technologies for their competitive advantage. Such firms invest in order to undercut the prices of foreign local competitors using out-of-date production methods, or to introduce completely new products to foreign markets.

DFI may involve vertical or horizontal integration, or the conscious diversification of the scope of a firm's activities.

Horizontal and vertical integration

Vertial integration means mergers or takeovers among firms in the same industry but at different stages in the chain of production or distribution, e.g. by taking over distributors or suppliers of raw materials. It can enable the linking up of technically related processes, and removes the profit margins and transactions costs associated with contracts between different companies. The firm might obtain total control over sources of supply, sales outlets, etc., and may acquire the ability to deprive competitors of low-cost inputs or convenient distribution systems. Horizontal integration, conversely, is the combination of firms operating in the same industry and at the same stage of the production/distribution chain. Growth through horizontal integration has the following advantages:

(a) It enables a firm with a mediocre performance record to improve its market position.

(b) Economies of scale might become available (e.g. bulk purchasing discounts, integration of production processes, extensive application of the division of labour, etc.).

171

(c) The business develops a 'critical mass' which could improve its competitive position.

(d) Opportunities for diversification (see below) might arise from the process.

The problem with both vertical and horizontal integration is that the business becomes locked into a specific market which, if it collapses, leaves the company in a perilous position.

4. The question of diversification

A basic strategic issue confronting an international firm is whether it should concentrate on the activities it performs (or could perform) best, to the exclusion of other lines of work; or whether it should diversify into different fields. Diversification can involve the supply of completely new products, entering fresh market segments (possibly using modified versions of existing brands), or imitating the products of other firms (subject of course to patent restrictions). Note how the latter practice can itself generate the inspiration and know-how necessary to develop completely new items. Reasons for diversification include the following:

(a) Attempts to strengthen a hold on a market by controlling diverse activities connected with it, e.g. a paper manufacturer diversifying into carton making, wallpaper production, gift wrapping manufacture, etc. This is an example of 'concentric' diversification, i.e. diversification involving a common technological base and market outlets. Similar marketing methods will (normally) apply to the firm's diverse outputs.

(b) Loss of traditional products or markets.

(c) Large seasonal variations in demand for a firm's existing product.

(d) Overdependence on a handful of customers.

(e) Successful research and technical development activities resulting in new products and applications.

(f) Existing products reaching the ends of their life-cycles.

(g) Increased competition within existing markets.

(h) Potential for the joint marketing of a wide range of goods.

(i) Spare capacity within the firm that can be utilised via the supply of fresh products.

Diversification versus specialisation

The basic argument for diversifying the firm's activities across numerous industries and nations is that it (hopefully) prevents the failure of a particular product or market from totally ruining the business. Diversification should lead – so its advocates argue – to a recession-proof company, with a slump in one market being offset by expansions elsewhere. Further advantages to diversification are that:

(a) Lucrative opportunities can be exploited as they emerge so that the firm's profit earning potential is extended.

(b) Profits earned in certain areas of a diversified company can be used to reinforce activities elsewhere.

However, extensive diversification necessarily turns a company into a conglomerate of unrelated businesses, possibly with a complete and unwieldy administrative structure that is difficult to manage. Invariably it requires significant changes to the firm's current organisation structure. 'Pure' diversification, i.e. that which extends the firm's activities to unrelated and unfamiliar products, is especially problematic and expensive, requiring the rapid acquisition of know-how and the deployment of large amounts of resources. New production and marketing methods have to be learned, and fresh relationships with third parties (input suppliers, agents, specialist consultancies, etc.) established. Further problems with diversification are as follows:

(a) Genuine opportunities for diversification might not be available.

(b) Faulty mechanisms for researching fresh market and/or product opportunities can lead to disastrous investment decisions that could ruin the firm.

(c) Diversification might result in the firm locking up large amounts of capital in particular technologies or administrative or distribution systems from which it cannot subsequently withdraw. Paradoxically therefore, diversification could reduce a business's flexibility and ability to cope with change.

These difficulties have caused a number of large MNCs to consolidate their activities, to specialise in one or two fields in which they possess a competitive edge, to focus on core businesses and discard subsidiaries and divisions regarded as peripheral to mainstream operations. Such companies used international takeovers to strengthen their hold on chosen technologies, markets and product categories. They purchased foreign firms with overlapping products but which served countries in which the takeover predator did not have a presence. Businesses possessing specific competencies that helped the parent consolidate its operations into narrower areas were also acquired. Specific advantages to specialisation are that:

(a) It develops great expertise in a particular area.

(b) Product specialisation can mean improved use of labour and equipment, the development of a strong corporate image based on a single product line, and a big reduction of stocks.

(c) The firm can maintain a position at the leading edge of the technology of its chosen field.

(d) Large volumes of similar items will be supplied, leading perhaps to economies of scale, better customer care and a higher level of product quality.

(e) It limits the range of problems that management has to confront, i.e. problems will relate to just one line of activity rather than diverse multi-market multi-product operations.

Difficulties with specialisation include the following:

(a) Outdated techniques and attitudes might be passed on from one generation of employees to the next.

(b) The strategy assumes that the firm can continue its current activities without hindrance and at peak efficiency, i.e. that no discernible threats from competitors, poor industrial relations, interruptions in supplies or impending technological developments exist or are likely to arise in the future. This might be a wholly inappropriate assumption.

(c) There is a presupposition that the more a management and employees know about something the better at it they become, which is not necessarily true.

(d) The firm could become inward looking and resistant to change. Managers might be uncritical and accept without question the prevailing status quo.

TECHNIQUES OF DFI

The advantages of buying an existing local business outright, as opposed to setting up an entirely fresh operation from scratch, include the avoidance of start-up delays and expenses, and the immediate possession of a functioning administrative system with staff, distribution arrangements, etc. This presupposes of course that a suitable local business can be found and that its price is reasonable.

On the other hand the acquired business has to be integrated into the parent firm's organisation and management systems; old and technologically out-of-date equipment may be acquired; and implementing change in the purchased firm's operating methods might prove difficult.

5. Acquisitions

Motives for acquisitions include:

- Removal of competitors
- Reduction of the likelihood of company failure through spreading risks over a wider range of activities
- The desire to acquire businesses already trading in certain markets and/or possessing certain specialist employees and equipment
- Obtaining patents, licences and other intellectual property
- Economies of scale possibly made available though more extensive operations
- Acquisition of land, buildings, and other fixed assets that can be profitably sold off
- The ability to control supplies of raw materials

- Expert use of resources, e.g. if one firm possesses large amounts of land and buildings and the other is exceptionally skilled in property management
- Desire to become involved with new technologies and management methods, particularly in high risk industries
- The potential ability of a larger organisation to influence local and national government
- Tax considerations, e.g. the carryover of past trading losses into the merged business
- Additional financial and other resources, including greater capacity to undertake research.

Mergers and acquisitions

A merger (or 'amalgamation') is a voluntary and permanent combination of businesses whereby one or more firms integrate their operations and identities with those of another, and henceforth work under a common name and in the interests of the newly formed amalgamation. Typically, the companies which combine jointly issue new shares in the freshly created organisation to replace existing shares in the merging organisations. This differs from a hostile 'takeover' situation whereby one business buys a majority shareholding in another company, against the wishes of the latter's management. MNCs need coherent and carefully thought-out strategies for acquiring other businesses (especially where hostile takeovers are involved) for a number of reasons:

(a) Failed acquisitions can ruin the entire company.

(b) The cost to the purchaser is invariably higher than the pre-bid valuation of the target, consequent to the purchaser's belief that the acquisition will improve overall group profitability.

(c) Rumours of an attempted cross-border takeover affect the current market prices of shares in the predator company as well as in the takeover target.

(d) Takeovers have numerous human relations implications. A major acquisition will lead to changes in the duties and responsibilities of significant numbers of employees of both the acquired and purchasing businesses. Managers and other personnel have to adjust their perspectives and working methods.

(e) Senior management might become totally preoccupied with the implementation of an acquisition, resulting in the neglect of other duties.

(f) The publicity surrounding a takeover can enhance or greatly damage a company's image.

6. Problems with acquisitions

The acquiring company has to accept the basic characteristics of the acquired firm as they stand. In other words the latter's location, contractual commitments, physical conditions, etc., are predetermined, in contrast with a completely new start-up whereby the business selects the most convenient site, erects purpose-built premises, and so on. Further problems with takeovers are as follows:

(a) Market conditions might suddenly change following a costly acquisition.

(b) New competitors may emerge (attracted perhaps by the publicity surrounding the initial merger or takeover).

(c) Resignations of key employees in the acquired business might occur.

(d) Control difficulties created by having to manage a large and diverse organisation could arise. Note especially the need to collect, analyse and interpret enormous amounts of management information data.

(e) The activities, working methods and organisation structures of the amalgamating firms may turn out to be fundamentally incompatible. Note that it is not necessarily the case that an acquired firm has to be integrated into the parent's organisation system. Indeed it may be far better to leave the acquisition as an autonomous profit-earning unit.

(f) Even if the smaller of the merging businesses is more efficient than the larger, it may have little or no influence on decisions taken by the amalgamated company after the merger.

(g) A firm which takes over another and pays for it in cash may subsequently become extremely short of liquid assets, whereas a company paying for another business in shares (e.g. two shares of the bidding company in return for one share in the target of the attempted turnover) could experience share dilution (i.e. reductions in earnings per share), to the annoyance of existing shareholders.

(h) Senior managers in one of the firms taken over might not be worth employing in the larger company, hence involving the new business in dismissals and consequent employee compensation claims.

(i) Increased size can lead to diseconomies of scale rather than improved efficiency; bureaucracy increases and internal communications become difficult.

Conditions for success

Successful implementation of an acquisition strategy requires the following:

(a) Clear specification of acquisition objectives.

(b) Establishment of meaningful criteria for the choice of the firm(s) to be acquired.

(c) Development of sound search procedures for finding suitable target businesses. This will involve the screening of candidate firms; analysis and investigation of targets; propositioning and negotiation with the managements of suitable companies. Note that the search should not be restricted to businesses that happen to be for sale; reluctant takeover targets should also be considered.

(d) Careful planning of the entire process, using expert outside assistance where appropriate. The characteristics, products, management styles, finances and business systems of target firms all need to be examined.

Selecting acquisition targets

A number of factors need to be taken into account when choosing takeover targets, such as the following:

(a) The target's long-term prospects. A company experiencing short-run financial problems will pay poor dividends and in consequence the market price of its share will fall. Yet the business might be fundamentally sound and thus represent a lucrative takeover opportunity.

(b) The calibre of the target's management team, and whether existing management will recommend shareholders to accept or reject a takeover bid.

(c) The number of shareholders in the target company. A business with just a few dominant shareholders who are anxious to sell their shares will be easy to take over, and vice versa.

(d) Share price of the target.

(e) The value of the target company's property and other assets (including its brands, goodwill and trademarks).

7. Divestment

This involves the sale or closure of operating units (usually subsidiaries or divisions) in order to rationalise activities, concentrate resources in particular areas, or downsize the organisation (though note how downsizing can occur via reductions in the size of the labour force rather than shutting down whole units). Reasons for divestment include:

- Financial losses attributable to specific operations.
- The decision to focus all the firm's attention on its core businesses, at the expense of peripheral activities. This might result from perceptions that resources will be better used if they are concentrated in particular areas and/or that management is not able to control a widely diversified enterprise.
- The need to raise large amounts of cash at short notice.
- Government insistence that a firm be broken up in order not to contravene state monopoly legislation.
- Predicted technological changes that will cause products to become outdated.
- Collapse of a market.
- Failure of a merger or acquisition.
- A subsidiary absorbing more of the firm's resources than management is willing to provide.

Note how the selection of a unit for divestment offers management a convenient scapegoat that can be blamed for all the company's past problems. Divestment strategies require careful attention to human resource planning within the organisation (redundancy consultations, redeployment, etc.), public relations, and the manner in which assets are discarded.

8. Cross-border mergers and takeovers in the European Union

The European Commission conducts periodic (usually annual) surveys of EU merger and takeover activity, the results of which are published in the Commission's *Annual Report on Competition Policy* and in the biennial *Panorama of EU Industries*. To date these surveys have concluded that the commonest reasons for acquiring other firms include: improvement of market share, desire to expand and obtain economies of scale, complementarity of the activities of the businesses involved in a takeover, and the need to reorganise and restructure enterprises. Further reasons for acquisitions and mergers, the Commission suggests, are:

- The opening up of national capital markets to businesses from other EU member states
- The acceptance by banks and other finance providers of higher ratios of borrowing to fixed assets within client companies than previously has been the case
- The fact that a growing number of European companies are being forced to adopt cross-border trading perspectives
- The increased willingness of large conglomerates to discard subsidiaries in order to concentrate on core business.

Unfortunately, statistics on the extent of cross-border acquisitions are generally unreliable, since there are no laws requiring that they be reported. Thus, press cuttings and *ad hoc* industry surveys have to be used to assess the current situation. It seems, however, that a very substantial increase in trans-national EU takeovers has taken place. According to the European Commission the volume of cross-border mergers and acquisitions (M&As) has equalled that of domestic M&As since the formation of the Single Market. The average real value of acquisitions is also rising, indicating that larger firms are being acquired (Hawk 1991; Hamill 1992).

9. Barriers to cross-border EU takeover activity

Banks and family financing, in conjunction with the absence of substantial equity markets in certain countries, have led to a shortage of companies for sale in these nations, and basic attitudes towards takeovers differ among member states. The higher reserves conventionally held by countries in some EU states result in their being better equipped to resist unwanted attempted takeovers. Belgian, French and German companies must, by law, create a reserve of at least 10% of their share capital. Italian companies have to retain a 20% reserve; in Denmark the reserve has to be 25%; and in Greece 33.3%. Additionally, the laws of many of these countries allow companies to create special tax-free contingency reserves during highly profitable years (to cover possible environmental risks, currency exchange rate uncertainties, etc.), and then to write these reserves back into the mainstream accounts in loss-making periods.

Arguably, the fact that in several Continental EU countries it is legally necessary for elected worker representatives to be given a say in company management may act as a barrier to mergers and acquisitions. Employee representatives on a Supervisory Board might argue against accepting a bid from another firm, and the legal requirement that employee representatives be informed and consulted on takeover attempts (as matters affecting their fundamental interests) causes delays that take the heat out of attempted takeovers. Indeed, in Germany and the Netherlands employee representatives have the legal right to delay decisions on mergers and acquisitions for several weeks (longer in certain circumstances).

Further barriers to M&As in certain EU countries include the following:

(a) Specific groups of shareholders can be given special voting rights. In Germany for instance, shares with high par values have more voting rights than shares with low par values. French law permits companies to grant more voting powers to longstanding shareholders. France, Germany, Belgium and the Netherlands permit companies to restrict the voting powers to any single shareholder to a low level (e.g. that no one person or institution may cast more than 10% of all votes, regardless of the magnitude of their actual shareholdings). This prevents individuals with large blocks of shares from transferring majority voting powers to takeover predators. Cross-shareholding deals among friendly companies, with each partner holding large blocks of votes in the other, are common in Continental European states.

(b) Lawful devices to conceal the names and addresses of shareholders are available in Belgium, France, Spain, Italy, Germany and the Netherlands.

(c) There is a lack of reliable financial information about target businesses in certain countries (especially in Italy and Spain).

(d) Bearer shares are used extensively in many EU states, which makes it difficult to identify shareholders willing to sell their equities.

These factors have meant that relatively fewer company takeovers have occurred in many Continental EU countries compared to the UK, and that UK style 'dawn raids', hostile takeovers, competing bids, and all the other thrills and spills of the UK takeover market are virtually unknown in other EU countries (Kay 1993). The *advantages* of this situation are as follows:

(a) Companies can adopt long-term perspectives, invest, expand and develop without constantly having to be on their guard against unwelcome attempted takeovers.

(b) It provides a stable foundation upon which the macroeconomy can build and prosper.

Disadvantages are that:

(a) Absence of a free competitive market for the buying and selling of companies could mean that resources are not allocated to their most profitable uses.

(b) There is no widespread market mechanism for valuing the worth of companies.

10. New start-ups

An entirely new business can be set up to satisfy precisely the owner's specific needs, and all the problems and pitfalls of mergers and acquisitions are avoided. Selection of a location for a fresh start-up is a major strategic decision. Factors relevant to the choice typically include the following:

(a) *Finance.* Availability of long-term funds (greenfield sites normally require more start-up capital than the development of existing manufacturing facilities); government grants, subsidiaries, and tax reliefs in various regions.

(b) *Labour.* Amount of skilled labour in the area. Local wage levels. Training facilities in nearby colleges.

(c) *Ancillary services.* Extent of local service industries, consultants, distributors, etc.

(d) *Operational factors.* Access to raw materials. Adequacy of energy supplies, water, road and rail networks, etc.

Once a location decision has been taken the firm commits itself to major capital expenditures. The establishment cannot be relocated in the short term.

A critically important decision is whether to lease or buy premises. Indeed, it may dominate all other criteria. Outright purchase of premises means the owner benefits from increases in the capital value of the property. Also, owned premises can be offered as security against loans. Conversely, leasehold premises require no capital outlay, and (of course) they cannot be seized by creditors if the business fails.

Progress test 10

1. Why was there an upsurge in direct foreign investment by US companies in Western Europe between 1946 and the mid-1960s?

2. On what grounds do countries sometimes prohibit direct foreign investment?

3. List four macroeconomic factors that have encouraged international DFI.

4. What are the advantages to an MNC of projecting a local image in a foreign market?

5. Explain the difference between product-driven and market-driven DFI strategies.

6. Define the term 'vertical integration'.

7. Why do some companies attempt to diversify their activities?

8. What are the advantages to buying an existing business outright, rather than setting up an entirely fresh enterprise?

9. List six motives for company acquisitions.

10. What is divestment? Why do firms engage in divestment?

11. A number of factors inhibit cross-border EU takeover activity. What are these factors?

12. List four considerations to be taken into account when selecting a location for a new business start-up.

11

INTERNATIONAL TECHNOLOGY TRANSFER

FUNDAMENTALS

1. Nature of technology

Technology means the utilisation of the materials and processes necessary to transform inputs into outputs. Understanding technology requires knowledge; operating a technology requires skills. Technology is created by people and it affects people; especially through the goods it produces and the working conditions (extent of the division of labour, employee involvement in operational decision making, use of discretion at work, etc.) it creates.

Changes in technology affect (i) physical devices (such as machines, tools, instruments and equipment); and (ii) techniques and working methods (procedures, routines, application of specific skills, etc.). Accordingly, technology usually influences:

- employee training needs
- the nature of employees' tasks
- organisation structures
- employee job satisfaction and attitudes towards work.

Management has to choose which particular devices and techniques are best for improving efficiency and for achieving organisational goals.

2. Technology transfer

Technology transfer is the transmission of innovations arising in one firm or country to others. Innovations might involve new products, processes or working methods, or the use of specialised know-how. In all cases knowledge passes from the innovator to one or more recipients, who thus avoid the need to conduct independent research, or to develop projects, or to test and evaluate the outcomes of research. International businesses are a primary vehicle for the transfer of technology between nations. Technology is a key factor in the economic and social development of nations, so the importation of new technology is actively encouraged by the governments of many states. The European Commission is also very keen to encourage technology transfer, in order to prevent the 'cartelization' of technology within certain EU regions and/or nation states (Germany and France for instance). Note how the transfusion of technology is frequently accompanied by an exchange of new management ideas and methods, although some techniques might have to be simplified to make them understandable to local workers.

'*Point-to-point*' technology transfer occurs when a single donor transfers a technology to a single recipient, e.g. firm-to-firm or from one research institute to another. '*Diffusion*', conversely, refers to the situation where there are many recipients all having easy access to the technology. Point-to-point technology transfer agreements require bilateral negotiations between the partners, and normally involve some contractual device for protecting the confidentiality of the transferred knowledge. The term 'hard technology' is sometimes used to describe patents, capital equipment, designs, technical specifications and other tangible items. 'Soft technology', conversely, is the management, organisation and administration of technical processes. Typically the intellectual property embodied within hard technology can be legally protected. Accompanying soft technology, however, is usually non-copyright and/or non-patentable. It is essential to realise that modern industrial technology is multi-dimensional and involves much more than patents, designs and the use of machines and computers. Crucial aspects of today's new technologies concern management and support services, ongoing R&D and product development, and the expertise *surrounding* production techniques and methods. Technology, therefore, is a package of activities that might include a preinvestment study, capital equipment, technical support services, the training of personnel, and the implementation of quality control systems, as well as the provision of designs, drawings and materials specifications.

Key issues in technology transfer

The basic issues that need to be addressed by donor firms are *how* to transfer technology to another country (*via* licensing, direct foreign investment, contract manufacture under patent, etc.); whether to undertake research and technical development in foreign locations; the choice of the technology that best fits the foreign environment; and how to maintain a technology-based competitive advantage over time. The latter will involve (i) measures to protect trade secrets, and (ii) ongoing R&D. Recipients of technology have to consider how best to integrate new technologies into existing administrative structures and working methods; the standards of skill required for their operation; the availability of training facilities in the local area; and the extent of local grants and subsidies for the introduction of new methods.

3. Reasons for technology transfer

Firms engage in technology transfer in order to:

- increase overall company profitability. Production may be cheaper abroad, and output does not have to be sent long distances to reach end consumers

- gain a competitive edge in foreign markets through supplying technically superior products (irrespective of short-run profitability considerations)
- obtain grants and subsidies from foreign governments. Note how certain underdeveloped countries *require* MNCs to bring with them the latest technology as a condition of being allowed to operate within the local market.
- overcome capacity limitations in the home country
- exploit superior capital markets, access to skilled labour and other inputs in foreign countries
- increase the competence and potential of foreign subsidiaries.

4. The debate on technology transfer

Political controversy has surrounded the question of whether the technologies transferred by MNCs to their production units in underdeveloped countries are appropriate for the latter's social and economic development needs. The technologies transferred by MNCs – it is sometimes alleged – are too capital intensive, and are geared to the supply of goods that are unsuitable for low-income consumers. In practice this means that the governments of Third World countries sometimes urge MNCs to export technologies that are more labour intensive than in developed nations, and which have a smaller scale. Yet when MNCs transfer older capital equipment and technical methods capable of producing cheaper output for the local market, they are accused of 'dumping' redundant technologies on Third World states, thus causing them to remain technologically dependent on Western nations and to continue to be economically underdeveloped (Thorelli 1966). Indeed, special import licences have been necessary for the consignment of secondhand machinery to certain developing countries. Note moreover that it is often impossible to alter the labour/capital mix of a given technology or, where substitution possibilities do exist, the costs of implementing them would be prohibitive. Also a shift from capital to labour intensive methods might cause the firm to become involved (unwillingly) in labour relations; to experience quality control problems and an increase in the level of waste; to have to implement employee training programmes; and to suffer the indignity of assuming a low-tech public image. Also the firm's ability to respond quickly to alterations in local market conditions might be adversely affected.

Host country governments sometimes attempt to influence the natures of the technologies used in MNC subsidiaries through making investment grants dependent on the recipient firm creating a specified minimum number of new jobs; by encouraging labour intensive foreign investment through keeping labour and other costs low and deregulating labour markets (removing employment protection and social welfare benefits for example); and by subsidising the development of less efficient (typically labour intensive) industries where the introduction of new methods will have the greatest impact (to the benefit of the investing foreign firms).

METHODS AND IMPLICATIONS

5. Technology transfer methods

Technology may be transferred via the following methods:

(a) Direct foreign investment.

(b) Licensing of patents, trademarks or know-how.

(c) Franchising.

(d) Management contracts and/or turnkey arrangements involving the transfer of key personnel.

(e) Contract manufacturing.

(f) Joint ventures, which enable firms quickly to acquire technical knowledge in fields not normally associated with their day-to-day operations (toolmakers requiring expertise in computer software for example) and thus shorten the gap between new product innovation and sale to the final consumer. Note how new technical developments that impinge on the work of a firm in one industry sector increasingly arise in other sectors, hence creating many incentives for businesses to enter into collaborative joint ventures aimed at transferring technologies across industries and national frontiers.

Successful technology transfer involves a learning process on the part of the recipient business. This is obviously more difficult in the case of transnational transfers because of differences in language, technical standards, production methods, perspectives on quality management, and national employee attitudes and behaviour. Dealing with these matters may require the creation of extensive documentation, control manuals in the local language, training programmes and ongoing communication mechanisms. The recipient's ability to benefit from the transfer depends on the calibre of its employees (especially their educational backgrounds), the flexibility of its operating systems, and the technological infrastructure (research activity, extent of trade and technical publications, availability of skilled labour, etc.) of the country concerned.

Major factors influencing the nature of the technology transferred by a multinational business to a foreign country include the following:

(a) *The scale of foreign operations.* Typically, the larger the market the more extensive will be the firm's investment in the country concerned and hence the bigger the scale of plant. Substantial operations create opportunities for the utilisation of automated capital intensive methods and the attainment of economies of scale.

(b) *The nature of the production process.* Certain types of machinery and equipment might be required regardless of any other circumstances, i.e. the necessary technology is 'fixed' and cannot be altered.

(c) *The relative costs of labour and capital.* Availability of cheap labour obviously encourages firms to substitute labour for capital wherever possible.

(d) *Extent of government grants and subsidies.*

(e) *The costs of adapting the technology used in the home country to meet foreign conditions.* Often it is easier simply to transfer technology as it is, without any attempt at varying the labour/capital mix, because of the cost and inconvenience of having to modify existing methods.

6. Licensing

Licensing is appropriate where the firm has legal control over its intellectual property (*via* registered patents and/or trademarks), where transport costs or the cost of establishing local manufacturing facilities would be prohibitive, or where rapid installation of a manufacturing capability in a particular market is necessary in order to beat the competition. Other circumstances in which licensing is likely to succeed are where:

- Images of locally produced items will improve sales.
- The licensee will have to purchase input components or materials from the licensor.
- The licensor is already exporting directly to more markets than it can conveniently handle.
- It is not technically feasible to establish a permanent presence in a particular country.
- The foreign market is small and does not justify the expense attached to alternative forms of market entry.
- The licensor is a small company with limited resources.
- There are possibilities for 'technology feedback' from the licensee.
- The technology transferred under licence is 'perishable' so that the licensor has considerable bargaining power through its ability to supply new technology in the future.
- Licensing can be a means for testing and developing a product in a foreign market, perhaps with a view to subsequent direct foreign investment.
- Auxiliary processes rather than a core technology can be licensed.

Licences can take many forms, ranging from a permit to exploit an existing patent, to extensive and complicated arrangements on industrial co-operation. There are a number of types of licensing agreement. With an *'assignment'*, for instance, a firm hands over all its intellectual property rights in relation to a particular patent, trademark, design or whatever, to a licensee. The latter may then use these rights as it wishes. If the firm issues a *'sole'* licence, however, it retains rights but agrees not to extend licences to anyone other than a single licensee during the period of the agreement. *'Exclusive'* licences require licensors not to use their patents, trademarks, etc., for their own businesses while licensing contracts are in force, leaving these rights entirely to licensees for pre-specified periods. *'Know-how licensing'* means the licensing of confidential but non-patented technical knowledge. The advantages of licensing are that:

(a) No capital investment is necessary.

(b) Licensees avoid research and development costs, while acquiring experience of manufacturing the item.

(c) The licensor has complete legal control over its intellectual property.

(d) A manufacturing capability can be quickly established in an unfamiliar market.

(e) Licensees carry some of the risk of failure.

(f) The nucleus of the parent organisation can remain small, have low overheads, yet control extensive operations.

Disadvantages to licensing are:

(a) Profits are sacrificed through allowing other firms to make the parent company's goods.

(b) The risk of a licensee company setting up in competition once it has learned all the licensor's production methods and trade secrets and the licence period has expired.

(c) Possible ambiguities and interpretation difficulties in relation to minimum and/or maximum output levels, territory covered, basis of royalty payments (including the frequency of payment and the currency to be used) and the circumstances under which the agreement may be terminated.

(d) Deciding how to control the licensee in relation to quality standards, declaration of production levels, and methods of marketing the product.

(e) Problems arising if the licensee turns out to be less competent than first expected.

(f) Possible failure of the licensee to exploit fully the local market.

(g) Acquisition by the licensee of the licensor's technical knowledge.

(h) The need for complex contractual arrangements in certain circumstances.

(i) The numerous opportunities that arise for disagreements and mis-understandings.

Normally the licensee will demand exclusive rights in the country concerned (possibly in several countries) and may request the right to sub-contract to other local businesses. Note how exclusive licensing necessarily restricts competition and hence could lead to the companies involved being in breach of the competition law of the host nation. In the European Union, two block exemptions (for both patent licensing and know-how licensing) cover the overwhelming majority of cases, namely where:

- the goods or services covered by an agreement represent less than 5 per cent of the total market for these goods or services; *and* (additionally)
- the aggregate turnover of the parties to the agreement is less than a certain threshold (currently 200 million ECUs)

For contracts exceeding these thresholds the exemption applies provided the agreements:

- contribute to improving the methods of producing or distributing goods or to the promotion of technical or economic progress; *and*
- give consumers a fair share of resulting benefits; *and*
- will not significantly reduce competition across the entire Single European Market.

These block exemptions are discussed further in **13** to **15** below.

Licence contracts

These need to specify royalty and other fee payments, criteria for and the timing of remittances, the geographical area to be covered, permissible selling prices, and provisions for terminating the contract. Procedures concerning quality control should be detailed, plus the licensee's ability to become involved with competing products and the remedies available if the licensee fails to meet its obligations. Sometimes the experience acquired by the licensee in operating the licence leads to further technical development and inventions, so it is essential to determine at the outset the ownership of any fresh patents that emerge. Other key elements that need to be included in the licence contract are:

- the licensee's capacity to sub-contract
- minimum production levels
- extent of the support services to be given by the licensor
- permissible selling prices
- termination and renewal arrangements
- confidentiality requirements
- procedures for settling disputes and which country's laws shall apply to the agreement.

7. Franchising

Franchising is a form of licensing whereby the franchisee adopts the parent company's entire business format: its name, trademarks, business methods, layout of premises, etc. The franchisor provides (in return for a royalty and lump sum fee) a variety of supplementary management services: training, technical advice, stock control systems, perhaps even financial loans. Hence it retains complete control over how the product is marketed, but the franchisee carries the risks of failure and the franchisor's capital commitment is typically low. Accordingly, international franchising allows companies to expand rapidly from a limited capital base. It combines the technical experience of the franchisor with the intimate local knowledge of the franchisee. Franchisees are self-employed, not employees of the parent company, and rarely possess rights against a parent organisation in the event of either the entire systems or just an individual outlet collapsing (Abel 1991; Welsh 1992).

Normally, franchisees must follow standardised business techniques, layouts of premises, and are subject to some control by the franchisor. Franchisees are sheltered under a protective umbrella of specialist skills, resources and experiences already possessed by the parent organisation. They obtain a well known name and set of activities with a proven reputation. Franchisees are required to protect the franchisor's good name through maintenance of minimum quality standards, adoption of a uniform appearance, adherence to standard opening hours, and so on. If the franchisor is a manufacturer, the franchisee is usually required to purchase supplies (for example, meat for hamburgers, spare parts, ingredients for alcoholic or soft drinks) from the franchisor at prices predetermined by the parent firm (which buys raw materials in bulk at big discounts).

Franchising began when investors of new machines, processes or business methods were forced by lack of finance or inadequate knowledge of the business world into allowing other parties the right to manufacture or otherwise adopt new inventions in exchange for a licence fee. Initially, therefore, business expertise was provided by franchisees. As the system developed however franchisors assumed responsibilities for business organisation, trade markets, advertising and sales promotion. Today, franchisors impose levies on franchisees to cover national advertising and servicing costs. The cost of local advertising is borne by franchisees. Successful franchising requires that the product or service involved has a distinct and unique image which is conceptually dissimilar to competing lines. Also, demand for the franchised product should be genuinely international, and expected to continue in the long term. Franchising is not suitable for fashion products with short lives. Business methods associated with the product, its presentation, ingredients, style and design, must be capable of standardisation.

8. Advantages and disadvantages of franchising

Advantages to franchisors include the following:

(a) As franchisees are self-employed (rather than employees of the parent firm) they will be highly motivated to succeed in their own business. There are no strikes, go-slows, work-to-rules, or other industrial problems.

(b) While franchisors retain control of distribution systems, new and unfamiliar market segments can be entered using the skills, experiences and local background knowledge of neighbourhood-based franchisees.

(c) Since large distribution networks are tied to supplies from single companies, there exist opportunities for bulk buying of raw materials at big discounts.

(d) As a franchise operation grows, trade marks, brand names and product styles become more widely dispersed and familiar to the public. The franchisor's name becomes internationally recognised.

(e) The nucleus of the franchisor's organisation remains small, and overheads are low. Large profits can result from a limited capital base, yet risks are shared with franchisees. Moreover, routine administrative problems are dealt with by outlets, not central office.

Similar benefits accrue to franchisees. A franchise can be purchased (often with a loan arranged by the franchisor) for less than usually has to be paid for an existing business. Outlets receive advice on book-keeping, tax liability, training of staff, stock control, layout of premises and related matters. Advertising is dealt with by franchisors, leaving outlets free to concentrate on day-to-day operations. Technical advice and training will also be available. Another advantage is the product and marketing research activities undertaken by franchisors, that small firms individually could not afford. Also, the competition faced by an outlet within a specific locality is restricted by the fact that franchisors will not permit more than one of their franchisees to operate there.

Drawbacks relate to the fact that franchisees' working methods are controlled. Product specification, quality, layout of premises and so on are predetermined. Little discretion is allowed. Royalty payments could be high, making unprofitable an otherwise successful business. Unjustifiably high raw material prices might be charged by franchisors, and interruptions in supplies (indeed, inadequate backup services generally) can ruin an individual outlet. Unlike ordinary businesses, franchised outlets cannot be sold without the franchisor's permission. Also:

(a) The brand image of the franchised product may deteriorate for reasons beyond the franchisee's control, including policy mistakes made by the parent organisation.

(b) Since royalties are invariably expressed as fixed percentages of turnovers, hard-working and successful franchisees will have to pay ever-increasing sums to their franchisors, thus discouraging the more able. Yet, franchisees who fail lose everything.

(c) Franchise contracts cover relatively short periods, normally five years. A successful franchisee who has increased the profitability of an outlet will find that it reverts to the franchisor following expiry of the franchise contract. The franchisor will then demand higher royalties in line with the increased value of the outlet. During the contract period, however, the franchisee is tied to a particular product, unable to modify the good or introduce alternatives.

Franchisors too face disadvantages. They control only the overall format of outlets, not day-to-day operations. Badly managed outlets offering poor quality and inadequate presentation of the product can ruin a carefully nurtured public image. Sometimes, franchisors insist on inspecting franchisees' premises, but this can arouse resentment and cause disagreements over how that outlet should be run. Franchisees are not employees, they cannot be dismissed, and termination of a contract might be difficult. Typically, franchisees regard themselves as owners of their outlets (which they are not) and begrudge interference from the parent firm. A common problem is that franchisees can learn a business from top to bottom while under contract, and then set up competing outlets (perhaps under disguised ownership) nearby the moment their contract expires. Franchisors must rely on outlets to declare honestly their monthly receipts (for the purpose of computing royalty payments), to promote their product vigorously, and to employ suitable staff.

Obviously, aggregate returns to a franchisor are less than would be available were all outlets directly owned and controlled since then all revenues would accrue to the franchisor, not just percentage royalties. On the other hand, franchisors avoid start-up and developmental costs, and they share any risk of failure. Relatively little administrative work is necessary, and fewer staff are needed within the parent firm.

9. Legal aspects of franchising

Since franchising is potentially a restraint on free competition, it could violate the competition law of many nations, particularly considering that franchisees are usually tied to supplies from the parent, at supply prices determined by the latter. In the European Union, however, there exists a block exemption to cover *distribution* franchise agreements, although at the time of writing there is no exemption in relation to industrial or manufacturing franchises.

Under the block exemption it is permissible for distribution franchise agreements to restrict franchisees' abilities to:

- sell or use competing products during or up to one year after the termination of the contract
- seek custom outside the designated territory
- decline to sell the entire range of the franchisor's products
- scale down the extent of the operations of their outlets
- engage in independent advertising
- disclose to outsiders the know-how gained during the period of the agreement.

Franchisees, moreover, can be compelled to inform the parent company of any new and additional know-how they acquire through their experience of operating the franchise (Mendelsohn 1993).

The European Commission has always sought to encourage franchising on the grounds that it improves the provision of goods and services within the EU and facilitates new business start-ups thus increasing inter-brand competition (Singleton 1995). Hence, the Commission has been extremely lenient when applying EU competition law to franchising agreements, and many more restrictive provisions are allowed under the franchising block exemption than under the corresponding block exemptions for exclusive distribution and purchasing. This has meant that it can be advantageous to distribute goods *via* franchise arrangements than by other means, so that firms have been tempted to pass-off what are in reality restrictive distribution contracts as 'franchise' deals. To qualify for the franchise block exemption the contract involved must include obligations concerning the application of a uniform presentation of premises, a common name or shop sign, the transfer of know-how and long-term provision of assistance by the franchisor to the franchisee. Otherwise it is treated as a normal distribution agreement. Franchise arrangements between companies producing similar competing goods are not allowed under the block exemption.

Types of franchise agreement

There are three basic forms of franchise agreement: unit, area development, and master (Mendelsohn 1993). A *unit agreement* covers the rights and obligations of a single franchised outlet, specifying the territory allocated, protection of intellectual property, duration of the contract, nature and extent of the services to be provided by the franchisor, etc. An *area development agreement* is appropriate for situations where a franchisee wishes to operate many outlets in the same area. In effect the franchisor hands over an entire territory for development by another party under licence. Hence this type of contract needs to contain details of:

- the legal protection afforded to the franchisee *vis-à-vis* his or her exclusive right to develop the region
- how and by when the franchisee will establish multiple outlets
- the development programme
- procedures for selecting and approving locations
- responsibilities for training and supervising staff in the various outlets
- who shall decide the number and distribution of outlets within the region
- whether the developer can sell his or her rights to a third party.

With a *master franchise agreement* the franchisor contracts to a sub-franchisor the right to create and subsequently dispose of individual franchised outlets for the main franchisor's product.

Withholding taxes

Bilateral tax treaties concerning withholding taxes on transfers between a parent company and its subsidiaries do *not* apply to payments from franchisees to franchisors, because in law the two parties are separate and independent businesses. Hence the tax position of a franchisor with franchisees in several countries can become extremely complicated. A major problem is that franchise fees are treated differently in disparate countries. In some nations they are regarded as royalties; elsewhere as straightforward profits, or as management fees or service income. The intellectual property transferred through a franchise contract is viewed as a capital asset in certain states; as a source of revenue in others. (This is important because money paid for capital assets can normally be offset against tax.) It could be tax efficient for a franchisor to set up a local subsidiary company to operate franchised outlets in particular countries (the Netherlands for instance).

10. Licensing in Third World countries

Protection of intellectual property is more difficult in underdeveloped countries than in the West, and there is widespread counterfeiting of patented products in certain nations. Western governments sometimes accuse the governments of Third World countries of deliberately turning a blind eye to blatant patent violations and of complying with requests for compulsory licences (see below) too easily. The governments of some underdeveloped countries allege, moreover, that patenting by large foreign companies gives them monopoly power in the local market. Note that the bulk of patents granted by developing countries are held by non-residents and that most of these patents are not actually worked in these developing nations (see below) but are simply used to block imports from businesses competing with the firm holding the patent. Another criticism of the role of MNCs in technology transfer is that large international firms possess excessive power when negotiating licensing and other contracts with businesses in recipient countries. Potential licensees lack information, choice and opportunities for redress if the MNC fails to meet its obligations.

Compulsory licensing

Patents registered in various countries need to be 'worked,' i.e. the patented product must actually be produced and/or sold periodically. Patents that are not exploited for a certain period (this varying according to the law of the country concerned – two years is typical) may be subject to 'compulsory licensing', i.e. another firm can apply to a Court for permission to utilise the patent under licence from the inventor. The Court can compel the latter to issue a licence on terms that the Court considers reasonable. The Courts of underdeveloped countries are frequently criticised by Western MNCs for accepting requests for compulsory licenses too readily.

11. Patent violations

The deliberate imitation of patents and/or branded products is big business in the international economy and is continuing to expand. Cosmetics, wrist watches, pharmaceuticals, chemicals, fashion clothing, books and computer software are particularly susceptible to copying. Low-quality copies of a company's product devalue the company's image (product guarantees on counterfeits are obviously worthless) and deprive it of income. MNCs can respond to the counterfeiting of their products by taking legal action, or by compromising and using the counterfeiters as sub-contractors (note that counterfeit production can be of extremely high quality and that significant quantities of counterfeit goods sometimes find their way into official distribution systems – selling alongside the originals). Counterfeiting is especially problematic in a number of underdeveloped countries (particularly in Asia) which have extremely lax laws where counterfeiting and the misuse of trade marks are concerned. Developing countries sometimes defend this on the grounds that it is unreasonable to expect them to establish highly expensive search and evaluation procedures for assessing the validity of applications for patents and trade marks. The Uruguay Round of the GATT negotiations changed GATT rules to enable countries with industries that fall victim of significant counterfeiting to impose severe retaliatory measures against offending nations and patent and trade mark holders to have counterfeit goods confiscated and sold off (Maskers 1993).

12. Protection of trade marks

Significant national differences apply to this matter, since in some countries the first user of a trade mark becomes its lawful owner, whereas in others formal registration with state authorities is required. Another important difference is between countries which require owners of registered trade marks to use them during specific time intervals (usually three to five years) or accept that other firms may appropriate them after the specified interval has elapsed. The fact that formal registration of a trademark is necessary in certain states means that 'brand piracy' might occur in these nations. Brand piracy is the practice of people other than the original brand name user registering the brand name of a company just about to enter a country in which formal registration is necessary and then 'selling' the brand name back to the company concerned. 'Passing off' is another problem, i.e. making a slight change in the lettering of a brand name or a cosmetic alteration to the design of a logo in order to pretend that the item is the same as the original branded product.

Because not all countries recognise the principle that the person or organisation first using a brand name, logo, etc., has legal ownership of the intellectual property it embodies, it becomes necessary formally to register the firm's trade marks in *every* nation in which the company intends doing business. This process can be extremely expensive, adding up to 15 per cent to the costs of new product development in certain circumstances. Legal actions to protect trade marks are also very costly. Note how in some countries it may be necessary to register a brand name at frequent intervals, with any brand name not reregistered in the correct manner becoming available to any other business.

13. Protection of intellectual property in the European Union

Patent protection is available within the European Union on a country by country basis or at the pan-EU level. A patent is nothing more than an official document granted to the inventor of an entirely new product or manufacturing process allowing the inventor a monopoly over the production, use or sale of the invention for a certain period from the date the patent application was filed. To obtain a patent the inventor must supply full details of the invention to a national patent office, which has to be satisfied that the invention contains original features. Patent holders may legally prevent other people from copying or using their inventions, may licence the patent, or sell or exchange it for money or goods. The temporary monopoly is given in recognition of the inventor having discovered the invention which, at the end of the patent protection period, enters the public domain (i.e. it can be copied by anyone). It is the responsibility of patent holders to enforce their rights, not the national patents office that grants patents.

Increasing competition, more R&D within European companies, free cross-border capital mobility across national EU frontiers, the free labour mobility of research workers, widespread introductions of new technologies to European firms, and a greater willingness to finance risky projects made possible by easier access to Europe's financial capital markets have led to sharp increases in the numbers of EU patent applications. Patents can be registered separately in individual EU nations, or throughout Europe *via* a single application under the 1977 European Patent Convention. The latter covers 17 West European countries including all EU states plus Switzerland, Monaco and Liechtenstein. To use this system the inventor must apply (through his or her national patents office) to the EU Patent Office in Munich specifying the EU countries the patent is to cover. The inventor then receives a bundle of national patents relating to those countries. Renewals of the patents can be undertaken through the inventor's national patents office. Applications can be in any one of three languages: English, German or French. On being granted, the patent is translated into the other two languages plus the languages of any other EU countries to which the patent is to apply. Opposition to the patent must be filed within nine months of when it was granted. Patent protection lasts for 20 years from the date of filing the application.

As the inventor receives a bundle of national patents rather than a single document, subsequent litigation must be carried out separately in each country. However the EU member nations have agreed a further Patent Convention under which EU-wide patents will eventually be granted. These will be subject to the rules of the Convention rather than national laws on patenting. Disputes will be resolved through special Patent Courts established in each state, the judgements of which will be binding throughout the Union. Advantages to the proposed EU patent include convenience, lower overall registration costs, the need to pay only one set of renewal fees, and the fact that actions to prevent infringement of a patent will have effect throughout the entire European Union (Maronick 1988).

Two important EU Regulations apply to intellectual property, as follows:

(a) The 1984 Regulation on Patent Licensing Agreements, which allows patent holders to grant territorially exclusive licences to other firms for periods of five years beginning from the date a new product is introduced to the EU. Limited exclusivity is permitted thereafter, provided the customer can easily obtain the item from other sources. Also, exclusive licences outside the scope of the block exemption can be notified to the European Commission through a special procedure and, if they are not opposed within six months, are automatically exempted.

(b) The 1988 Regulation on Know-How Licensing Agreements. This allows the insertion of territorial restrictions in know-how licensing agreements so as to prevent licensees from exploiting the licensor's know-how in territories not covered by the contract.

14. Trade marks in the European Union

Trade marks may be registered separately in every country where protection is required (except for Belgium, Luxembourg and the Netherlands, which have a common registration procedure giving protection throughout the Benelux union). Alternatively, pan-EU protection can be acquired *via* the EU Trade Mark Regulation agreed in 1993 and currently being implemented. This does not interfere with national trade marks already registered in each EU country, but instead creates a procedure that enables nationals of EU (and certain other) states to obtain from a central EU Trade Mark Office (EUTMO) an EU Trade Mark that is valid and enjoys identical legal protection in all EU countries. An EUTM can be obtained as an alternative to a national trade mark registration. For existing trade marks, the equivalent national trade mark registration systems will continue to co-exist alongside the EUTM scheme, which is voluntary.

Applications for EU Trade Marks can be made through national patent offices or direct to the EUTMO in Alicante in Spain. Registration will be refused if the trade mark is not sufficiently distinct, in order to differentiate it clearly from competing trade marks, or if the name is likely to mislead the public or is otherwise contrary to EU public policy. Obviously the name must not already be in use within an EU state. It is up to aggrieved parties to petition the EUTMO for prohibitions on the use of their trade marks by other firms. Appeals against the decision of the EUTMO are heard first by a Board of Appeal and then by the European Court of Justice. Civil actions for damages resulting from an infringement of a registered EUTM are heard in the national courts of the country in which the violation allegedly occurred.

Owners of registered EUTMs enjoy all the legal rights available to the owner of intellectual property in any EU country. These rights may be transferred, offered as security against bank loans, or licensed (for use in the entire European Union or just certain parts of it) to other businesses. An EUTM will have a life of ten years from the date of registration, and is renewable. Registration empowers an EUTM holder to prevent any other person or organisation from using the same trade mark for similar goods or services or from imitating the trade mark, e.g. by changing a few letters in the name while retaining its essential character so as to 'pass off' products. Other firms are not permitted to exploit the commercial value of the trade mark, e.g. by mentioning it in the promotional literature of other businesses. EUTMs cease to have effect if they are not used for five years, or if the acts or omissions of the EUTM's owner allow it to become a generic product title. It is up to a third party to make a formal application to the EUTMO to have a EUTM revoked.

The EUTM Regulation was preceded (and made possible) by a 1988 Directive on the harmonisation of trade mark legislation, which obliged countries to harmonise national rules *vis-à-vis* the rights conferred on registration of a trade mark and the tests applied when deciding whether a trade mark can be registered.

National versus EUTMO registration

There will be cases of course where firms will have to continue registering national rather than EU trade marks, e.g. if businesses in different parts of the EU are independently using the same trade mark. Also national registration can be cheaper than using the EUTM scheme, especially if the firm operates predominantly within just one or two EU countries.

15. International agreements concerning intellectual property

A number of international agreements have been concluded in order to facilitate the protection of intellectual property abroad. The longest established is the International Convention for the Protection of Industrial Property, originally signed in Paris in 1883 and repeatedly revised since then. This Convention has over 100 signatories and covers patents, models, trade marks and industrial designs. According to the rules of the Convention, an inventor who obtains a patent in one member country must then apply for protection under the national patent laws of other member countries, pay additional fees, and run the risk that these further applications may be refused. However, the applications take priority in these other countries over subsequent competing applications, provided they are filed within one year (six months for trade marks) from the date of the application in the inventor's home country. The owner's rights over the intellectual property are automatically maintained during this period. Signatory nationals are obliged to extend to inventors from foreign member countries all the rights, protections, privileges and remedies as are available to home country nationals. No compulsory licence may be granted within three years from the grant of a patent, even though the patent has not been worked.

The Madrid Agreement 1982 established the World Intellectual Property Organisation (WIPO) with headquarters in Geneva and through which trade mark holders in participating states can obtain protection in about 30 countries. On receipt of an application for registration, the WIPO circulates the trade mark to all signatory nations, where it is processed according to local intellectual property law. When the exercise has been completed the applicant receives a bundle of national trade mark registrations, at much lower cost than if a series of separate applications had been registered. A Protocol to the Agreement was signed in 1988, representing in effect a completely new Treaty with less stringent membership conditions than the earlier Agreement. This was necessary because the national intellectual property laws and practices of certain states (including some EU countries) were incompatible with the provisions of the original Agreement, even though these nations wanted to participate in the system. Under the Protocol, intergovernmental organisations can become members of the WIPO, despite particular states belonging to these intergovernmental organisations not themselves having signed the Madrid Agreement. The EU intends joining the WIPO as an intergovernmental organisation. Thus, any holder of an EUTM will be eligible to apply for WIPO protection in non-EU countries even if the holder's home state is, for technical reasons, not a signatory to the Madrid Agreement.

16. Management contracts

The term 'management contract' is sometimes applied to the situation whereby a firm in one country provides a team of expert managers to an enterprise in another for a fixed period under contract. Typically the team will install a new system, train local personnel and then hand over the entire system to local control. (The latter procedure is referred to as a *turnkey* arrangement.) Otherwise the contract might cover an *ad hoc* project or technical service agreement. A management contract could be used to supplement a separate licensing, joint venture or contract manufacturing arrangement and may be tied in with an agreement from the contracting firm. Equally a firm might provide management expertise to one of its major suppliers. Here the management team will be drawn from one of the parties to the agreement, which might result in that firm's managerial resources being overstretched (Welch and Pacifico 1990). The advantages of management contracts are that:

(a) Technologies are transferred very quickly.

(b) Clients have new systems installed to a predetermined specification known to have succeeded in other places.

(c) Supplying firms incur few overheads.

(d) Returns to the company supplying the expertise are known with certainty.

(e) There is little risk of expropriation by host country governments.

(f) For turnkey contracts, there is a lower risk of failure for the client business.

Potential problems associated with management contracts are the possibility of disagreements between the foreign management team and local managers over what constitute the best working methods and that local employees might be untrainable. Also the arrangement may be more expensive for the client than simply bringing in outside consultants on an *ad hoc* basis, and the contractor might not be genuine in its commitment to training local personnel. For turnkey contracts, moreover, the contractor might be slow in 'turning the key' (i.e. training up local workers to the level necessary to take over the plant) and the client becomes totally dependent on the contractor's goodwill.

Progress test 11

1. Define technology.

2. Why is the European Commission anxious to encourage technology transfer between EU states?

3. Explain the difference between diffused technology transfer and point-to-point technology transfer.

4. What is 'soft technology'?

5. Why do companies engage in technology transfer?

6. List the basic methods of technology transfer.

7. What are the essential requirements for successful technology transfer?

8. List the factors that normally influence the nature of the technology transferred by a multinational company to a foreign company.

9. Explain the difference between an assignment and a sole licence.

10. Outline the key elements of a typical licensing contract.

11. What are the main disadvantages of franchising?

12. Explain the term 'compulsory licensing'.

13. How can an MNC deal with firms that counterfeit its products?

14. What is meant by 'brand piracy'?

15. What is a 'management contract'? In what circumstances might a management contract be useful?

12

INTERNATIONAL LOGISTICS AND DISTRIBUTION

1. Logistics

Logistics involves the co-ordination of the movement and storage of inputs and outputs in order to satisfy customer demand in the right place at the right time at the lowest cost. Hence it concerns the analysis of the costs, efficiencies and feasibilities of the various modes of transport and temporary storage needed to move goods to their destinations, safely and with minimal pilferage and materials loss. Specific issues covered by logistics management are:

- Scheduling the arrival of materials and other inputs
- Warehousing and inventory control, including the strategic choice of international warehousing facilities
- Production scheduling and monitoring the progress of items through the production process
- Packaging, transportation and final delivery to customers
- Transport cost analysis, i.e. the critical examination of various alternative modes of transport available in relation to customer needs (speed and frequency of delivery, reliability of delivery dates, convenience of collection, etc.). The costs involved include freight charges, insurance, intermediate handling and storage (warehousing for example), special packaging costs, documentation expenses, expected pilferage, spoilage rates, stockholding costs and the interest on capital foregone through having money tied up as goods in transit for various journey times.

TRANSPORTATION

2. Sea transport

Seafreight is cheap compared to most other options, but slow, and transhipment (i.e. having to unload and reload consignments between different modes of transport) may be necessary. In certain parts of the world, port congestion frequently delays the unloading of cargoes. Seafreight is flexible in the sense that there is usually a choice of ships going to the required destination, although it is necessary to book space well in advance of the shipment and substantial documentation is needed. There are 'liner services' that set sail and arrive according to a strict time table and which charge uniform freight rates regardless of the particular shipping company concerned; and 'tramp' ships that leave port only when they have a full cargo and which are liable to call at intermediate ports *en route* to load and unload *ad hoc* cargoes. Hence there is no firm commitment that a tramp service will arrive at a particular end destination within a pre-specified period. Freight charges for tramp ships vary *between* vessels. Two main documents are connected with sea transport, as follows:

1. *The standard shipping note (SSN)*, which is a form used to advise the shipping company about what is to happen to the goods on arrival at the foreign port, e.g. who will collect them, who is to pay unloading charges, whether the consignment is to be placed in a warehouse within the docks, etc. The document also acts as a formal request to the destination port authorities to receive and handle the shipment.

2. The *bill of lading*, which is the shipping company's receipt for the goods specifying whether they were loaded in a satisfactory or damaged condition. A 'clean' bill of lading refers to goods received on board in apparently good condition and with no shortages. Otherwise the bill is 'dirty' and will detail the shortfalls or damage to goods observed. A 'short form' bill of lading is one that does not show the shipping company's terms and conditions on the back. In the absence of any other evidence, the holder of a bill of lading is entitled to collect the consignment from the docks on its arrival, i.e. the bill is a *de facto* document of title. Without a bill of lading the customer can only obtain possession of the goods by giving the shipping company a bank letter of indemnity which protects the shipping company against subsequent claims. The bill of lading is the contract between the exporter and the shipping company and is a highly legalistic document. For small loads and/or short journeys, however, the shipping company might issue a 'data freight receipt' (sometimes called a sea waybill) rather than a bill of lading *per se*. DFRs act merely as receipts for goods and as evidence of contracts of carriage. They do not relate to the ownership of goods.

A contract under which an *entire ship* is hired to a user is called a Charter Party (CP). There are two forms: *non-demise* CPs whereby the shipowner provides the vessel *and* crew, and *demise* CPs which furnish the vessel only. A 'voyage CP' is for a specific journey(s); a 'time CP' contracts the ship for a stated period.

3. Air transport

Airfreight journey times are very short, although services are subject to weather delays, labour disputes at airports, and diversions are sometimes necessary. Air transport is not suitable for heavy, non-perishable consignments, although modern aircraft are increasingly capable of carrying heavy loads. Advantages to air transport include:

(a) Less stockholding and speedier settlement of invoices in consequence of faster delivery of goods.

(b) Avoidance of certain intermediate warehousing costs as consignments can move straight from the airport to customers' premises (the cost of warehousing can be as much as one third of the value of stored items).

(c) Its usefulness from the viewpoint of customers operating Just-in-Time production systems (*see* 14:7), because it becomes possible to satisfy small and frequent orders immediately.

(d) Convenience and ease of administration. Space can be booked direct with an airline or through a cargo agent. Either will help consignors to arrange shipments and documentation, and will organise goods collection services if required.

The basic document used in air transport is the 'air waybill', which is nothing more than a consignment note – it is not a document of title. Airfreight prices are fixed internationally *via* the International Air Transport Association (IATA), although competition does occur through a variety of special discounts offered to customers. Also IATA rates do not apply to consignments large enough to justify chartering an entire aircraft, charges for which depend on the urgency of the trip and the time of year the aircraft is needed. Note however that the charter has to pay for the entire round trip if the chartered plane returns empty.

4. Rail and road transport

Rail transport is suitable for bulky consignments sent over long distances. The cost-effectiveness of the method increases the longer the journey, especially in Continental Europe where there are many high-speed services. A problem with rail transport is the need for transhipment, although this can sometimes be avoided for consignments large enough to use 'swap body' containers, i.e. self-contained trailers on their own wheels that can be exchanged between vehicle cabs, as opposed to 'flat' trailers on to which containers have to be loaded. The entire swap body can be uncoupled from a cab, rolled on to a train for long haul rail transport, and rolled off and attached to another cab at its final destination. Empty containers are re-routed by national railway companies *via* an internationally agreed system. The document under which goods are transported by rail is the 'International Consignment Note' which lays down internationally agreed standard conditions of carriage.

Road transport offers door-to-door collection and delivery of goods. There is no need for transhipment and minimal intermediate goods handling, thus reducing handling costs and pilferage losses. Lorries can go to remote rural areas, and may be re-routed at will as circumstances alter. Loads can cross national frontiers without customs interference in consequence of an international transport agreement, known as the TIR (Transport Internationaux Routiers) convention which enables road hauliers to seal their vehicles in the exporter's country, travel across national frontiers and have all customs documentation processed at the final delivery point. The contract of carriage between an exporter and the road haulier is evidenced by a CMR note (Convention de Marchandises par Route), which acts as a receipt for the goods but does not provide evidence of ownership of the consignment. Under the CMR convention there are standard international contractual conditions for road transport, covering liability for loss or damage to goods and the maximum value of insurance claims against the haulier. Problems with road transport are its slowness over long distances; its vulnerability to bad weather; limited load sizes; and the fact that lorries often have to return empty.

Road and ferry

Road transport is often used in conjunction with Roll-on Roll-off (Ro-Ro) ferries which carry complete vehicles or the trailers of articulated lorries. Goods handling is reduced to the absolute minimum (no lifting gear is required, and marshalling is easy), so that ferries can turn around extremely quickly. Ro-Ro facilities exist along the entire European and North American coastlines and in all the major ports in the major trading nations of the Pacific Rim.

5. Choice of transport method

Speed, cost and reliability are the main factors that have to be balanced when selecting a particular mode of transport for international consignments. Accordingly the consignment needs to consider:

- how quickly the goods are required by final consumers
- the weights, sizes and handling characteristics of transported items
- the value of consignments (which affects insurance costs and the likelihood of pilfering)
- the consequences for customers of late delivery (the impact on Just-in-Time production systems for example)
- costs of intermediate goods handling and storage, packaging, spoilage of perishable items, documentation, and the income foregone through having working capital tied up as goods in transit during long journeys.

One option is for the consignor to engage a freight forwarder to handle all its international transport and associated documentation. Freight forwarders specialise in the international movement of goods and advise clients on packaging and labelling, warehousing, and which modes of transport are most suitable for carrying a client firm's output. They will assume full responsibility for documentation and insurance; will book air freight or ferry space for consignments; arrange for the collection of goods from sea ports, railway stations or container depots in other countries; and organise final road delivery.

6. INCOTERMS

Standard definitions of common export delivery terms have been drafted by the International Chamber of Commerce. These INCOTERMS, as they are known, can be incorporated into contracts of sale, price quotation, letters of credit, etc., and specify precisely the duties and obligations of buyer and seller and, in particular, the exact moment at which ownership of (and hence responsibility for) goods passes from one party to the other. Hence legal arguments about who is responsible for what, when and where, may be avoided as all these matters have already been defined in the INCOTERM that the contracting parties agree to apply. INCOTERMS are widely quoted and have a legal status in some countries. The commonest INCOTERMS are as follows:

(a) *Ex Works (EXW)* which requires the customer to collect the goods from the exporter's premises.

(b) *Free on Board (FOB)*, where the buyer takes delivery when the goods are loaded on to a ship in the exporter's country.

(c) *Cost, Insurance and Freight (CIF)*, whereby the exporter pays all transport and insurance costs to a named foreign destination.

(d) *Delivered Duty Paid (DDP)* where the exporter assumes *all* costs and risks involved in delivering the goods to the customer's premises. Increasingly, this is the standard requirement for export sales.

Variations on the above include Free on Rail (FOR); Free on Truck (FOT); and Cost and Freight (C&F) which parallels CIF except that the buyer rather than the exporter is responsible for insurance. Additionally there are special INCOTERMS to cover multimodal transport. For example, Free Carrier (FRC) is the same as FOB but for any form of carrier. Ownership of the goods passes from supplier to purchaser when the consignment is handed to the carrier at a specified place. Likewise, 'Carriage and Insurance Paid to' (CIP) matches CIF but for any means of transport. The INCOTERM 'Delivered at Frontier' (DAF) means the customer takes responsibility for the goods the moment they pass through a named national frontier.

7. Warehousing

Companies can warehouse goods in their own premises or in (frequently subsidised) warehouses owned by airports and by docks and harbour authorities. Freight forwarders and large road hauliers also provide warehousing facilities. Factors influencing the decision where to warehouse goods include the whereabouts of concentrations of customers, likelihoods of breakage and pilferage, depot rental or acquisition costs, and the ease of transportation both to the warehouse itself and from the warehouse to major outlets, taking into consideration local road and rail links, traffic congestion, etc. A firm that warehouses its goods in multiple locations can get its products to customers very quickly, but only at higher administrative and storage costs. Also average overall inventory holding will be higher than if a single warehouse was used for a particular region.

Bonded warehouses, freeports and freezones

Bonded warehouses are buildings to which goods may be sent without paying import duties. While in a bonded warehouse goods may be blended, repackaged or otherwise modified. Duty is payable only as goods are released, and not at all if they are re-exported. National customs authorities exert tight control over bonded warehouses. Use of bonded warehouses is especially valuable where the imported goods are subject to a quota restriction, since the exporter can be sure that consignments will not be refused entry to the country on arrival if a quota threshold happens to have been exceeded. The items can be stored duty free until the next quota period.

A 'freeport' fulfils the same function, but comprises a designated wider area at a seaport where goods can be stored and manipulated free of duty. Inland 'freezones' are equivalent to freeports but usually located near airports. Today there are several hundred freeports/zones throughout the world. They vary in relation to the extent of tax relief afforded to the firms operating within them. In several Pacific Rim countries freezones offer total exemption from *all* forms of taxation (not just customs duties), and have minimal health and safety regulations. Significant investment incentives (cash grants, generous depreciation allowances, etc.) might also be available to firms prepared to start new businesses in freezone areas.

Advantages and disadvantages of freezones

Freezones provide employment for local workers and contribute to the economic development of the regions in which they are situated. Also the local infrastructure is stimulated. Creation of freezones removes much of the bureaucratic paperwork attached to customs and other import procedures, and concentrates export processing services and facilities (insurance, packaging and labelling, pre-shipment inspection and certification, etc.) in a small area. To be successful, however, freezones need to be located at or near to international ports or airports, or on major shipping routes, and to have excellent local banking, telecommunications and other commercial services. Unfortunately some national governments have deliberately established freezones in economically depressed areas with poor local facilities, hoping that new investment will occur and local jobs be created. This has not always happened. A major criticism of freezones is that in many cases they serve merely to divert to certain locations activities that would have occurred anyhow, and thus deprive governments of tax revenue.

INTERNATIONAL DISTRIBUTION

8. Distribution channels

A distribution channel is a route from the producer of a good to the final consumer. Functions of a distribution channel include the physical movement of goods, storage of goods awaiting transit and/or sale, transfer of title to goods, and their presentation to final purchasers. There are four main categories of distribution system, as follows:

(a) *Direct to consumers*, e.g. mail order or if the supplier owns and controls its own outlets. No intermediaries are involved, so prices can be lower and the firm can ensure that its goods are properly presented to local consumers. The method is commonest among companies (i) with very large volumes of international business (and thus able to justify establishing a separate sales organisation), (ii) with technically complicated products, and (iii) where customers are geographically concentrated and place high value orders.

(b) *Producer to retailer.* Here the retailer bears the cost of storing goods awaiting sale. The supplier must employ salespeople to canvass retail outlets and to merchandise the product. Retailers sell the goods, possibly offer credit, provide product information to customers, and ensure that goods are available in small quantities throughout the year. Franchising (*see* 11.7) is a special case of this method.

(c) *Producer to intermediary.* The advantages of selling to an intermediary (export merchant for example) include (i) less administration (there is no need for a salesforce, no warehousing costs, fewer deliveries, and negligible invoicing and debt collecting) and (ii) the transfer of the risk of product failure from the supplier to the intermediary. However, final prices will be higher and intermediaries typically handle competing lines.

(d) *Through agents* (*see* 12).

International distribution differs from its domestic counterpart in the following respects:

(a) The range of available options is more varied. An MNC can establish its own distribution system (purchasing or setting up from scratch its own distribution subsidiaries in various countries) or may opt to use locally controlled channels. In the former case a further decision has to be taken regarding whether to manage distribution subsidiaries through expatriate or locally recruited staff. Standardisation of the methods and procedures used by an MNC for international distribution is extremely difficult because of the big differences that exist in national distribution systems. Hence the MNC's task is to identify and utilise that combination of directly owned foreign sales subsidiaries, wholesalers, import agents and other intermediaries, and retailers necessary to ensure that its products are available to customers where and when they are needed and at a reasonable price.

(b) Distribution channels are usually longer than for domestic business.

(c) Delays and holdups at various points in international distribution systems are common.

(d) Wholesaling and retailing systems differ markedly from Continent to Continent.

Factors influencing national distribution systems include:

- Consumer demand patterns. Shoppers in some countries insist on buying their goods in small quantities from nearby stores which they visit frequently; elsewhere people prefer to shop in large retail outlets on (say) a weekly or fortnightly basis.
- Wage levels paid to retail workers.
- Competition rules within the country (which might discourage the development of large retail chains).
- Entrepreneurial attitudes within the nation. In Japan, for example, buying a shop is a popular second career for many business executives who retire in their early fifties.

- Local laws restricting the size and nature of retail outlets.
- Popularity of mail order buying.

9. Choice of system

In selecting a distribution system the producer should consider the following characteristics in respect of each alternative:

(a) Cost of the channel. This is affected by the need to give discounts, salespeoples' salaries and travelling expenses, costs of credit given, inventory holding costs of unsold output, and administrative costs (invoicing, debt collection, bad debts, etc.).

(b) Extent of the control that can be exercised over the channel.

(c) Whether the channel improves or worsens the image of the goods (e.g. high-quality expensive output would not be congruent in a low-price cash and carry discount store).

(d) Geographical coverage of the channel.

(e) Reliability of distributors in relation to:

- product presentation and the provision of information to customers
- ensuring continuity of supply
- adequacy of customer care and after-sales service.

(f) Consequences for the duration of the total order cycle, i.e. the period likely to elapse between the customer placing an order and the actual delivery of the goods.

(g) Probabilities of the non-availability of the product in certain markets through using certain channels and the impact on long-run sales that occasional stockouts will exert.

10. Use of intermediaries

The advantages to an international business of handling its own distribution rather than engaging intermediaries include total control over the entire distribution process, the development of management skills in the international distribution field, the absence of commissions and discounts payable to outsiders, and possibilities for economies of scale and economies of scope in the distribution process. (Economies of scope are unit cost reductions resulting from a business undertaking a wide range of activities and thus being able to provide common services useful for each activity.) The staff involved will (or should) be committed to the well-being of the company, and there is continuity of the personnel involved in distribution matters. Staff are completely familiar with the firm's products and how they need to be presented, and have detailed knowledge of all the company's operations. They are fully accountable for their actions and their careers within the organisation depend substantially on the success of their work.

Advantages to using intermediaries, conversely, are as follows:

(a) The firm does not require an extensive foreign sales organisation.

(b) Intermediaries should be more objective in their assessments of the prospects for sales of the product in a particular region.

(c) The company does not need to train and develop in-house staff in specialist distribution functions.

(d) Savings on overheads should be available.

(e) Intermediaries have extensive contacts with experts in their field, and ought to possess up-to-the-minute knowledge of foreign market situations.

(f) Many (though not all) intermediaries take full possession of the goods and assume all the risks of foreign non-payment.

(g) Intermediaries have wide-ranging experience of the distribution problems of firms and industries other than their immediate clients and this experience should enable them to identify appropriate solutions and appreciate all the options available and difficulties involved.

Note moreover that a number of the benefits of using in-house staff to handle distribution assume that the people involved are competent and highly motivated. This is not always the case: staff might be apathetic and/or incapable of undertaking complicated duties. They might lack the specialist expertise and independent perspectives of high-calibre intermediaries.

Considerations that an international business should take into account when deciding whether to handle its own distribution rather than engage intermediaries include the following:

(a) Volume of sales. If sales within a particular market are modest it is rarely worthwhile handling the distribution of the goods internally within the firm.

(b) Nature of the product. High-tech items that require complex after-sales service are likely to be distributed direct by the producing company.

(c) Availability of good calibre distribution outlets in the local area.

(d) The ease with which feedback on how well the firm's products are selling in the local market can be obtained from local distributors.

(e) Whether the scale of sales can be increased substantially via intermediaries in the country concerned.

Selection of intermediaries

Major criteria to be examined when selecting an intermediary include the candidate's geographical coverage, product and market expertise, required margins, size of salesforce, credit rating, track record, corporate image, customer care facilities and ability to promote the supplier's products in an effective way.

11. Piggybacking

Smaller firms engaged in international business sometimes 'piggyback' on larger companies that already operate in certain foreign markets and are willing to act on behalf of other businesses that wish to export to those markets. This enables larger companies to use fully their sales representatives, premises, office equipment, etc., in the countries concerned. The carrier will purchase the goods outright or act as a commission agent, and may or may not sell the rider's product under the carrier's own brand name depending on the form of the agreement. Sometimes the carriers will insist that the rider's products be similar to its own in view of the need to deal with technical queries and after-sales service 'in the field'. The rider obtains access to all the carrier's facilities and resources, and can conveniently sell its product without having to establish its own distribution systems. 'Carriers' also benefit. They are able to sell items that fill gaps in their own product lines, without having to manufacture additional products. Economies of scale in bulk distribution become available, and the carrier's overall business image may improve. Problems with piggyback arrangements are the possible lack of commitment by the carrier to the rider's products; possible failure of the rider to supply the carrier on a continuous basis; and the fact that the rider becomes locked into the carrier's selling methods and territorial coverage.

Another means whereby a smaller business can distribute its products easily in foreign markets is to enter into 'sister company' agreements with foreign firms. A sister company is a business in another country offering similar products and which is of a similar size and nature to the one looking for a partner. Such firms act as a foreign agent, advise on local market conditions, translate documents, etc. Usually the sister company is engaged in complementary rather than directly competitive lines of work.

12. Agents and distributors

Agents differ from distributors in that whereas the latter actually *purchase* a supplying firm's products (assuming thereby full responsibility for their condition, sale, and any bad debts), agents simply put their clients in touch with third parties but then 'drop out' of resulting contracts – so that the agreements are between the agent's client and third parties, without the agent being further involved. An agent will (for a commission) find foreign customers for a company's products, but if the goods are defective, damaged or delivered late it is the client and not the agent who is responsible. In practice, however, the distinction between an agency and a distribution agreement can become blurred, especially if the agent takes physical control over the goods. Distributors typically demand exclusivity. Note how exclusivity clauses in a distribution agreement can create legal difficulties, because exclusive trading arrangements are not generally permitted under the competition laws of most industrialised nations.

Rules on agency

Certain rules apply to agents in all countries, as follows:

(a) The agent cannot act for a third party as well as the client without disclosing the fact to everyone concerned.

(b) Agents are obliged to maintain strict confidentiality regarding their clients' affairs, and to transmit to them all relevant information.

(c) If an agent does not pass on money deposited with the agent but owing to a third party, the client is still liable for the third party debt.

(d) The client is liable for damages to third parties for wrongs committed by an agent 'in the course of his or her authority'.

(e) Clients are obliged to indemnify their agents for expenses incurred while reasonably exercising their duties.

13. Use of agents

Agents operate on a commission basis and may either be *brokers*, who simply bring together buyers and sellers without ever taking physical possession of the goods; or *factors* who do possess the goods until customers are found and who sometimes sell under their own names at prices they think best (Christou 1990). A *del credere* agent is one who, in return for a higher commission, indemnifies the supplying firm against customers' bad debts.

14. Choice of agent

Agents need to be fully familiar with local business conditions and practices, and capable of conducting local market research. Other criteria to be adopted when choosing an agent should include the following:

(a) Whether the agent has contacts with local businesses capable of supplying specialist services to the exporting company (repair and after-sales service for example).

(b) How easily the agent can be contacted.

(c) Whether the agent will represent a competing firm and, if so, the incentives that are needed to encourage the agent to promote the exporter's products enthusiastically.

(d) How much information and feedback on matters such as consumer responses to the product, the quality of local delivery arrangements, whether local translations of operating instructions are satisfactory, etc., the agent can provide.

(e) How easily the calibre of the agent's work can be evaluated.

(f) The agent's track record, how long the firm has existed and its general business reputation.

(g) How extensively the agent covers the market; how many branch offices it has and their location and whether the agent can genuinely cover an entire country.

(h) Whether the agent possesses sufficient resources for the task: staff, showrooms, technical competence, storage facilities, etc.

(i) The ease with which the firm can control and motivate the agent. Normally the agent will be asked to prepare quarterly sales forecasts and to explain significant deviations of actual sales from those predicted. The agent should keep a record of enquiries received, calls made, customer complaints, etc. and submit details on a monthly basis.

(j) Whether the agent requires a large amount of technical training about the product and sales training for promoting it effectively.

15. Support of agents

Supplying companies can support and motivate their agents through the provision of technical advice and training; regular meetings in the principal's country paid for by the supplying firm; regular circulation of information about the supplying firm's current activities, changes in personnel, new product developments, marketing plans, etc.; and significant local advertising and brand awareness development by the supplying company. Other devices for supporting agents include:

- Incentive schemes such as competitions with cash prizes, free holidays, etc., for intermediaries with the highest sales.
- Setting up regional offices to coordinate communications with the firm's agents or distributors in a particular area.
- The principal's involvement in local exhibitions and trade fairs in conjunction with the local agent.
- Field visits to the agent.

16. Agency contracts

Agency agreements should be in writing and detail the parties to the agreement, duration (including the length of any probationary period), products and territory involved, confidentiality requirements, arbitration provisions and which country's law shall apply to the contract. Other matters that need to be specified are:

- termination arrangements
- the agent's discretion to offer special terms to customers
- the principal's right to inspect client's accounts
- requirements to disclose all relevant facts
- responsibility for credit checks on potential customers and for collecting debts
- commission rates
- extent of the agent's authority.

The agent's commission details must be tightly specified in relation to when exactly commission is payable (on receipt of an order, on delivery of the goods, or on payment of the resulting invoice); whether commission is still payable if an order is eventually cancelled; and whether the principal will pay commission on orders received from the agent's territory that did not pass directly through the agent but which might be indirectly attributable to the agent's work (repeat orders, for example).

17. Distributors

Since distributors actually purchase the supplier's goods they assume full responsibility for selling the item and for all credit risks. An important potential advantage is that a local image for the product might be projected. Also the distributor has to pay for storing the goods. Note how the contract between supplier and distributor can specify precise selling prices and marketing procedures that the distributor is obliged to follow.

Distribution contracts need to cover most of the items mentioned in **16**, plus clauses on discounts allowable, which party is to be responsible for defective items, selling prices (where appropriate), arrangements for after-sales service, and (importantly) exclusivity details. Note how exclusivity clauses can create legal difficulties, because exclusive trading arrangements are not generally permitted under the competition laws of most industrialised nations. And even if no exclusivity arrangement is specified a distributor will almost certainly insist on receiving more favourable terms than other purchasers, again causing legal problems. European Union approaches to this matter are discussed below.

18. EU law on agency

Agency law in the European Union has been harmonised via the Commercial Agents Directive 1986, under which any individual or company acting as an agent (excluding bankruptcy receivers and insolvency practitioners; partners, employees or officers of firms; or commodity dealers) has the right to receive the following on termination of an agency agreement:

(a) Full payment for any transaction predominantly attributable to the agent's work during the period of the agency, even if the transaction is concluded after the agency has been terminated.

(b) A lump sum not exceeding the agent's average commission for one year. To complete this average the agent's earnings over the last five years are considered (or less if the agency has not been in force for five years). The lump sum could be payable if the agency has ended because of the death of the agent.

(c) Damages for losses (e.g. loss of goodwill) in appropriate circumstances (Whittaker and Roney 1993).

The above represents the minimum levels of compensation payable; national governments may impose further requirements if they so wish. Thus, for example, French agents are legally entitled to one month's notice for each year of service up to a maximum of three months and up to two years' past average commission is payable. In Germany, principals must give agents one to six months' notice, depending on the duration of the agreement. Dutch agents are entitled to four month's notice plus one extra month if the agreement has lasted for three years; two extra months if the agreement has lasted for six years, and may obtain payment for contributions to the principal's goodwill up to the value of one year's commission.

19. EU law on exclusive distribution

The European Commission has issued a block exemption releasing virtually all small to medium sized business from EU legislation in the exclusive distribution field. Under the exemption, agreements between pairs of undertakings, whereby one agrees to supply exclusively to the other pre-specified goods for resale in a certain area and which require the distributor to obtain goods only from the other party, are legal provided:

(a) There is an alternative local source of supply for the type of product involved in the agreement.

(b) The supplying firm's output is available from at least one other source than the distributor, e.g. from a distributor in another territory or direct from the supplier's own premises.

(c) One of the parties to the deal has an annual turnover of less than ECU 100 million.

(d) The goods supplied under the agreement have a market share of less than five per cent.

Also, manufacturers of the same type of product cannot appoint each other as exclusive distributors in order to carve up the total European market, e.g. if a British manufacturing firm has its French counterpart as its exclusive distributor in France, and *vice versa*, so that consumers only have one source of supply in either country.

Distribution to selected distributors (dealers) whereby the supplier is prepared to sell only to particular dealers who then promise not to resell to anyone other than end users, are not generally covered by the distribution block exemption because of the control over prices they might allow. However, the Commission has agreed not to take action against suppliers so long as:

(a) The agreement is 'reasonably necessary', e.g. by virtue of the needs for special facilities for selling the product, for after-sales service, or for technical expertise among distributors.

(b) Quantitative limits are not placed on the number of approved dealers within a specific area (a city for instance).

(c) Selection criteria are objective and applied uniformly. Examples of suitable yardsticks are the dealer's technical knowledge, calibre of premises or extent of facilities.

(d) Competition within the market is not adversely affected.

213

20. Special distribution problems

National distribution systems differ radically between richer and poorer countries. Major disparities include:

(a) The degree of access to supermarkets and department stores (as opposed to smaller and more general outlets).

(b) Sizes and frequency of consumer purchases. Customers in poorer countries tend to be geographically scattered, immobile and to purchase in small units.

(c) Extent of specialisation in retailing. Rural retailing in poor countries is mainly non-specialist, with outlets that supply whatever goods are demanded and can be paid for by the local community at a particular moment in time. Specialised retailers are found only in towns with a large number of middle-class families.

(d) Lengths of distribution channels. Retailers in underdeveloped countries are served by a plethora of import agents, national wholesalers, local wholesalers in towns and in rural areas, travelling sales vans and local food produce markets. Wholesalers sell to retailers frequently and in small units.

(e) The intensity of competition among retailers. This tends to be very high in Third World countries because of shortages of the capital and skilled labour needed to set up manufacturing businesses, so that single-person retailing is a popular outlet for entrepreneurial activity in these nations.

(f) Transport systems and storage and handling facilities. Poor transport restricts the catchment areas of retail outlets, since the latter are dependent on customers who reside within a reasonable travelling distance. The worse the local transport system the fewer the number of customers' shopping trips and the more difficult are deliveries made to customers from the retail outlet.

Progress test 12

1. Define logistics.

2. What is a bill of lading?

3. List the advantages of air transport.

4. What is a CMR note?

5. State the main factors to be taken into account when selecting a mode of transport.

6. Define the following INCOTERMS: cost and freight, ex-works, delivered duty paid.

7. What is a freezone? List the advantages of freezones.

8. What is a distribution channel? List the main types of distribution channel.

9. How does international distribution differ from domestic distribution?

10. What factors influence national distribution channels?

11. State the advantages of using intermediaries to handle the international distribution of goods.

12. What is meant by the terms (a) piggybacking and (b) sister company?

13. Explain the difference between an agent and a distributor.

14. How can principals support and motivate their agents?

15. Outline the main provisions of the EU Commercial Agents Directive 1986.

13

ORGANISATION OF INTERNATIONAL BUSINESS

BASIC ORGANISATION

1. Organising for export

Exporting means the sale in a foreign market of an item produced, stored or processed in the supplying firm's home country, as opposed to the supplier being involved in foreign manufacture or processing of goods. In practice, however, the distinction between pure 'exporting' on the one hand and wider foreign operations on the other has become increasingly blurred as more and more businesses internationalise their activities. There is nevertheless a distinct set of commercial practices and techniques with which the would-be exporter has to become familiar. These techniques relate in particular to foreign trade documentation, transport and logistics, and methods for getting paid. It follows that companies which export significant amounts of their outputs need to establish export departments to undertake the specialist aspects of export work. Note however that the size and character of an export department will depend on how many of the practical tasks attached to exporting the firm decides to complete itself and how many it leaves to intermediaries (*see* 12:**10**). If the bulk of export duties are undertaken in-house the department will need people/ sections to look after the following functions:

- Documentation relating to transport, insurance, finance and customs entry
- International marketing research and research into foreign technical standards and packaging requirements
- Distribution, including the control of agents and distributors
- Marketing and selling: international advertising, mail order sales, international sales promotions and the control of export salespeople.

Firms that choose to engage outsiders to perform the majority of export tasks must still co-ordinate intermediaries' contributions, maintain the links between various stages in the export process, and dovetail export activities into the company's overall corporate plan. And there are certain export duties that cannot be completed by third parties (e.g. dealing with enquiries, preparing quotations, expediting confirmed orders, and so on).

Export departments are generally more self-contained than other administrative units, and export managers are necessarily involved in a wide range of functions: foreign market research, negotiation of agency and distribution contracts, product modification for foreign markets, arranging credit, packaging, organising after-sales service in foreign countries, etc. Note that a small, compact and specialist department can have advantages over a larger unit. Export administration might be completed more efficiently if just a handful of people are involved. If a few specialists handle all aspects of export orders – documentation, transport and payments arrangements, insurance, customs clearance and so on – then there is less likelihood of error and, when mistakes do occur, they can be rectified more easily. General advantages to having an export department are that relevant skills are collected and developed in a single section, that department members will be genuinely committed to increasing the firm's export effort, and that it can act as a cost and profit centre in its own right. Problems are that the department might not be taken seriously by the firm's senior management, that through its self-contained nature it might pursue its own objectives rather than those of the wider enterprise, and there may be difficulties recruiting high-calibre staff possessing relevant skills.

2. The international division

A firm that sets up branches and/or subsidiaries in other countries and which has substantial foreign operations (possibly including manufacture, licensing and joint venture arrangements) may decide to establish an 'international division' (perhaps as an upgrading of an export department as foreign activities expand). The international division will assume full control of all foreign operations and take over some functions previously undertaken by various departments (cross-border marketing, finance of international transactions, transport, etc.). Expertise in all aspects of international business is concentrated in the division, which takes significant decisions about product and distribution policy and is increasingly involved in the firm's strategic affairs. Major decisions that need to be taken when setting up an international division are:

- To whom the head of the division shall report. Is this to be the chief executive of the company, or some other person?
- The extent to which the division will determine the firm's international business strategies and policies.
- How the division will relate to other parts of the enterprise.
- Whether the division is to be empowered to borrow money in foreign capital markets.

Benefits derived from having an international division are that:

(a) Specialist experience and expertise in international business are acquired.

(b) The firm obtains a convenient device for developing a multinational strategy.

(c) Decisions on international aspects of the enterprise's work are taken at the heart of the enterprise.

(d) Centralised control of domestic and international operations is facilitated.

(e) Staff from the international division can make valuable contributions to the work of domestic divisions.

(f) The division can act as a 'champion' to further the cause of the firm's international activities when resources are being allocated at the company level.

Disadvantages associated with international divisions include:

(a) The possibility that they will not be able to handle increasingly diverse and complex international operations in isolation from the rest of the firm.

(b) Possible conflicts between domestic and international divisions.

(c) The potential for the 'marginalisation' of an international division within the wider enterprise, with senior management not taking the work of the international division seriously.

(d) Heavy reliance on assistance from domestic divisions, especially in relation to R&D, new product development and quality control.

(e) Conflicts regarding the prices at which the international division will transfer goods to other divisions, and *vice versa*.

(f) Duplication of activities within international and domestic divisions.

(g) Overspecialisation within the international division leading to narrow perspectives and a failure to recognise the needs of the enterprise as a whole.

ORGANISATION STRUCTURES FOR MULTINATIONAL COMPANIES

The nature of multinational enterprise is discussed in Chapter 9. Organisation structures for MNCs need to integrate their worldwide operations within a single administrative system that optimises the use of company resources and enables the firm to take full advantage of opportunities wherever they arise (Goshal and Nohria 1993). A number of problems attach to the construction of a sound organisation system for a multinational company, notably:

- having to co-ordinate the activities of units in many geographically distant countries
- differences in the cultural orientations of employees, distributors, etc., in foreign nations
- the multiplicity of interest groups (governments, consumers, local representatives, intermediaries and so on) that need to be appeased in each state
- possible wide discrepancies in the motivations of staff in various subsidiaries
- having to cope with an enormous volume of information generated by worldwide operations.

A common feature of MNC organisation is that senior managers have world-wide responsibilities. Thereafter, however, a range of organisational models may be applied, as outlined in **3** to **8** below.

3. Functional structure

Here the firm seeks to accommodate its international activities within its existing functional structure, so that departments responsible for sales, market research, promotion, etc., generally would handle international aspects as well. This is a convenient form of organisation for a firm with a small number of products, which operates in a stable competitive environment, and which needs an organisation structure suitable for maximising scale economies and for adapting its products for markets in various parts of the world.

Intense functional specialisation might develop expertise of such a high calibre that it creates an important competitive advantage for the company. All international activities can be controlled by a handful of line managers; there are no conflicts between profit centres and duplication of effort is avoided. However, functional organisation is not usually the best way to administer multinational operations, for a number of reasons:

(a) It cannot be usefully applied within a firm that makes and sells numerous products internationally, because functional managers would need to possess specialist expertise in each of the company's products, or certain individuals would have to concentrate on particular product lines within functions (hence creating a *de facto* product organisation structure – *see* **6**).

(b) A separation of marketing and production could arise.

(c) Responsibilities for specific international business activities might become confused, as some cross-border operations might not fit neatly into existing functional categories.

(d) Functional line managers' knowledge of foreign markets and business practices may be inadequate.

(e) Senior line managers can become overwhelmed with work. Each functional department has to deal with several diverse territories (each possessing unique problems and characteristics) as well as with the international dimension (documentation, need for special packaging, etc.) of the particular function concerned.

4. Regional structure

This involves setting up regional divisions, each responsible for a certain part of the globe (Europe, South America, the Pacific Rim, etc.). Strategies are determined at headquarters, leaving regional managements in day-to-day control. The head of a regional unit assumes responsibility for all functions within his or her area and must co-ordinate marketing, production, transport and other duties therein. Operations can be specifically designed to suit regional conditions.

Advantages of this form of organisation are that:

(a) The importance of regional variations in culture, business methods, consumer characteristics, etc., is recognised. A major argument for organising on a geographical basis is the increasing economic integration of the world's main regions (NAFTA and the EU for example). As business methods and consumer behaviour harmonise within these trading blocs it makes sense to regard each region as a single unit. Staff within a regional department acquire extensive knowledge about regional characteristics, the nature of the competition, customer preferences, local business norms and cultures, and so on.

(b) It is especially useful for situations where operations at the regional level generate economies of scale but where minor modifications of (for instance) packaging and promotional messages are appropriate (as in the food processing, oil and pharmaceutical industries for example).

(c) The system is clear, logical and easy to apply.

(d) There is close co-ordination between production and marketing in each region.

Problems with regional organisation structure include:

(a) The difficulty that some managers have in adopting a totally international perspective on the enterprise's worldwide activities.

(b) Insufficient emphasis on new product development.

(c) The appropriate determination or boundaries for each region. NAFTA, for example, is a single trading bloc, but there are big differences in the cultures and market structures of its three members. Differences within major regions (such as Western or Eastern Europe, North or South America) are so huge that it is not possible for individuals to become experts on all the countries that a region contains.

(d) Heavy demands placed on the managers in charge of each geographic division, who need to acquire a wide range of general management skills.

(e) Regional units improperly favouring operations within their own particular regions (e.g. by always procuring inputs from within their region) at the expense of global considerations.

(f) Duplication of activity within regional units.

Geographical structure is commonest when the countries covered by a division are in close proximity and the same product is being marketed in the area concerned. It is especially suitable, perhaps, where firms have technically simple products and operate in stable environments; where regional customer groups have different needs and/or special difficulties (complex documentation and distribution arrangements for example) apply to the area; and where product modification, different packaging and pricing policies, and different customer service activities are needed for each geographic market. Normally, advisory departments at head office will provide staff support for personnel, marketing, etc., leaving day-to-day line management in the hands of managers of regional departments. The latter have total responsibility for secondary activities (contract manufacturing and so on) in the relevant region.

5. International subsidiary structure

This has two versions:

1. Each of the firm's foreign subsidiaries reports directly to head office, without intermediary layers of management (i.e. there is no regional headquarters, international division or other lesser authority responsible for subsidiaries' affairs). Subsidiaries exercise a considerable degree of autonomy.

2. The parent firm retains responsibility for its subsidiaries' functional activities, but sets up a board of management for each subsidiary to oversee local operations and to develop the local market.

Advantages associated with either form of subsidiary structure are that they:

- represent simple and inexpensive approaches to international organisation which provide for local responses to changes in local conditions
- are useful for the training and development of managers within subsidiary units
- provide a career structure for local nationals employed by subsidiaries
- ensure that international issues are considered at the highest level of management within the organisation
- facilitate the co-ordination of international operations.

Problems with subsidiary structure include the large amounts of information and requests for assistance emanating from subsidiaries (resulting perhaps in important matters being overlooked), the need for extensive liaison between subsidiaries, and the tendency for subsidiary boards to mirror (perhaps inappropriately) the structure of the main company. Incorrect strategies might be imposed on subsidiaries, and local managers could lose sight of the global objectives of the organisation. Also the system becomes complicated and unwieldy as the number of subsidiaries increases. Conflicts between subsidiary boards and head office functional specialists might emerge.

6. Product structure

Businesses that supply several unrelated types of product or which have products that require significant modification for various markets might decide to organise around product divisions. Each division controls all activities associated with the product, including purchase of raw materials, processing, administration, and the sale and distribution of the final output.

Product structure is appropriate for multiple-product multiple-market situations, especially if products are purchased by disparate categories of end users. It is also suitable for high technology items and when tariff or transport considerations necessitate foreign manufacture. No distinctions are drawn between domestic and international operations. The advantages of product structure are that:

(a) The managers of product divisions acquire a wide range of general managerial skills as well as expert knowledge of the problems associated with the particular product. Hence it provides an excellent means for training managers for higher-level posts.

(b) Since employees must necessarily acquire a wide range of skills in order to succeed in a product department, they become flexible and hence can be quickly shifted from one type of work to another.

(c) The work of the department is varied and thus possibly more interesting for employees.

(d) The firm can quickly add or discard product divisions as new products emerge or existing ones disappear.

Problems with this approach are that:

(a) Product managers might be experts in the technical aspects of the firm's output, but lack experience of international business.

(b) Co-ordination across product divisions may be difficult.

(c) The importance of international marketing might not be properly recognised and that important regions could be overlooked. A product that sells worldwide requires global co-ordination of marketing activities, which could be difficult to implement in a product structure. The allocation of marketing overheads to product divisions becomes problematic.

(d) Within a product division, international activities might have to compete with other elements of the division for attention and resources. Hence important opportunities for developing international sales might be missed.

7. Strategic business units (SBUs)

An SBU is a grouping of a business's activities which are then treated as self-contained entities for the purposes of strategic planning and control. Hence an SBU could be a division of a company, a department, a collection of departments, a subsidiary, or a function undertaken within the firm (e.g. all the firm's marketing activities might be regarded as an independent SBU). Often SBUs cut across existing divisional, functional and departmental boundaries. Having defined SBUs, management then gives each unit a budget and the authority to administer its own resources. Criteria for establishing SBUs might involve:

- similar markets or product types
- shared resources
- shared know-how
- common concerns (with customer care or impending government legislation for example).

The idea was invented by the US General Electric company which, dissatisfied with its existing divisional structure, rearranged all the enterprise's activities into SBUs, some of which bore little relation to traditional departments, divisions or profit centres. Thus, for instance, a number of food preparation appliances previously manufactured and sold through several independent divisions in various parts of the world were merged into a single 'housewares' SBU. Similarly, a firm might produce television sets in one division, radios in the next, and car stereos systems in another. Yet for strategy and planning purposes all three activities could be conveniently lumped together into a self-contained administrative unit.

To make sense, an SBU should:

- comprise compatible elements each possessing a direct and identifiable link with the unit as a whole
- be easy to appraise (which requires that its performance can be compared with something similar within or outside the organisation)
- contribute significantly towards the attainment of the organisation's goals.

SBUs are most appropriate for highly diversified businesses, the activities of which can be grouped under distinct headings. The advantages to the creation and uses of SBUs are that:

(a) They reduce the number of administrative units that senior management has to monitor and control.

(b) Use of SBUs enables management to operate two levels of strategy: overall corporate decisions that affect the nature and direction of the enterprise, and unit level strategies relevant to specific operating environments. This facilitates the linking up of strategy development with strategy implementation.

(c) Important decisions can be taken in discrete business units.

(d) SBU organisation provides a planning framework that cuts across organisational boundaries.

(e) Units are encouraged to behave entrepreneurally.

(f) Decision making can be related to specific consumer groups and resource categories.

The main problems with SBUs are how to co-ordinate many disparate activities simultaneously and how to assess the financial and other contributions of various activities to a particular unit. SBUs are not suitable for vertically integrated companies supplying a limited range of products.

8. International matrix organisation

Matrix organisation is a means for creating project teams that cut across departmental boundaries. Individuals are seconded from their 'home' departments onto various project committees and thus have a number of bosses – their head of department and the team leaders of the groups to which they are temporarily attached. This can create problems, of course, in that individuals may receive conflicting instructions from different bosses, each insisting that the work of their particular team be given top priority. Teams cut across product, geographical market and functional lines. They are multi-disciplinary and provide numerous opportunities for employee participation in decision-taking and the rapid development of general managerial skills. The system is extremely flexible (teams can be set up and disbanded at will). Matrix structures are especially useful for:

(a) Managing complex projects where immediate access to several highly specialised professional skills is required.

(b) Managing strategic business units (*see* 7). Often, SBUs do not correspond to existing divisions or departments so that it becomes necessary to establish a team representing each aspect of the work of the unit to oversee its activities.

Advantages and disadvantages of matrix approaches

Matrix organisation offers a practical and coherent device for analysing the make-up of an enterprise. Company organisation is related to the needs of internal decision-making processes, ensuring that every section which ought to be involved in a particular decision is adequately represented. Personal and departmental contributions to the organisation are systematically classified and crucial activities that absorb large amounts of effort and resources are highlighted.

The method is commonly used where several departments performing related duties are grouped together into an international division. In this way, interdepartmental communications are enhanced and duplication of effort can be avoided. Further advantages are that:

(a) There is much face-to-face communication between managers with interests in the same projects.

(b) Project teams can be immediately disbanded following a project's completion.

(c) Departmental boundaries do not interfere with the completion of projects.

(d) Team leaders become focal points for all matters pertaining to particular projects or functions.

(e) Flexible attitudes are encouraged.

(f) Specialised professional knowledge relevant to a project or function is instantly available.

(g) Interdisciplinary co-operation is facilitated.

(h) Junior managers develop broad perspectives on problems and issues.

(i) Top management is left free to concentrate on strategic planning.

The essential problem with the matrix approach is perhaps its sophistication and complexity, leading to the need for managers who are trained and competent in the system and committed to making it work. Other difficulties are the duplication of effort created, the time spent in committees (with consequent effects on the speed of decision-making), and possible disputes regarding who should do what and who is in charge of whom.

Team leaders are responsible for projects, though heads of department retain executive authority over their staff. In consequence, team members might receive conflicting instructions from heads of department on the one hand and project team leaders on the other! Thus, it is important to establish at the outset (i) who, ultimately, each individual should obey, and (ii) whether subordinates are to regard themselves first and foremost as members of a department or as members of a particular project team. (Usually, departments take precedence since projects last only for limited periods, and individuals will normally be assigned to a number of projects at the same time.) Other problems are that:

(a) Matrix systems are more complicated and costly to administer than other forms of organisation.

(b) They might offer fewer discrete promotion opportunities than do hierarchical systems.

(c) Teams rather than individuals are appraised (unsatisfactory employees may thus be difficult to identify).

(d) Unofficial links between members of various project teams may emerge which subvert teams' abilities to achieve their objectives.

(e) Staff need to be trained in the methods of matrix management and the cost of such training could be substantial.

(f) Conflicts may occur between the decisions of individual line managers and the collective decisions of project teams (which normally are given their own budgets and authority to implement decisions).

(g) Matrix structures might encourage managers to develop their political and negotiating skills at the expense of their managerial abilities.

(h) The system may severely overwork certain key managers.

(i) Team members may be unclear about the precise nature of their roles in the team and in the organisation.

9. Designing the international organisation structure

Organisation structure is an important *means* whereby a company can attain its objectives. The latter change over time, so the firm's organisation system might also need to change in order to keep in step. The essential purposes of an organisational structure are:

- to have the right people taking the right decisions at the right time
- to establish who is accountable for what and who reports to whom
- to facilitate the easy flow of information through the organisation
- to provide a working environment that encourages efficiency and the acceptance of change
- to integrate and co-ordinate activities.

Organisation structure must balance order and innovation. On the one hand, it needs to avoid the duplication of effort, to standardise procedures, monitor the quality of work, etc. On the other hand, it should encourage initiative among the staff and generate job satisfaction in employees through presenting them with an interesting variety of disparate tasks. There is no single ideal structure that is universally applicable to all international businesses. What works in one firm may not be suitable elsewhere because of differences in mission, strategies, and the calibre of personnel. In the ideal situation:

(a) Each unit will act as a self-contained cost/profit centre.

(b) Information about units is readily available (meaning they can be controlled without difficulty).

(c) Work passes from one unit to the next in a logical sequence.

(d) The resource needs of each unit are clearly visible so that resources may be deployed where they are most urgently required.

Manifestations of an inappropriate organisation structure include:

- poor internal communication
- slow decision making and frequent bad decisions
- lack of motivation among staff
- poor co-ordination of the work of various divisions and departments
- high administrative costs due to inefficiency and/or duplication of effort
- bad relations between line and staff managers
- management not being able to appraise the efficiencies of certain functions (accounting, marketing, etc.), or activities (e.g. launching a product, changing a production technique) because of the complexity of organisational interrelationships within the firm
- staff not knowing the organisation's true objectives
- absence of procedures for interdepartmental consultation and/or joint departmental decision-taking
- a single favoured department dominating others, even to the extent that other departments feel they require its permission prior to initiating certain actions
- conflicts between individual and organisational goals, and the pursuit by individuals of personal rather than company objectives
- slow and inefficient decision-taking within the business
- excessive numbers of meetings necessitated by people not being sure what they are expected to do
- poor co-ordination of projects
- non-implementation of strategic plans.

The final choice

Factors influencing the choice of organisational form should include the extent of the company's foreign operations and experience of international markets, the size of the business, the number and technical nature of its products, and its aspirations regarding further international expansion. Other factors to be considered are:

- the number, size, types and complexity of operating units in various countries
- ability levels and experience of the MNC's staff in each country, especially their capacities to think strategically and plan for the long term
- ease of communication with and control of operating units
- availability of local finance and other resources
- stability of local markets (the more uncertain the local market, the greater the need for local control).

In selecting a structure an MNC needs to ensure that the organisation has an unambiguous chain of command, is capable of coordinating worldwide activities, can take decisions quickly at the most appropriate level, and provides for fast and effective communication between units. The structure chosen needs to motivate and develop employees, facilitate international communications, planning, decision-making and control, create a clearly defined accountability and delegation system, and make it as easy as possible for the company to satisfy customer demand. It is particularly important that managers of all units (subsidiaries, divisions, product groupings or whatever) have a common perception of the firm's overall goals and how they should be pursued. It is important to note that there is no reason in principle why a business's structure should not be an *ad hoc* mixture of product, geographic and other systems. This leads to complex communication and accountability procedures but could be just what the company in question actually needs.

10. Spans of control

Determination of the widths of senior managers' spans of control is a key decision when structuring a multinational company. A manager's span of control is the number of immediate subordinates who report directly to that person. Narrow spans involve just two or three subordinates; wide spans have perhaps twelve or fifteen subordinates reporting to a single manager. Most analysts suggest that any more than six or seven subordinates represents too wide a span of control because of the complex relationships and competing demands on the controlling manager's time that result, especially in the context of international operations. Five factors are relevant to the choice of a span of control: organisational diversity, complexity of work, geographical coverage of the company's activities, and the calibres of the manager and his or her subordinates.

Organisational diversity affects the efficiency of internal communication. If face-to-face contacts between manager and subordinates are impossible, communication has to depend on telephone calls, letters, memoranda and similar indirect methods. Interruptions in information flows and other communication breakdowns cause loss of effective control, especially if people and departments are geographically separated. Complex work means that managers need time to assess the reports and suggestions of subordinates in foreign subsidiaries, and they ought not to be overburdened with minor problems. A narrow span of control is appropriate in this case. Note however that the imposition of narrow spans of control throughout the organisation necessarily creates many more

227

levels of authority than in 'flatter' structures, resulting perhaps in long channels of communication and in important information not being passed up and down the chain of command. Hence top management may lose touch with what happens at lower levels within the organisation.

Some managers are better able to handle large numbers of subordinates than others, depending on their training, experience and personal qualities. The degree of authority given the manager is also relevant to this point. Similarly, well-trained, enthusiastic and competent subordinates need less control and supervision than others, so that wide spans of control may then be applied. Narrow spans of control recognise that an individual's capacity to supervise others is limited and that it is better to deal with a small number of subordinates properly, than to have contact with many subordinates but only in casual ways. However, wide spans also offer advantages – they force managers to delegate (so that subordinates acquire experience of higher levels of work), subordinates may experience a higher degree of job satisfaction, and the cost of supervision is low. On the other hand, co-ordination of subordinates' activities may be poor. Communication between subordinates of equal rank could be inadequate and lead to much duplication of effort.

11. Tall and flat structures

Narrow spans of control create numerous levels of authority within the organisation and hence long chains of command. The advantages of a 'tall' organisation with many levels between top and bottom are as follows:

(a) Managers may devote their full attention to the demands of their subordinates in various countries.

(b) There is proper supervision and (hopefully) effective control.

(c) There is less need to co-ordinate the activities of subordinates than in a flat structure.

(d) Duplication of effort among subordinates is unlikely.

(e) Communications are facilitated.

(f) Employees are presented with a career ladder and thus can expect regular promotion through the system.

(g) It facilitates specialisation of functions and the creation of logically determined work units.

Flat organisations have the following advantages:

(a) Managers are forced to delegate work, so that subordinates acquire experience of higher-level duties.

(b) Morale may improve on account of the majority of employees being on the same level.

(c) Low supervision costs.

(d) Subordinates are given more discretion over how they achieve their objectives.

(e) Fewer personal assistants and staff advisors are necessary because there are fewer levels.

(f) Managers and subordinates communicate directly without having to go through intermediaries. Hopefully, therefore, information will not be lost or misinterpreted as it passes up and down the organisation.

(g) Managers remain in touch with activities at the base of the enterprise.

12. Bureaucratic versus flexible structures

An MNC operating within a rapidly changing international environment may have to alter its organisation at short notice and for all aspects of its work. Consider for instance a computer manufacturing company which finds that a competitor has introduced a cheaper and superior model. This business must completely reorganise its design, production, marketing and administration systems almost at once. Thus, it should adopt flexible organisation structures possessing total labour mobility, overlapping responsibilities, and fragile and transitory departmental structures that can be altered at will. The employees of such a company must be capable of taking on different types of work at short notice, and be culturally attuned to accepting change.

Conversely, organisations in relatively stable environments, or which employ poorly educated and/or apathetic staff, or which are concerned with routine assembly line or equally mundane activities that cannot be made more interesting, may opt for rigid, formal and bureaucratic organisational forms. Rules will exist covering every aspect of the firm's work. There will be clear divisions of work and close supervision. All procedures will be standardised and stated in writing: workers will not be allowed discretion over how they undertake their tasks. Relationships are extremely formal in such a system; everyone knows their place and exactly what they are expected to do.

Such measures relieve employees of the burden of having to think for themselves, and there is certainty that work will actually be completed. But individual initiative is stifled and this type of organisation is not capable of accommodating change: people 'pass the buck' whenever they are confronted with new ideas.

13. Strategy and structure

'Structure follows strategy' in the sense that once a strategy has been selected the organisational framework of the business will usually have to be amended in order to implement that strategy. Thus, expansion abroad may lead to the creation of an international division; diversification can result in the establishment of foreign subsidiaries and SBUs (*see* 7); new product development might necessitate a change in departmentation, and so on. Examples of how strategy can affect structure include the following:

(a) Divisionalisation of a firm may create a large number of levels in its overall management hierarchy, and widen the spans of control (*see* 10) of individual senior managers. The former is due to the imposition of an extra layer between the chief executive and operational units in conjunction with the inevitable emergence of employee grading systems within divisions themselves; while the latter results from the proliferation of specialist staff advisers at head office, all reporting to a handful of senior executives.

(b) Diversification strategies can greatly increase the numbers of departments and divisions within a firm.

(c) The size of a company's core business might depend on the extent to which it is diversified.

(d) Acquisition strategies determine how many quasi-independent subsidiary units a firm has to operate.

(e) Doing business in geographically separated and culturally disparate markets can cause a business to organise itself in a distinct and complex way. It is especially important for structure to follow strategy, perhaps, in high-tech firms operating in conditions of rapid change. Here, structure needs to keep up with the requirements of the latest technological innovations, so that the business's organisational infrastructure must be flexible and capable of speedy alteration as circumstances change.

14. Problems of organisation design

Detailed and protracted attention to organisational design might result in the drafting of a theoretically perfect organisational model which in reality is so impractical that it can never work. Further problems with organisation design are as follows:

(a) The people who design an organisation might not themselves subsequently have to work within the structure.

(b) Staff implementing the structure might not possess any knowledge of the theories on which it is based, leading perhaps to contradictory and inconsistent organisational policies.

(c) Informal or 'shadow' organisational structures might grow up alongside to subvert the official system. The formal organisation is that established by management and embodied in organisation charts, official hierarchies, company rule books, operating manuals, etc. Formal organisation is intended to be permanent, to contribute directly to the attainment of organisational goals, and to facilitate the smooth flow of work. Informal organisation, conversely, arises naturally and spontaneously as individuals begin to interact. Thus, informal groups emerge to represent people with common interests, each group possessing its own norms, perceptions and internal communications. Informal organisation is important because the informal structures that emerge may develop goals and work routines that run contrary to the interests of the formal system.

Progress test 13

1. List the main duties and responsibilities of a typical export department.

2. What are the advantages of having an in-house export department?

3. Why do firms sometimes set up export divisions? What are the main problems likely to be experienced by an export division?

4. The functional organisation structure is usually considered inappropriate for a multinational business. Why is this the case?

5. How does an international subsidiary organisation structure operate?

6. What is an SBU? What are the advantages of an organisation system based on SBUs?

7. List six advantages and six problems of matrix organisation.

8. What are the key purposes of an organisation structure?

9. If an organisation structure is inappropriate for the needs of an enterprise, certain problems are likely to emerge. What are these problems?

10. List the main factors that should influence the choice of an organisation structure.

14

INTERNATIONAL OPERATIONS MANAGEMENT

1. Operations management

Operations management concerns the transformation of material resource inputs into outputs of goods and services. It is normally associated with manufacturing; but might equally involve, for example, transport operations, warehousing, or the deployment of physical items such as shelving, refrigerated cabinets and checkout tills in a retail outlet. Operations management is particularly associated with techniques of production, i.e. the conversion of raw materials and/or components into finished items. Special factors that apply to international (as opposed to domestic) operations management are as follows:

(a) Widely disparate economic, technological and social environments influence the production process in various states.

(b) Co-ordination of the activities of production units in different parts of the world may be difficult and complex.

(c) Material and other inputs often have to be moved between countries. This could be expensive and involve lengthy delays.

(d) Wage costs in developed and underdeveloped countries differ enormously.

International operations management strategy

This needs to derive from the firm's overall corporate strategy and has many crucial implications for the financing of an international business, for its organisation, management style and human resources. A successful operations management strategy is one which results in the supply of the correct amount of output in the right places at the right quality, cost and time. Absence of a coherent operations management strategy is likely to result in loss of market share, high worldwide inventories, expensive and inefficient working practices, use of inappropriate production methods in various countries and ineffective management. Issues that need to be addressed by an international operations management strategy include the following:

(a) The technologies to be used in manufacturing.

(b) International make versus buy decisions (*see* **6**).

(c) Criteria for selecting capital investment projects in various countries.

(d) How host country workforces are to acquire appropriate technical skills.

(e) When to introduce new technologies and how quickly.

(f) The calibres of the plant and equipment to be employed in manufacturing.

(g) The natures of the quality control and quality assurance procedures to be used in foreign subsidiaries and how these are to be monitored.

(h) How to integrate international manufacturing activities to marketing.

(i) How best to integrate computer assisted manufacturing into the firm's overall organisation system.

For manufacturing businesses (as opposed to providers of services) operations management is a key MNC function if only because of the large proportion of a company's expenditures that it will absorb. Apart from operating costs (raw materials, wages, electricity, etc.) there are the capital costs of fixed plant, equipment, vehicles, warehouses, and so on. Also, operations management has to be totally integrated with the work of other divisions, departments or sections of the firm since production decisions normally involve marketing (*what* goods should be produced); finance (*how* production is to be paid for); personnel (recruitment, training and control of staff); and a variety of other departments – security, secretariat, legal services, etc. The range of tasks undertaken by the staff in charge of operations management is extremely varied. In managerial grades, professional engineers, designers and functional specialists are employed, together (usually) with their administrative and clerical support units. At the other end of the spectrum are workplace supervisors, skilled, semi-skilled and un-skilled workers, and maintenance and inspection personnel in subsidiaries throughout the world. Note moreover that, very often, senior operations management staff possess more technical knowledge and are better qualified academically than colleagues in other fields, especially in high-technology industries.

2. International standardisation of production facilities

Some companies use the same production methods, degree of capital intensity, layout of plant, control systems, etc., in all the countries in which they operate. Others deliberately customise their facilities to suit local conditions in each nation, e.g. by using relatively labour-intensive techniques in low-wage areas. Standardisation normally involves the use of specialised equipment designed for long production runs, as opposed to multifunction machines that make items in batches. A related issue is specialisation versus diversification of operations in particular countries. Diversification enables the firm to respond quickly to changes in demand in local markets, but could result in higher costs of production.

Advantages to standardisation of production methods include the following:

(a) Interchangeability of components across plants and the ability to shift production between countries easily and quickly.

(b) Less need for production planning and design, as much of this will be a straight repetition of previous activities.

(c) Simplicity of the comparison of the performances of production units in various countries.

(d) Less worldwide stockholding and more efficient inventory management at the international level.

(e) The capacity to transfer technical support staff between plants, since they will already be familiar with all the equipment and working methods being applied.

(f) Transfer of technical knowledge and improved methods for operating the common equipment found in all units.

Further benefits are that the parent firm can have a simple organisation structure (*see* Chapter 13), that procurement procedures (*see* **5**) can be standardised and centralised, and that the company's worldwide logistics can be consolidated into a single system. Also the establishment of new plants is facilitated as experience of installing the necessary equipment and procedures will already have been accumulated in other regions. Standardised designs and production methods can be quickly implemented. Disadvantages to standardisation are that production costs may be higher than necessary in certain countries (due to the use of inappropriate methods relative to local resources – availability of very cheap labour for example); host country government investment grants and subsidies might be lost through not installing specific types of grant-attracting capital equipment; and local labour forces might not be able to cope with the company's standardised technology. Note moreover that local technical standards and employee safety requirements might necessitate the customisation of the production techniques applied in specific subsidiaries.

3. Robotics and flexible manufacturing

Computerisation and the use of robots have revolutionised manufacturing and enabled a wider range of items to be produced within the same factory. Specialisation of tasks, standardisation of output and long production runs to secure economies of scale are in many cases no longer necessary in order to reduce manufacturing costs. This is crucially significant because today's circumstances demand fast responses to rapidly changing environments, close attention to quality, customer-driven product design and characteristics, a wide range of models to place before customers, and speed of delivery as well as an attractive price. Increasing international competition has resulted in consumers throughout the world being presented with numerous product options. MNCs must therefore be more customer oriented than in the past and willing rapidly to adapt their outputs to meet consumer requirements.

Flexible manufacturing

A flexible manufacturing system comprises a collection of computer-controlled machine tools and transport and handling systems, all integrated *via* the use of a master computer. This enables the manufacture of small batches of output each modified to suit the requirements of particular market segments, while continuing to obtain manufacturing economies of scale. The essential advantage of flexible manufacturing is that it enables new product specifications to be implemented immediately, thus allowing frequent and rapid modifications to output for different orders (necessary to satisfy the needs of various markets and consumer categories). It becomes possible to implement dozens (even hundreds) of alterations in product specification simply through reprogramming factory robots – as opposed to having to retrain manual workers. Robots, moreover, can work at levels of intensity and accuracy not physically possible when the work is done by humans.

Use of robots and flexible manufacturing enables the MNC to attack small market niches in specific countries by adapting a basic product to satisfy local tastes. The firm can use sub-assemblies of components from several of its own subsidiaries, thus enhancing its attempts to optimise operations at the global level. Overall performance can be improved *via* rapid responses to new market opportunities as they arise in various parts of the world. Note however how flexible manufacturing has increased the capacities of small host country businesses to compete effectively against MNC outputs, eroding the technological dominance of MNCs in a number of nations and industries while increasing the market shares of small local enterprises.

4. Contract manufacturing

Contract manufacturing is an important alternative to direct foreign investment (*see* Chapter 9), licensing (*see* 11:6), and export of domestic production. With contract manufacture the MNC places orders with local foreign businesses for the production of goods which it then sells locally or exports. Local manufacture can be dovetailed to the needs of local distribution arrangements and numerous cost savings may be obtained. A 'home-grown' image is attached to the goods, and delivery and customer service mechanisms should improve. Further advantages to contract manufacture include:

- easy withdrawal from markets that do not live up to expectations
- not having to invest large sums of money in capital equipment
- the potential to undertake large-scale operations from a small capital base
- avoidance of involvement in industrial relations with foreign manufacturing workforces.

Contract manufacture can only occur, of course, if foreign firms with the skills and capacity to undertake contracts operate within relevant areas. It is particularly suitable for companies with high-level marketing skills and facilities but little experience of physical production, or where:

- existing production facilities are overloaded
- there is a shortage of suitable licenses in foreign markets
- high tariffs or other barriers to imports apply to the country concerned.

Problems with contract manufacture include the difficulties of monitoring and maintaining quality levels, of protecting any intellectual property embodied within the manufacturing item, and preventing the other firm setting up in competition (perhaps covertly) once it is has acquired expertise in making the product. Note moreover that the company to which the contract is awarded may require substantial technical back-up, possibly extending to the training of its employees.

5. International procurement

Effective procurement policies will ensure the arrival of the right inputs, at the right time, in the correct quantities at the most competitive price. A crucial decision that needs to be taken is whether to set up a centralised purchasing office to buy in bulk for subsidiaries throughout the world; leave procurement to local units; or use a mixture of central and local purchasing, with some items being bought locally and others by a central purchasing facility (Fagan 1991; Kotabe 1993). Centralised sourcing is more likely, perhaps, for basic items that can be used in an unmodified form in subsidiaries in all countries, and in firms based on continuous-flow technologies. A centralised international purchasing unit can be organised according to types of material purchased, or by particular areas of operation. In the former case, each purchasing officer will buy just one variety of product, thus developing intimate knowledge of the category of item and its worldwide suppliers. Otherwise, purchasing officers will supply all the requirements of specific subsidiaries or production operations, covering many different product categories. Staff will collect current price lists, catalogues, details of delivery times, and data on material availability. The unit's managers should be capable of obtaining emergency supplies at short notice (even at significantly higher procurement cost), and will constantly be on the lookout for new sources of supply and cheaper, better, or quicker deliveries (Swamidass 1993).

Advantages to centralisation include the high discounts available on very large orders, the ability of head office purchasing staff to seek out the best suppliers on the global level, and the immense bargaining power possessed by a big MNC's centralised purchasing office. The MNC's worldwide stockholding levels should diminish; the scheduling of deliveries can be centrally controlled. Note also that apart from advantages relating to purchase price, bulk buying allows an MNC to specify minimum quality standards and perhaps even design specifications. Centralised systems moreover can apply common administrative procedures and documentation to all buying activities. Close liaison between a central purchasing unit and the MNC's subsidiaries is essential – buyers not immediately connected with specific subsidiaries may be tempted to substitute cheaper but inferior goods for those really required. Centralised purchasing officers should never ignore subsidiaries' requests for supplies of a particular type simply because of procurement expediency.

With decentralised procurement, staff in local subsidiaries who possess detailed knowledge of immediate requirements place orders without reference to a central control. The method is quick and convenient, but does not allow bulk purchases; and higher prices may be paid through ignorance of alternative sources. Decentralised buying enables subsidiaries to obtain the inputs best suited to their requirements, and local managers can use their detailed knowledge of local business conditions to negotiate favourable supply contracts with local firms. Responses to changing market situations can be fast and effective.

Choice of system

Whether an MNC should have a centralised or decentralised procurement system should depend on a number of factors, as follows:

(a) Host country local content rules (*see* 9:8), which might require a MNC's subsidiary to purchase a certain value of its inputs from local sources.

(b) The technical complexity of the inputs to be purchased.

(c) Economic and political stability of host nations. Local sourcing is less appropriate within volatile environments.

(d) Import duties on items transported to subsidiaries from other parts of the world.

(e) Extent of currency exchange controls in host nations. Stringent controls might prevent a subsidiary from paying for imported inputs in hard currency.

(f) Whether the staff of the MNC's subsidiaries possess the importing skills necessary to obtain supplies from other countries.

6. Make or buy decisions

Large multinational companies have the choice of making their own component inputs or buying them from other firms. In the former case the MNC needs to decide whether to produce the item in the same country as that in which it will be used, or in another country followed by its export to the user nation. A firm that produces its own components enjoys complete control over their specification, design, quality and time of delivery. Also, there is no profit margin as with supplies purchased from outside. External suppliers however will normally have produced far more units of output than those delivered to the individual purchasing firm, and thus will experience scale economies (and hence lower costs) not possible in firms producing their own components. Moreover, internal production of supplies often requires additional investments in manufacturing plant, and extra labour might have to be employed. A firm could invest heavily in plant and equipment needed for component manufacture only to find that outside firms offer these components for sale at prices lower than internal production costs.

Factors influencing the make/buy decision include:

- Currency exchange rates between various nations.
- Production costs in different locations.
- Quality levels of alternative suppliers.
- How quickly inputs need to be delivered.
- Comparisons of foreign and local firms' prices, product features, technical support and after-sales service, reliability and (where appropriate) ability to supply on a continuous basis.

- The extent to which a particular input is crucial for the firm's survival.
- Local content requirements.
- Whether internal economies of scale in the production of inputs are possible.
- The number of external suppliers of the input. If there is but a handful of supplying firms then the incentive to make the item internally increases.
- The number of buyers of the item relative to the number of sellers. Oligopolistic situations mean that suppliers can increase their prices to very high levels following an expansion of market demand. If conversely there are many suppliers and few buyers then competition should ensure that prices remain stable (or even fall).
- Set-up costs for each production run.
- The need to protect intellectual property. For example, the staff of an outside firm commissioned to supply highly specialised components might be able to infer the characteristics of the main product to which the component is an input, and the purchasing company might want to keep these details secret.
- Whether management wishes to maintain continuity of employment for the firm's workers.
- Investment grants, subsidies and tax allowances possibly available from national governments for installing and using the machinery needed to make components in-house.

Products that are most likely to be purchased are:

- Labour-intensive items that require large amounts of unskilled labour, as the latter is much cheaper in certain parts of the world.
- Simple products the design, specifications and product technologies of which are unlikely to change over time.
- Items for which internal company demand is unpredictable, so that it becomes useful to be able to purchase the product 'off-the-shelf' rather than having to set up intermittent production runs.
- Products with numerous suppliers. Hence strikes and/or other disruptions in particular outside firms will not prevent the purchasing company's schedules from being met.

Advantages to purchasing inputs from abroad rather than locally are that the most suitable and cost-effective items may be procured, and that contacts with a wide range of suppliers can be developed (so that the purchasing firm does not become overly reliant on too small a number of outside businesses). On the other hand, it has been argued that the just-in-time (JIT) procurement and production methods (see below) increasingly used by multinational business make it imperative to source many inputs locally, rather than importing them from abroad.

7. Just-in-time methods

In a JIT production control system, work is planned so that each production unit delivers to the next unit precisely the input it requires in order to proceed with the next stage of manufacture (or processing) and delivers the input just in time for the work to begin. In consequence, few if any stocks of inputs are carried, and there is no bunching of production lines or queues anywhere in the system.

The method requires precise scheduling of raw materials procurement, production processing and despatch. And there has to be a predictable daily demand throughout the entire sequence of manufacture, with minimal change over time and extremely reliable equipment. Moreover, successful application of JIT methods implies the need to simplify products and rationalise product lines to avoid having to carry numerous different components and other input stocks.

Applied to purchasing, the JIT philosophy implies frequent, regular, small deliveries combined with long-term contracts with supplying firms. Hence, purchasing staff spend little time looking for the best deal for each order and instead devote their attention to helping suppliers improve the design and quality of inputs. Since JIT methods demand the uninterrupted supply of materials and input components to the manufacturing firm, foreign sourcing creates significant risks for the purchaser. Long journeys from foreign supply points may be involved, and the longer and more complex the journey the greater the likelihood of delay and disruption. Also JIT requires the regular arrival of small batches of items (in order to minimise average holdings of inventory), and foreign suppliers may not be willing to despatch small consignments to customers abroad. Exchange rate fluctuations, moreover, will frequently alter the import price of foreign supplies.

8. Location of production operations

A major characteristic of MNCs is their ability to transfer production between nations. Host governments of the countries in which operations are terminated dislike this intensely (as it increases unemployment and weakens the local technological infrastructure), but there is little they can do. Relocation of activities from one country to another creates problems for the MNC itself, however, including:

(a) The need to start a new business or expand and reorganise an existing subsidiary in another nation.

(b) A fresh configuration of transport and procurement costs.

(c) Possible changes in employment protection and other business laws in the new host country which remove the cost advantages of the original decision to relocate.

(d) The likelihood that a new start-up in a foreign country will require the importation of capital equipment into the host country. Government restrictions on firms' abilities to import capital equipment can create difficulties in this regard. Also the maintenance of complex capital equipment could be problematic in certain countries.

(e) The fact that continuity in the supply of electricity cannot be guaranteed in some areas.

Choice of location

A firm could attempt to serve all its foreign markets from plants in just one or two countries, or establish specialised manufacturing units in various states (each making a particular product), or have foreign manufacturing subsidiaries that produce multiple items for diverse international markets. Accordingly, an MNC must balance the lower costs available in some countries against the possible need to transport goods over long distances and perhaps lack of skill among workers in low-cost nations. Other factors affecting the location decision include:

- the availability of natural resources in various regions
- possibilities of foreign governments imposing controls on the repatriation of profits and/or the availability of foreign exchange
- industrial and commercial infrastructures within specific countries (roads, power, communications, etc.)
- levels of import duties and other protective measures in particular markets
- ease of access to new technologies
- rents and land prices in different areas
- availability of government grants, loans, tax reliefs and subsidies
- extents of business services industries in particular countries (marketing services, consultants, financial services, etc.)
- the desirability of projecting a local image
- the sizes and profitablities of local markets
- degrees of political and other forms of risk
- labour productivity
- local availabilities of skilled workers, and technical and managerial personnel
- stability or otherwise of industrial relations within various countries
- possibly the desire to threaten rival firms on their own territory in certain nations.

Much depends on the nature of the firm's product and the technology used in its supply or manufacture. Items that absorb large amounts of natural resources might usefully be made in countries abundant in these resources (although in practice this is frequently not the case – materials are shipped long distances to heavily industrialised regions). Firms with products that require employees possessing a wide range of technical skills are likely to locate in developed countries which have extensive education and vocational training systems. If the supply or manufacture of a product needs just one or a few skills then the producing company could locate in a low-wage nation and train local workers in the requisite competencies. Items that can be produced using unskilled labour can be made in whichever low-wage country has an industrial infrastructure capable of supporting the firm's operations. Note however that large MNCs are sometimes capable of providing their own infrastructure services (electricity generation, road constructions, etc.) so that wage costs might be the dominant determinant of where to locate plant.

Notwithstanding the above, no specific sets of factors comprehensively explain MNC's location decisions. Firms with similar characteristics and supplying the same type of product operate in widely disparate countries and economic environments. It seems that the processes behind location decisions are highly complex, and that a multitude of factors can affect outcomes. Locational disadvantages in some respects could be more than offset by advantages in others. Bad management and lack of know-how can wipe out country-specific cost benefits. Equally, high calibre entrepreneural skills might enable a firm to compete successfully in a high-cost location.

9. Internationalisation of research and technical development

Research and development (R&D) concerns the acquisition of new technical knowledge, particularly regarding new products, processes, materials and working methods. Activities might be initiated by an MNC's marketing staff (having identified new consumer demands) or by production personnel as they seek new methods of manufacture. 'Pure' research is normally funded by the state or an entire industry. Its aims are exploratory and very general; immediately applicable results are not expected. Applied research, in contrast, investigates specific practical questions. Applied work is typically initiated and paid for by the individual company. The aim of applied research is quick improvement of a particular situation. 'Development' means the practical application of the results of research.

The need for R&D arises from the dynamic nature of contemporary business and the inescapable fact in many international commercial situations that materials and competitors' outputs are constantly improving, leading to a sharp reduction in the average life of the typical product. Extensive R&D spending implies the needs for large markets (to absorb the costs of heavy research expenditure). It also carries the danger of triggering 'R&D wars' as competitors respond to a firm's innovative behaviour in international markets. Key MNC decisions concerning R&D include:

- the minimum returns that must result from R&D projects in a prespecified time period if the projects are not to be terminated
- whether R&D personnel are to be involved in the determination of the MNC's overall corporate strategy
- whether to undertake basic or applied research, or a mixture of the two (and if so then in what proportions).

Basic strategic options are as follows:

(a) Purchase patents and know-how from external sources.

(b) Seek to invent entirely new products in-house.

(c) Commission other organisations to invent new products.

(d) Improve existing products.

(e) Engage outside bodies to develop existing products.

Foreign-based R&D

Host countries often put pressure on multinational companies to locate R&D activities alongside their production facilities. This should improve the overall technological capacity of the host nation *and* help the MNC in question gain a competitive edge in the local market (Cheng 1993). Further advantages to undertaking R&D abroad are that:

(a) The process of technology transfer from the parent MNC to its foreign subsidiary is facilitated.

(b) Products and processes can be developed to suit local conditions.

(c) Foreign R&D units can provide technical services to local customers.

(d) Specialist knowledge and skills that might only be available in a particular foreign country can be utilised.

(e) Employees of the foreign R&D unit will understand the specific needs of the local market.

(f) Substantial state investment grants and subsidies might be available for research-based activities.

Problems with establishing a foreign R&D facility include the following:

(a) The resulting research unit might not be large enough to be economically viable.

(b) Necessary technical skills may not be available in the local population. This is a major problem in underdeveloped countries that have few institutes of higher education.

(c) It could require the reorganisation of the administrative structure of the entire company, in order to relate production and marketing activities to localised R&D.

10. International quality standards

Adherence to internationally recognised quality assurance (QA) standards is an increasingly important tool for gaining fresh markets in both developed and developing countries. Quality assurance concerns the total system needed to assure customers that certain minimum quality standards will be satisfied within the supplying firm. Formal QA standards have been drafted by various bodies (including the British Standards Institute's BS 5750) which specify that supplying firms must implement definite procedures for ensuring that appropriate 'quality environments' are maintained, e.g. that the tools used on certain jobs be of a particular type and that only qualified and certified staff be employed on certain projects.

A QA system might invite supplying firms to improve as well as provide contracted items, and themselves to initiate alterations in the appearance, design or durability of requisitioned products. Suppliers need therefore to know the purposes of the articles they are invited to produce, and the operational circumstances of their use. Hence, a clear statement of purpose by the purchaser – leaving technical details (including perhaps the choice of input materials) to the discretion of the supplying firm – might have greater long-term value than precise and detailed specifications of weights, sizes, machine tolerances, etc.

ISO 9000

BS 5750 is the UK version of the international quality assurance standard ISO 9000, which itself is based in large part on BS 5750. ISO 9000 is a detailed and extensive document with several parts and appendices. It requires the supplier to demonstrate its ability to design and supply products in predetermined ways. Apart from design procedures, the specification covers the supplier's own procurement systems: its inspection and testing methods, the means by which customers may verify its claimed quality systems, how customers can check the supplier's records and other documents relating to quality procedures and how customers may confirm the nature and extent of quality-related training given to the supplier's staff. The aim of ISO 9000 is to provide suppliers with a means for obtaining certificated approval that their quality management systems are up to scratch. Customers throughout the world may then have confidence in a company's ability (i) to deliver goods of a prespecified quality and (ii) to maintain the quality of its output at a consistent level. This should increase the saleability of the firm's outputs. Further advantages to ISO 9000 certification (which is granted by national standards authorities, such as the UK's BSI, France's ANFOR, or Germany's DIN organisation) are that it:

- demonstrates the company's commitment to quality
- requires the standardisation of quality procedures throughout the organisation
- facilitates the identification of problem areas
- improves the image of the firm
- may increase operational efficiency
- leads to greater awareness of customer needs
- can cause staff to be better motivated.

Problems with obtaining ISO 9000 accreditation for an MNC's subsidiaries in disparate nations include the financial costs of altering (perhaps perfectly reasonable) existing quality control methods to meet ISO 9000 standards (these costs could be enormous relative to the overall improvement in quality that results) and thereafter of maintaining the new systems, and the fact that firms seeking ISO 9000 accreditation *themselves* determine the level of quality of output. ISO 9000 applies to the procedures for maintaining a certain quality level, even if the quality of the final output is intentionally low.

11. Time-based competition

'Time-based' manufacturing strategies are those which focus on the rapid development of new models. In other words, MNCs might prefer to produce new products faster rather than make them better or more cheaply. The rationale for this is that in order to succeed in today's highly competitive world a new product not only needs to possess novel and attractive features; it must also be introduced quickly. Note how product life cycles are in many countries shortening significantly for the majority of product categories, with large numbers of product offerings now being judged as much on novelty and fashion as on any other purchasing criterion (Stalk 1990). Firms' capacities to engage in time-based competition are greatly facilitated by the use of flexible manufacturing (*see* 3), which means that they can produce small batches of items customised to meet the requirements of specific groups of customers. Companies employing flexible manufacturing do not need to rely on economies of scale from mass production in order to obtain competitive advantage. Hence frequent introduction to a market of small outputs of alternatives of a core product may be feasible and what the market requires.

Advantages claimed for time-based competition include the following:

(a) Accelerating the pace of innovation can generate fresh ideas and thinking that lead to important new inventions.

(b) Firms can behave opportunistically, exploiting lucrative market segments as they appear.

(c) Speeding up the production process generally leads to savings in inventory and working capital.

(d) Parallel sequencing of product development and production activities is often possible.

(e) As research and technical development is so costly, the shorter the period the firm is spending money on this the better. Sometimes an item is 'good enough' even though further technical research on it would be beneficial. Also there is a tendency in certain companies to overload their product research and development departments with too many disparate projects.

Possible disadvantages to time-based competition are that it could lead to inadequate market research and product testing and poor quality output. Also the cost of rapid new product development could be extremely high, and the administrative procedures necessary for time-based competition might be extremely complex and/or overstretch the organisation's resources.

Progress test 14

1. Define operations management.

2. What are the main items that need to be included in an international operations management strategy?

3. List the main advantages of the international standardisation of production methods and facilities.

4. What is meant by the term 'flexible manufacturing'?

5. List the advantages and disadvantages of contract manufacturing. In what circumstances is the use of contract manufacturing to be recommended?

6. What are the benefits to a multinational company of the centralised procurement of inputs?

7. List six factors that a firm should take into account when deciding to make rather than purchase its input components.

8. Explain the implications of just-in-time production systems for the procurement policies of multinational businesses.

9. What factors should influence the choice of location for a firm's manufacturing operations?

10. List the major decisions that a multinational company has to take in relation to research and technical development.

11. What is ISO 9000 and what is its purpose?

12. Explain the term 'time-based competition'. What are the advantages of time-based competition?

15

INTERNATIONAL FINANCIAL MANAGEMENT

THE INTERNATIONAL FINANCIAL ENVIRONMENT

1. The international monetary system

The role of the International Monetary Fund in the development of the post-Second World War international monetary system was briefly discussed in 1:9. Today's international monetary system is based on flexible exchange rates, but with substantial government intervention on foreign exchange markets intended to maintain currency exchange rates at levels compatible with the realisation of national economic goals. Thus, market forces of supply and demand for particular currencies determine currency prices, with national governments themselves buying large amounts of their own currencies in order to bid up the price when this is considered too low (using the country's stock of reserves of foreign currencies to finance the purchase), and selling when the exchange rate is deemed to be excessive (hence increasing the country's export prices with consequent problems for the balance of payments). At the time of writing the majority of European Union countries are attempting to fix their exchange rates against each other, while allowing them to float against the rest of the world. This is occurring through:

- National EU monetary authorities intervening in foreign exchange markets so as to keep their exchange rates at predetermined parities with other member countries (within certain limits); *and*
- Member nations depositing 20 per cent of their international reserves with the European Monetary Co-operation Fund (EMCF) on a three-month basis in return for access to credit facilities for financing balance of payments imbalances with other member states.

The aim is to have fixed European currency exchange rates immediately prior to the formation of the common European currency (see **4**). Unfortunately, countries regularly leave and then re-enter the system as their circumstances alter, e.g. in consequence of heavy speculation driving down a currency's value to very low levels.

Theories of exchange rate determination

To the extent that exchange rates are permitted to find their own market levels, the question arises as to what exactly determines the value of a particular currency. A country's short-run balance of payments situation obviously plays an important role, as does currency speculation. It is known, moreover, that differences in interest rates and differences in inflation rates between any pair of countries will exert powerful influences on movements in the currency rate of exchange between the two nations, as follows:

(a) *Differences between interest rates.* If one country has a rate of interest significantly higher than the other then financial investors in the low interest rate nation will close down their interest earning accounts, convert the money into the high interest rate country's currency and make new deposits in the high interest nation. This sale of the low interest country's currency will drive down its price until there is no financial benefit to be had from the relocation of interest earning deposits, because so few units of the high interest nation's currency can be obtained when making the conversion. Note how the slide in the low interest country's exchange rate (which makes imports more expensive thus contributing to domestic inflation) may prompt its government to raise the rate of interest in that nation.

(b) *Differences between inflation rates.* Suppose that the rate of inflation in the first country is significantly above that in the second. Exports from the former nation to the latter will fall, because the prices of the goods exported are so high. Hence the high inflation country will experience a balance of payments deficit, the other country will run a surplus, and the latter's exchange rate will rise. This proposition is referred to as the 'purchasing power parity theorem'.

In practice changes in exchange rates are very difficult to forecast accurately because governments regularly intervene on foreign exchange markets deliberately to distort the influences of supply and demand for their currencies.

2. Fixed versus flexible exchange rates

Whether it is better for the world economy to have fixed or flexible currency exchange rates is a much discussed question. The system established *via* the International Monetary Fund in 1947 (otherwise known as the 'Bretton Woods' system after the town in New Hampshire, USA, which hosted the meeting that set up the IMF) was based on fixed exchange rates, which at that time were considered superior given the experience of the widespread disruptions seemingly caused by flexible exchange rates during the 1930s. However, the world moved towards flexible exchange rates in the 1970s and 1980s, although particular groupings of countries (notably the European Union) have attempted to operate fixed exchange rate systems within specific trading areas.

Arguments in favour of flexible exchange rates are as follows.

(a) The forces of supply and demand should create an objectively correct rate of exchange for any given currency without the need for government intervention.

(b) Countries are not required to hold stocks of international reserves of gold and foreign currencies which in a fixed exchange rate system would be used to intervene on foreign exchange markets when their exchange rates were falling.

Reserve holding has a cost: the money could instead be used for industrial and/or infrastructure investment, for the provision of better public services, etc.

(c) Governments do not have to spend money on the administrative bureaucracies and information-gathering activities that otherwise would be necessary to manage interventions on foreign exchange markets.

(d) The state does not need to have a 'balance of payments policy' as such. Policy decisions relating to the balance of payments (particularly the mix of policies appropriate for correcting balance of payments deficits) are taken by politicians and civil servants, and are frequently wrong. The cost to the nation of bad decisions in this field can be enormous, as the resulting measures (tax and interest rate rises, reductions in public spending and so on) affect all aspects of domestic economic activity. In a fixed rate system civil servants are required to estimate the 'correct' currency exchange rate for the country concerned: a seemingly impossible task in view of the complexity of the (numerous and fast changing) variables that might be relevant. With flexible exchange rates, conversely, the interplay of market forces determines the rate of exchange in an objective and politically neutral manner.

(e) Nations can pursue their own independent policy objectives without having to worry about the effects on currency exchange rates. Suppose for example that a government decides to 'go for growth', seeking to expand domestic incomes and employment through tax reductions, cuts in interest rates and increases in public expenditure. This will generate higher spending on imports and hence a balance of payments current account deficit. Also the lower interest rate will cause foreign investors to deposit their money in other countries, so that financial capital leaves the nation. Accordingly the exchange rate will then begin to fall and, under a fixed rate system, the authorities will have to use their international reserves to enter the foreign exchange markets and purchase domestic currency in order to bid up its price. But a country only has a certain amount of international reserves, and when they start to run out the government must introduce economic policies designed to remove the underlying balance of payments deficit that is causing the drain on reserves. Hence, taxes and interest rates are increased and other deflationary measures have to be imposed, effectively *reversing* the initial growth strategy! With flexible currency exchange rates, conversely, a payments deficit caused by an economic expansion will result in a fall in the exchange rate of the expanding country, so that its export prices fall and its imports become more expensive. Exports should rise and imports go down until a new stable exchange rate is established. At this new exchange rate domestic consumers will be worse off in that they have to pay more for imported goods, but the government's expansionary economic policies do not have to be terminated.

(f) In principle a country should not be affected by an economic depression occurring in one of its major trading partners. Under fixed exchange rates a slump in one country will reduce domestic inflation and cause firms to shed labour, cut costs and rationalise production systems so that export prices to other nations will become highly competitive. This might result in a serious balance of payments deficit in another country which, in consequence, will have to deflate its economy in order to stabilise its currency exchange rate. With flexible rates, however, the slump in the first economy will lead to a rise in its exchange rate, and will not automatically transmit the depression to other nations.

(g) The activities of currency speculators in a flexible exchange rate system should be beneficial rather than damaging. During the years that exchange rates were fixed, certain currencies (notably sterling) were persistently weak and had to struggle to maintain their predetermined parities. The balances of payments of the countries involved were frequently in (heavy) deficit and there was constant danger of formal (and internationally agreed) devaluation. This presented currency speculators with a 'one way option', in that there was absolutely no possibility that such currencies would rise in value, but a high probability that they would fall. Not surprisingly, therefore, there were periodic waves of speculative selling of weak currencies, sometimes resulting in their devaluation. With flexible rates, so the argument goes, speculation should be stabilising, since in order to make money the speculator must buy a currency when its price is low and sell when the price is high. Hence, speculation will bid up the exchange rate of a currency the price of which is objectively too low, and bid down the price when it is too high according to rational criteria.

(h) Exchange rates adjust quickly to changing circumstances. This prevents the accumulation of large balance of payments deficits the removal of which will require harsh remedial action in the longer period.

(i) A sudden fall in the exchange rate immediately alerts a nation's government to the fact that something is wrong. Flexible rates provide the authorities with a fast and effective economic information system.

(j) There is no *a priori* reason to suppose that a flexible exchange rate should *of itself* be unstable. To the extent that significant fluctuations occur they result from instability in the underlying economy of the country concerned, and it is these matters that need to be addressed, rather than the question of the exchange rate.

Problems with a system of flexible exchange rates include the following:

(a) *Instability and uncertainty of internal prices.* As a country's exchange rate fluctuates so too does its domestic rate of inflation, consequent to changes in import prices.

(b) *Increased costs of international transactions.* Exporters who price their outputs in foreign currencies cannot be sure how much the sales of their products will be worth in terms of domestic currency. Hence they need to take out forward cover (*see* **13**) against their foreign currency revenues. Importers too must hedge against the possibility of having to pay more for foreign purchases in consequence of exchange rate depreciations. All this costs money and imposes much administrative work on firms.

(c) *Continuing decline in the balance of payments.* A fall in the exchange rate of a country that imports large amounts of 'necessary' goods (i.e. basic items that the country cannot do without – food or energy for example) can be disastrous for the nation, since these goods will still have to be imported regardless of their higher prices.

(d) *Competitive devaluations resulting from many countries attempting to expand their economies simultaneously.* The mechanism outlined in **(e)** above is useless if several nations all decide to implement growth policies. As exchange rates fall the resulting increases in import prices have dire inflationary consequences. A reduction in one country's exchange rate means a rise in that of at least one of its trading partners. Exporters in the latter will thus have difficulty in selling their goods abroad, with consequent unemployment. Hence the country's government might retaliate by introducing policies intended to lower its exchange rate, perhaps triggering a series of competitive devaluations leading to soaring inflation in all participating countries.

(e) *Possibilities for destabilising speculation (see [g] above).* Not every speculator buys low and sells high (otherwise *all* speculators would amass unlimited fortunes); mistakes occur and their effects on particular currencies can be devastating.

(f) *Reduced capital inflows.* Uncertainty of exchange rate levels could discourage foreign investment.

(g) *Loss of an important benchmark against which national governments can anchor their economic policies.* Defence of the exchange rate can be used to justify politically unpopular but necessary economic policy decisions. Flexible exchange rates arguably allow the avoidance of deflations that should not be avoided.

(h) *Encouragement of governments to pursue their national self-interests* and adopt 'beggar-my-neighbour' policies, leading in the long term to higher inflation and unemployment than otherwise would be necessary.

There are, of course, counter-arguments and counter-counter-arguments to all the above-mentioned propositions.

3. Common currencies

Endeavours by countries to implement fixed exchange rate systems can be regarded in a sense as attempts to achieve some of the benefits that would accrue if a single currency were used for international transactions: stability, certainty, easy transfer of resources, etc. There are however obvious differences between a system of fixed exchange rates and a single unified currency, namely the administrative costs and inconveniences of having to convert one currency into another, the risk of devaluation, and the fact that tariffs may be payable as goods move across national frontiers. In what circumstances should groups of countries seek to create a common currency for use in all member states? The European Union has already taken the decision to introduce a single currency by the end of the decade, and a number of other regional economic groupings (*see* 1:5) are actively considering this matter.

Optimum currency areas

Much of the debate on the desirability of having a common currency within particular regions focuses on whether these regions constitute 'optimum' currency areas. According to some writers (see for example Mundell 1961; Magnifico 1973; Barrell 1990), internal factor mobility and regional wage/price flexibility are the crucial determinants of whether a common currency area will succeed. If one country within the area is prosperous and experiencing inflation while another has price stability but is economically depressed, then a decision by the currency area's monetary authorities to raise interest rates in order to cure the inflation occurring in the prosperous country will, because the interest rates rises will apply throughout the common currency area, increase unemployment in the depressed nation and hence make that country's overall economic situation significantly worse! Thus, labour and capital must be able and willing to move from poor to wealthy areas hence equalising unemployment and economic growth rates in various regions.

Any decision by the central monetary authority will make some regions better off while harming others, so that wages and prices in disadvantaged areas must fall relative to those in prosperous regions in order to attract new business start-ups and to encourage additional capital investment by existing firms. Otherwise, factor immobility and wage/price rigidity will result in endemic mass unemployment and low living standards in those parts of the common currency area the economic interests of which have not been prioritised by the region's Central Bank. Unfortunately, national attitudes towards what represents an appropriate inflation/unemployment trade-off differ considerably from state to state. Some national governments prefer a higher rate of inflation but with more jobs; others have price stability as the dominant policy objective. Inevitably, therefore, some areas are sure to be left with unwanted inflation/ unemployment situations.

Advocates of common international currencies assert, however, that their advantages for industry and commerce are overwhelming and not necessarily related to wage/price flexibility or factor mobility concerns. Governments of all nation states face dilemmas *vis-à-vis* the regional effects of central economic policy decisions. All that differs in relation to an international common currency is the magnitude of the results. Losers must be compensated by gainers and helped to mitigate adverse effects. Within any common currency area (such as the present United Kingdom of England, Scotland, Northern Ireland and Wales) the central government may tax its citizens and then channel resources – in the form of grants, subsidiaries, preferential interest rate arrangements and other forms of regional development aid – towards those areas badly affected by central monetary and other economic policies. Thus, to the extent that factors of production are not perfectly mobile and wages and prices are in practice inflexible it becomes necessary for a central governmental authority for the entire common currency area to tax the area's residents in order to raise the funds necessary to assist depressed regions.

4. The single European currency

All possibilities for speculation against particular European currencies will cease the moment a common currency is introduced. All prices will be quoted in single currency terms so that consumers within the common currency area will be able directly to compare in the same currency unit the prices of similar items in various states. A single currency means pan-European price labelling and packaging, and the absence of currency conversion costs for businesses in nations that are members of the scheme. Companies outside the common currency area (CCA), conversely, will need separate prices, packaging and labelling for domestic and CCA markets, and must incur the (substantial) expense of currency conversion. CCA firms engaged in cross-border trade will not have to maintain temporary foreign exchange balances: use of a common currency will enable cash received from several different countries to be lumped together instantly and without conversion and deposited in the highest interest earning country, and cross-border cash transactions will be executed faster on average than in the past. Firms operating within the CCA will experience easier comparison of input costs relating to suppliers in various CCA countries and be better able to assess potential customers' creditworthiness. All published accounts, reports from credit factoring companies, etc., will be evaluated in the same currency units thus facilitating evaluation. Another benefit will be improved access to equity finance for medium-sized businesses wishing to expand.

Share prices in CCA companies will be quoted in the same currency units everywhere, facilitating pan-European share trading and access to CCA Stock Exchanges by investors and companies throughout the common currency area, a major advantage to businesses seeking external funding. Also the fact that having a common currency will expedite intra-CCA cash transfers will lead perhaps to far wider *pan-European* ownership of company shares than previously has been the case. Common currency company reports, share price quotations and flotations will enable investors to compare directly the financial performances of enterprises in all CCA nations.

Importing costs might fall for certain CCA companies, as the single European currency is sure to be widely used for financing international trade outside the European common currency area. Many non-EU exporters (especially in Eastern Europe) will be prepared to accept the new currency in payment of invoices, so that firms within the currency area will be saved the expense of raising foreign exchange for non-CCA transactions. Businesses will be able to record and compare all accounting values in one unit, making for easy identification of the most costly and the most profitable activities in various markets. Hence there will be less need for book-keeping for companies with transactions in several CCA states, since no foreign exchange calculations will be necessary. Clearer and better information on competitors should become available.

Consequences for human resources management

Wages, national insurance and superannuation contributors will be expressed in the same monetary units across the CCA so that each employee will be able to compare his or her remuneration with that of someone doing exactly the same work in another CCA country. Disparities will be obvious, leading perhaps to demands for explanations of the differences (often due to variations in productivity between regions) and perhaps to pan-CCA management/ union collective bargaining and the cross-border harmonisation of wages within particular occupational groups. Employees in low-wage countries are likely to exert pressure on their employers to improve productivity in order to enable wages to increase. Note moreover that if unions and managements in one member nation agree extremely high wage increases, while wage deals in another member country are very low, then (productivity and all other things held equal) many firms in the former nation will go into liquidation, creating unemployment which itself exerts downward pressure on pay. Also, transparency of labour costs could induce a larger number of businesses to relocate in low-wage regions than otherwise would be the case, and the migration of labour from less prosperous to more affluent areas might be encouraged.

Business planning

Firms within the CCA should be able to plan their activities more effectively as there will be less uncertainty concerning prospective returns on foreign CCA activities. Firms will know exactly how much revenue will result from invoices issued to foreign CCA customers: there will be no need to take out expensive forward cover against the possibility of currency depreciations. Note how the risk of currency depreciation is a deterrent to cross-border long-term investment because it means that both the capital value of an investment and the flow of income generated are likely to fall in terms of domestic currency. Business planning should also benefit from the inherently stable monetary environment likely to emerge from the intended system.

The single currency will be managed by a pan-European central bank with a board comprising a politically independent president plus the governors of the national central banks of countries participating in the scheme. Thereafter, national central banks will act as local operating arms of the European central bank (ECB). All EU countries have already agreed that price stability should be the ECB's key objective. Decisions on national taxes, public spending and borrowing will remain with national governments, subject to co-ordination and guidance from the ECB. No government may spend or borrow beyond limits prescribed by formulae applied equally to all participants. Hence, interest rates should fall throughout the common currency area and fluctuations within them diminish.

5. Problems with a single European currency

It will take some time for people to become culturally attuned to using a new form of currency. For retailers, the major practical problem with the introduction of a common currency is likely to be the cost of re-equipping with new cash handling equipment. Staff training will be necessary in order to familiarise employees with new cash units, money handling arrangements, etc. Further problems that might be experienced by businesses as the common currency is introduced include:

(a) Possible labour relations difficulties as employees compare their single currency remunerations with those of workers in comparable firms in other CCA states.

(b) Fresh price labelling requirements, the cost of publishing new price lists and related promotional literature, and the consequences of changes in credit costs as national interest rates converge.

(c) Negative consumer reactions to the discovery that a firm is charging different prices for the same product in various nations.

(d) Increased competition as firms find it easier to analyse foreign competitors' performances and compare them using common criteria.

Companies in West European countries outside the CCA but which undertake large amounts of trade with CCA businesses will find their positions especially problematic. Such firms will need to incur foreign currency hedging and conversion costs and to have dual price labelling and contract documentation arrangements. It will be less convenient for CCA residents to buy from these businesses (as people living within the CCA can buy from firms using their own single currency cheques) and non-CCA firms may be ascribed a 'foreign' image. The difficulties will be compounded if a country is initially outside the CCA but shortly thereafter decides to participate in the common currency scheme, since standard money handling equipment and systems will already have been selected and implemented to suit the fast-track nations. Firms located in incoming countries will have to adopt these standards.

INTERNATIONAL CAPITAL MARKETS

6. The world's main financial markets

Most of the world's major capital markets are located in large cities such as London, New York, Tokyo, Singapore, Paris and Hong Kong. Within these cities there are concentrations of banks, stock exchanges, underwriters, currency traders, financial experts and international financial organisations. Certain centres additionally provide 'offshore' financial services in currencies other than that of the host nation. The offshore function is also undertaken in a number of small countries such as the Bahamas, the Caymen Islands, the Antilles and Bahrain. Offshore centres provide extensive facilities for foreign currency deposits and loans and supply large amounts of funds to international firms. Liberal regulatory and tax environments apply to foreign (though not necessarily to domestic) transactors in these markets.

The international bond market

A 'bond' is a document that evidences a loan to a government or to a company. Normally, bonds carry a fixed rate of interest and are redeemable after a certain number of years. A loan to a company that is secured against the company's assets is called a 'debenture'. Domestic bonds are issued by governments or companies within their own national borders and denominated in the domestic currency. 'Foreign' bonds are issued outside the borrower's country and denominated in the currency of the country in which they are sold, e.g. a UK company may sell Deutschemark denominated bonds to German lenders. The term 'Eurobond' is used to describe a bond denominated in a certain currency and placed on the European bond market by a borrower, underwritten by a syndicate of banks from different countries, and sold in several nations. For example, a UK firm might sell Deutschemark denominated bonds in France, Italy and Spain. If sufficient buyers come forward the syndicate of banks stands ready (at a price) to take whatever bonds are left over from the initial offer. Many Eurobonds are denominated in US dollars. Like the Eurocurrency market generally (see below), Eurobond issue and trading is largely unregulated. All Eurobonds are issued 'offshore' so that no national withholding taxes apply to interest payments. Purchasers of Eurobonds do not need to register their ownership with any central body. Note how this enables Eurobond holders to avoid declaring interest receipts to their national tax authorities.

7. The Eurodollar market

This began in the late 1940s when the Soviet Union and Eastern bloc countries closed their dollar accounts in the USA, for fear of confiscation. Instead they deposited their dollars with London banks, which then re-lent them to non-US residents who needed dollars to purchase imports from the US. At this time the USA was the world's economic powerhouse and the US dollar was the dominant international currency, acceptable in all countries. Hence there was a big demand for dollars to finance international transactions, so that exporters to the US were delighted to be paid in dollars rather than in their home country currency. Firms acquiring dollars would lend them to other businesses that required dollars in order to buy US products, using the London banks as an intermediary. The growth of the London Eurodollar market was phenomenal, for four main reasons:

(a) Whereas national banking systems were heavily regulated during this period, there were no government controls over the Eurodollar market. In particular there was no 'reserve requirement', i.e. every single dollar deposited in London could be onlent; banks did not have to hold back any of their dollar deposits as reserves. Hence, profit (in the form of interest) could be obtained on the total value of each deposit. Because of the high profits on Eurodollar deposits the banks were able to offer attractive rates of interest on dollar deposits, further stimulating the market.

(b) In the 1950s and 60s the US authorities restricted the rates of interest that US banks located in the US could pay on time deposits. Hence dollars were shifted to London from the US whenever US interest rates were below London Eurodollar market levels. (Note that by this time many of the London Eurodollar banks were in fact subsidiaries of US parents.) American banks lost deposits, and replenished them by borrowing dollars from London (often from their own subsidiaries) which they then onlent to US customers at (uncontrolled) higher rates of interest.

(c) In 1965 the US government introduced exchange controls and taxes which effectively prohibited the export of long-term capital from the USA. The only way in which an American firm could raise the money to invest directly in a foreign country was to borrow on the Eurodollar market and convert the dollars obtained into the currency of the relevant foreign country.

(d) The large and persistent US balance of payments deficits of the 1960s fed dollars into the world economy, some of which found their way back to the USA via the Eurodollar market. As the US dollar was at that time the major international unit of currency, acceptable throughout the world, so American importers could purchase goods from abroad and pay for them with dollars printed by the US government. Thus, US deficits provided many of the dollars which ended up on the London Eurodollar market.

The supply of Eurodollars comes from private individuals, from enterprises which have exported to the US and been paid in dollars, and private or state-owned banks and other financial institutions which wish to utilise part of their dollar reserves as Eurodollar deposits. Arguably the existence of the Eurodollar market facilitated 'hot money' flows between nations through providing a safe base currency for speculative transactions. Individual countries faced the possibility that rapid and massive liquidations of foreign holdings of their own currencies in favour of Eurodollars could occur, so that their own interest rates had to be held at levels at least equal to those available on Eurodollars. It followed that to all intents and purposes these countries lost control over their domestic monetary policies.

As the Eurodollar market developed so too did trading in other currencies outside their home countries: Eurodeutschemarks, Eurofrancs, Eurosterling, etc. This trade became known collectively as the 'Eurocurrency market'. Eurodollars constitute between 65 and 85 per cent of the total Eurocurrency market, the actual percentage fluctuating from year to year. The market is essentially unregulated.

Eurocurrency transactions are very large and involve governments, banks, multinational companies, international organisations and public sector corporations. Most deposits are short term (90 per cent have a maturity of less than six months), although Eurocurrency loans are generally for longer periods. This creates substantial risk, as Eurocurrency institutions are 'borrowing short and lending long', and thus need to rely on a continuous inflow of short-term deposits to enable them to meet their obligations. The term 'Eurocredit' is used to describe Eurocurrency borrowing with a period of maturity of more than one year. Loans are usually made at a certain percentage above the London Inter-Bank Offer Rate (LIBOR), i.e. the interest rate that banks charge each other for loans. The rate of interest charged on a particular loan will depend on the creditworthiness of the customer and the cost to the lender of arranging the transaction.

INTERNATIONAL FINANCIAL MANAGEMENT

Major issues in international financial management include:

* administration of working capital and cash flows

- selection of sources of funds
- choosing whether to centralise or decentralise financial decision making
- profit repatriation policies
- the management of foreign exchange risk.

8. Management of working capital

Working capital comprises current assets (stock, debtors and cash) minus current liabilities (typically short-term borrowings). The objectives of working capital management are to ensure that sufficient cash, inventories and short-term credit are available to support the firm's worldwide operations, while minimising the costs involved. Subsidiaries require cash in order to finance day-to-day transactions. They do not (normally) need to hold reserves, as additional cash can always be transmitted from head office if an emergency occurs. Note moreover that head office rather than the subsidiary can settle the latter's bills in appropriate circumstances.

The essential issues are (i) whether to pool money in a central location (which could be the headquarters country, or a 'tax haven' in some other part of the world) or leave cash in local subsidiaries, and (ii) whether to centralise or decentralise financial decision making.

Centralisation

The essential justification for centralised MNC financial decision making is that since multinational companies seek to maximise their profits at the global level, financial strategies and policies should be determined by a single central authority able to adopt a genuinely international perspective. Specific benefits of the centralised approach include:

(a) The ability to switch financial resources to their most profitable uses at short notice. It is important to withdraw cash from nations with high rates of inflation (which erode the purchasing power of local currencies) or where currency devaluation or the imposition of exchange controls are likely to occur.

(b) Development of specialist skills by head office financial managers.

(c) Easier cash flow forecasting for overall company operations. Head office can prepare a *company-level* cash flow forecast, facilitating the minimisation of the aggregate amount of cash necessary to finance the firm.

(d) The ability to offer to banks a single large deposit may enable the parent to obtain a higher rate of interest than would apply to numerous smaller amounts.

(e) The absence of risk of confiscation of cash balances by foreign governments.

(f) The dovetailing of the use of cash balances to the overall corporate strategy of the firm.

(g) The capacity to convert cash into earning assets more quickly. Excess liquidity should be eliminated.

(h) Improved management of currency exchange rate risk (*via* the use of financial futures for example – *see* **13**).

(i) Economies of scale in borrowing, i.e. a large MNC can borrow huge amounts in order to finance its worldwide operations and thus secure a lower interest rate from the lender.

(j) The capacity to control and co-ordinate subsidiaries' activities more easily.

(k) Possibly the more objective and professional appraisal of foreign investment projects.

Problems with centralised financial management are that:

(a) The precise financing requirements of particular subsidiaries might be overlooked by headquarters managers who are more concerned with the global picture.

(b) The morale of a subsidiary's managers might diminish, as the subsidiary has no control over its financial destiny.

(c) Application of head office financial policies might bring the firm into conflict with host country governments.

(d) Headquarters staff are likely to possess less knowledge of local capital markets than subsidiary managers.

(e) Local managers might be the best people to know which financial reporting, control and cash management systems are most appropriate for local operations.

(f) Cash flow decisions will be taken less quickly than under a decentralised system.

(g) Subsidiaries might become less flexible and competitive than if they were allowed to manage their own finances.

(h) Head office staff may be overburdened through having to plan subsidiaries' cash flow situations. Note how the centralisation of financial decision making means the preparation of three sets of financial documents: one for monitoring the subsidiary's cash flows, another for reporting current financial performance to head office, and a third for managerial decision making 'in the field'.

In practice an MNC may adopt a mixture of approaches to cash management; centralising the administration of cash emanating from certain countries while leaving some subsidiaries to manage their own financial affairs.

9. Sources of funds and the repatriation of profits

An MNC can finance its operations through equity issues and borrowing by the parent organisation (including Eurocurrency borrowings), intracompany loans and transfers among subsidiaries, or loans raised by subsidiaries from local sources. Financing subsidiaries through intra-company transfers is cheap, flexible and convenient, but not suitable if there is a high degree of political risk in the host nation (local borrowing is more appropriate in this situation). For general information on debt and equity financing, see the M&E title *Management*. In the international context the following should be noted:

(a) Borrowing in multiple national markets exposes the company to risks arising from exchange rate fluctuations.

(b) The rate of tax deducted at source on interest payments (i.e. 'withholding tax') by subsidiaries to their parent organisation differs from country to country.

(c) Some nations impose limits on the level of dividend that may be sent abroad.

(d) Share issue is normally only possible in advanced industrial countries. Developing countries rarely posses capital markets capable of supplying the necessary funds.

Local borrowing is most appropriate where there is significant exchange rate risk *vis-à-vis* the host country's currency (because borrowings in other currencies would have to be converted into that of the nation concerned), and where it is desirable to borrow locally for political reasons.

Repatriation policies

An international business can remit funds from a foreign subsidiary *via* dividends on shares, interest on loans from the parent organisation, transfer pricing (*see* 17:**13**), or through management fees paid directly to headquarters. Tax and/or exchange control considerations typically determine the precise form in which profits are repatriated. *How much* is remitted from the subsidiary to headquarters will depend on the interest rate differential between the two countries, how urgently funds are needed for operations in other parts of the world (and the costs of financing these operations from local sources), host country limits on the amounts that may be repatriated, actual and expected currency exchange rate fluctuations, the rate of inflation and the degree of political risk in the host nation. Further relevant considerations include:

- growth prospects in the host country
- costs of borrowing in the host country
- currency conversion costs
- the desirability of projecting a favourable 'local company' image to the host country's government.

10. Accounting systems

International financial management is more complex and difficult than for domestic operations in part because of differences in national accounting standards in the various countries in which an international firm does business. These differences cause problems for the company's financial information system, compounded by the need to conduct business in multiple currencies. Nevertheless, the efficient management of an MNC depends critically on the calibre of its internal accounting system. MNCs must transfer assets between nations and hence require reliable information on the natures and values of those assets. Financial reports are needed to ascertain the profitabilities of various projects, subsidiaries and types of operation; and for presentation to host country governments, shareholders and prospective investors. At the subsidiary level the system needs to generate useful information for decision making and control, and the information itself must be in a format that can be understood by local managers. Equally, the parent organisation must be able to compare meaningfully its operations in various countries and consolidate subsidiary accounts into enterprise-wide financial statements.

Subsidiary accounts are prepared according to local disclosure laws and accounting practices and enable local and head office managers to compare a subsidiary's performance with comparable firms in the local area. Another set of subsidiary accounts must then be assembled that are easily translated into the format required at the enterprise level. Consolidated company-wide accounts may have to be distributed beyond the head office country, particularly to the tax authorities of nations in which the company has branches (*see* 16:5).

National accounting standards

These vary widely from state to state, creating numerous difficulties for international businesses because accounting standards determine the basic frameworks through which companies complete transactions in various countries. The main difference in national accounting systems is between countries in which the principal purpose of financial accounting is to satisfy the requirements of government tax authorities, and nations with developed equity capital markets where meaningful published accounts are necessary in order to provide information to shareholders. Accounting regulations and practices in nations where tax considerations predominate are highly legalistic and follow government rules rather than standards established by professional accounting bodies. This makes the accountant's job more straightforward, but the depth of the financial information generated is not as extensive in these countries as in other states. A critical consequence of the distinction between the two approaches is that whereas accounts prepared for tax purposes tend to understate a company's performance in order to save tax, the reverse follows if the intention is to raise capital from external sources! This situation results in the book profits of companies in some countries (Ireland, the UK, and the Netherlands for example) consistently appearing higher on average than in other nations. Another influence on the extent of detail contained within company accounts is the role of local banks in supplying business finance, since the extensive use of bank financing reduces the impetus for firms to produce sophisticated accounts for examination by alternative investors.

Notable examples of differences in national accounting rules include the following:

(a) In some countries (Denmark, Sweden, Germany and the Netherlands for example) company accounts must reveal the extent to which any or all of a business's assets have been pledged as security against loans. This does not apply in (for instance) Luxembourg or Portugal.

(b) In the majority of nations, companies do not have to disclose their expected future obligations *vis-à-vis* the payment of retired employees' company pensions. Yet this is a formal requirement in Denmark, Ireland, Finland and Sweden.

(c) In Germany, inventions may be valued using a wide variety of methods other than the conventional 'lower of cost or market value' (which is legally necessary in the majority of nations).

(d) The book values of profits in UK firms are frequently reported as being higher than in the accounts of comparable Continental European businesses. Wider shareholding and equity financing in the UK means that companies must appear to be profitable in order to defend their share price and attract new investment. The bank and family financing of companies that is common in many other countries removes this need.

(e) 'Creative' accounting is virtually unknown in the Netherlands, where accountants have traditionally adopted a strict 'economic' approach to the valuation of assets. It is difficult also in France and Germany, where accounting is effectively a branch of the law and where there exist detailed legal prescriptions over how accounts have to be presented.

(f) In the Netherlands, fixed assets are always valued at their replacement cost rather than at historical cost as is the general Continental European practice.

Factors influencing national accounting practices include:

- The influence of a country's company law on accounting practice
- Managerial attitudes towards 'conservatism' in valuing assets and disclosing income
- The extent of the financial information required by local capital markets
- Degree of inflation within the country (accounting practices in nations where asset values are constantly deteriorating in money terms in consequence of high rates of inflation will necessarily differ from practices in other states)
- Whether managements are legally obliged to give financial information to employee representatives
- Tax considerations
- Size and influence of the accounting profession
- Cultural attitudes towards the role of business in society (which will affect the degree of business regulation and hence the amount of financial information a firm has to disclose)
- The country's membership of a regional economic grouping (such as the EU) which imposes trans-national rules on accounting practice.

Note how the accounting practices of many developing nations follow those previously imposed by the former colonial power. Also a number of countries have chosen to base their accounting systems on the US model in consequence of the spread of American influence (especially *via* direct foreign investment by US firms) in the post-Second World War era.

Differences in national accounting systems create many problems for the multinational company, including the following:

(a) Financial managers in subsidiaries in disparate countries will have different perceptions of the meaning of the same item in a financial report, creating international communication difficulties among financial executives.

(b) The company has to prepare several sets of financial statements based on different accounting principles. Then it must prepare a consolidated set of accounts using identical accounting concepts and measurement criteria and encompassing all the firm's subsidiaries in various countries in order to compare their performances and take global investment decisions.

(c) Share issue documentation used to raise money in one country may be completely inappropriate for other nations, as investors and financial analysts will be looking for different things in different countries.

(d) Host country governments may demand detailed information on a particular subsidiary's financial situation, fearing that an MNC's normal published accounts are concealing tax liability, improper transfer pricing (*see* 17:**13**), unfair competitive practices, etc. Equally the government of an MNC's headquarters nation might suspect that the company's consolidated accounts hide tax loopholes, large-scale movements of foreign exchange to other countries, and so on.

International accounting standards

The International Accounting Standards Committee (IASC) was established in 1973 by the national professional accounting institutes of a number of leading industrialised countries (including the USA, Japan, the UK and Germany). Each national professional body is obliged to ensure that any guidelines, Codes of Practice or national standards that it imposes on its members conform to standards agreed by the IASC. The adoption of comparable standards, methodologies and financial reporting procedures in all states should enable investors and others to compare like with like when analysing companies in various nations; newly established firms should be able (through examining competitors' accounts) to identify the most profitable fields of operation; and national governments would be able to adopt common positions on the taxation of companies.

Although some international accounting standards have been agreed and implemented, progress towards genuine harmonisation has been slow, essentially because:

(a) Professional bodies do not have the legal power to set binding standards (only national governments may do this).

(b) Fundamental differences in the legal and tax environments of disparate countries continue to exist.

(c) Some member organisations of the IASC have very many members, other only have a few, so there are major disparities in the status of IASC member bodies in various nations.

(d) It can be extremely difficult to devise harmonised standards that satisfy the company law and tax requirements of all the countries represented by IASC members, especially in view of the fact that accountants (and others) in various nations have different views on the *fundamental purpose* of financial statements.

(e) International enforcement of agreed standards is virtually impossible.

The OECD (*see* 1:**7**) recommends that MNCs disclose the following in their annual accounts:

- Principal activities in each country.
- Sales and profits by country.
- New capital investments by country.
- Transfer pricing policies.
- Average number of employees by geographic area.
- The accounting principles used in preparing financial statements.

Note that the above are merely guidelines and are purely voluntary. Also OECD does not specify any criteria for actually measuring the items under the various headings.

11. Tax considerations

An MNC has to pay taxes in the headquarters country and in the nations where its subsidiaries are situated. National tax regimes affect MNC decisions concerning the location of manufacturing capacity, the legal structures of foreign operations (branches versus subsidiaries for example – see 16:5), the financing of foreign subsidiaries (loans, equity issue, etc.), and practices *vis-à-vis* transfer pricing intended to minimise the book value of profits of subsidiaries in high tax countries. Special tax problems confronting the international business are as follows:

(a) Double taxation may occur (see below) because income generated in host countries could be taxed by both host and headquarters country governments.

(b) The moment at which tax liability arises differs between nations, offering many opportunities for tax deferred *via* careful planning of the timing of operations in various countries.

(c) Disparate rates of corporation and other forms of tax apply in different states. In most nations, tax rates on distributed profits (dividends, interest payments or royalties) are lower than on funds retained within the firm, on the grounds that the recipients of distributed profits will have to pay further tax on their incomes.

(d) The tax base (i.e. who is subject to tax and in what circumstances) varies among countries.

(e) Calculations regarding the treatment of tax losses, windfall income and capital gains, depreciation, taxes on intra-company transfers, and many other issues differ markedly from state to state.

In the great majority of industrialised nations MNCs pay corporation tax on home country earnings plus revenues from operations abroad. A small number of countries, however, do not tax foreign income.

Double taxation

The purpose of a double taxation treaty is to prevent firms being taxed twice on the same remittances: once by the foreign government on a local subsidiary's payments to head office (usually through withholding taxes on dividends, interest and royalties) and then by the head office country as corporation tax on the revenues received. (Withholding tax is the percentage of dividends, interest payments, etc., deducted at source as tax by the host nation's fiscal authorities.) Numerous bilateral tax treaties exist whereby withholding taxes on foreign subsidiaries' (or branches') repatriations of profits to head office in another nation are either exempt from withholding tax entirely or pay at a special reduced rate. The exemption or reduction applies for payments in both directions between the two nations. Note how bilateral treaties may specify different rates of reduced withholding tax for various pairs of countries, so that it may be worthwhile transferring money between subsidiaries in disparate nations prior to final repatriation. For example, a tax treaty between countries A and B might provide for 15 per cent withholding tax on transfers between the two nations; whereas treaties between B and C and A and C could specify withholding tax at just five per cent. Hence money could be sent from B to C (at five per cent tax) and then from C to A (again at five per cent) giving a total tax liability of just ten per cent (assuming country C does not tax the incoming revenue).

Such complexities make it essential for MNCs to plan international cash transfers with the utmost care and to take full advantage of tax benefits available in various countries.

12. Tax havens

These are small countries that do not impose corporation taxes on foreign companies. The Bahamas, the Cayman Islands, Panama and Liberia are examples. Foreign firms only need establish a nominal residence and may then receive money from abroad without having to disclose it, and are legally entitled to conduct their business in secret. Another use of a tax haven is as an intermediary for purchasing. Suppose for example that a UK firm buys a foreign product for £10 per unit and resells it at £15 per unit, generating a £5 profit on which tax is payable. This firm might set up a nominal subsidiary in a tax haven (that has no business taxes whatsoever); the subsidiary rather than the parent could make the purchase (again at £10 per unit), sell the product to the parent in the UK at (say) £14 per unit, thus enabling the parent to sell to the final customer at £15 but only record a taxable profit of £1. The reason behind the creation of a tax haven is the hope that foreign firms will spend money in the local area and will stimulate the country's banking and financial services infrastructure. For a tax haven to succeed it needs to have political stability, excellent communications with the outside world, no exchange controls, and minimum regulation of its financial services industries.

Arguments against the use of a tax haven are that:

(a) The administrative and other costs of shifting funds and maintaining secrecy may outweigh a company's tax savings.

(b) Interest rates on money held in a tax haven might be lower than available elsewhere.

(c) A growing number of countries refuse to recognise the existence of tax havens where fiscal matters are concerned, i.e. they *assume* that funds deposited in a tax haven are in fact an integral part of the firm's home country assets and tax them as such. The USA, Germany and Japan are examples of nations in this category.

(d) Transfers to tax havens are likely to lead to investigations into the remitting company's financial affairs by the home country's tax authorities.

Note moreover that tax haven nations do not have any bilateral tax treaties with other states and hence are excluded from the benefits resulting from such arrangements. Note moreover that an MNC may actually choose to pay a substantial amount of tax in its head office country in order to foster good relations with the nation's government.

FINANCE OF FOREIGN TRADE

13. Management of foreign exchange risk

A business which invoices its foreign customers in terms of local foreign currency, or which accumulates foreign currencies for some other reason, runs the risk that the exchange rates of these foreign currencies will depreciate in value relative to the firm's home country currency between the moments that contracts are signed and when the money is actually received. Hence less domestic currency is obtained for a given amount of foreign currency after the exchange rate has moved in the home country's favour. To avoid this risk the exporter can sell to its bank, in advance, the foreign currency that its customers have been invoiced to pay. The bank will quote a fixed forward exchange rate for these transactions, which will apply to the conversions regardless of the actual spot exchange in force one month or three months (say) from today.

The bank will demand a reward for its services and therefore will quote an exchange rate for forward currency transactions which differs from the current spot exchange rate by an amount sufficient to cover the bank's exposure to risk and make a profit. This obviously represents a (significant) cost to the exporter.

An exporting firm that invoices in local currency and which expects the spot exchange rate to move in its favour (so that it stands to raise more domestic currency when it eventually comes to convert than if it converted today) may decide not to bother with forward cover. Another possibility available to exporters scheduled to receive foreign currency payments over a long period is to enter into an *option contract* with its bank whereby the exporter is given the right to sell to the bank foreign currency up to an agreed limit at a predetermined rate at any time within the next 12 months. If the spot exchange rate moves in one direction the exporter will exercise the option; if it moves in the other the option will not be taken up, forfeiting thereby the fee paid to the bank to purchase the option.

Further devices for avoiding foreign exchange risk include the following:

(a) 'Swap arrangements' whereby two or more firms in different countries agree to lend their surplus cash to each other on a reciprocal basis. Suppose for example that a French company needs US dollars to pay for imports from the US. It might have an arrangement with an American business whereby the latter lends (at low interest) to the French firm the dollars necessary to settle the import transaction. When the US company imports from France and requires francs it borrows these from the French firm. The two loans will then be balanced-off against each other at a predetermined currency rate of exchange. This can be cheaper than using the forward exchange market and (importantly) may be used to circumvent national exchange control regulations.

(b) Inclusion of 'renegotiation clauses' in all sales contracts to enable an exporter automatically to change the contract price in the event of significant exchange rate fluctuations.

(c) Accumulation of (interest earning) foreign currency balances in various countries, to be exchanged for other currencies at appropriate moments or used to purchase local products for subsequent exporting to other markets. Note how this imposes additional costs and inconvenience on the exporting company relative to locally based rivals.

14. Settlement of international transactions

Payment by cheque or credit transfer is known as 'open account' settlement. Exporting businesses that are not prepared to accept the risks of customer default attached to open account trading may be able to use bills of exchange or letters of credit (see below) to finance international transactions. Alternatively, the exporter can use the services of an export 'credit factoring' company which will purchase, at a discount, invoices issued to foreign customers as the goods are supplied. This is discussed in **19** below.

Bills of exchange

A bill of exchange is a written instruction sent by an exporter to an importer ordering the importer to pay to the exporter, or anyone specified by the exporter, a certain sum of money either on receipt of the bill, or at a specified date in the future (e.g. in three months' time). A bill that requires payment immediately or within three days of acceptance is called a sight bill or draft; one that is to be settled in the future is referred to as a term, usance or tenor bill. The seller is the 'drawer' of the bill, the buyer the 'drawee', the seller's bank is known as the 'remitting' bank and the importer's bank the 'collecting' bank.

15. Uses for bills of exchange

Bills of exchange can be used for acceptance credit transactions, for documentary collections, or for forfaiting (*see* **16**). Acceptance credit transactions occur when the exporter sends a bill of exchange to a foreign importer, who 'accepts' it (by signing the bill) and returns it to the exporter. Once accepted the bill becomes a 'negotiable instrument', i.e. it can be sold to another party. Hence one possible way of dealing with an accepted bill is for the exporting firm to sell it to its own bank at a discount. The bank then collects the money when the bill matures. Thus the bank assumes the risk of non-payment. A documentary collection involves the exporter handing over a bill of exchange to its own bank, together with various documents (e.g. the insurance certificate, invoice, transit documents) required by the customer prior to taking delivery. The exporter's bank now sends the bill to the customer for acceptance. If the bill is a sight bill, the customer settles it at once. If it is a term bill, the customer accepts it and returns it to the exporter's bank, which now becomes responsible for collecting the money. All the documents which provide title to the goods are handled by the exporter's bank, which will only release them to the customer at the time of payment.

It is of course open for the exporting firm to keep the bill until it falls due for payment and itself collect the money, or borrow money from its bank using the accepted bill as security. In the latter case the bank might want a guarantee that the bill will definitely be settled, e.g. by requiring the importer's bank to promise to honour the bill if the importer defaults. The term 'avalised bill of exchange' is applied to a bill that carries such an undertaking. If the bill is not avalised and the buyer defaults then the bank will still expect the exporting company to repay the loan. This is known as 'with recourse financing', i.e. the bank can demand compensation from the exporter if the customer defaults.

In the event of a customer defaulting on a bill of exchange the first step towards recovery through local courts is to have the bill protested. This means getting a notary public (i.e. a local person legally qualified to attest and certify documents) to ask the customer for payment or reasons for non-payment. The latter are put into a formal deed of protest which is then placed before a local court as evidence of dishonour.

16. Forfaiting

A company engaged on a long-term and expensive project with a large customer can have the latter accept a bundle of bills of exchange, each maturing on a different date. The first bill could be payable after six months, the second after 18 months, the third after three years etc., up to the last bill maturing on completion of the project. These accepted bills may now be discounted *en bloc* with the company's own bankers.

The advantages of forfaiting are that it is financing without recourse (although the exporter's bank may insist that the bills of exchange be avalised) and that since bills of exchange are sold to the bank at today's known rate of discount the exporter pays what is in effect a fixed rate of interest on the money raised. The amount available to the exporter is known with certainty and there is no risk of currency exchange rate depreciation so that forward planning is facilitated.

Problems with forfaiting include the loss of revenue resulting from discounting the bills, bankers' administrative fees, and the need to persuade customers to accept bills of exchange issued for work that will not be completed or goods that will not be supplied until a long time in the future.

17. Letters of credit

Foreign importers who are little known in the exporter's country will experience difficulty in ordering goods because suppliers (and their bankers) will fear non-payments of accounts. Thus, importers commonly arrange for established banks (preferably in the exporter's country) to guarantee final payment. Banks which agree to do this will issue to foreign importers 'letters of credit' in which they formally assume responsibility for settling importers' debts, subject to the conditions laid down in the letters of credit. These conditions normally relate to the receipt by the importer's bank of a number of properly completed documents (including documents of title) relating to the transaction, notably the transport document (bill of lading, air waybill or whatever), the invoice, insurance certificate and (where appropriate) dangerous goods notices, packing lists, pre-inspection certificates, bank indemnities, and so on. A bill of exchange might also be included in the bundle. A 'confirmed' letter of credit is one the settlement of which has been guaranteed by a bank in the exporter's own country. The exporter is paid by its local confirming bank, which then collects the money from the foreign bank issuing the credit. The confirming bank has no claim on the exporter if the credit is not honoured. Currently, nearly all letters of credit are irrevocable, meaning that they cannot be arbitrarily cancelled by the customer.

18. Settlement by letter of credit

The first step in letter of credit settlement is for the foreign customer to approach its bank (called the 'issuing' or 'opening' bank) and ask it to open a letter of credit in the exporter's favour. The letter of credit will specify when payment is to be made (e.g. on presentation of documents or at a later date) and which documents must be submitted prior to the paying bank releasing the money. On issuing the letter of credit the bank assumes liability for the debt. Then the exporter or its bank (known as the 'advising' bank) is informed that the credit has been opened and of the exact conditions to be met prior to releasing the money. The goods are now sent off and the documents forwarded to the bank that is to pay the money. A bill of exchange may or may not be included in the documents depending on the precise terms of the credit. On receipt of the documents the paying bank checks them and, if they are in order, releases payment. Alternatively, if payment is to be through a bill of exchange, the bank accepts and returns this on behalf of the customer. In the latter case it is the bank and not the customer that honours the bill of exchange when it matures.

19. Factoring

Factoring involves the outright sale (at a discount) of debts owed to the company to an outside body in exchange for cash. The factor takes over the administration of the client company's invoices, collects the money and (importantly) assumes the risk of customer default. How much is paid for the invoices is subject to negotiation but will depend ultimately on the magnitudes of debt involved, the degree of risk, and the extent of the paperwork needed to collect payment. A variation on the technique is 'invoice discounting' whereby the exporting company receives a cash payment (effectively a loan) from the invoice discounter against the value of the invoices issued to customers, but retains responsibility for debt collection and for an agreed proportion of bad debts.

Credit factors are expert in the laws and techniques of international debt-collection. Usually they operate through international networks of factors, providing reciprocal services for fellow members. These networks enable factors in various countries to communicate with end customers in the latter's own language and to apply collection procedures appropriate to the country concerned (Hawkins 1993). The client receives an 'up front' cash payment and incurs minimal administrative debt-collecting costs.

Problems with factoring and invoice discounting

While convenient, factoring and invoice discounting can be expensive compared to the interest payable on loans. Also, the client company is usually expected to sign a 12-month agreement with the factor or discounter so that it becomes locked into using factoring/discounting services. A problem with factoring is the client company's loss of contact with its customers where debt settlement is concerned. Either the factor will collect debts under its own name – which might irritate the client's customers – or under the client's own letterhead. In the latter case, however, it will still pursue long-outstanding debts vigorously – in the client's name – regardless of possible damaging effects on customer relations.

Progress test 15

1. What is the purchasing power parity theorem?

2. List the arguments in favour of flexible exchange rates.

3. What is an optimum currency area?

4. How will the introduction of a common European currency affect human resources management?

5. Explain the difference between domestic bonds and foreign bonds.

6. How did the Eurodollar market originate?

7. List the major issues in international financial management.

8. What is the main argument in favour of centralising financial decision making within multinational companies?

9. How do differences in national accounting systems cause difficulties for international businesses?

10. What are the main influences on national accounting practices?

11. What is a double taxation agreement?

12. List the arguments against the use of tax havens by multinational firms.

13. Explain the operation of an 'option contract' in the context of foreign exchange.

14. What is meant by 'open account settlement' of international debts?

15. What is a documentary collection?

16. What is a letter of credit? How can a letter of credit be used to facilitate the settlement of import transactions?

16

MARKET ENTRY

Businesses can enter foreign markets *via* exporting, use of agents and/or distributors, licensing and franchising, joint ventures, management contracts, contract manufacturing or direct foreign investment. Also the firm might wish to establish branches in various nations. Exporting, joint ventures and the operation of branches are dealt with in this chapter: other forms of market entry are covered elsewhere.

TYPES OF MARKET ENTRY

1. Exporting

Exporting means the sale abroad of an item produced, stored or processed in the supplying firm's home country. Some firms regard exporting as little more than a convenient way of increasing total sales; others see it as a crucial element of overall corporate strategy. 'Passive' exporting occurs when a firm receives orders from abroad without having canvassed them. 'Active' exporting, conversely, results from a strategic decision to establish proper systems for organising the export function and for procuring foreign sales. Exporting may be direct or indirect. With direct exporting the exporter assumes full responsibility for the transfer of goods to foreign customers, for customs clearance, local advertising and final sale of the goods. Indirect exporting uses intermediaries. *Export merchants*, for example, reside in the exporter's country, acting as principals in export transactions (that is, buying and selling on their own accounts). They are wholesalers who operate in foreign markets through their own salespeople, stockists and, perhaps, retail outlets. Exporters are relieved of administrative problems, documentation, shipping, internal transport and so on, and do not carry the risks of market failure. However, they lose control over the presentation of their products, and foreign sales may fall because of poor foreign retailing.

Advantages and disadvantages of exporting

Exporting is cheap and convenient to administer and carries no risk of failure of direct foreign investments. The revenues from foreign sales accrue entirely to the exporting company (rather than it having to repatriate profits from foreign subsidiaries), and the firm builds up a network of contacts with foreign agents, distributors, retail outlets, etc. Direct exporting provides total control over the

voids the need to share know-how with foreign partners; and
ve intermediaries. Exporting can be highly profitable, although
t of an export facility can place a severe strain on the business's

ns for not actively exporting, on the other hand, include:

- Cost of financing long periods between obtaining export orders, delivering the goods to distant destinations and getting paid
- Problem of acquiring and retaining staff competent to undertake the extensive paperwork associated with international marketing (except for EU firms selling within the Union) and who possess the linguistic and specialist foreign trade skills necessary for selling abroad
- Managerial resources necessary to have people visit foreign markets regularly, monitor and control agents and distributors, meet important customers, attend foreign exhibitions, etc.
- Costs and inconvenience of finding foreign agents and distributors and of investigating the market characteristics and trading rules of various foreign countries
- Difficulty of forecasting sales in foreign countries rather than in the firm's home nation. Sales forecasting can be far more difficult for foreign countries than in the firm's home base. Changes in the political, legal, social and economic superstructures of other nations are hard to predict, as are the behaviours of actual and potential competing companies.
- Higher degree of risk typically involved in selling abroad rather than in the home country.

Note moreover that the resources needed to sell abroad might be more profitably employed in building up the home market, and that foreign sales may encourage a company to delay introducing new products and/or to ignore the threat of domestic competition. Direct exporting in particular takes time (to establish the necessary procedures), money and commitment. The firm needs to be willing to adapt its products to meet foreign requirements and to research the needs and characteristics of foreign customers. Failure to devote sufficient resources to active exporting can result in disaster. Common problems experienced with exporting are that:

(a) A firm's export department might not be taken seriously by senior management. Note how export managers are necessarily involved in a wide range of functions: foreign market research, negotiation of agency and distribution contracts, product modification for foreign markets, liaison with foreign advertising media, transport, arranging the clearance of letters of credit, packaging, organising after-sales service in foreign countries, and so on. Export management, therefore, should be seen as a responsible and demanding function worthy of high status within the organisation.

(b) In consequence of its self-contained nature the export department might pursue its own objectives rather than those of the wider enterprise.

(c) Staff possessing the requisite (specialist and wide-ranging) export skills are difficult to recruit. A frequently experienced difficulty is that foreign sales increase substantially, but without any attempt to enlarge and reconstitute export department, resulting in its staff assuming widening responsibilities for which they are not properly prepared.

Use of intermediaries

The engagement of intermediaries to handle the export of a company's products has a number of advantages, including:

- Their expert knowledge of export markets and procedures. Intermediaries may be more objective when assessing the probabilities of the exporter's products succeeding in various foreign markets. Their wide-ranging experience of the export problems of other firms and industries enables them to identify solutions quickly and to appreciate all the options available and the difficulties involved.
- Not having to train in-house staff in the details of the export function
- Savings on the overheads associated with a large export department
- The fact that intermediaries are driven by the need to make a profit (rather than simply drawing on employee's salary)
- Their extensive contacts with other specialists in the export field.

The exporting firm need not possess any knowledge of export methods and procedures, or assume any financial risk of non-payment. It does not require a foreign sales organisation or visits to foreign markets. The disadvantages are the cost, and loss of control over final selling prices and marketing methods.

In-house export departments

Advantages to having the firm's in-house staff assume total control over exports include the accumulation of skill within the export department and (hopefully) employees' genuine commitment to expanding export sales. Staff should possess detailed knowledge of all aspects of the company's products and operations; control is straightforward, and there is continuity in the personnel employed on export work. Use of in-house facilities is perhaps most appropriate where (i) the firm has a limited number of clearly identified customers, (ii) the costs of export marketing are easily controlled, and (iii) little after-sales service is required. In-house staff know exactly where to look for information within the company and (importantly) are fully accountable for their actions in the long term: their careers within the organisation substantially depend on the success of their work. Disadvantages to using in-house staff include the following:

(a) Internal employees are not subject to penetrating expert criticism from outside. Mistakes made by in-house employees in consequence of lack of specialist skills and knowledge might never be revealed.

(b) Staff usually have limited experience of other industries and firms.

(c) Internal staff might be apathetic and lack the management skills and innovative attitudes needed to complete an unusual or exceptionally difficult project on time.

(d) The export department might become obsessed with export methods and procedures, regardless of the profitability of export sales.

273

res

Vs) are collaborative arrangements between unrelated parties ? or combine various resources while remaining separate and ;al entities. There are two types of JV: equity and contractual. The 5 each partner taking an equity stake in the venture (e.g. through setting up a joint subsidiary with its own share capital); the latter rely on contractual agreements between the partners. Joint ventures are an example of the wider concept of the 'strategic alliance', which embraces knowledge-sharing arrangements, mutual licensing, measures to control and utilise excess capacity, etc. Usually JVs are formed to undertake a specific project that has to be completed within a set period. JVs are a flexible form of business arrangement; can be quickly entered into and shut down; enable the sharing of costs; yet are frequently just as effective a means for entering markets as more direct forms of foreign investment (Lorange and Roos 1992). Often they are used to establish bridgeheads in a foreign market prior to more substantial operations within the market by individual participants. Advantages to joint ventures include the following:

(a) Firms can expand into several foreign markets simultaneously for low capital cost.

(b) Shared cost of administration.

(c) Partners can avoid the need to purchase local premises and hire new employees.

(d) Shared risk of failure.

(e) JVs may be available in countries where outright takeovers of local firms by foreigners is not allowed.

(f) Less costly than acquisitions.

(g) Higher returns than with licensing/franchising.

(h) Firms can gain instant access to local expertise and to partners' distribution systems.

(i) Possibly better relations with national governments in consequence of having a local partner.

Problems with JVs include the possibility of disagreements over organisation and control, and over methods of operation and the long-term goals of the venture. Other disputes might arise concerning pricing policy, the confidentiality of information exchanged between members, and about how underperformance by any one of the participants is to be dealt with (e.g. whether equal compensation is to be payable to each of the parties if the project is abandoned). Further possible difficulties are listed below.

(a) Partners may become locked into long-term investments from which it is difficult to withdraw.

(b) Possible arguments over which partner is responsible for budg overspends and how these should be financed.

(c) Problems of co-ordination.

(d) Profits have to be shared with partners.

(e) Possible differences in management culture among participating firms.

(f) Completion of a JV project might overburden a company's staff.

(g) Need to share intellectual property.

(h) Difficulties associated with the integration of a JV into an overall corporate strategy.

(i) Partners are not free to act independently.

(j) The corporate objectives of partners may conflict.

(k) Transfer pricing problems may arise as goods pass between partners.

(l) The importance of the venture to each partner might change over time.

3. Criteria for selecting JV partners

Local partners in a foreign country should have proven knowledge, expertise and experience of local business conditions and practices. A prospective partner should be able to conduct or commission local market research and needs to possess extensive contacts with local banks, businesses and providers of special-ist services. Obviously the partner must have resources (staff, technical facilities, management systems, etc.) sufficient to undertake the collaboration (Harvey and Lusch 1995). Further selection criteria are (i) the firm's track record, how long it has existed and its general business reputation; and (ii) how readily the quality of the potential partner's work can be appraised. Ideally, participants should be able to pool complementary skills. For example, one partner might supply the technological know-how, another raise the necessary finance, while the third provides local marketing expertise and facilities. Crucial to the selection process is the exercise of 'due diligence' in relation to an intended collaborator. This means verifying the other business's value and activities and will normally involve an assessment of its creditworthiness (probably undertaken by an international credit reference agency), inspection of its accounts, and the evaluation of its technical and managerial competence.

The due diligence process

The due diligence process usually commences with a preliminary questionnaire being sent to the proposed partner. This questionnaire will seek to identify and evaluate the commercial and legal matters which are material to the decision whether or not to proceed with the business proposed. Due diligence typically involves a thorough examination of the following aspects of a potential partner's affairs:

(a) *Creditworthiness.* The assessment of creditworthiness can be undertaken on by a local reference agency, which will confirm the business's ...ss, search through local Court records to establish whether it ...ents or defaults outstanding against it, and take up references ...bankers and from businesses with which the firm in question ...redit account. Also the agency might be able to collect press cutting... ...other published materials about the potential partner's past activities.

(b) *Verification of the business's accounts.* The accountancy body of the country in which the potential partner is situated will supply lists of local accountants prepared to do this work. National accountancy bodies can be contacted *via* local chambers of commerce. There are, moreover, many large international accounting firms with branch offices in most economically developed states.

(c) *Assessment of the firm's technical and managerial competence.* A local accountant might be able to arrange for a technical expert to appraise the calibre of the firm's managerial, technical and marketing capacities.

The final choice

Criteria for making the final choice should include the following:

(a) Whether the prospect is genuinely interested in the proposed venture, rather than seeing it as just another deal.

(b) The potential partner's ability to understand the firm's aims and problems.

(c) Whether taking on the project will overburden the partner's staff.

(d) How easily the firm will be able to communicate with the partner.

(e) Whether the prospect's proposal directly addresses the firm's specific requirements.

(f) How closely the partner's contributions can be monitored.

(g) Whether the ability and motivation levels of executives in the two enterprises are compatible.

4. Choice of market entry method

Criteria for selecting a market entry method should relate to the organisation's overall corporate strategy and the extent, depth and geographical coverage of its present and intended foreign operations. The firm's management needs to ask itself whether it wishes the company to have long-term involvement with international markets; or merely to exploit opportunistic export sales (Kwon and Kopona 1993). Major factors that should influence the choice include the following:

(a) How quickly the firm wishes to commence operations in the market (outright purchase of a fully operational local business is usually the speediest method).

(b) Volatility of competition and competitive intensity in the countries concerned.

(c) The ease with which intellectual property can be protected (th particularly important for licensing and joint ventures).

(d) The degree of market penetration desired (deep penetration normally requires a permanent presence within the relevant country).

(e) The firm's experience and expertise in selling and operating abroad.

(f) Sizes of the margins taken by intermediaries in particular nations.

(g) Tariff levels, quotas and other non-tariff barriers to market entry.

(h) Availability of trained and competent personnel for staffing foreign subsidiaries.

(i) Political stability of the foreign countries the firm wishes to enter, and other risk factors.

(j) The business's financial resources and hence its capacity to purchase or set up foreign establishments.

(k) Physical and technical characteristics of the product (simple products are easy to manufacture abroad).

(l) Availability of marketing, financial and general business services in target foreign markets.

(m) Ease of communication with intermediaries (agents, consortium buyers, etc.) in specific countries.

(n) Local constraints on the foreign ownership of businesses and/or licensing arrangements involving foreign firms.

In practice, many large companies with extensive foreign operations adopt a variety of market entry methods: exporting to some countries, licensing or operating joint ventures in others, or purchasing manufacturing plant elsewhere. A mixture of these might be applied within a particular foreign state so that, for example, export to a country and licensed manufacture within that country occur side by side.

5. Branches and subsidiaries

As a firm's international activities expand, the inadequacy of exporting as a means for doing foreign business might become progressively evident. The firm will (or should) have acquired detailed knowledge of foreign markets and export procedures and thus might be capable of dispensing with export intermediaries. Accordingly, the company may set up its own branches and/or subsidiaries, possibly to oversee production operations in other countries. The difference between a branch and a subsidiary is that whereas a branch is regarded in law as a direct extension of the parent firm into a foreign country (so that the parent is legally responsible for all the branch's debts and activities), a subsidiary is seen as a separate business from the parent company. A subsidiary is responsible for its own debts and (unlike a branch) is subject to exactly the same taxes, auditing, registration and accounting regulations as any other local business.

easy to set up and to dismantle, but complicated tax situations
e some nations relate the amounts of tax payable by branches to
profits of their parent companies. Normally branches are con-
e transport and storage of goods, marketing, the provision of
ice; and liaison with local banks, advertising agencies, suppliers
rs, and so on. Local assembly and/or manufacture is normally
undertaĸᴇ.. _ / other means. In most (but not all) countries the existence of a
foreign branch has to be registered with local governmental authorities. Usually
the registration is straightforward, comprising the deposit of a simple form plus
translated documents attesting the whereabouts and solvency of the parent
company.

Advantages to operating a branch rather than a subsidiary are that:

- A branch need not have its own capital or directors.
- Assets can be transferred from the parent to the branch without incurring tax liability.
- No company formation or winding-up procedures are required.
- Losses can be offset against the parent's profit.

Factors that might encourage the establishment of a subsidiary rather than a branch include:

- Limited liability
- The ability to apply for government regional development assistance and R&D grants on the same terms as any other local business
- A local identity
- The capacity to raise capital in the subsidiary's own name and (importantly) to sell shares to outsiders
- Not having to disclose the annual accounts of the parent organisation
- The ability to undertake internal reorganisations without having to report this to the foreign authorities.

SELECTION OF MARKETS

6. Locating export markets

There are two approaches to the location of suitable foreign markets. The first
seeks to define characteristics of customers who will be attracted to the product,
and then go through a list of countries picking out those most likely to contain
significant numbers of that customer type. The other approach involves exporting only to predetermined easy markets (say because of a common language or
ready convertibility of local currencies) and adapting output to meet local needs.

In principle, every country in the world is a candidate for market entry. It is
necessary therefore to reduce the list of possibilities to manageable dimensions.
Criteria for eliminating countries offering little chance of success include the
following:

(a) *Demographic factors*. Large populations may be essential for sales of low-value mass-produced items. Age structures could be crucially important for products that appeal to particular age groups.

(b) *Local incomes.* There is little point in exporting to a poor country whose residents cannot afford the goods offered for sale. National income might be unevenly distributed with a small handful of people owning nearly all the country's wealth. An even distribution of income and wealth is desirable for marketing consumer durables and other basic products; uneven distribution might help sales of extremely expensive, superluxury items. Another relevant factor is the country's rate of inflation, which determines real (as opposed to nominal) changes in standards of living.

(c) *Existence of local competitors.* Foreign markets already serviced by many suppliers are, of course, difficult to enter. Note also that existing local firms often enjoy easy access to local capital markets and may control local distribution channels.

(d) *Tax policies in the importing country.* Import duties reduce export profitability. Additionally, high internal sales taxes may be imposed.

(e) *Local laws and customs.* Consumption of certain goods (alcohol for example) is illegal in some countries. Local religious or cultural norms may prohibit particular products: pork for instance is not eaten by members of several religious groups. Invariably, countries at war will not allow importation of goods that have passed through enemy territory. Local laws could demand special guarantees, after-sales service, safety standards, and so on, not required in the exporter's country.

(f) *Potential market growth.* Early entry to a foreign market that is expected to expand can offer lucrative rewards, since distribution networks capable of excluding competing firms can sometimes be set up.

(g) *Storage and transport facilities.* The climatic conditions that prevail in certain countries make them unsuitable for particular products. Some motor cars, for example, cannot withstand extremely cold winters. There are drinks and foodstuffs that need refrigeration which may not be commonly available locally. Road and railway systems might be inadequate for effective distribution of the exported good.

Other relevant factors include geographical proximity of potential foreign markets, strengths of foreign firms, occupational patterns, buying habits, and so on. It may be possible to group together several countries according to common religion, language, or degree of industrialisation. The latter is particularly important because it largely determines the lifestyles of populations – spending habits in one highly industrialised country typically parallel spending patterns in others.

7. International marketing research

Discovery of overseas marketing opportunities requires the assembly of information about the following:

(a) The size of various market segments, their buoyancy and prospects for expansion.

(b) Demographic structures of prospective markets in terms of age, sex composition, family structures, geographical spread of the population, etc.

(c) Market stability, local rates of inflation and economic growth.

(d) Whether local cultural norms and values might affect consumer perceptions of the firm's product, and if so the implications of this.

(e) Foreign tastes, lifestyles and spending patterns.

(f) Average local incomes and the distribution of wealth; living standards, housing and education.

(g) Number of competitors, their strengths and weaknesses and modes of response to other firms' activities.

(h) Competitors' prices, product quality, credit terms, delivery periods, after-sales service, etc.

(i) How easily the firm will be able to monitor competitors' behaviour (price changes, product modifications, etc.).

(j) How frequently competitors change their prices (this is a crude indicator of the stability of the local market and whether local firms do actually compete).

(k) The selling points that competitors stress in their local advertising, and why these characteristics are emphasised.

(l) Local technical product standards and labelling requirements.

(m) Local preferences regarding package size, colouring and design, weights and volumes, shapes and ease of package disposal.

(n) Local taxation; investment grants for establishing subsidies and/or owned distribution outlets.

(o) Nature of local distribution channels.

(p) Availability of commercial services (advertising agencies, debt collectors, warehousing facilities and so on).

(q) Frequency and whereabouts of local trade fairs and exhibitions.

International businesses can commission international marketing research from large agencies in their home countries (these agencies having international connections), or from local research firms based in foreign markets. Research companies apply the full range of MR techniques to their international work, including the following:

(a) Consumer sampling through questionnaires and interviews (undertaken by local employees of the research company).

(b) Market surveys.

(c) Test marketing.

(d) Canvassing competent local business people about a product's likely appeal.

(e) Interpreting foreign statistics (e.g. knowing what products are included in various statistical classifications, assessing data reliability, etc.).

(f) Conducting local telephone surveys.

(g) Estimating the market shares of local competitors.

(h) Obtaining details of the ownership and control of competing firms.

(i) Assessing growth prospects in the local economy.

(j) Establishing why competitors choose to distribute their products through certain channels.

(k) Measuring local consumers' reactions to the firm's brand name and images.

(l) Providing sales estimates for each of several possible selling prices.

(m) Determining the costs and benefits of various distribution options.

(n) Assessing the cost effectiveness of local advertising media.

(o) Investigating various promotional possibilities.

(p) Conducting local retail audits (i.e. continuously monitoring a panel of selected local retail outlets to check the level and periodicity of sales of the client firm's product).

8. Purposes of international marketing research

International marketing research should help the firm improve the quality of its marketing strategies in each of the countries in which it does business. As a management tool international marketing research can assist the firm reduce its exposure to risk, avoid errors, identify foreign opportunities, decide which foreign markets to enter and the best mode of entry (exporting, licensing, joint ventures, etc.) to each nation. It should help the firm to determine which advertising messages to transmit, the prices to charge, which distribution channels to use and whether to modify existing products. Also it assists product positioning (*see* 17:9) within various national markets, and in the choice of the advertising media to be used in each country.

Problems of international marketing research

The specification of objectives for international marketing research are typically more complex than for domestic research exercises, and the execution of the research is difficult. The research design has to be modified in each country according to local cultural, economic, social and institutional factors. Questionnaires have to be translated or completely fresh ones devised; new sampling frames (e.g. electoral registers, telephone books, etc.) must be defined. Data collection procedures will vary from area to area. Also it is more difficult to establish an appropriate unit of analysis at the multi-country level than for domestic research. For example, it may be necessary to examine the same market segment across several nations, an entire regional grouping of countries, specific sectors within particular nations, etc., depending on corporate objectives and product category. Further problems are that:

(a) Field experiments are difficult to replicate in different countries in consequence of the influence of cultural factors.

(b) Survey methods have to be varied according to literacy and education levels, consumer responsiveness to being asked questions and the communications media available in various nations (Malhotra 1988).

(c) It is difficult to compare research results from one country with those of others.

(d) Lack of familiarity with foreign data sources and the inability to assess the reliability of the information they supply may lead to bad decisions.

9. Organisation of international marketing research

Co-ordination and control problems may arise from the need to conduct research across national frontiers, especially when there are different research objectives in different countries. Because information relating to several countries (each possibly possessing a unique marketing environment) has to be gathered, a decision is needed regarding whether the research is to be managed at the head office or local level. The problem with centralisation is that head office is forced to rely heavily on secondary data when evaluating issues, and could miss important factors. If, on the other hand, research is subcontracted to local research companies (which themselves might be subsidiaries of international research groups) then extra costs are incurred and the commissioning firm could lose effective control over the process.

Local versus international research companies

An MNC might contract a large international research company to undertake research tasks, or use smaller independent and locally based research firms. The latter will be closer (culturally as well as geographically) to local customers than international research firms and might therefore be better able to assess local consumer attitudes and tastes. However, close inspection and control of the research firm's work may be required. The advantages of using a big international research company are that it will provide 'one-stop shopping' (a large research company should be capable of supplying all the client's research needs), and that it will possess wide-ranging experience of similar assignments already completed for other businesses. Hence the client benefits indirectly from other companies' research efforts. Note that the large international research firms sometimes subcontract assignments to local independent research companies. The problems for the client arising from this situation are that not only does the client lose control over the work, but also its brief to the international research company may not be comprehensively and accurately transmitted to the latter's contact abroad. Also there is no easy way to establish whether the local subcontractor is performing satisfactorily.

10. International market segmentation

Market segmentation is the process of dividing the total market into sub-units and then modifying the product and/or the way it is packaged, advertised or otherwise promoted in order to satisfy the particular customer requirements of each market segment. Traditionally, markets have been segmented with respect to geographical location, socio-economic structure, age, sex, ethnic origin, religion, etc. Increasingly, however, attention is paid to the behaviourial aspects of target segments, especially the relationship between spending patterns and the life styles (actual or desired) of various consumer groupings (Day *et. al.* 1988).

Data on consumers' ages, sex, income levels, occupations, educational backgrounds, marital status, and social class can be extremely useful in identifying the whereabouts of potential markets. Each time a fresh variable is added to the analysis the narrower the target market becomes. This results in a more precise specification of the customer type being sought, hence enabling the firm to identify an assortment of promotional methods which cater for this segment (Baalbak and Malhotra 1993). A problem arises in that the market definition may become so narrow that a large number of genuine prospects are excluded, so that messages are not drafted to appeal to these consumer groups. The objective, therefore, is to subdivide the market accurately *without* precluding bona fide opportunities.

Demographic segmentation

Demographic variables include the sex, age, income, household size, occupation, physical whereabouts, social status, etc., of prospective customers. A serious difficultly here is the incompatibility of various countries' definitions of social class. In Britain, for example, the official census divides people into six categories: A, B, C1, C2, D and E. Grades A and B contain the upper middle class, professional and managerial people and others on high incomes; categories B and C1 are the middle and lower middle class, including clerical and administrative workers on above-average incomes; C2 is the skilled working class earning average incomes; D comprises unskilled manual workers with below-average income levels; class E contains the elderly, the unemployed and other poor people.

This UK categorisation is convenient, well established and widely used by private research organisations outside the UK. Many Continental publications and television/radio companies analyse their audiences in ABC1, etc., terms, although beyond the marketing services industry the classification is not generally applied. For instance, The Netherlands' national statistical office divides the Dutch population into categories of Professional and Higher Managerial, Intermediate Managerial, Clerical and Skilled Manual, and Pensioners and the Unskilled. The German authorities segment Germans in terms of monthly household income. France combines 'senior management' with the

283

self-employed, and has further classes for professional, white collar and blue collar employees. Greece divides its population according to residence in urban, semi-urban or rural areas. Further definitional and measurement discrepancies apply in many other demographic fields.

It is necessary to think creatively when segmenting markets demographically. Pharmaceuticals firms, for example, should establish the countries and regions within countries that have higher than average numbers of doctors and dentists per thousand population (e.g. all of Italy, the south of France, and the southern parts of Germany and The Netherlands). Suppliers of household furniture need to take an interest in average household size, and in the typical number of rooms per household in each state (highest in Denmark, Belgium, Luxembourg and central Germany). There are pockets of extremely high income consumers in the south of England, north Holland, north Germany, Denmark, central and southern France, and so on.

Psychographic segmentation

Consumer attitudes, perspectives and purchasing behaviour can differ remarkably within market groups possessing nearly identical demographic characteristics. For example, two households may be located in the same area and have equal incomes, yet exhibit enormous differences in their consumption patterns according to their lifestyles, attitudes and aspirations. Hence the incorporation into the analysis of a psychosocial dimension to reflect consumer lifestyles, personality type, interests, leisure activities, perspectives and opinions may be needed in order to reduce the extent of the markets under review. The term 'psychographics' refers to the systematic study of consumer lifestyles, attitudes, interests, opinions and prejudices as they affect purchasing behaviour. Psychographics seeks to sketch profiles of particular consumer groups and hence identify demands for certain products from key variables that characterise various consumer types. For instance, an outdoor type who enjoys sport, fast cars, action-packed television programmes, etc., may be attracted by products with rugged images that correspond to these conceptions. This kind of analysis distinguishes between consumers in terms of their activities, interests and opinions; particularly *vis-à-vis* their use of leisure, mental priorities, stances on ethical and social issues, and attitudes towards themselves and the environments in which they exist. Psychographics can be a useful supplement to demographic analysis, enabling the supplying firm to segment a market more precisely.

Effective segmentation depends on detailed and accurate marketing research. Inevitably therefore international firms wishing to undertake segmentation exercises in foreign countries are disadvantaged through their geographical remoteness and possibly by inability to interpret foreign data correctly. The essential purpose of segmentation is the detection of unsatisfied needs among hitherto unexplored market sections. Thus, analysis should focus on the identification of needs and consumer motivation factors rather than on the peculiarities of particular foreign countries. The aim is to isolate relatively homogeneous consumer groups within wider markets. Marketing mixes are then adjusted to satisfy the needs of the identified market segments.

Problems with psychographic market segmentation

All lifestyle and attitudinal taxonomies rest on the basic assumption that consumers have *consistent* values, beliefs and attitudes that are not subject to sudden and unpredictable change. Casual observation of human behaviour suggests that this is not always true. Other problems include the following:

(a) The psychosocial categorisations used in psychographics are highly subjective and open to numerous interpretations. What *exactly* is meant by terms such as 'sophisticated', 'reflective', 'persuadable', 'refined', etc?

(b) Psychographic analysis for products that are used by a wide range of types of consumer is a waste of money.

(c) Implementation of campaigns resulting from segmentation exercises requires the existence of highly specialised media vehicles capable of carrying specially devised messages to narrowly defined target groups.

(d) Obtaining information on the whereabouts of foreign consumers exhibiting specific psychographic characteristics can be difficult (although increasing amounts of lifestyle data are becoming available).

Critics of the psychographic approach might argue that it adds little of *practical* value to supplying firms, and that relating psychographic concepts directly to consumer behaviour is extremely problematic. What does emerge, however, is that even in the richest and poorest countries there are substantial consumer groups with near identical lifestyles and aspirations, and it is certainly the case that differences between the market sectors *within* specific member states greatly outweigh differences in consumer behaviour *between* many nations.

Progress test 16

1. Explain the difference between active exporting and passive exporting.

2. List six problems associated with exporting.

3. Why do many firms use intermediaries to handle the export of their products?

4. Explain the difference between an equity joint venture and a contractual joint venture. What criteria should be applied to the selection of joint venture partners?

5. List six factors that should influence the choice of market entry method.

6. What is the difference between a branch and a subsidiary?

7. List the advantages and disadvantages of operating a branch rather than a subsidiary.

8. Define the term 'psychographic market segmentation'.

9. List six sets of variables that need to be researched when searching for foreign market opportunities.

10. There are two basic approaches to the location of foreign countries suitable for market entry. What are they?

17

INTERNATIONAL MARKETING

FUNDAMENTALS

1. Nature of international marketing

L.S. Walsh (see the M&E title *International Marketing*) defines international marketing as:

(a) The marketing of goods and services across national frontiers; *and*
(b) The marketing operations of an organisation that sells and/or produces within a given country when:
(i) that organisation is part of, or associated with, an enterprise which also operates in other countries; *and*
(ii) there is some degree of influence on or control of that organisation's marketing activities from outside the country in which it sells and/or produces.

The essential principles of marketing apply to international operations as much as they do to domestic trade, although a global outlook is required and the problems of international marketing are more extensive than for internal trade. International marketing requires multilingual communications, and numerous cultural factors have to be taken into account. Information on foreign markets will often be in foreign languages; may be hard to obtain; and is frequently difficult to interpret. Further problems that arise in the course of international (as opposed to domestic) marketing are as follows:

(a) Products and promotional methods may have to be modified to suit the needs of specific countries.

(b) Foreign market environments might be turbulent and unpredictable.

(c) Distribution channels are sometimes very long and involve many intermediaries.

(d) International marketing managers require a wide range of marketing skills.

(e) Diverse national laws on advertising, consumer protection, sales promotions, direct marketing, etc., need to be taken into consideration.

(f) Pricing decisions have to take account of currency exchange rate fluctuations.

(g) Market research is more expensive than for domestic marketing, and can be extremely problematic.

(h) Competitors' behaviour may be difficult to observe.

(i) Special packaging and labelling might be required.

2. The international marketing concept and the international marketing mix

The 'marketing concept' is the idea that a firm should seek to evaluate market opportunities before production, assess potential demand for the good, determine the product characteristics desired by consumers, predict the prices consumers are willing to pay, and then supply goods corresponding to the needs and wants of target markets. Adherence to the marketing concept means the firm conceives and develops products that satisfy consumer wants. For international marketing this means the integration of the international side of the company's business with all aspects of its operations, and the willingness to create new products and adapt existing products to satisfy the needs of *world* markets. Products may have to be adapted to suit the tastes, needs and other characteristics of consumers in specific regions, rather than it being assumed that an item which sells well in one country will be equally successful elsewhere.

The marketing mix

Marketing is a collection of activities that includes selling, advertising, public relations, sales promotions, research, new product development, package design, merchandising, the provision of after-sales service, and exporting. The term *marketing mix* describes the combination of marketing elements used in a given situation (Borden 1965; McCarthy 1981). Appropriate mixtures vary depending on the firm and industry. Major elements of the marketing mix can be listed under four headings:

(a) *Promotion* – including advertising, merchandising, public relations, and the utilisation of salespeople.

(b) *Product* – design and quality of output, assessment of consumer needs, choice of which products to offer for sale, and after-sales service.

(c) *Price* – choice of pricing strategy and prediction of competitors' responses.

(d) *Place* – selection of distribution channels and transport arrangements.

A firm's marketing mix will normally (but not necessarily) have to be adapted for international (as opposed to purely domestic) marketing in consequence of the many national differences that exist in relation to stages of economic development (manifest in income levels and lifestyles), social systems, technological environments, legal frameworks, competitive situation, business practices and cultural perspectives. Promotion policy, for example, has to consider disparate laws and regulations on advertising and sales promotions, while pricing policies need to take into account wide variations in norms relating to credit and delivery terms in various states.

288

Approaches to international marketing

Differentiated international marketing strategies involve the modification of products and promotional messages to take account of cultural, linguistic, legal and other national characteristics. An *undifferentiated* marketing strategy, conversely, means the application of an identical marketing mix in all countries, and is normally cheaper to implement than the differentiated approach. Here the firm offers exactly the same product using identical promotional images and methods in a wide range of markets. Differences in market segments are ignored. Products are designed and advertised in order to appeal to the widest possible range of consumers. *Concentrated* marketing involves focusing all the firm's attention on a handful of markets and applying a different marketing mix to each market. The markets involved could be particular countries, or types of customer with common characteristics but resident in several different countries.

3. International product policy

A fundamental decision that has to be taken by companies operating internationally is whether to supply to foreign markets the firm's existing product, or modify the product to suit the needs of each foreign country. Product modification is appropriate where there exist:

- Significant differences in local consumer taste
- Intense competition in foreign markets (creating the need to differentiate a firm's output from that of foreign rivals)
- Special local requirements in relation to package size, technical standards, consumer protection laws and customer care facilities
- Differences in local climate, living conditions, literacy and technical skill level of users, customer buying habits, incomes (buyers in poor countries might need low quality products), and in the uses to which the product might be put in various markets.

Hopefully product modifications will increase worldwide sales of the firm's core products through (i) the satisfaction of different customer needs in various regions, (ii) retention of existing customers by keeping the product up-to-date, and (iii) matching the product attributes offered by competing firms. Complementary products might be introduced to stimulate sales of existing lines, e.g. by improving the usefulness of currently produced items (gardening tools or DIY power accessories for example). The need for extensive product modification is a common impetus for firms to establish local manufacturing or assembly facilities in foreign countries, as it could well be cheaper to set up a new establishment to produce what is essentially a new product near to end consumers rather than make major changes to existing production lines and procedures at home.

The case for standardisation

A number of problems apply to product modification, notably that:

(a) Extra promotional costs have to be incurred.

(b) There is duplication of effort within the business.

(c) The company may possess insufficient experience and technical know-how of different products and how to market them.

(d) Technical research and development efforts might become fragmented as increasing amounts of resources are devoted to issues pertaining to the special requirements of particular national markets.

Supplying a single unmodified product can provide several advantages: economies of scale in production, concentration of technical research methods, fewer staff training requirements, and so on (Whitelock 1987). It leads to reduced stockholding costs (because demand in any market can be met from a single inventory of the same item), facilitates the development of technical expertise in a narrow area, and allows the interchangeability of spare parts and input components between supply points in various locations. Accordingly, firms sometimes attempt to create universal products (hopefully) suitable for all markets in all regions. This might be suitable where:

(a) The essential need that the product aims to satisfy is basically the same in all national and market segments.

(b) After-sales service is easily standardised.

(c) There exists a large market across several countries and cultural differences do not necessitate adaptation.

(d) The product has a strong international brand image. Note how a particular national image can help sell an unmodified product in several markets. Japanese goods, for instance, are generally regarded as reliable, high quality and technically excellent: positive images that will help an overtly Japanese item to sell in *any* country.

INTERNATIONAL PROMOTIONS POLICY

4. International advertising

The key issue in international advertising is whether the firm should standardise its advertising messages or adapt them to meet the requirements of particular foreign markets (Alexander 1993; Van Hulle 1993). Some advertising messages are applicable to several countries, others are relevant to only one. Much depends on the degree of homogeneity of target consumers in various countries, their lifestyles, interests, incomes and tastes (Anholt 1993; Agrawal 1995). The advantages of uniformity are that it:

- requires less marketing research in individual countries
- is relatively cheap and convenient to administer
- demands less creative time to devise advertisements; a single message is constructed and used in all markets.

Customisation, conversely, might be necessary in consequence of:

- cultural differences between countries and/or market segments
- translation difficulties between different languages
- differences in the educational backgrounds of target groups in various countries
- non-availability of certain media (specialist magazines, for instance) in some regions
- differences in national attitudes towards advertising.

To the extent that alterations are needed they may take one or more of the following forms:

(a) Different media. For instance, listeners to commercial radio in different countries might typically belong to different socio-economic groups.

(b) Changes in symbols, e.g. using a male rather than a female model as the dominant figure in an advertisement. This might be necessary if males are the primary purchasers of the product in one market and females in another.

(c) Changes in advertisement headlines and body copy.

(d) Changes in the fundamental selling proposition. For instance, presenting a bicycle as a leisure item in one market, a fashion accessory in another, and as a commuting vehicle elsewhere.

5. Laws and regulations on advertising

These vary from country to country. Comparative advertising, for example, is unlawful in many nations. (Comparative advertising involves the comparison of an advertised item with competing products and/or mention of rival firms.) The use of superlatives in advertising copy is allowed in the UK, Belgium and Italy, but not in Germany or France (at least not on television). In the Netherlands, superlatives have to be backed up by factual evidence. There are severe constraints on the use of pornography and/or sexual innuendo in advertisements in a number of countries: advertising in foreign languages is sometimes banned. Other legally sensitive areas in the international advertising field include the use of children as models; the creative approaches that may be employed (for example, it is illegal in many countries to instil fear in consumers' minds in order to advertise products); the media permitted to carry advertisements; and the amounts of advertising allowed in each medium (e.g. the number of minutes of advertising permitted in each hour of television broadcasts). The advertising of 'health' goods, pharmaceuticals, war toys, alcohol and tobacco are subject to stringent control in the great majority of nations (Hegarty 1993; CEC 1993).

6. International direct marketing

Direct marketing covers direct mail, telephone selling, catalogues, and 'off-the-page' selling via cut-outs in newspaper and magazine advertisements. Direct marketing is the USA's third largest advertising medium, after newspapers and

TV. In Western Europe direct marketing accounts (according to the European Commission) for about a quarter of all commercial communication expenditure (Baines 1995).

Direct mail is the dominant force of direct marketing, and is buoyant throughout the world. It offers a flexible, selective and potentially highly cost-effective means for reaching foreign consumers. Messages can be addressed exclusively to a target market; advertising budgets may be concentrated on the most promising market segments; and it will be some time before competitors realise that the firm has launched a campaign. Also the size, content, timing and geographical coverage of mailshots can be varied to suit national circumstances, and there are no media space or airtime restrictions and no copy or insertion deadlines to be met. All aspects of the direct mail process are subject to the company's immediate control, and it can experiment by varying the approach used in different countries.

A number of factors have contributed to the increasing use of direct marketing for international campaigns, as follows:

(a) The widespread availability of freefone telephone facilities in most nations, so that it is possible to quote an international 0800 freefone telephone number to enable customers to ring free of charge in response to direct mail (and other) advertising campaigns.

(b) The growing number of independent households in many countries resulting from falling birth rates, higher divorce rates and increasing longevity.

(c) Increasing levels of female employment throughout the world. This has stimulated the use of direct mail as a primary means of selling to women who now go to work rather than spend large amounts of time shopping.

(d) New possibilities for the identification of distinct market segments among various types of family group.

(e) Vast improvements in the availability of mailing lists both for households and for business-to-business customers. Lists can be purchased or rented from commercial list brokers who now operate in all major trading nations.

(f) Greater competition among the providers of international mail despatch services.

7. International sales promotions

Sales promotion covers the issue of coupons, the design of competitions, special offers, distribution of free samples, etc. The objectives of sales promotion campaigns include:

- stimulation of impulse purchasing
- encouraging customer loyalty
- attracting customers to the firm's premises
- penetration of new markets
- increasing the rate at which customers repeat their purchases.

Promotional techniques need to relate to the specified aims of the exercise (free samples to enter new markets, reduced-price offers to encourage repeat purchase, money-off coupons to attract customers to the premises, etc).

The use of sales promotions as a marketing weapon has expanded rapidly throughout the world. Unfortunately, however, international businesses wishing to employ sales promotions for cross-border campaigns face a number of serious practical difficulties, because in many nations the use of certain sales promotions techniques is regarded as unfair competition, and as such is subject to stringent legal control. Indeed, conflicting laws sometimes apply to these matters in various countries. Money-off vouchers, for example, are legal in Spain but not in Germany; 'lower price for the next purchase' offers are legal in Belgium, illegal in Denmark and could be illegal in Italy depending on the circumstances of the offer. Cross-product offers (buy one item and get a big price reduction on something else) are illegal in Luxembourg; while free draws are illegal in Netherlands. In Germany and certain other countries free gifts are forbidden if they constitute a genuine incentive to buy. The justification for the latter is that the distribution of free gifts can be interpreted as a form of 'dumping', undertaken merely to force rival companies out of business. Other criticisms of the use of sales promotions suggested by the governments that severely restrict or ban them are that the true value of the promoted item is concealed since consumers are improperly influenced (arguably misled) by the special offer accompanying the sale, and that consumers cannot meaningfully compare the prices of similar competing goods because of the distortions and distractions that sales promotions introduce. Some governments allege moreover that large firms which possess the resources necessary to plan and implement extensive sales promotion campaigns enjoy an inequitable advantage over smaller rivals.

INTERNATIONAL BRANDING

8. Nature of branding

A product is anything a business has to sell, whether this be a physical good or a service. 'New' products could be completely fresh innovations, or modifications of existing products, or copies of other firms' products (Littler and Schlieper 1995). *Branding* a product means giving it a trade name and/or logo and then seeking *via* advertising and other sales promotion to associate certain attractive characteristics with the branded item. Customers then *recognise* the product and, having once been satisfied by it, need not subsequently re-evaluate its worth. Thus, little fresh information about the product has to be provided to the customer after it has been branded. Note that failure to brand a product convincingly can result in the waste of much of the firm's advertising, since advertisements will promote the *generic* product category (including competitor's versions) to which the item belongs rather than the output of the firm in question.

Brand images encapsulate whole collections of product attributes and special features. Consumers come to know what the brand represents and may thus satisfy their requirements without careful thought or research. Also they can avoid repurchasing unsatisfactory branded items. If the firm sells several products in the same foreign country it must choose whether to allocate separate brand names to individual products or establish a generic 'family' brand covering all versions of its output. The latter approach can be highly cost effective, especially if the various products are closely related through associated usage (toiletries for example) or a common channel of distribution, a common customer group or similarity of prices. This is because the entire product range may then be advertised under a single brand name, thus cutting the cost of advertising individual brands separately. Moreover, additions to product lines are introduced easily and inexpensively since no extra advertising or promotions need be incurred. The new product is simply incorporated into existing advertising literature – the firm does not have to establish a completely new individual brand image. Separate brands are essential, nevertheless, if the firm wishes to appeal to different market segments (e.g. in consequence of cultural differences) or where products are markedly dissimilar.

Choice of brand name

Brand names used in foreign markets need to be internationally acceptable, distinct and easily recognisable, culture free, legally available and not subject to local restrictions. A brand name is far more than a device to identify the supplier of a product; it is an advertisement in its own right and a means for arousing in consumers a set of emotions and mental images conducive to selling the item. Short, simple, easily read and easy-to-pronounce brand names are usually best for foreign markets. Such names can be used in several countries simultaneously, for family branding, and may be supported within advertisements by a wide variety of pictorial illustrations.

9. Brand positioning

Market positioning involves finding out how customers think about the firm's products in relation to competing products, with a view either to modifying the product (plus associated advertising and other publicity) to make it fit in with these perceptions, or to changing the product's position in consumers' minds (Johansson and Thorelli 1985). Positions depend on the nature of the product, competing products and on how consumers see themselves (the lifestyles to which they aspire, role models, etc.). The essential issue is whether to attempt to position a brand similarly in all the nations in which the firm wishes to sell its outputs or to attempt different positions for the item in each country. A number of factors should influence the decision whether to opt for a single or different position in various countries, as follows:

(a) The degree of direct and immediate substitutability between the advertised output and locally supplied brands (if this is high the appropriate position for the product should be self-evident).

(b) The scope of the product's appeal: whether it sells to a broad cross-section of consumers (in relation to their ages, sex, income level, lifestyle, etc.) or only within small market niches.

(c) The extent to which a product's selling points are perceived similarly in different nations.

(d) Whether the item fulfils the same consumer needs in each market.

(e) Whether the brand name and/or product features need to be altered for use in disparate markets.

Positioning a brand in the same location in all foreign markets has a number of practical advantages, as follows:

(a) The firm can concentrate all its creative efforts on a handful of variables equally relevant to all markets.

(b) Standardisation of advertising is facilitated, leading to many cost savings.

(c) A similar price can be charged in each market, so that common price lists, catalogues and other price-sensitive promotional materials can be printed. Also the firm is not open to accusations of unfairly charging too high a price in certain markets.

(d) Similar demographic and lifestyle variables will be researched in each country. Hence, the firm only needs to monitor a few key statistics in the nations in which the product is sold.

Sound reasons for seeking different brand positions in various countries include:

(a) The existence of numerous possibilities for national stereotyping (e.g. precision and reliability in Germany, flair and elegance in France, style in Italy and so on). Stereotyping enables the advertiser instantly (and cheaply) to associate desirable national images with certain brands. Consumers' perceptions of a brand may be significantly influenced by the image of the country with which it is associated.

(b) The availability of extensive creative possibilities when drafting advertisements with nationalistic themes (windmills in The Netherlands, *haute couture* in France, pasta in Italy, etc.).

(c) Local customers' possible perceptions that locally produced goods are superior in quality (Belgian, French and German consumers are known to exhibit this characteristic for certain products).

10. Valuation of brands

Brand names are valuable assets in their own right. They can be sold, mortgaged, assigned to others or licensed in return for a royalty or lump-sum payment. Increasingly, firms prefer to acquire local firms that already possess strong brand images in foreign countries rather than incur the expense of introducing and developing their own brands in unfamiliar markets. Also, brand values often appear as intangible assets in company balance sheets, and the amounts stated have significant implications for the borrowing powers of the firm.

Ultimately, the only way to value a brand is to sell it to the highest bidder on the open market. Unfortunately, there is typically no genuine competitive market when a brand comes up for sale: bilateral haggling between the brand owner and a single possible buyer normally applies. The vendor will probably begin the negotiation from a brand valuation based on the worth of the brand when used in the vendor's own business, which will depend on factors such as:

- The amount that has been spent on introducing and developing the brand (market research and advertising costs, agency fees, sales promotions expenses etc.)
- The competitive situation and the risk of new brands entering the market
- Whether the brand is a market leader or a market follower
- The number of countries in which the brand can be used without significant adaptation
- Trends in consumer fashion likely to affect brand performance
- An estimate of the difference between the retail price made possible by selling the firm's output under the existing brand name and the price at which it would have to be sold if unbranded
- The long-term stability of demand (and hence of output and the use of productive capacity) created by consumer loyalty towards the brand
- Relations between the brand image and the firm's overall corporate image.

A firm considering purchasing an existing brand, conversely, will be concerned with:

- Fluctuations in annual sales and the expected life of the brand
- The brand's ability to stand alone and create good profits without having to rely on the sale of other goods, brands or services
- The brand's market position
- Consumer brand awareness and brand loyalty, independent of the company owning the brand
- The magnitude of the flow of income expected to be generated by the brand in comparison with the return to be had from investing in some other form of asset.

INTERNATIONAL PRICING

11. Determinants of selling prices

The price a firm may charge for its output depends on many factors, including the following:

(a) Consumers' perceptions of the attributes and quality of the product.

(b) Total demand for the good (which depends on consumer income, the size of the market and seasonal and demographic factors).

(c) The degree of competition in the market.

(d) Price elasticity of demand for the product (i.e. the extent to which a price change leads to an alteration in sales).

(e) Competitors' likely reactions to a price cut.

(f) Consumers' knowledge of the availability of substitute products.

(g) The product's brand image and the degree of consumer loyalty.

(h) Costs of production and distribution.

Special problems apply to international (as opposed to purely domestic) pricing, particularly in relation to lack of information, uncertain consumer responses, foreign exchange rate influences and the difficulty of estimating all the extra costs (including overheads) associated with foreign sales. These extra costs might include translating and interpreting fees, export packaging and documentation costs, insurance payments, clearing agents' fees, pre-shipment inspection and wharfage costs, and many other items. Credit periods are very long in some countries. Government price controls apply in certain states.

12. Pricing strategies

A number of pricing strategies are available, as follows:

(a) *Penetration pricing*, whereby a low price is combined with aggressive advertising aimed at capturing a large percentage of the market. The firm hopes that unit production costs will fall as output is expanded. The strategy will fail, however, if competitors simultaneously reduce their prices. This is a long-term strategy intended to build market share. It is expensive and normally involves substantial expenditures on promoting the product. Pricing at low levels in certain foreign markets might also be necessary in consequence of lower income levels of local consumers; intense local competition from rival companies; or weak demand for the product.

(b) *Skimming*, which is a high-price policy suitable for top-quality versions of established products. The firm must convince high-income consumers that the expensive model offers distinct improvements over the standard version. This policy requires the existence in the local market of significant numbers of high-income consumers prepared to pay top prices. Products should be designed to appeal to affluent consumers, offering extra features, greater comfort, versatility or ease of operation. The firm trades off a low market share against a high margin. A foreign image can help a product sustain a premium price, providing the image involves special qualities or features not available in home-supplied competing goods.

(c) *Cost-plus pricing* whereby the supplying firm predetermines the length of a production run, adds up all its anticipated costs – fixed and variable – and divides estimated total cost by planned output. Some percentage mark-up is then added to get a unit price. Cost-plus pricing is problematic for firms producing several different products. Allocations of overheads to the various items will be arbitrary to some extent, so that individual products may be over or underpriced. Also not all of a production run will necessarily be sold. Some units may have to be put into stock or scrapped, hence altering the unit production costs of the remaining items. And how should an international firm serving many foreign markets relate its overheads to particular markets? For example, what proportion of senior management time should be assumed to be taken up by the firm's foreign operations? Should the business seek to cover *all* its costs including overheads ('full-cost' pricing) or merely the *variable* costs of foreign sales, regarding the latter as a bonus that contributes to total revenue but need not absorb overhead expenditures.

(d) *Product life-cycle pricing.* Here the price is varied according to the stage in the product's life cycle. Initially, a high price may be set to cover development and advertising costs. The price might then be systematically lowered to broaden the product's appeal.

13. Transfer pricing

Transfer pricing means the determination of the 'prices' at which an MNC moves goods between its subsidiaries in various countries. A crucial feature of large centralised MNCs is their ability to engage in transfer pricing at artificially high or low prices. To illustrate, consider an MNC which extracts raw materials in one country, uses them as production inputs in another, assembles the partly finished goods in a third, and finishes and sells them in a fourth. The governments of the extraction, production and assembly countries will have sales or value added taxes; while the production, assembly and finished goods countries will impose tariffs on imports of goods. Suppose the MNC values its goods at zero prior to their final sale at high prices. The government of the extraction country receives no revenue from sales taxes because the MNC's subsidiary in that country is selling its output to the same MNC's subsidiary in the production country at a price of zero. Equally the production country raises no income from import tariffs on this transaction because the raw materials are imported at zero price! The only tax the MNC pays is a sales tax in the last country in the chain. Transfer pricing at unacceptably low values has been a major problem for many developing nations. Sometimes, therefore, the government of the country in which an MNC operates will insist that a government official shall decide the price at which the MNC exports its output, and not an employees of the MNC itself. Thus, the government of the host country will ensure that it receives an appropriate amount of sales tax. Similarly, importing countries might impose quantity-based instead of price-based import duties to ensure a reasonable revenue from taxes on imports of an MNC's goods.

Tax considerations aside, transfer prices need to be realistic in order that the profitabilities of various international operations may be assessed. Possible criteria for setting the transfer price include:

- the price at which the item could be sold on the open market (this is known as 'arms length' transfer pricing)
- cost of production or acquisition
- acquisition/production cost plus a profit markup (note the problem here of deciding what constitutes an appropriate profit markup)

- senior management's perceptions of the value of the item to the firm's overall international operations
- political negotiations between the units involved (a high or low transfer price can drastically affect the observed profitability of a subsidiary). Note the problems that arise if the 'buyer' happens to be the head office of the firm.

Normally the solution adopted is that which (seemingly) maximises profits for the company taken as a whole and which best facilitates the parent firm's control over subsidiary operations. Arm's length pricing (*see* above) is the method generally preferred by national governments and is recommended in a 1983 Code of Practice on the subject drafted by the Organisation for Economic Co-operation and Development (OECD). Note how a subsidiary that charges a high transfer price will accumulate cash, which might be invested more profitably in the selling country than elsewhere.

Problems with setting a realistic transfer price are as follows:

(a) Differences in the accounting systems used by subsidiaries in different countries.

(b) Executives in operating units deliberately manipulating the transfer price to enhance the book value of a subsidiary's profits.

(c) Disparate tax rates and investment subsidy levels in various countries.

(d) Possible absence of competition in local markets at various stages in the supply chain. Thus a 'market price' in such an area may be artificially high in consequence of the lack of local competition.

(e) There might not be any other product directly comparable to the item in question, again making it difficult to establish a market price.

(f) If a price is set at too high a level the 'selling' unit will be able to attain its profit targets too easily (at the expense of the 'buyer') and lead perhaps to idleness and inefficiency in the selling subsidiary.

Special problems arise when goods are being transferred among the partners of a joint venture. Should the various members of the venture be regarded as 'subsidiaries' or as independent businesses required to pay a market price?

Progress test 17

1. Define international marketing.

2. What are the special difficulties attached to international marketing compared to domestic marketing?

3. Explain the marketing concept.

4. How should a firm's marketing mix be adapted for international (as opposed to domestic) marketing?

5. Explain the difference between a differentiated marketing strategy and an undifferentiated marketing strategy.

6. In what circumstances is it appropriate for a firm to modify its products when selling in foreign markets?

7. List the main advantages of product standardisation.

8. Give six examples of matters in relation to which there are national differences in laws on advertising.

9. What major factors have contributed to the rise in the use of international direct marketing that has occurred in recent years.

10. Why is it extremely difficult to use sales promotions for international marketing campaigns?

11. Why do firms brand their products?

12. Define the term 'market positioning'.

13. How can the monetary value of a brand be established?

14. List the main pricing strategies available to an international firm.

15. What is transfer pricing?

18

INTERNATIONAL HUMAN RESOURCES MANAGEMENT

FUNDAMENTALS

1. Human resources management

Human resources management (HRM) concerns the human side of the management of enterprises and employees' relations with their firms. Its purpose is to ensure that the employees of a company, i.e. its human resources, are used in such a way that the employer obtains the greatest possible benefit from their abilities and the employees obtain both material and psychological rewards from their work. A key element of HRM is, of course, 'personnel management' which is that part of human resources management concerned with staffing the enterprise, determining and satisfying the needs of people at work, and the practical rules and procedures that govern relationships between employees and the organisation. In particular it involves (according to the UK Institute of Personnel and Development's published definition of the subject) the development and application of policies governing:

- Human resources planning, recruitment, selection, placement and termination
- Education and training; career development
- Terms of employment, methods and standards of remuneration
- Formal and informal communication and consultation both through the representatives of employers and employees and at all levels through the enterprise
- Negotiation and application of agreements on wages and working conditions; procedures for the avoidance and settlement of disputes.

However, whereas personnel management is practical, utilitarian and instrumental, and mostly concerned with administration and the *implementation* of policies, human resources management has *strategic* dimensions and involves the total deployment of human resources within the firm. Thus, for example HRM will consider such matters as:

(a) The aggregate size of the organisation's labour force in the context of an overall corporate plan (how many divisions and subsidiaries the company is to have, design of the organisation, etc.).

(b) How much to spend on training the workforce, given strategic decisions on target quality levels, product prices, volume of production, and so on, in order to ensure that the organisation has the competencies necessary to survive and prosper.

(c) The desirability of establishing relations with trade unions from the viewpoint of the effective management control of the entire organisation.

(d) The wider implications for employees of the management of change (not just the consequences of alterations in working practices).

The strategic approach to HRM involves the integration of personnel and other HRM considerations into the firm's overall corporate planning and strategy formulation procedures. It is proactive, seeking constantly to discover new ways of utilising the labour force in a more productive manner thus giving the business a competitive edge. Practical manifestations of the adoption of a strategic approach to HRM might include:

- Incorporation of a brief summary of the firm's basic HRM policy into its mission statement
- Explicit consideration of the consequences for employees of each of the firm's strategies and major new projects
- Implementation of programmes for changing organisational cultures
- Designing organisation structures to suit the needs of employees rather than conditioning the latter to fit in with the existing form of organisation.

Formulation of a human resources strategy implies recognition of the crucial importance of the HR function and the need therefore to have HR specialists in the senior management team, e.g. as members of the firm's main and/or subsidiary boards of directors.

2. National differences in HRM practices

A wide range of factors determine national HRM practices: social and economic circumstances, national culture, labour market characteristics, laws and customs, nature of the workforce (skills, attitudes, educational backgrounds, etc.), sizes and structures of business enterprises, identities of the main stakeholders in firms, levels of prosperity, role of the state in social affairs, and so on. Important national differences arise in relation to:

- The extent of employee participation in management decision making
- Legal regulation of employee relations (especially the roles of trade unions and collective bargaining)
- The importance of market forces in fixing wages and conditions of service
- Attitudes towards individualism and collectivism
- Backgrounds of persons engaged in the HRM function. In some countries (Germany for example) HRM professionals tend to have legal qualifications; elsewhere HRM is seen as a matter of financial efficiency, or in terms of sociology and human relations, or in certain nations as an occupation suitable for the 'gifted amateur'.

- Whether HRM is seen as a specialist or a general line management function.

Workers doing comparable jobs in different countries vary with respect to their motivation (e.g. whether there exists a 'work ethic' in a particular nation), commitment to employing organisations, wage levels, technical skills and educational backgrounds. Other determinants of national differences include the extent of unemployment (which often affects workers' attitudes towards their firms), age and sex distribution of the population, and expectations regarding working hours, holidays, etc. Managerial attitudes and behaviour also vary between nations. Differences in managers from disparate countries might relate to preferred management style (authoritarian approaches are more common in certain countries), values, personal objectives, approaches to problem-solving, salary expectations, use of management models and 'scientific' techniques, willingness to delegate, and attitudes towards risk. Planning and strategy formulation are more widespread in some countries than in others. Attitudes towards punctuality and the need to complete work on schedule can also differ among nations.

3. Management styles

The term 'management style' has two (related) meanings. One is the demeanour that a manager adopts when dealing with employees; the other is the collective approach of the management of an entire organisation to questions of leadership, worker participation in management decisions, control of employees, and to interpersonal relations between managers and basic grade workers. In the former context the particular style chosen will depend on personal inclinations, training and experience, and on environmental factors. It will affect managers' relations with their subordinates, group productivity, and patterns of interaction among employees. In the macro-organisational sense, management style helps determine formal structure, line and staff relationships, whether the firm uses project teams, the frequency and character of interactions with workers, and so on.

4. National differences in management style

In some countries the prevailing management style is highly formal and authoritarian, in others it is the reverse. National disparities result from the following:

(a) *Cultural* factors such as religion, attitudes towards industry and towards management as an occupation; and community views on efficiency, the role of profit, savings and investment. Achievement in business is rewarded more in some societies than in others. Willingness to accept risk also differs markedly between countries.

(b) *Social* factors such as:
(i) Whether there exists a *work ethic* in the country. Higher incomes and increasing productivity create possibilities for greater amounts of leisure, yet in some communities managers (and others) choose to work extremely hard and take little time off regardless of their large remunerations.

(*ii*) *Social class systems.* A high degree of class and/or occupational mobility results in individuals from a wide variety of class and income backgrounds reaching the top in management positions. Class systems affect recruitment policies and procedures and promotion and salary grading schemes. Rigid class structures cause an oversupply of trained, educated and competent people in lower-level management jobs, since social barriers prevent their moving up the hierarchy.

(*iii*) *Attitudes towards authority.* Paternalistic management styles and highly formal interpersonal relationships between managers and subordinates are likely in countries where deferential attitudes are valued for their own sake. The psychological distance between managers at different levels affects communication, problem-solving and decision-making systems.

(*iv*) Existence or otherwise of *strong desires to accumulate wealth.*

(c) Variations in the institutional frameworks within which businesses operate, particularly company structures.

(d) Average sizes of enterprises and their forms of ownership.

(e) Contrasting management training systems.

(f) Differing economic conditions and stages of economic development.

(g) Differences in legal environments in relation to employment protection, health and safety regulations, etc.

5. Education systems

The quality of a country's education system determines the overall calibre of the managers of its businesses. Some important consequences of good or bad basic education systems are as follows:

(a) Poorly educated managers will not be able to understand and apply the latest management techniques, particularly those with a quantitative dimension, and may tend to resist change. They are not likely to read current trade and technical journals and hence may be unfamiliar with the latest technical developments.

(b) Ill-educated individuals frequently possess hostile attitudes towards other groups and cultures. This has implications for recruitment, selection and performance appraisal procedures, and for general equal opportunity matters.

(c) If females receive a different sort of education from males (e.g. girls being taught only non-technical subjects) it becomes difficult for women to enter certain managerial occupations.

(d) It is difficult to introduce technically complex products and processes to organisations where the top management is inadequately educated.

(e) If irrelevant subjects are taught in schools and colleges the country will eventually experience skills shortages in key areas.

(f) Badly educated managers often find it difficult to communicate with (better educated) managers in other countries, leading to fewer export orders.

6. Religious factors

Religion affects culture and may itself be an important determinant of individual behaviour and management style. The following influences are particularly significant:

(a) Religion can form the basis for a class system and hence create a barrier preventing certain groups from obtaining management jobs. The Hindu caste system, for instance, once allocated members of each caste to *specific* occupational and social roles. (Discrimination based on caste is now forbidden by the Indian constitution.) Catholic minorities in Protestant countries and Protestant minorities in Catholic countries sometimes complain of discriminatory treatment where appointment to managerial positions is concerned.

(b) The ease with which women can enter management may be affected by religious considerations.

(c) Religious principles can determine attitudes towards the morality of the pursuit of material wealth.

(d) A community's dominant religion might directly affect business practices. Islam is a case in point.

(e) Religion can engender patriotic attitudes among business leaders. Japanese Shinto, for example, emphasises respect for the state, for the Japanese people and for national authority. Such influences might encourage co-operation among employee groups and aggressive attitudes towards export marketing.

STRATEGIES FOR INTERNATIONAL HRM

7. Need for HRM strategies

An international or multinational business's success or failure depends to a large extent on its ability to select, train, motivate, develop and manage its human resources and it is axiomatic that no business can attain its mission without employees who are competent to complete the necessary work. Specific reasons for having a human resources strategy include the following:

(a) Firms with the most productive workforces possess an international competitive advantage over rivals.

(b) Expenditures on personnel typically represent a very large proportion of an MNC's total spending.

(c) An MNC's capacity to adopt new technologies, enter fresh markets and/or undertake different lines of work frequently depend more on the capabilities of its people than on capital investment.

(d) Computerisation of manufacturing and administrative processes has greatly influenced the nature of work and the structure of employment within enterprises. Communication and control systems have altered; there is less demand for unskilled employees completing routine duties. Strategic HR planning is necessary to cope with the resistance to change that new technologies might engender and the possible displacement of labour that might result.

(e) Increasing organisational complexity requires a suitable mix of specialist skills which cannot be obtained overnight.

(f) Extensive employment protection legislation in many countries imposes constraints on how managements may treat their workforces.

Through formulating a human resources strategy, management places human relations at the top of its agenda, hence encouraging a professional approach to human resources issues throughout the firm. HR activities should be better co-ordinated: personnel policies and procedures can be standardised in all divisions and subsidiaries if this is desired (although some MNCs leave personnel matters to local subsidiary discretion and control).

Problems with human resources strategies include the following:

(a) Strategies are sometimes formulated ritualistically, without genuine commitment to their implementation. Management might be as much concerned with *being seen* to possess an HR strategy as actually having one *per se*. Statements to the effect that organisations are 'equal opportunities employers', for example, may be made cynically and with no intention of applying the principle in practice (the real purpose being to create a good image with government equal opportunity agencies and other outside bodies).

(b) Major differences of opinion over what constitutes an effective HR strategy may emerge between head office personnel specialists on the one hand and subsidiary managers on the other.

(c) There is little point in having an HR strategy if it is not properly communicated to *everyone* working for the firm throughout the world. Lack of management/worker communication and employee involvement in HR management issues can make the implementation of HR strategies extremely problematic.

(d) Although a company may have an HR strategy 'on paper' and under the overall supervision of a head office personnel department, line managers might simply ignore the strategy at the subsidiary level.

(e) Difficulties caused by failures in an MNC's human resources strategy might not be as obvious as, say, the consequences of a collapse in financial strategy – at least not in the short term.

Note how immediate crises in human resources management can often be overcome by short-term measures such as compulsory early retirement for everyone above a certain age, extensive overtime working to meet staff shortages, emergency recruitment etc., but only at a heavy long-term cost to the firm.

8. Standardisation versus local control

The advantages to applying standardised HRM practices in all subsidiaries in all parts of the world include the integration of all HRM activities into a coherent whole, the creation of shared values and a common work culture, establishment of targets that are understood throughout the organisation, and the implementation of straightforward procedures for setting individual targets, appraisal and monitoring work. Nevertheless, many MNCs devolve responsibility for HRM to their foreign subsidiaries. Reasons for delegating HRM to local units include the following:

(a) The desire to relate employee remuneration to performance levels achieved in *local* operations.

(b) Increasing competence in the human resources management field of the line managers employed in the foreign subsidiaries of large MNCs, consequent to more extensive training and better staff development than in the past.

(c) The trend towards overall decentralisation and diversification of activities in large MNCs, with quasi-autonomous profit centres, budgetary control by local managers, decisions on industrial relations management being taken at the establishment level, etc.

(d) Effective teamwork within a local unit can be accompanied by team-based bonus systems.

(e) Local circumstances can be taken into account during collective bargaining.

(f) The possible strengthening of managerial authority at the local level.

(g) Unit-level communictions between management and employee representatives are facilitated.

(h) The suitability of local control of HRM for international companies with foreign subsidiaries that undertake differing types of work and hence employ disparate categories of employee, each with its own special problems and set of terms and conditions of employment.

Disadvantages to local control include duplication of activity among subsidiaries, fragmentation of procedures, heavy dependence on *ad hoc* unwritten rules, and the formulation of policies by subsidiary managers with little expertise in HRM. Changes in working methods and terms and conditions of employment might be introduced to local units in an uncoordinated and haphazard manner. Also the issues discussed during decentralised negotiations are likely to become parochial, ignoring matters relating to global corporate strategy, planning and investment. A major problem with devolution of personnel and/or HRM work to non-specialists in subsidiaries is that non-specialists may be neither competent nor interested in personnel or HRM issues, and might not be motivated to complete HRM duties properly so that critically important personnel tasks are neglected. Bad HRM decisions lead to a poor corporate image, higher long-run costs and loss of output due to industrial conflict. Also subsidiary managers might focus all their attention on immediately pressing personnel problems, at the expense of long-term HRM planning, and it could result in HRM considerations not influencing strategic management decisions. Effective devolution requires:

- the provision of back-up services in relation to technical problems arising from contracts of employment, legal aspects of redundancy and dismissal, union recognition, etc.
- acceptance by everyone that subsidiary managers' workloads will have to increase following their assumption of personnel responsibilities
- training of line managers in HRM techniques and concepts.

Decentralisation of the HRM function to foreign subsidiaries is more likely where:

(a) There is little integration between the production systems of decentralised units (as sometimes happens when a business has expanded *via* mergers and acquisitions of other firms).

(b) The company has many products and operates in multiple markets.

(c) The impact of technical change is felt predominantly at the local workplace rather than at the company level.

(d) There is no overall corporate identity to which workers in subsidiary units can relate.

(e) The skills and competencies needed to undertake a subsidiary's work are found in local rather than national labour markets.

(f) There are big regional disparities in wage levels.

(g) A company's activities are spread over many nations.

Sometimes MNCs introduce two-tier devoluted HRM systems with basic policies being determined centrally, leaving incentive schemes, working hours, holiday entitlement, etc., to be decided locally. Note how the decentralisation of HRM requires a more active personnel department than otherwise might be the case. In particular, the personnel department needs to:

- provide expert help and advice to decentralised units
- develop schemes for training local managers in the skills of personnel management
- implement disciplinary, grievance and disputes settlements procedures at the local level.

9. Strategy formulation

When devising an HRM strategy for a large international or multinational company it is important to assess the size, nature, scope and human resources requirements of the *future* organisation (rather than the business as it stands) and to define the measures necessary to supply the human resources needed to attain company goals. Human resources strategies should be formulated *after* other major functional strategies have been determined. Thus the firm must decide its strategic objectives; specify its production and marketing strategies, organisation structure and operational plans; and *then* address the issue of how best to manage the human resources required to implement the chosen options. Next, the firm must compare its present human resources with the demands implied by its overall corporate plan. The comparison needs to examine:

- existing and desired organisational climates (cultures), including leadership style and employee participation mechanisms
- the types of people required in terms of skills, attitudes and performance capabilities
- motivation and reward systems
- current and anticipated skills requirements
- the firm's training and employee development capabilities.

Further matters requiring consideration include potential obstacles to the efficient use of the firm's human resources, the quality of internal company communications, techniques for measuring performance, and general personnel policies. Gaps between actual and desired situations will become apparent. Measures for bridging these gaps should now be defined.

10. Influences on international HRM strategy

HR strategies are necessarily affected by a variety of environmental factors. *External* influences include the following:

(a) *The legal framework.* Laws on collective bargaining in various countries, the right to strike, employment protection, employee participation in management decisions, minimum wage levels, etc., in each of the nations in which the company does or intends to do business.

(b) *Political factors.* Host country government attitudes, guidelines and Codes of Practice on employment matters. The general ambiences of host nation governments towards industrial relations and employment matters.

(c) *Economic factors.* Unemployment and inflation rates in host nations (both these variables affect employee demands for wage increases), competition within industries (intense competition implies the poaching of rival firms' staff), growth prospects, and so on.

(d) *Social trends.* Extents of female participation in national labour forces, amounts of part-time working, attitudes towards work and working hours, demands for improvements in the quality of working life, changes in living standards, educational opportunities, etc.

(e) *The technological environment.* Changes in working methods, needs for reskilling and greater flexibility of labour, and the implications of various technologies for management style.

Internal factors affecting international HR strategy are the degree of decentralisation of the organisation; the present state of morale; whether jobs can be completed by unskilled people; the natures of host country workforces in terms of background, education, perspectives, etc., the degree of trade union activity within subsidiaries; the attitudes of the company's principal shareholders towards employee relations; and the perspectives of individual senior managers.

INTERNATIONAL EMPLOYEE RELATIONS STRATEGIES

11. Employee relations

The subject 'employee relations' deals with all the formal and informal relationships of an interpersonal nature that arise from management/employee interactions in working situations. The modern approach to the management of employee relations is to emphasise co-operation rather than conflict and to integrate employee relations policies into the overall corporate strategy of the firm. This requires that management recognise the critical importance of harmonious relations with its workforce in various countries, and relate its employee relations policies to the achievement of increased competitiveness in the international field. Major decisions that have to be taken when formulating an employee relations strategy include:

- whether to recognise trade unions
- managerial approaches to personnel policies and procedures that affect employee relations (recruitment and promotion; appraisal; selection of workers for training, redundancy, etc.)
- whether management is prepared to use external bodies to arbitrate and help resolve disputes
- the basic formulae to be applied to the division of the firm's profit between the owners of the business and workers
- the methods to be used for communicating with employees
- the degree to which employee representatives are to be involved in management decision-making (EIRR 1994).

Few multinational companies even attempt to impose standardised employee relations policies on subsidiaries in different countries because of the wide variations in national labour law, norms and labour relations practices among nations. Nonetheless, the parent company is necessarily concerned with the state of employee relations in its subsidiaries, in order to control labour costs and ensure the continuity of operations. Accordingly headquarters staff are likely to fulfil an advisory and/or mediating role whenever employee relations problems arise. Hence, HQ will advise on:

- the company's overall philosophy on management-worker relations, the role of trade unions, and so on
- alternative solutions to employee relations problems that might be pursued
- cost constraints necessitated by overall company strategy
- the employee relations policies of subsidiaries in other countries and whether they have been successful
- wage rates and employment conditions in various nations (bearing in mind an MNC's ability to shift its operations across national boundaries)
- productivity improvement measures introduced in other countries.

The aim is to apply consistent (though not necessarily identical) policies in subsidiaries throughout the world. Managers within particular subsidiaries should know precisely where they stand in respect of employee relations matters, and policies affecting employees should be dovetailed into an overall company plan.

12. MNC relations with trade unions

An MNC's ability to shift production between countries gives it an important advantage in negotiations with local trade unions in host nations. Further problems for unions that have to deal with MNCs include the difficulties of obtaining information, of interpreting financial data and of identifying key decision makers within the parent firm. Note how transfer pricing (*see* 17:13) can be used to make a subsidiary's profits appear very low for the purpose of collective bargaining with employee representatives. And there seems to be little enthusiasm on the part of workers in MNC subsidiaries in one country for taking strike action in support of workers in dispute with the same MNCs in other parts of the world. Nevertheless, trade unions are themselves increasingly internationally-minded and willing to co-operate across national frontiers (especially in the European Single Market). Also unions in one country may look at precedents relating to pay and working conditions set in other nations when formulating demands, thus forcing an MNC to co-ordinate its employee relations strategies centrally in order to present a consistent front. Little transnational employer/union collective bargaining has (to date) occurred, however, mainly because trade unions are quintessentially *national* organisations, with minimal experience of international affairs.

The OECD Code of Practice on industrial relations in MNCs

In 1975 the Organisation for Economic Co-operation and Development issued a set of guidelines for the conduct of industrial relations within MNCs. This is a purely voluntary Code, which recommends:

- that the right of employees to join and be represented by trade unions be respected and that MNCs engage in collective bargaining with employee representatives
- the provision of facilities to employee representatives to help them conduct collective negotiations
- that MNCs give employee representatives meaningful information for the purpose of collective bargaining, including relevant financial information
- observe standards of employment not less favourable than local norms in the host country
- the training and, wherever possible, promotion of local workers
- that MNCs give adequate notice of intended closures and/or relocations of production and discuss with employee representatives measures for mitigating the adverse consequences of closures
- equality of treatment of all groups of employees in relation to recruitment, dismissal, pay, promotion and training
- that MNCs not use the threat of transfer of an operating unit to another country as a bargaining weapon when negotiating with unions.

INTERNATIONAL COMPARISONS OF HRM PRACTICE

13. HRM in the European Union

The needs to recruit, motivate, appraise and control employees are common to organisations throughout the world. How HRM is implemented, however, differs substantially from state to state. Major disparities occur in relation to terms and conditions of employment; the extent of the casualisation of national workforces; the availability of special leave for maternity, career breaks and for compassionate matters; and in recruitment and dismissal procedures. For example, in France and Belgium it is illegal to use press advertisements for job vacancies for implicit corporate image advertising (offering jobs that in reality do not exist). Additionally, French job advertisements cannot lawfully specify an upper age limit for applicants for the vacant post. Application forms for French jobs cannot lawfully include questions concerning union membership, religion, politics, or family situation (Dany and Torchy 1994).

German firms' selection methods must be approved by their works councils and are subject to much Federal legislation. Applicants are legally entitled to privacy, the right to be treated with dignity, payment of interview expenses, and may not be asked 'improper' questions. The latter include questions concerning the candidate's politics or family situation. Italian job advertisements have to comply with the state Workers' Statute, which forbids mention of political views, union membership, racial or religious criteria.

Several Continental EU countries legally require employers to pay part-time workers pro-rata to full-time employees and not to discriminate against part timers in relation to working conditions, selection for dismissal, etc. Night work is strictly controlled in a number of EU states. Greek night workers must be paid at least time and a quarter of normal rates; double time at weekends. Spain and Portugal also have a statutory minimum rate of 125 per cent for night work. Spain bans night work for anyone under the age of 18. The Netherlands prohibits night work entirely unless the firm involved obtains a special licence from the Dutch Ministry of Labour. In Belgium night work has to be voluntary, approved by employee representatives, and only undertaken by permanent full-time workers. Additionally, some countries set down minimum wage premiums for overtime working. French, Greek, German and Irish workers are entitled to at least time and a quarter for overtime; Portuguese employees have to be paid at least time and a half for the first hour of extra working and time and three-quarters from then on. In Spain all overtime attracts a 75 per cent statutory bonus. For further and more detailed information on national differences in European HRM practices see the M&E titles *Human Resources Management* and *Employee Relations*.

14. HRM in the United States of America

US human resources management emphasises the importance of individual initiative and responsibility, selection and promotion on merit, the assumption that employees should and will be loyal to the employing organisation, and willingness to dismiss workers whose performance does not come up to scratch. Motivation often depends on (substantial) rewards and penalties. There is open vertical and horizontal communication among employees compared with many other countries, and relatively informal personal relationships.

United States employment law and practice is based on the doctrine of 'employment at will,' i.e. the freedom of employers to hire and fire as they please and to terminate an employee's job at any time and for any reason – subject to that person's contract of employment. Market forces determine the pattern of most US economic activity (apart from the nation's extensive defence industries). Vigorous competition and the regular business shut-downs/start-ups that it implies have led perhaps to a greater willingness to accept change than in some other countries and to a workforce that is prepared, on the whole, to move to areas and industries where jobs are available.

Collective bargaining has traditionally taken place at the enterprise rather than the industry or national level. Also, American unions negotiate on a far wider range of matters than their West European counterparts, especially regarding fringe benefits (health and welfare schemes, extended holidays, occupational pension, etc.). US unions' successes in negotiating with managements in relation to fringe benefits derive in part from the Wagner Act which empowers the US National Labour Relations Board (NLRB) to compel employers to bargain with unions on a multitude of issues.

15. Japanese approaches to HRM

William Ouchi has suggested that the Japanese approach to HRM comprises three strategies and six associated techniques (Ouchi 1981). The strategies are as follows:

- Commitment to life-long employment
- Projection of the philosophy and objectives of the organisation to the individual worker. Making workers feel they belong to a clearly defined corporate entity.
- Careful selection of new entrants and intensive socialisation of recruits into the existing value system.

These strategies are implemented through six techniques:

(a) Seniority-based promotion systems. Recruits expect to spend their entire careers with a single firm. They acquire experience of various aspect of the business through job rotation and steady (but slow) progression through the management hierarchy. Since there is but limited opportunity for promotion, most transfers are lateral. This develops generalist rather than specialist management skills, and well-rounded management personalities.

(b) Continuous training and appraisal which, combined with guaranteed job security, enable managers to construct long-term career plans. Managers might experience less stress than their Western counterparts.

(c) Group-centred activities. Tasks are assigned to groups rather than individuals.

(d) Open communications both within work groups and between management and labour. Managers and workers dress alike and eat in the same works canteen.

(e) Worker participation in decision making, based on consultation with all who will be affected by the proposed change.

(f) A production-centred approach with, nonetheless, great concern for the welfare of the employee. There is no great social divide between management and worker.

In Japan, payments systems are seniority based. The longer an employee has been with the firm the more he or she is paid. Another important feature of the Japanese corporation is that it will usually have just one trade union representing all its employees.

Japanese approaches to employee relations have attracted much attention in recent years because of formidable successes achieved by Japanese industry and the contrasts offered by Japanese management styles relative to those applied in Western countries. Japanese firms, moreover, seem to have obtained the co-operation of foreign workers, even in countries where industrial strife is commonplace.

STAFFING THE MULTINATIONAL COMPANY

16. Recruitment of managers

An international business may engage home country staff to fill managerial positions both in the base country and abroad; or it could staff home country jobs using home country personnel while employing host country nationals for foreign positions; or have no concern for the particular nationalities of persons occupying key managerial roles within the organisation. Advantages to using host country nationals as managers of foreign subsidiaries are their fluency in the local language, absence of cultural adjustment problems, and the fact that no relocation expenses are incurred. Individuals will already possess relationships with local business services (banks, advertising agencies, etc.) and government officials. Also there will be continuity of management style within each foreign subsidiary, and a local business image will be generated. Another reason for employing host country nationals is that foreign governments may prefer MNCs to use locally recruited managers on the assumption that they will behave in the best interests of the host country rather than the MNC's headquarters nation (Brewster 1991).

However, a host country national might experience difficulty when communicating with headquarters managers (because of differences in culture, background, attitude and perspective), and he or she may lack the product knowledge and managerial expertise of expatriate staff (Weiss and Gripp 1992). A locally recruited manager, moreover, might 'side' with the government of the host country on matters involving conflict with the parent firm. And once the individual has reached senior management level in the host country then (unless the person is transferred to HQ) he or she has nowhere else to go and may become demotivated.

An alternative both to using host country nationals and to employing expatriate home nation staff is to engage third country nationals who have already proven their ability to adapt to foreign environments, and thus will be able to settle-in more quickly and at lower cost. In the European Union for example the total freedom of movement and residence of labour has given rise to a new class of 'Euro-executives' who regularly take management jobs in different EU countries. The characteristics of Euro-executives are discussed below.

17. Euro-executives

These are multi-lingual managers who feel at home in any European country, are familiar with EU business laws and practices, and regularly move between companies and countries. Qualities of Euro-executives include:

- Cultural adaptability, i.e. the ability to blend quickly into the local culture of any EU member nation
- Wide-ranging experience of European business management resulting from several changes of jobs and location
- Possession of generalist rather than function-specific management competencies
- Ability to communicate effectively and to exercise interpersonal management skills
- Knowledge of individual EU markets
- Selling and negotiating skills, and the ability to conduct hostile negotiations in more than one language
- Familiarity with EU product standards
- Knowledge of the documentation and procedures attached to cross-border EU marketing, including those needed for transport and distribution across the Union
- Willingness and ability to cope with rapid technical, organisational and environmental change
- Capacity to get on with fellow workers of different nationalities and to contribute to multinational project teams
- Acceptance of a lifestyle involving much foreign travel, frequent relocation and disruptions to normal family routines.

Problems attached to the employment and use of Euro-executive are as follows:

(a) Their high salaries (resulting from their short supply) which create large differentials between Euro-executives and other managers. Euro-executives are hired in consequence of their superior competencies and will demand remuneration packages comparable to those available in other countries. Additionally, they could demand compensation for the high cost of accommodation in prosperous areas (London for instance), for the cost of sending children to private schools that cater for a particular nationality, and for the loss of a spouse's earnings.

(b) Fitting them into conventional line and staff organisation systems, which might stifle their initiative and creativity.

(c) A high probability of their being headhunted by other firms.

(d) Their lack of intimate knowledge of their employing companies and associated products or of the local economy and local business cultures. Euro-executives might not stay in a country long enough to develop networks of contacts with local business people, banks, ancillary services, etc.

(e) Possible conflicts arising from different approaches to business adopted by Euro-executives compared to locally-recruited managers.

Euro-executives, moreover, could experience significant domestic problems that might reduce their usefulness to employing firms, for example:

- Reluctance to accept a fresh assignment in another EU country because the manager's children have only just settled into a local school
- Opposition to an intended move from the manager's spouse, who may regard it as interference with his or her own career
- Traumas and tribulations attached to regularly moving house and resettling in other cultures
- Practical problems connected with finding suitable housing, arranging for pension transfers, tax arrangements, etc.

18. Expatriate staff

Use of home country staff for foreign assignments ensures that senior management has full knowledge of the capabilities, experience, attitudes and perspectives of those in charge of foreign operations; that managers are fully conversant with company policies and procedures; and that communications will be fast and efficient (Boyacigiller 1991). The local subsidiary will be run precisely as headquarters wishes, and since the expatriates themselves will depend on the parent organisation for future career advancement they can be relied upon to further the parent company's interests. Expatriates might have greater product knowledge and managerial expertise than local nationals.

Disadvantages to using expatriates include:

- Their lack of familiarity with the local language, culture and business practices
- The period needed for them to settle-in to a new environment (up to a year in some cases) during which a manager's productivity will be lower than he or she achieved at home
- Dangers that individual biases and prejudices towards certain racial or other ethnic groups might emerge during a foreign posting, even though such negative attitudes were not apparent during the manager's home country service
- The possibility that expatriates might impose an inappropriate management style on host country employees rather than adapting to the local environment

- The blocking of promotion opportunities for locally recruited staff, the most able of whom may well leave the firm.

Settling-in

Settling-in difficulties might result from the expatriate's family not adjusting to local conditions, children not making progress at school, or a spouse not finding local employment. Experience suggests that female spouses frequently experience greater difficulty in adjusting to a foreign environment than their male partners, essentially because expatriate communities tend to be male dominated (the husbands' jobs representing the reason for the existence of the expatriate community) and since female spouses lack the continuity and stabilising influence provided by a job (Black and Gregersen 1991). The female may have given up work in order to accompany her spouse to the foreign country, and has to cope with new experiences in all aspects of life: accommodation, friendships, house care arrangements, etc. A spouse will probably find it easier to settle-in to a foreign country that already has a large expatriate community from the spouse's home country. This community can provide help and support to and share its experience with the individual in question; create immediate opportunities for social intercourse; and will generally insulate the spouse from the shock of having to cope with a new environment.

Expatriate training programmes

These normally include the provision of information on the host country, housing, educational and medical facilities, living conditions, social norms, etc.; language training; and job specific matters relating to local business laws and regulations, the tasks to be undertaken, performance targets, methods for communicating with head office, and so on. The programme might include visits to the country, briefings by other employees recently returned from abroad, and the supply of information to family members who will accompany the person to the new location (Carusgil *et al* 1992). While abroad, the expatriate might be kept in touch with head office affairs *via* the appointment of a mentor (typically a senior head office manager) who periodically meets with the expatriate to discuss the latter's progress and what is likely to happen to the expatriate on his or her return. Further training might be needed to prepare the person and his or her family for repatriation (Moynihan 1993).

Expatriate remuneration

Salary levels need to be of a level sufficient to attract, retain and motivate expatriate staff of a suitable calibre. This could involve paying expatriates salaries that are considerably higher than those of locally recruited managers, causing much resentment among the lower paid staff. Supplements to base salary are common, and could take the form of expenses payments (for cars, drivers, hire of domestic servants, etc.), special cost of living allowance to compensate for higher taxes, housing costs and so on encountered abroad. Alternatively a straight percentage premium on basic salary might be payable during the foreign posting. An important issue is the currency in which the expatriate is remunerated, since changes in currency exchange rates will affect the conversion value of local currency savings. Sometimes the expatriate is paid partly in local currency and partly in the currency of the host nation.

Repatriation

It is crucially important to plan the orderly re-absorption of a former expatriate into the head office organisation system following his or her return from abroad. Problems frequently experienced by returning expatriates include reductions in their real standards of living (loss of paid accommodation, termination of financial assistance with school fees, etc.), boredom (a headquarters job may be less varied and carry less responsibility), and 'reverse culture shock' as the individual adjusts to changes in the home country environment. The returning expatriate has to cope with head office organisational changes that will have occurred during his or her absence, possible communication difficulties with head office colleagues, new technical developments and alterations in head office management methods.

19. Selection of staff for foreign postings

Managers may be attracted to a foreign posting through prospects for a higher salary, long-term promotion (though often these are not actually realised), broader responsibilities and the acquisition of experience not available in the home country. Such aspirations could cloud an individual's judgement *vis-a-vis* the problems that expatriate assignments are likely to involve, and obscure the fact that expatriate work can be extremely demanding. The ideal expatriate is perhaps one who, in addition to being adaptable, is good at foreign languages, self-reliant and independent, emotionally stable and in excellent physical health, is sensitive to foreign culture, technically competent and genuinely enjoys working abroad. He or she needs to possess a working knowledge of business methods, cultures, organisation and policies in various countries and of best practice in foreign firms and be able quickly and easily to transfer his or her knowledge and skills between firms and operational cultures. The person should be a good communicator, capable of exercising interpersonal management skills in multicultural situations; willing and able to cope with rapid technical, organisational and environmental change; and capable of working with fellow managers of different nationalities and of contributing to multinational project teams.

Few managers possess all these qualities, and great care is necessary when selecting staff for foreign postings. Factors influencing the choice of individuals for expatriate jobs might include:

(a) *Individual characteristics*: qualifications and experience, track record, perspectives, adaptability and attitude, family situation (and whether the candidate's family genuinely want the person to work abroad), language and area expertise, career plans and personal preferences.

(b) *The host country environment*: local business norms and cultures, degree of employee participation in management decisions, calibre of the foreign subsidiary's employees, how easily a foreigner will be able to 'blend in' with the local environment.

(c) *Company-specific factors*: technical sophistication of the business, nature of the industry, status of international (as opposed to headquarter's country) operations, organisational culture.

(d) *Equal opportunity considerations*: sex discrimination against women in employment continues to exist to a number of countries, sometimes with an (allegedly) religious base. This can affect a female manager's ability to function effectively in the host country. Inevitably companies must consider the moral and ethical issues connected with possible decisions to deny female managers the opportunity of interesting and potentially career-enhancing foreign postings simply because they are women.

20. Management of an international sales force

Many international businesses employ international salespeople to travel the world looking for orders. Sending representatives to foreign destinations is expensive, but still far cheaper than establishing permanent presences in other countries, especially when the total value of orders is likely to be small. A number of HRM problems arise from the engagement and use of an international sales force. In particular the recruitment of suitable people is extremely difficult because of the special abilities that international salespeople need to posses. They require all the skills expected of a domestic salesperson; plus linguistic abilities, the capacity to work alone and without supervision, the patience necessary to cope with long periods spent travelling, a cool temperament and the ability to cope with stress. Note the high level of responsibility that the international salesperson has to assume. He or she will negotiate with customers and have to take significant decisions. The person represents the top management of the company and cannot be seen to be constantly referring back to head office for instructions (otherwise there is little point in sending a salesperson in the first instance – the deal could just as well be concluded by correspondence). Other qualities required of the international salesperson include:

- a detailed knowledge of the product
- the ability to acclimatise quickly to unfamiliar cultures, customs and business practices
- maturity and dependability
- a neutral stance on political issues. The person cannot afford to have national prejudices: foreign cultures and organisations must be accepted *as they are* and without challenging foreigners' behaviour or attitudes.

Long periods spent travelling abroad can cause social problems for the individual involved. Personal relationships with colleagues and customers during an assignment will usually be of a strictly formal business nature, leading perhaps to loneliness, boredom and the collapse of personal motivation. Permanent friendships in foreign countries are difficult to establish because the salesperson will not be in one place for a period long enough to build up social relationships outside work.

Some of these problems can be overcome through employing salespeople who live and work abroad but report directly to and are controlled by head office. The individuals involved may be recruited in the head office country or in the nations in which they operate. This approach reduces salespeoples' travelling time and expenses and enables individuals to become fully familiar with business customs and cultures in the areas they cover and with local transport arrangements (an important consideration in remote regions – knowledge of road networks, railway systems and timetables, etc., can greatly improve an export saleperson's efficiency in the field). Also the local salesperson will be fluent in the local language. Note that no internationally travelling salesperson can possibly be fluent in the language of *every* country that he or she will be called upon to visit, and thus will have to rely on interpreters. The ability to speak the client's language is extremely desirable as it greatly improves the flow of communications, avoids misunderstandings and enables the salesperson to understand properly the customer's requirements.

Progress test 18

1. Define human resources management

2. Explain the strategic approach to human resources management.

3. What is meant by the term 'management style'? Give six examples of factors contributing to national differences in management style.

4. List the advantages to a multinational company of applying standardised HRM policies and practices in all its subsidiaries in all parts of the world.

5. What factors should a firm consider when formulating a human resources management strategy?

6. Outline the major provisions of the OECD Code of Practice on industrial relations in multinational companies.

7. According to W. Ouchi, the Japanese approach to human resources management comprises three strategies and six associated techniques. What are these strategies and techniques?

8. What is a Euro-executive?

9. List the main problems associated with the management of expatriate staff.

10. What criteria should be applied when selecting staff for foreign postings?

11. List the major difficulties attached to the management of an international sales force.

19

STRATEGIES FOR INTERNATIONAL BUSINESS

THE SCOPE OF STRATEGIC MANAGEMENT

1. Nature of strategic management

Strategy concerns the determination of a general direction for the enterprise and the formulation of overall business policies. Examples of strategic decisions are the choice of products a company will supply, the markets in which it is to operate, how many divisions and departments the firm is to have, whether to operate at the top or bottom ends of markets in various countries, whether to acquire other businesses, and how to finance operations. Strategic decisions are the most important that senior management has to take, as they commit extensive resources and have substantial consequences for the life of the organisation. Decisions made at the strategic level set precedents for lower echelons and cascade down to affect functional, divisional and subsidiary operations. Strategic management is more difficult at the international than the domestic level because international businesses have to deal not only with the conventional strategic considerations of markets, technologies, competitors, etc., but also with questions of host country regulations, company/host government relationships, and international politics. And the environments in which strategic decision making takes place are more complex and varied than for home country operations.

Strategies frequently (but not always) lead to the specification of 'objectives'. An objective is a statement of something a business needs to accomplish in order to succeed. The more concrete are the company's strategies the easier it is to determine objectives, since the strategies selected impose constraints on policies and generally define the lines of activity the firm will pursue. Typically, objectives relate to such matters as financial returns, rates of growth, market shares, introduction of new products, efficiency improvements, cost cutting programmes, removal of competitors, and so on.

Strategy and tactics

Tactics comprise the practical methods for implementing strategic decisions. Responsibility for tactics often lies with executives who are not themselves concerned with strategy determination. Examples of tactical management are decisions concerning:

- selection of distributors in various countries
- use of outside consultants rather than internal staff to oversee projects
- choice of international advertising agent
- whether to purchase or lease premises for subsidiaries in particular nations
- whether local subsidiaries should operate on overdrafts from local banks rather than borrowing working capital from head office.

Note how an MNC with sound and effective strategies has a good chance of succeeding in the longer period even if it makes tactical errors. The converse is not true however. For more information about the nature of strategic management see the M&E text, *Corporate Strategy and Business Planning*.

2. Advantages and problems of strategies

The collapse over the years of so many businesses (domestic and multinational) that invested heavily in sophisticated strategy formulation and business planning procedures has led in some quarters to cynicism about the entire subject of strategic management. Note particularly how in all major industrial countries the list of the top 100 companies is liable to rapid and drastic alternation. Profitable business, arguably, is about beating current trends, spotting imminent changes in consumer sentiment, responding to environments, and certainly not about adhering to predetermined strategies. Today's commercial world is so uncertain and turbulent that it is unrealistic – so critics of corporate strategy allege – to expect the realisation of any medium to long term plan.

It is certainly the case that a number of international businesses that have devoted relatively little attention to the precise specification of formal strategies have performed better than the average within their particular fields; yet no international or multinational business can afford to dispense entirely with strategic management. The risks associated with not having a strategy are simply too great to make this a viable option. Companies need not only to react and adapt to change; they should actively look for and wherever possible create change and this is rarely possible without an overall strategy. Note moreover that the existence or otherwise of a corporate strategy is but one of numerous variables affecting a firm's success or failure. Observed performance (good or bad) depends on a myriad of interconnecting factors, making it difficult to trace out cause and effect. Presence or absence of a distinct corporate strategy within an organisation that performs well or badly does not necessarily mean that one causes the other.

Specific advantages to having strategies include the following:

(a) Co-ordination of divisions, subsidiaries, and other component parts of the organisation is made easier. The existence of a strategy provides a focal point towards which all the firm's energies may be directed.

(b) Strategy formulation forces management to think through the possible future actions of major competitors and hence to prepare reactions to changes in competitors' behaviour.

(c) Strategies provide the business with definite criteria against which to evaluate the performance.

(d) The process of formulating a strategy forces the company to analyse its position and hence identify and remedy internal weaknesses.

(e) External threats and opportunities are identified.

(f) The company can decide in advance how it will respond to predictable changes in customer tastes and spending patterns in various countries.

(g) Speculation about possible future events and circumstances may cause the firm to discover ways of influencing the future for its own benefit.

(h) Important decisions are taken only after considering all the facts, not in chaotic short-run crisis situations.

(i) A firm with a coherent strategy should be able to deploy its resources more effectively and monitor the efficiency of its working methods and rate of growth against predetermined standards.

The case against spending large amounts of money on formulating strategies rests largely on the turbulence of international commercial environments and hence the high probability that business forecasts will be wrong. Further reasons for not having extensive formal strategies might include the needs to react instantly to competitors' actions and to seize fresh opportunities as they arise, and the likelihood that the circumstances pertaining to an important strategic decision are likely to be unique. In the latter case there is no precedent to follow and consequently a significant likelihood that the decision will be incorrect. Erroneous strategic decisions could result in squandering large amounts of resources. Arguably therefore it is better simply to await change and respond to it as its consequences unfold.

3. Forecasts

Forecasts are predictions of future situations or events, in contrast to 'plans', which frequently (but not always) contain statements of predetermined responses to anticipated future eventualities. Forecasts may be based on past events, or involve pure speculation (e.g. when there are no data on relevant previous occurrences or when something completely novel and unprecedented is foreseen). Short-term predictions are normally more accurate than long-term projections. The latter are subject to greater uncertainty, so larger margins of error must be allowed. Hence, many firms prepare both short and long term forecasts; the former in detail, the latter only in outline. It is not worth spending enormous amounts of money on long-term predictions of highly uncertain events.

Both internal and external forecasts might be necessary. Internal forecasts could relate to subsidiary units' expenditures, equipment breakdowns, maintenance requirements, labour productivity, plant utilisation, materials costs and usage, overheads, working capital requirements, returns on capital employed, cash flows, etc. External forecasts might involve national economic growth rates, price levels, foreign exchange rates, consumers' expenditure and other macro-economic variables, plus market share and assessments of competitors' likely future behaviour. Often the forecaster's task is to identify connections between variables (i.e. 'what causes what') and hence to generate predictions of future outcomes. Hopefully this will enable management to determine the conse-quences of its intended policies and thus select the best course of action. In a formal forecasting procedure the pre-assumptions of the exercise are clearly laid out, so that inaccurate forecasts can be examined in order to establish which of the assumptions were incorrect. Then it becomes possible to learn from past mistakes and so improve future forecasts.

4. Reasons for forecasting

Senior managers inevitably have to take certain decisions the consequences of which depend on the states of environments and factors that are not known at the time the decisions are made. In these circumstances, managers typically apply their experience of similar past situations to the decision-making process. The need for forecasts arises wherever decisions have to be made in conditions of uncertainty, so that managers cannot really avoid forecasting because un-certainty is an essential ingredient of business life: numerous decisions have to be taken on the basis of incomplete information and on inadequate knowledge of the factors that cause a situation.

A major reason why forecasting is inevitable in many international business situations is that strategic decisions often take several years to exert their full effects, especially capital investment decisions and matters pertaining to the introduction of new products. This type of decision needs to be taken not in relation to current conditions but rather in the context of the situation that the decision taker believes will apply at the time the results of the decision begin to be felt. Therefore, future conditions have to be considered when making such major long-term commitments. Further justifications for forecasting are as follows:

(a) Forecasting facilitates the co-ordination of policies.

(b) Arguably, effective planning is impossible without sound forecasting procedures.

(c) Forecasting encourages strategic vision. Proactive managers are naturally curious about the future. Logically-constructed projections will assist them to think clearly and sensibly and to weigh up all alternative possibilities.

(d) Forecasting need not be prohibitively expensive. Straightforward and low-cost forecasting methods are frequently as good as (indeed often outperform) complex and sophisticated statistical techniques.

(e) Clear patterns and relationships among variables can be observed in many international business situations, so it makes sense to utilise them to the best advantage. The problem, of course, is predicting breaks in trends and/or the precise timing of turning points in trend cycles.

(f) The alternative to forecasting is to take decisions on the basis of current conditions, which is inappropriate in a fast-changing world; there will always be some aspect of the future situation that differs from anything experienced in the past.

Long-range forecasts

Long-range forecasts are needed to facilitate decision making *vis-à-vis* such matters as major long-term investments in capital equipment (especially the introduction of new technologies), plans for acquiring or merging with other businesses, research and development projects, new product development and introduction, and the withdrawal of existing products. A long-range forecast is as much an act of faith as a statistical prediction – it is a statement of intent, not a prognostication. Plans extending over several years will never be realised unless positive measures (human resource policies, management by objectives procedures, new product development, management training, etc.) are initiated to secure their achievement. Yet because of the numerous and severe difficulties necessarily attached to long-term planning and forecasting, and the uncertainty of the benefits likely to result from the exercise, these matters are frequently overlooked. Management becomes preoccupied with shorter-term problems and ignores the need to consider longer-term issues.

5. Strategic objectives

Objectives are statements of what management wants to achieve. The clearer the statement of a company's objectives, the more obvious are the policies necessary for their attainment. All businesses have at least two common objectives: to break even, and in the longer term to offer to owners a reasonable rate of return. Thereafter however different firms typically possess differing base objectives. Some seek maximisation of immediate financial returns, others want to build for the future and are willing to sacrifice short-term profits in exchange for long-term security. Examples of primary (strategic) objectives include attaining a prespecified overall rate of return on capital employed within the business; increasing shareholders' earnings per share to a certain level; or becoming the market leader in a particular field. The particular strategic objectives chosen typically result from the 'mission' of the firm (see below).

Strategic objectives are determined by a company's board of directors in accordance with pre-established corporate strategies and the company's mission statement. Note how the objectives actually set within a business often emerge from the interplay of a number of divergent influences, corresponding to the interests of the various stakeholders in the enterprise. Stakeholders' bargaining power, access to information, knowledge of issues and interest in outcomes will help determine the weights attached to the preferred objectives of each group. The formal specification of objectives has a number of benefits:

(a) All the firm's activities are jointly directed towards the attainment of common goals.

(b) Criteria are established for the effective utilisation of existing resources.

(c) Resource deficiencies are identified.

(d) Objectives provide guidelines for the preparation of human resource plans and budgetary controls.

(e) Individual managers' roles and task expectations are clarified.

Further advantages to having corporate objectives are that they should infuse a sense of direction among senior employees, facilitate the co-ordination of diverse activities and establish benchmarks against which actual performance may be appraised. Hence they act as motivators, guides to action, and a device for exercising managerial control.

Problems with setting corporate objectives are that:

(a) Competitors may hear of them and initiate activities designed to prevent their accomplishment.

(b) They might impose rigidities on the firm's operations and inhibit its ability to respond immediately to changes in market trends.

(c) Objectives can interact and multiply, resulting perhaps in the firm's inability to cope with numerous objective-related activities.

6. Mission statements

A mission statement is a declaration of an organisation's fundamental purpose: why it exists, how it sees itself, what it wishes to do, its beliefs and its long-term aspirations. Thus it is a statement of intent, combined perhaps with an outline of the basic ground rules that management has determined will govern the firm's behaviour. Normally a mission statement will define the company's core business(es) and its strategic aims and objectives – but without going into detail. Accordingly, the statement has a dual purpose: to provide guidance on how the business will operate on a day-to-day basis, and to map out its desired future situation.

The statement needs to be broad in order to accommodate (i) necessary changes in strategies resulting from altered circumstances and the emergence of fresh opportunities, and (ii) the requirements of interested parties such as shareholders, employees, functional departments, outside regulatory bodies, etc.

Why have a mission statement?

The discipline of preparing a mission statement compels management to clarify basic issues affecting the organisation, relate the firm's strengths and weaknesses to its competitive environment, identify external constraints, and develop a central focus for all the company's activities. Advocates of mission statements argue that only through careful analysis of a business's mission may effective strategies be devised: the more concrete the mission statement the more obvious are the strategies needed to satisfy the firm's mission. Also the possession of a mission statement affirms the organisation's long-term commitment to essential values and activities, and generates an aura of confidence and credibility to the outside world. Other advantages to having a mission statement are that:

(a) It encourages top management to adopt a strategic vision derived from a coherent philosophy concerning what the business is about, where it is headed and what it needs to do to get where it wants to be.

(b) It acts as a 'corporate constitution' against which the firm's behaviour (including acts with ethical and social implications) may be evaluated.

(c) It presents the firm and its employees with the challenge of attaining the mission, hence facilitating the implementation of change.

(d) It enables total company resources to be allocated according to the priorities explicit or implicit in the organisation's mission.

Once management has decided what the organisation exists to do it can then devise appropriate strategies and plans and is in a position to detail the corporate skills needed to attain key objectives.

Contents of a mission statement

A mission statement should outline the firm's strategies at the highest level of generality, succinctly summing up the purpose and major intention (to customers, shareholders, suppliers and employees) of the enterprise. The mission statement of a particular firm might contain much technical, product, market and other information and extend to several pages. Equally it may occupy a single short paragraph and emphasise just a couple of key concepts. Examples of extracts from a few actual mission statements are given below:

(a) Our mission is to be the worldwide leader in automotive and auto-related products and services as well as in newer industries such as aerospace, communications and financial services.

(b) This business will produce and sell low-cost, functional lighting systems to television studios throughout the world and will install these whenever required.

(c) This company seeks to be the market leader in the passenger car entertainment business and will achieve this through the frequent introduction of new models of high-quality, top-end-of-the-market car radios, speakers, cassette players and related equipment.

(d) Our mission is to search for oil and produce, refine and market petroleum and petroleum products throughout the world (multinational oil company).

(e) Our mission is to be a major factor in the worldwide movement of information (US telephone company).

(f) Our purpose is to search continuously for fresh opportunities for developing measurement control technology and constantly to improve the quality of and reliability of our products.

Everyone who works for the enterprise should support its mission. In practice, however, different managers may interpret a business's mission in entirely different ways. Thus it is essential that the mission statement be precise, explicit, neither too broad nor too narrow, and written in language that all interested employees can understand.

7. Strategy formulation

Strategies can be formulated once the business has determined its mission. The first step in the process is to conduct a situation analysis to establish the company's internal strengths and weaknesses and the environmental threats and opportunities that it confronts. Strengths and weaknesses might relate to functional activities (such as marketing or finance), the firm's product range, plant and equipment, delivery and distribution systems, R&D activities, human resources, and so on. Examples of opportunities are: prospects for developing new markets and/or introducing new products, for cost-cutting programmes, taking over competitors, buying up sources of supply or distribution networks, etc. Threats can emanate from competitors, governments, risks of economic depression, changes in laws, product obsolescence or changes in public taste.

Hopefully the analysis will indicate the direction in which the company needs to move (the markets in which it ought to be operating, whether it needs to diversify its product range, etc.) and what precisely it has to do to get to its desired destination. Then plans can be devised and implemented and the consequences observed. The results might cause the firm's management to look again at the feasibilities of its core objectives, the adequacy of its resources and the relevance of current operational activities in relation to the attainment of the company's mission.

PRODUCT PORTFOLIO ANALYSIS

8. Origins of product portfolio analysis

Firms with a range of products and which operate in multiple markets need criteria for determining which products should receive most resources and which should be abandoned. Typically a multi-product international business will possess three types of product: 'safe' products which generate a steady cash inflow; 'developing' products which are increasing their market shares in expanding markets; and 'declining' products which contribute little to company profits, say because they are at the ends of their life cycles or in consequence of fresh competition from other firms. Thus a multi-product international company should aim for a balanced portfolio of products in order to ensure (i) a continuous inflow of cash, (ii) that new products are available to take over from those in decline, and (iii) that all the company's activities are not exceptionally risky.

One of the earliest analyses of this issue was by the Boston Consulting Group, which classified products according to two variables: the product's share of its total market, and the rate of the market's growth. The best products, obviously, were those with high market shares of buoyant markets, experiencing high rates of growth, and the firm's strategy should be directed, therefore, to promoting these. Figure 19.1 illustrates the so-called 'Boston grid'.

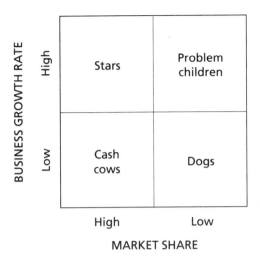

Figure 19.1 The Boston grid

Each of the firm's products is allocated to an appropriate position in one of the four quadrants. *Cash cows* are products with high market shares and thus are assumed to earn the cash needed for new investment in other lines of work. *Problem children* (also referred to as 'question marks') are not generating cash because of low market share, but have potential and are in high growth market sectors. Investment in these products can yield rich dividends. *Stars* have high market share in a buoyant market. They generate cash but may require further investment to maintain their market positions. *Dogs* do not earn any cash; indeed their continuing existence might actually absorb money.

According to the Boston Consulting Group, cash cows should be maintained but not receive significant investment. The cash received should be spent mainly on stars, with the balance being devoted to *selected* problem children. Typically, stars become cash cows as the growth rates of their markets decline, although some may end up as dogs. Market share is measured in relation to that of the firm's largest competitor. Thus, if the firm in question has 60 per cent of the market and its biggest competitor has 30 per cent then its relative market share is two. This is supposed to indicate a company's relative competitive position. High market share is assumed to result in high profitability and consequent generation of large amounts of cash.

Business growth rate means the rate of expansion of the market. For a national market this is provided by the rate of growth of domestic product of the country concerned. Otherwise industry growth rate or some other relevant proxy is used. The higher the business growth rate then, *ipso facto*, the easier it is for the firm to develop its activities and to succeed in the market. Break-points between 'high' and 'low' categories for market share and business growth rate are selected subjectively and are, of course, somewhat arbitrary. For business growth rate, the average GDP of Western countries might be used to define the boundary between high and low. The Boston Consulting Group suggested a value of 1.5 for the boundary between high and low relative market share.

9. Developments of the Boston Grid

A number of organisations developed the Boston Consulting Group approach. Among the most important was the General Electric Company's 'Business Screen' method which uses the variables 'market attractiveness' and 'organisational strength' to categorise products. Market attractiveness depends on the size, growth rate, profitability and competitive intensity of the market and on how easily it can be served. Organisational strength involves the quality of the firm's products, the firm's efficiency and the effectiveness of its marketing. Consider for example a company with three products, A, B, and C as shown in Figure 19.2. The areas of the circles indicate the relative sizes of the markets for each product, while the wedges in each circle show the firm's share of that particular market. It can be seen that although the market for product A is large and highly attractive, the company is weak in its ability to serve this potentially lucrative segment, implying the need for further investment in this field. Product B should probably be discarded, while product C presents a 'question mark' about how to proceed. There is a large market for product C, the firm can supply it easily, and the company already has a large market share. But the market for C is stagnant and profit margins are low.

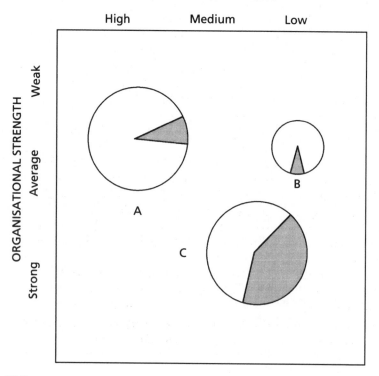

Figure 19.2

10. Advantages and problems of portfolio analysis

Portfolio analysis became a widely used tool for formulating the corporate strategies of multi-product multinational companies in the 1970s and early 1980s. Doubts concerning its effectiveness began to emerge however, and today it is less widely employed. Portfolio analysis is a useful aid to decision making that compels management to analyse its present situation. It is a simple, logical and convenient device for taking a bird's eye view of the firm's activities, for varying the marketing mix applied to specific products, for corporate planning, departmental structuring of the firm, and for deciding which individuals shall assume responsibility for which products (managing a rapidly developing product requires skills different to those needed merely to maintain a stable situation). It is conceptually straightforward and easy to use. Graphical presentation enables the rapid communication of the results of the exercise. Management is compelled to think carefully about each of the firm's products; to set objectives and to allocate resources in a rationally determined way. Hence it facilitates strategy formulation and the budgeting process. The technique has been criticised, however, for being simplistic and for encouraging managements to ignore complex yet crucially important environmental variables. Further problems are that:

(a) Market growth and market share are not necessarily associated with cash flow and profitability.

(b) Skilful management might turn around the fortunes of a product which a portfolio analysis might suggest be discarded. Categorisation of products as cash cows or dogs can lead to self-fulfilling prophesies, as resources might be withdrawn from products that in fact have reasonably bright prospects. A major problem with the application of the product portfolio approach to the assessment of foreign subsidiary operations is that a change in host country conditions can turn a star into a dog (or vice versa), or a cash cow into a question mark, almost instantly, e.g. through the imposition of government controls on MNC activities (see Chapter 9).

(c) Strategies implied by the analysis may not be technically feasible or might be too expensive to implement.

(d) Portfolio analysis can give the impression of scientific rigour, when in fact the entire analysis is based on subjective value judgements.

(e) It is not always clear which particular market a product is actually serving. Measurement of market share and industry growth rate can be meaningless in such circumstances.

(f) The analysis has little quantitative rigour.

(g) Empirical evidence to back up the fundamental propositions of the analysis is sparse. There are very many important examples of firms experiencing *declines* in profitability as market share has expanded.

(h) Human aspects of organisation and management are ignored.

(i) The analysis is only relevant for firms with a number of diversified products sold in different markets.

(j) Objective circumstances can prevent a firm altering its product range.

(k) Market attractiveness can change suddenly, unpredictably and in consequence of factors beyond the company's control.

(l) Numerous factors contribute to 'organisational strength' and 'market attractiveness'. Selection of which to consider is necessarily arbitrary to some degree.

The analysis is static rather than dynamic, representing a 'snap shot' of a situation at a particular moment. It *describes* a firm's situation rather than telling management what it can do. In particular it has nothing to say about the *risks* associated with various options. Note how a market that happens to be expanding at a rapid rate today might be stagnant in the near future, and that high growth, high risk and environmental turbulence are frequently inter-related.

COMPETITIVE STRATEGY

11. The work of M.E. Porter

The theory of competitive strategy results largely from the work of M.E. Porter, who defines competitive strategy as 'the art of relating a company to the economic environment within which it exists' (Porter 1980). According to Porter, five major factors determine this environment:

- Ease with which competitors can enter the industry
- Bargaining power of customers
- Bargaining power of suppliers
- Ease with which substitute products can be introduced
- Extent of competition among existing firms.

(a) *Ease of entry.* New firms will find it difficult to enter the industry where:
- Economies of large-scale production exist so that entrants must enter the industry on a large scale and hence assume great risk in order to gain a foothold in the market.
- There is much product differentiation through branding, differing designs and different product make-up in various market segments hence requiring potential entrants to spend large sums on advertising and sales promotion.
- Expensive capital equipment is needed before starting production.
- Entrants have limited access to existing distribution channels and thus need to invest heavily in establishing their own retail outlets, dealership networks, etc.
- Government policy restricts entry to the industry through, for example, quality regulations, licensing arrangements, and so on.
- Miscellaneous factors create cost advantages for existing firms:

experience of the industry; favourable locations, easy access to raw materials and similar benefits.

(b) *Bargaining power of buyers.* The bargaining power of a purchasing firm depends on (i) the number of buyers and the sizes of their orders, (ii) customers' knowledge of the product and competitors' prices, and (iii) how easily buyers can switch from one source of supply to others.

(c) *Bargaining power of suppliers.* Suppliers have more power if there are few of them and if the item supplied is unique. Sometimes the client firm is 'locked into' the supplies of a certain business. This occurs where the client has designed its own production system to accommodate the special features of a certain input, so that high costs must be incurred to change the source of supply.

(d) *Availability of substitutes.* Firms producing an item for which many readily available substitutes exist lose their ability to raise prices by significant amounts, since to do so would certainly cause them to lose trade.

(e) *The extent of competition.* Firms can charge higher prices in industries where businesses avoid competing with each other. In such industries, companies set similar prices, and steer clear of competitive advertising.

Porter suggests the following general principles of inter-firm competition:

(a) Rivalry between firms increases as the market share of existing firms become more equal. Severe competition is unlikely in 'market-leader, market-follower' situations.

(b) Competition intensifies as the rate of expansion of the total market slows down.

(c) Since goods which are perishable or difficult to store must be sold quickly, industries supplying such products will experience intense competition.

(d) Firms will compete most aggressively when they have much to lose from the activities of competing businesses (e.g. because of extremely large investments in plant and equipment).

(e) Competition becomes fierce when competing products acquire more and more similar characteristics, and is greatest in industries supplying homogeneous products.

A firm's competitive position depends on its market share, product quality, brand and corporate identities, distribution arrangements, and on its ability to expand or contract its operations at short notice.

Successful strategies, Porter argues, must involve at least one of the following elements:

(a) Cost leadership, e.g. through economies of scale or especially efficient production methods.

(b) Product differentiation, i.e. making the firm's output appear somehow different and superior to that of competitors.

(c) Supplying a particular market segment, i.e. finding a profitable niche in the market not yet serviced by competing firms.

How any one of these desirable characteristics can be achieved depends on the industry concerned, particularly on its age and the number of competing units. Thus, businesses in young industries might seek product differentiation, whereas for firms in mature industries the need to reduce costs may be seen as paramount.

A firm with many competitors might attempt to buy out as many other firms as possible in order to expand operations and hence achieve economies of scale. Conversely, businesses in declining industries may choose to divest subsidiaries and unprofitable divisions in order to focus all their efforts on small (but nevertheless profitable) market segments.

12. Criticisms of the theory of competitive strategy

Problems with the theory of competitive strategy include the following:

(a) Although it is sensible for a firm to have a competitive strategy, the environment in which it is applied will be constantly changing. Competing firms learn from each other's mistakes and emulate rivals' successes. Note that international competitive strategy is far more complicated than for domestic operations because of the increased numbers of rival firms, environmental variables, and diverse geographic markets that are involved. For example, it may be necessary to retain a presence in a low-growth low-profitability country simply to prevent the expansion in that market by international competitors, or to accept losses for several years in order to establish a sound base in a region in anticipation of long-term growth.

It follows that it is perhaps more important to possess a well-developed framework for generating fresh ideas regarding suitable strategies as circumstances alter, particularly as competitors respond to the company's strategic actions. It is not possible to know today what tomorrow's competitive strategy should contain.

(b) Implementation of a competitive strategy might involve spending large amounts of money purely on the assumption that if the money is not spent then a rival firm might behave in a certain way. Yet there is no guarantee that the rival will behave in that manner if the resources are not in fact committed.

(c) Competitive strategy relies on speculation about competing companies' intentions, abilities and commitments to particular markets, not on hard evidence.

(d) Sometimes, firms have few strategies in the early years of their operations; yet managers have important decisions that commit resources in various ways. This process establishes a *de facto* competitive strategy that eventually becomes the formal strategy statement of the firm. In the meantime however the entire competitive environment may have altered so that the enterprise is pursuing a competitive strategy no longer appropriate to its needs.

(e) Effective competitive strategies are consistent yet flexible; they should not be altered immediately problems appear, yet need to be changed quickly whenever significant environmental change does occur. But where exactly should the line between continuity and responsiveness be drawn? There is no a priori method for determining this matter. Porter's model implies that firms should choose a specific strategy route. Yet businesses that simply react to current events can be more flexible, responsive to change and profitable than firms with distinct (and perhaps rigid) strategies.

(f) Businesses often change the 'industry' in which they operate. The criteria defining a particular industry sector are likely to alter (e.g. through technical innovation), and as the firm finds itself in new competitive environments so its competitive strategies will need to change. Industry structures are dynamic, so that the basic units of analysis is constantly shifting.

(g) The model describes situations at a particular moment in time (rather like a snapshot of the early part of a horse race), but its ability to predict outcomes is questionable.

(h) Companies that score highly in terms of Porter's model (i.e. which face few rivals, substitute products, threats from new entrants, etc.) often fail, and vice-versa. Many organisational and efficiency factors determine whether a firm is successful.

13. Sources of competitive advantage

Competitive strategy means the development of those elements of the firm's overall activities that relate to beating the competition in the field. Firms obtain a competitive edge *via* their possession of particular assets, abilities or characteristics. Examples of factors possibly contributing to a business's competitive advantage include:

- ownership of patents, brands, know-how or other intellectual property
- superior product offer, novel product design features, high quality output and/or excellent customer care facilities
- economies of scale, efficient organisation and/or the possession of modern machinery, equipment or premises
- effective distribution systems, ability to service niche markets, an attractive corporate image, good public relations and customer loyalty to the firm's brands
- abilities to alter the firm's organisation structure quickly and to introduce new models at short notice
- easy access to financial capital or high levels of financial reserves
- well-qualified and highly motivated employees
- ownership of raw materials or other input suppliers and of distribution outlets
- superior R&D facilities
- access to low-cost labour.

Some businesses choose to develop just one source of competitive advantage, and allocate company resources accordingly. More commonly however, firms identify a combination of areas in which they need to excel and address these as a whole.

14. Critical success factors

Formulation of a competitive strategy involves a careful analysis of the strengths and weaknesses of the firm in question and of its rivals; identification of key success factors in the markets in which the business is to operate; and the precise definition of consumer attributes, demands, attitudes and behaviour. 'Critical success factors' are the variables that determine whether a company can beat its rivals in the market concerned. Some common critical success factors are:

- fast and reliable delivery
- product quality and customer care
- the ease with which a product can be modified, has appealing features, fulfils a clear need and has multiple uses
- the rate of expansion of the market and whether it is concentrated in accessible areas
- brand images and the location of products in their life cycles.

A firm's competitive edge could emerge from intangible rather than non-quantifiable factors, such as:

- senior management's intuitive grasp of which strategic issues are most important
- a chief executive's desire to achieve excellence, regardless of any other consideration
- creativity in the strategy formulation process, leading to imaginative new ideas.

Progress test 19

1. Why is strategic management more difficult at the international rather than domestic level?

2. List the advantages to a multinational company of having corporate strategies.

3. What is a 'strategic objective'? Give examples of strategic objectives.

4. How did product portfolio analysis originate?

5. What are the main problems associated with product portfolio analysis?

6. How does M.E. Porter define 'competitive strategy'?

7. What are the difficulties attached to Porter's theory of competitive strategy?

8. List six examples of factors that might contribute to a business's competitive advantage.

9. What are 'critical success factors'? Give examples of common critical success factors.

10. What is a company mission statement? Why do businesses prepare mission statements?

20

PLANNING AND CONTROL OF INTERNATIONAL OPERATIONS

THE SCOPE OF PLANNING

1. Nature of planning

Planning means the deliberate and systematic determination of what a company should do in the future in order to fulfill its mission and meet its objectives, given certain predicted or intended conditions. Whereas *strategies* define the general path a business is to follow, *plans* state precisely how it intends its strategies to be realised. Strategy concerns ideas, creativity and grand conceptions; plans involve the mundane and instrumental measures for the efficient allocation of human, material, financial and other resources within the organisation.

The planning process

Planning involves the decomposition of problems and issues into their component parts, application of rational analysis to the interpretation of information, and the selection of actions to achieve predetermined ends. Plans can be as general or as specific as the situation requires; strategic, tactical or operational; long, short or medium term. The planning process can begin as soon as the firm's mission and core objectives have been formulated. Thereafter, planning necessarily *precedes* other managerial activities, so that changes in organisation, staffing and so on follow from planning decisions.

Purposes of planning

The essential purposes of planning are to:

- relate the business to its environment, i.e. to ensure that environmental changes do not destroy the firm; through engaging in planning a management becomes aware of environmental factors and the influences they might exert
- co-ordinate complex activities
- utilise the talents of a range of people when taking important decisions
- improve organisational efficiency and facilitate the implementation of change.

2. Strategic plans

Strategic planning means the determination of how, in practical terms, the firm will attain its strategic objectives. Thus, strategic plans derive from the company's overall corporate strategy, from observed gaps between necessary and likely outcomes and resources, risk assessments, and from a situation analysis. Strategic plans might relate to such matters as divestment, business expansion, diversification, acquisitions of other businesses. research and technical development, and so on. They set out the detail of how and when the firm will enter new markets, increase existing market share, improve productivity, delayer the management hierarchy, etc. The strategic plan is wider in scope and will have longer time horizons than tactical or operational plans. Its purpose is to assess the future implications of current decisions, to develop a framework for adjusting operations to changes in the wider business environment, and to link and control the various elements of complex organisations.

Strategic planning is especially important for the international business in view of the diversity of its operations. Co-ordination and integration of activities are essential, and cannot normally be achieved without the creation of a comprehensive strategic plan. Further reasons why strategic planning is crucial for the international firm are:

- The intensity of competition at the international level
- Fresh opportunities for doing business in hitherto 'difficult' markets in Eastern Europe, China, Southern Asia and other parts of the developing world
- The need for large enterprises with diverse foreign activities periodically to rationalise and reorganise their operations, acquire foreign businesses and/or divest in certain countries
- For European firms, the threats and challenges arising from the existence of the single European market.

3. Advantages of planning

Planning is difficult and expensive: difficult because it requires forecasts of future environments and events; expensive since it ties up significant numbers of highly paid senior executives. There are, however, a number of advantages to formulating business plans. The process of planning compels management to prepare for future eventualities, to clarify its priorities, to develop criteria for monitoring performance and to think ahead in a systematic way. Further specific benefits to planning are that:

(a) Resource deficiencies may be identified.

(b) Staff participating in planning exercises should be motivated towards achieving planned objectives.

(c) All the firm's activities will be integrated and co-ordinated.

(d) Management is forced to consider its own strengths and weaknesses.

(e) Careful consideration of possible future events may uncover new and profitable opportunities.

(f) Measures to influence future events can be initiated by the company.

(g) Criteria are established for the effective utilisation of resources.

(h) Activities are jointly directed towards the attainment of common objectives.

(i) The firm is better equipped to respond to environmental change.

(j) Inefficiencies and duplicated effort may be identified.

(k) Team spirit is encouraged.

(l) The feasibilities of objectives are studied in depth.

(m) Important decision are taken unhurriedly using all the data available and considering all possible options.

(n) It encourages strategic thinking and a rational approach to taking decisions.

(o) The specific actions needed to achieve corporate objectives are (hopefully) identified.

(p) Barriers to the implementation of strategies will be revealed.

4. Problems with planning

Managers sometimes avoid involvement in planning processes, for a number of reasons:

(a) Lack of knowledge of and training in planning methods, leading to lack of self-confidence in being able to gather accurate information.

(b) Cynicism resulting from a belief that resources will not be made available in quantities necessary to implement the plan.

(c) Inadequate information about internal operations and/or external change.

(d) Assumptions that other people have already formulated the firm's plans.

(e) The desire to retain the ability to act flexibly and not to be constrained by rigid plans, especially at the subsidiary level.

(f) Realisation that individuals are likely to be criticised for not achieving targets established in the company's plans.

Rigid planning systems generate bureaucracies that can inhibit creativity and lateral thinking. Plans beget plans until, eventually, a 'plan of plans' might be necessary. Each failure has to be analysed, requiring more research, more personnel, more meetings, sub-committees, etc. Indeed, 'half-baked' planning is arguably worse than no planning at all. Planning is bound to fail if proper attention and resources are not devoted to the process. Further criticisms of planning are as follows:

(a) Strategic planning is not the same as strategic thinking, and the former does not necessarily facilitate the latter.

(b) The mechanics of the planning process are administratively burdensome and as such might be delegated by top management to subordinates who do not possess the breadth of knowledge or experience necessary to complete these duties. Also the very act of delegating the planning function might be seen as an expression of senior management's disinterest in planning by middle and junior executives.

(c) Plans rely on data rather than market instinct to make important decisions. Data relate to the past; instincts to the future.

(d) Markets are so unpredictable that it is a waste of time bothering to plan.

Special difficulties apply to international as opposed to purely domestic business planning, including shortages of information on foreign markets, translation problems, currency fluctuation, political uncertainties, and differences in market characteristics and business methods among nations.

5. Principles of planning

There exist certain fundamental principles of planning that should always be applied, as follows:

(a) As far as possible, plans should be based on facts and not opinions.

(b) Plans should incorporate some degree of flexibility to accommodate unforeseeable events.

(c) A plan should be as detailed as expenditure constraints allow.

(d) Plans should not extend too far into the future; accurate prediction of the distant future is simply impossible.

(e) All alternative courses of action should be considered.

(f) Side effect and implications of the actions envisaged should be examined.

(g) Instructions to individuals and departments must be incorporated into the plan.

(h) Plans should be concise and easy to understand.

(i) As the plan is executed its effectiveness in achieving stated objectives should be monitored. Differences between actual and desired positions must be quickly identified and remedial measures introduced.

(j) Targets embodied in plans should always be reasonable. Overambitious targets can never be achieved and lead to low morale and cynicism among employees. Equally, targets that are too low have no operational significance.

(k) While all aspects of the firm's operations need to be considered when developing plans, the greatest emphasis should be placed on identifying and examining the key factors that are crucial to the company's success.

PLANNING SYSTEMS

6. Types of planning system

Systems may be formal or informal; quantitative or intuitive (or a mixture of both); have short period horizons or extend a long way into the future. Further differences in systems relate to the sophistication (and costs) of the techniques applied, the degree of involvement of employee representatives, and relations with individual performance appraisal and management by objectives schemes.

Formal versus informal planning procedures

Formal planning procedures establish set rules for how plans are determined and should lead to consistency (all plans are developed to the same format) and ensure that relevant issues are analysed in depth. Advantages to having formal procedures are that:

(a) Everyone concerned with the planning process will have a common understanding of how plans are to be formulated.

(b) The drafting of procedures requires discussion and open communication among relevant employees.

(c) There is continuity in procedures. Note how promotions, resignations, transfers and retirements of staff mean that the managers concerned with planning will change from time to time.

Formal planning systems within MNCs are frequently based on pro forma documents circulated to subsidiaries and to divisions and heads of functional departments. Headings for a pro forma based planning system might include:

- perceived subsidiary/departmental/divisional objectives
- opportunities and threats and the actions needed to exploit opportunities and avert threats
- the risks involved in intended activities
- evaluation criteria to be used.

The main disadvantage to the formalisation of procedures is perhaps that it reduces flexibility, since precedents established through following formal rules must be adhered to in future cases. Further reasons sometimes advanced for not having formal written plans are that to possess them stifles creativity and innovation, discourages entrepreneurship, and generates inflexible attitudes. Another problem is that executives (at both head office and subsidiary levels) might feel intimidated by the need to accept the responsibilities that the precise specification of formal plans implies. Excessively formal planning procedures can become ritualistic: ends in themselves rather than aids to facilitate better management. Arguably, moreover, standardisation of the layout of the forms used to formulate plans can lead to standardisation of thought and a lack of creativity within the planning process. Also, pro forma headings in planning documentation may, by leading a manager's thinking, introduce bias and distortion to the results.

Informal planning

Despite their not being written down, informal plans may be well thought out and accurately relect the vision and aspirations of the management of the organisation. Informal planning, if sensibly applied, can have definite advantages:

(a) It recognises the need for flexibility in planning processes.

(b) The organisation becomes more adaptable, responsive and attuned to change.

(c) Fewer head office preassumptions are imposed.

(d) The people operating the system might be just as likely to think seriously about serious important planning issues as in a formal planning system.

(e) There is no inappropriate stereotyping of procedures.

(f) Large numbers of alternatives are considered.

Problems with informal procedures include the following:

(a) The absence of pro forma guidelines means that first-class managers are needed to operate the system.

(b) Large amounts of planning information are held in the heads of individual executives, whose resignation, illness, etc., could disrupt the informal procedures.

(c) Long-term problems might be ignored.

(d) The process may degenerate to the application of ill-conceived hunches.

(e) Plans are likely to be unco-ordinated.

7. Gap analysis

Here management sets targets based on what it believes to be attainable in the longer term and then compares these targets with forecasts of future achievement taken from projections of current activities – assuming that present circumstances continue. Divergences are then analysed, and measures implemented to bridge the gaps. Thus, gap analysis seeks to analyse disparities between potential and performance. Gaps might be identified, *inter alia*, in the following areas:

(a) Distribution, caused perhaps by shortages of intermediaries or outlets, or poor control over agents.

(b) Product offer, including product features, quality level and facilities for customer care.

(c) Market share, in that planned market share has not been achieved.

(d) Research and technical development, possibly involving large expenditures that have failed to generate tangible results.

(e) Rates of profitability, returns on capital employed in various subsidiaries, growth of assets and profits.

Consequences of gap analysis might include:

(a) Continuation of existing strategies, ignoring any minor divergences between actual and potential performance that might have been revealed.

(b) Introduction of new strategies specifically designed to bridge observed gaps, while keeping the firm's core strategies intact.

(c) A complete overhaul of the strategic orientation of the enterprise.

Problems with gap analysis are:

(a) Gaps may be the result of hopelessly optimistic assessments of what is possible, leading to the introduction of inappropriate policies and the pursuit of meaningless objectives.

(b) The difficulty of accurately quantifying the magnitudes of gaps.

(c) That the basic assumptions regarding future environments may be false.

(d) Actual future performance will depend on a whole range of factors apart from current strategies (entry or withdrawal of competitors for example).

Gap analysis requires the systematic examination of the various international environments in which the company operates. This is known as environmental scanning.

Environmental scanning

Environmental scanning is the process of searching for and gathering information on significant changes in the company's environments. Its purposes are to facilitate planning, monitor the relevance of current strategies, and identify the implications of environmental change for the firm's operations. International environmental scanning needs to encompass such matters as:

- behaviour of competitors
- trends in demographic and sociocultural factors
- political risk and instability
- currency stability
- economic variables including growth rates, inflation, consumer expenditure patterns and so on
- changes in market structure
- availabilities of labour, materials and financial capital in various countries.

Effective environmental scanning requires:

(a) A definition of which environments are most important to the company. Not all environmental factors can be investigated (there are too many of them) so a handful of relevant external variables must be selected for research.

(b) A sound international management information system.

(c) Precise identification of critical environmental issues, including assessments of which issues might develop into major opportunities or threats.

There are two approaches to searching for relevant environmental change. The first is to predict the external changes that might occur and then detail: (i) how the organisation would be affected by them; and (ii) how the organisation should respond. Alternatively, the planner may begin with a list of the firm's functions, followed by a listing of all the environmental factors that might affect these functions. The latter course is usually the easier of the two since it is concrete, and named individuals can be made responsible for listing relevant factors in each functional department. However, some important variables may be overlooked.

8. Top-down versus bottom-up planning

Top-down planning involves tight supervision of the entire planning process by head office, and has two alternative forms:

1. Senior management determines and hands down plans to subsidiaries and functional departments without the latter's participation in their formulation.
2. Top management expresses its initial expectations and issues broad guidelines to subsidiaries and departments, which then translate these aspirations into concrete action plans.

Top-down planning facilitates the co-ordination and control of activities, and decisions can be made quickly. Head office takes the initiative in devising plans, defines problems and imposes solutions. Problems with the approach are that:

(a) It can result in the domination of the planning process by people who are ill-equipped for the task.

(b) Managers preparing the plan might be remote from the realities of subsidiary operations.

(c) Lack of involvement in the formulation of plans by subsidiaries and functional departments could lead to plans not being implemented.

With *bottom-up planning*, conversely, subsidiaries and departments generate their own plans for achieving broadly defined objectives. Hence the company's overall corporate plan is built up from a series of components prepared by operating units. Typically a head office planning unit devises a general format to be followed by operating units when initiating proposals, and then co-ordinates the suggestions that emerge. It remains the case, however, that certain key plans still have to be prepared by the central planning unit, notably plans for new product introductions, organisational restructuring, joint ventures and other projects not assignable to individual departments of subsidiaries.

The discussions leading to statements of departmental subsidiary or divisional goals can be extremely time consuming in a bottom-up planning system, and could generate an extensive bureaucracy. Further problems are that:

(a) Consolidation of subsidiary plans may in practice amount to little more than adding them together, without any genuine attempt at integrating or co-ordinating intended actions.

(b) Subsidiary planners might believe that their plans are creative and innovative, whereas in fact they are wholly unrealistic in the context of the strategic management of the company as a whole.

(c) Managers of subsidiaries and departments may not have the expertise necessary to formulate sensible plans.

(d) Subsidiary executives might not be familiar with the work of other sections or with the firm's general situation.

(e) Each subsidiary department, division or other operating unit is likely to have its *own* set of aspirations.

(f) Subsidiary plans will be accompanied by requests for resources for implementing the plans in the relevant units, and the total amount of resources requested might exceed the level available within the organisation. Hence resource requests will be reduced according to some formula determined by top management, possibly resulting in unsatisfactory resource allocations for many units.

(g) The aggregated corporate plan resulting from bottom-up planning may lack coherence.

(h) The need for confidentiality in planning precedures relating to certain matters (attempts to out-manoeuvre competitors for instance) might prevent subsidiaries from being given all the management information needed to formulate effective unit plans.

(i) Bottom-up planning is out of place in an organisation in which it represents the *only* form of lower-level participation in mangement decision making.

(j) It invariably generates a great deal of (costly) activity but does not necessarily lead to any major decisions.

(k) Critical strategic decisions might be made outside the procedure (because of the latter's protracted nature) leading to disillusion with the system.

Advantages to the bottom-up approach are that:

(a) It utilises the skills and experiences of the subsidiary staff who will be responsible for implementing the plans.

(b) It motivates individuals towards the achievement of emerging targets.

(c) It should facilitate the development of a common purpose within the organisation.

(d) It develops decision making abilities among subsidiary managers.

(e) It encourages responsible and flexible attitudes among employees and positive responses to change.

(f) It enables management to receive valuable feedback from subsidiary managers about day-to-day operations.

(g) It involves a greater number of people in taking decisions and hence a lower risk of important factors being overlooked.

Implementation of plans

In practice a mixture of top-down and bottom-up approaches is likely to emerge, with regular interaction between senior management and operating units. Implementation of a plan will involve:

- allocation of responsibility for completing various tasks
- preparation of budgets
- scheduling of activities
- co-ordination of work
- establishment of review points at which progress will be evaluated
- determination of procedures for altering the plan as circumstances change.

CONTROL OF INTERNATIONAL OPERATIONS

9. Nature of control

Control has three aspects: establishing standards and targets; monitoring activities and comparing actual with target performance; and implementing measures to remedy deficiencies. It links inputs to outputs and provides feedback to those in command. Control systems are needed for both strategic and operational purposes. Strategic control involves establishing benchmarks for determining whether current strategies should be altered and, if so, how and when. Thus strategic control information on key external events and environments, and the data collected, has to be far more wide-ranging than that necessary for operational control. An effective control system will enable the rapid deployment of resources to their most efficient uses; disperse management expertise throughout the organisation; and generate comprehensive information on the activities of subsidiary units.

Control of international operations is more difficult than for domestic activities because of the large geographic (and sometimes cultural) distances between units, the diversity and complexity of the activities of the typical MNC, the fast-changing nature of international business environments, political and other uncertainties surrounding subsidiaries' actions, and the fact that there are so many extraneous variables beyond the company's influence.

Further control problems are that:

(a) Language differences can distort communication between head office and subsidiaries.

(b) Local cultural factors may cause the failure in some countries of motivational incentive systems that were enormously successful elsewhere.

(c) Host country governments might pressurise the management of a local subsidiary to act in the interests of the local economy at the expense of the parent company (e.g. by demanding that inputs be procured from local suppliers at higher cost than from another of the MNC's foreign subsidiaries).

(d) Managers in local subsidiaries might have difficulty in understanding the control information requirements imposed by head office.

(e) The costs of implementing control mechanisms are much higher than for a domestic firm.

10. Control systems

MNC control systems differ with respect to their attention to detail, inclusion of qualitative rather than quantitative criteria, degree of centralisation (*see* 13), level of sophistication (often related to the number of managers needed to operate the system), and the status of the head office personnel to whom reports are submitted. The ideal control system will measure subsidiaries' performances accurately, identify their strengths and weaknesses, establish meaningful operational priorities, and generate useful information for planning and investment decisions. It will facilitate the co-ordination of all the enterprise's activities, highlight potential pitfalls, and provide a basis for evaluating the performances of individual managers.

Controls may be direct or indirect. The former can be exercised via the strict application of standardised operating procedures; through frequent face-to-face meetings between subsidiary and head office staff (at which problems are discussed and future actions determined); by having expatriates occupy key positions in all foreign subsidiaries; or through visits to subsidiaries by senior head office executives. Indirect controls, conversely, occur at arm's length through budgeting procedures; the submission of detailed reports to head office; and/or requiring subsidiaries to adhere to preset financial and other ratios.

Use of standard procedures

'Procedures' are standard ways of doing things. The main advantages to having standard procedures are that unqualified and/or recently appointed employees can complete tasks without having to set up administrative frameworks or take decisions, and that duplication of effort may be avoided. Further benefits are that:

(a) There is no need for staff in subsidiary units to exercise discretion when undertaking tasks.

(b) Written records of standard procedures can be kept in a manual.

(c) There is less scope for argument between people in head office and in subsidiaries regarding how work should be completed.

Problems with the application of standard procedures arise when:

- They become out of date but are still utilised.
- Personnel apply them without any thought and in inappropriate situations.

- Procedures are regarded as convenient devices for solving problems that in fact require careful analysis and discussion.
- They become part of a rigid bureaucracy, stifling innovation and creativity.

Procedures should be reviewed periodically in order to assess their value and to determine which should be revised or discarded.

The process of control

In general, the less expensive the control process the better. Thus, automatic control systems that require minimal intervention are normally more efficient than systems which require constant supervision. Control systems need to contain three major elements: information input, data evaluation, and feedback to the controlling authority. Rapid feedback is essential; otherwise problems could develop faster than the controller's capacity to correct them. Action should always be taken when targets are not achieved, since there is little point in installing a sophisticated control mechanism only to ignore the deficiencies it reveals.

The first stage in the control process is the careful description of all current activities. Achievements are compared with targets and, if necessary, corrective action is taken or targets are amended to more realistic levels. Problems inevitably occur. Among the more substantial are the possibilities that:

(a) Current activities may not be reported accurately, comprehensively, or in sufficient detail.

(b) Inappropriate criteria might be used when setting performance objectives, resulting in unattainable targets which render the entire system inoperable.

(c) Historical records of relevant activities could be inadequate.

(d) Information retrieval systems may be faulty.

11. Principles of control

The more clearly specified are a company's mission, strategies, and policies then the more obvious and consistent will be the plans it produces, and hence the more self-evident the types of control mechanism it needs to apply. The following general principles should be adopted when devising a control system:

(a) Controls should focus on the key variables that determine the success or failure of the business. Obviously the control of routine subsidiary duties is important, but the consequences of inadequate control will be nowhere near as catastrophic for the organisation as a whole as neglecting to control success factors that are absolutely critical for the well-being of the entire company.

(b) Reports submitted through the system should relate to issues rather than individual performance. Inaccurate information will be submitted if a report might reveal failure to meet standards, with consequent penalties for the person or subsidiary concerned.

(c) Early feedback on problems should be generated.

(d) The control system should itself be subject to control. Performance of the system should be regularly monitored, especially in relation to its ability to co-ordinate the work of various sections and departments.

(e) Control information needs to be presented to people in formats that appeal to them and which they fully understand.

(f) The system should be financially cost-effective.

(g) Control mechanisms need to be sufficiently flexible to operate effectively even if corporate plans have to be altered.

(h) The information on which a control system is based must be as accurate and comprehensive as possible and directly relevant to the firm's activities.

12. Control by exception

A common approach to the control of international operations is the application of the principle of 'management by exception' (MBE), i.e. the practice of subsidiaries submitting to head office only brief condensed reports on normal operations but extensive reports on deviations from past average performance or targets set in corporate plans. Once established, standards are monitored by picking out significant deviations from predetermined norms. Exceptionally good or bad results are analysed in detail and explanations supplied, but the day to day functioning of the organisation within reasonable divergences from normal practice is not questioned.

MBE enables head office managers to devote their full attention to major strategy issues and avoid becoming immersed in routine subsidiary administration. However MBE does have disadvantages, as follows:

(a) Delays occur between the moment a problem arises at the subsidiary level, the moment it is noticed, and the time remedial action is implemented.

(b) Since 'acceptable deviations' from target performance are tolerated without investigation, it is possible for a subsidiary to be perpetually above or below standard by a relatively small amount without the fact ever being reported.

(c) The administrative work involved in preparing summary statistics to ascertain whether operations are within acceptable limits can itself be extensive.

Note how the revolution in telecommunications and the computerisation of business systems has removed the need for many management by exception proceures. MBE was popular in years past because of the enormous volume of information continuously generated by subsidiaries and the physical impossibility of continuously monitoring their activities. Thus, data was collected continuously but analysed periodically (monthly, quarterly, annually). Today, however, continuous monitoring by head office of all of its foreign subsidiaries' ongoing activities is technically possible. Information on costs, outputs, revenues, and other relevant variables can be fed into a subsidiary's computerised system and instantly transmitted to head office, which can immediately analyse the data and update summaries at once. Head office managers can requisition information at will and order its presentation in any one of a variety of alternative forms.

13. Headquarters–subsidiary relationships

An MNC must decide whether to centralise significant decision making to subsidiary units, or devise a joint headquarters/subsidiary decision making system somewhere between the two extremes. Factors affecting the choice include the following:

(a) *Size and complexity of the enterprise.* Large companies with extensive activities need centralised units to co-ordinate worldwide operations.

(b) *Value of capital assets.* Head office may be loath to delegate authority to local units if extremely expensive capital equipment is involved.

(c) *Ownership of the firm.* If a company is largely owned by one or just a handful of shareholders then its management may feel obliged to centralise its administration. Diverse shareholding – especially if large shareholders are to be found in host countries – could favour decentralisation.

(d) *Nature, extent and intensity of local competition.* Highly competitive environments require immediate responses at the local level, without having constantly to refer back to head office for direction.

(e) *Opportunities for achieving production and administration economies of scale through centralisation.*

(f) *Degree of interdependence among subsidiaries.* If units in some nations require inputs from subsidiaries in others then close central control and co-ordination will be needed.

(g) *Level of sophistication of the technology used in production.* Technological complexity and/or the need to protect intellectual property favour centralisation of decision making.

Centralised decision making is encouraged by rationalisation of production and marketing policies and systems and the standardisation of products and promotional campaigns. Other influences favouring centralisation include:

- the need to co-ordinate the firm's logistical systems
- low levels of diversification
- stable commercial environments.

It is unlikely, moreover, that a firm which sets up its own foreign subsidiaries from scratch will be more centralised than one which purchases existing self-contained businesses.

Factors favouring *decentralised* MNC decision making include:

- The fast rate at which economic, social, financial and political conditions are changing throughout the world, resulting in head office managers not being able to keep abreast of current developments.
- Differences in market characteristics, management style and employee relations norms and systems in various nations.

- Inability of head office managers to cope with problems arising at the subsidiary level.
- Legal requirements imposed by host country governments that local nationals have executive control over specific matters.
- Diversity in the company's range of products.
- Lack of knowledge, skills and managerial competence among head office managers.
- Significant international differences in marketing mix requirements for the company's outputs.
- The need to develop and motivate managers in subsidiary units.

14. Advantages and disadvantages of decentralised decision making

Decentralisation of decision making to subsidiaries has the following advantages:

(a) Senior executives can devote their time to strategic planning while leaving operational matters to expert local managers. Those at the top can take an overall bird's-eye view of the situation.

(b) Local initiative is encouraged.

(c) The organisation becomes responsive to local conditions.

(d) There is less red tape and hence faster decision taking.

(e) Local circumstances are taken into account when policies are determined.

(f) Managerial jobs in decentralised units become more interesting so that the organisation can attract better-quality managerial staff.

(g) Decentralised managers acquire the experience needed for more senior positions.

In a *centralised* decision making system, subsidiary managers are bound by fixed rules and directives and exercise little discretion in the course of their work. The advantages of centralisation include the following:

(a) All major decisions can be directly related to the core objectives of the enterprise.

(b) There are no possibilities for disagreements and haggling between different decentralised units.

(c) All the firm's activities are subject to direct and immediate control.

(d) There is fast decision taking with little red tape or duplication of effort in subsidiary units.

(e) Co-ordination of activities is enhanced.

(f) Correct working methods can be imposed on all parts of the organisation.

(g) The administrative system is clear and (hopefully) uncomplicated.

Disadvantages of centralisation are as follows:

(a) The organisation becomes inflexible and possibly unable to adapt to change.

(b) Senior managers might receive so much complex information from subordinates that important matters may be overlooked.

(c) Orders issued at the top of the organisation may be so irrelevant to the needs of component units that junior managers in charge of these units may simply ignore them.

(d) The initiative and expertise of junior managers in daily contact with local operations might not be fully utilised. Local circumstances might not be considered when policies are determined.

(e) Strategic problems may be ignored through top management spending too much time on operational issues.

In practice a two-tier mechanism might be feasible with tight and centralised monitoring and control of some subsidiary units and functions, and the adoption of an arms-length approach elsewhere. It is likely in this case that decisions on functions with company-wide implication (financial management, strategic planning, resource allocation for example) will be centralised at head office, leaving routine decisions concerning local market research, pricing within particular markets, local procurement, personnel matters, etc., to be taken at the subsidiary level. Certain decisions will require meetings and consultations between managers from subsidiaries and from headquarters. These might relate to international advertising and sales promotions, manufacturing strategies, performance standards and monitoring, quality management and so on. Sometimes head office will take the majority of decisions during the early stages of the life of a subsidiary, gradually devolving higher levels of autonomy to it as it matures and its local managers gain experience.

A further possiblity is for an MNC to establish regional offices which take over certain headquarters functions. Regional centres might be located in major foreign markets (to minimise communication and travel expenses), especially in areas with extensive local commercial services (capital markets, agents, insurance and transportation companies, advertising agencies, import/export merchants and so on). Decision making is decentralised to regional offices, which themselves control local subsidiaries in a centralised fashion.

15. Appraising the performances of foreign subsidiaries

The purposes of appraising foreign subsidiaries are to identify best and worse practices across the entire operation; to direct resources to their most efficient uses; inform local managers about how well they are performing relative to units in other regions; and facilitiate human resources planning (promotion, training, redundancy, etc.). Effective appraisal of a subsidiary relies critically on accurate measurement of its performance. Typically, head office will establish standards and measure and establish the reasons for deviations from these norms.

Standards might be set for each particular subsidiary, and performance assessed against these unique yardsticks, or an indentical set of standards could be applied to all subsidiaries, so that the performance of each unit can be evaluated against the performance levels achieved by the others. The advantage to the latter method is that standardised record keeping and reporting procedures may be applied to all subsidiaries.

Evaluating the relative performances of diverse foreign subsidiaries can be extremely difficult. MNCs frequently engage in transfer pricing in order to maximise returns to the company *as a whole*, and they shift cash between nations so as to minimise aggregate worldwide tax liability. Such actions obviously affect the book profits (and hence percentage tax returns on investment) recorded by particular subsidiaries. Also the profitabilities of foreign subsidiaries will be affected by many factors beyond the parent company's control. Returns in one country may be much lower than in others through taxes, laws, regulations, etc., specific to that country, not through inefficiency in the subsidiary. It is a fundamental principle of international management that individual subsidiary managers not be penalised for the detrimental effects of local environmental conditions beyond their control.

Specific problems that arise when appraising foreign subsidiaries are as follows:

(a) *Choice of currency for measuring profits.* Evaluation against hard quantitive criteria is obviously desirable, but comparisons of subsidiaries' achievements in monetary terms (levels of sales, costs, wage payments, etc.) may not be meaningful because rates of inflation vary enormously between countries. If values are measured in local currency terms, managers in countries with the highest rates of inflation will show the best performances. Why not, therefore, measure monetary variables in real terms expressed in local currency units? The difficulty here is that to compare one operation with others it is necessary to convert the real performance achieved in local currency into some other base currency. Suppose for instance a UK-domiciled MNC has plants in Spain, Nigeria and Hong Kong and the profitabilities of these are to be compared. Spanish profits (albeit measured in real terms against some base year) are expressed in pesetas. Nigerian profits in naire, Hong Kong profits in Hong Kong dollars. Meaningful comparisons between the three are not possible unless monetary values are converted into a base currency, say sterling. But then the reported results will depend crucially on fluctuations in the rates of exchange between local currencies and the chosen base. Conversions into the base currency can be made at the spot rate prevailing at the moment of conversion, a forecast spot rate for some time in the future, or an average spot rate calculated over (say) the previous six months. Inflation in the home country will affect currency exchange rates with other countries depending on the extent of the home country's foreign trade with them. Note moreover how a currency devaluation by a host country government makes it easier for a subsidiary to export its output (since foreign selling prices can be reduced in consequence of the devaluation), and *vice versa* for an increase in the host nation's rate of exchange.

(b) *Differing accounting conventions in host countries.* Accounting conventions vary throughout the world (see Chapter 15 for information on this matter). There are different rules governing share issue, disclosure, debenture arrangements, etc., between nations. Such conventions may be so fundamental that the creation of an entirely separate set of books for the MNC's own auditing might be impossible, or at least extremely difficult. Another question is how to measure a subsidiary's net income. Should this include service fees and overhead charges imposed by headquarters?

(c) *Delays in reporting.* Despite vastly improved communications and the increasing availability of international computer linkages, long delays in the transmission of important data might occur. Subsidiaries might not realise the significance of a particular piece of information for the global strategy of the parent corporation, and thus report it late or exclude it altogether.

(d) *Differences in the quality of the workforces available in various regions.* These can be enormous, and might greatly affect productivity levels achieved by subsidiaries in disparate nations.

Appraising an international division
Difficulties similar to those encountered when appraising subsidiaries arise when evaluating the performance of a firm's international division. These problems include:

- Deciding whether divisions should manage their own cash balances or turn them over to a central treasury for investment outside the division (externally or elsewhere in the company)
- Overhead allocations in relation to shared common services (administrative premises for instances) and matching these to estimates for divisional rates or return on capital employed
- Assessing the effects of company policies on the profits made by a particular division (e.g. the effects of artificially low input prices from other division)
- Choice of criteria for measuring profitability (absolute money values, rates or return on capital employed, etc.)
- Deciding whether each division is to be regarded as a cost centre in its own right ('buying in' materials and services from other divisions).

Progress test 20

1. Define planning.

2. What are the advantages of planning?

3. List the problems associates with informal planning procedures.

4. What is the purpose of gap analysis?

5. What is meant by the term 'environmental scanning'?

6. Explain the difference between the top-down planning and bottom-up planning.

7. Control has three aspects. What are they?

8. State the characteristics of an ideal control system for an MNC.

9. What is a 'procedure'?

10. Explain the concept of control by exception.

11. List the main advantages of centralised MNC decision making.

12. What are the major problems that might arise when appraising foreign subsidiaries?

REFERENCES AND BIBLIOGRAPHY

Abell, M. (ed) (1991), *European Franchising: Law and Practice*, Waterlow.

Agrawal, M. (1995), 'Review of a 40-year Debate in International Advertising: Practitioner and Academician Perspectives on the Standardisation/Adaptation Issue, *International Marketing Review*, 12(1), 26–48.

Alexander, D. (1993), 'A European True and Fair View', *European Accounting Review*, 2, (1), 59–80.

Anderson, O. (1993), 'On the Internationalisation Process of Firms', *Journal of International Business Studies*, Vol.24(2).

Andersen, S.S. and Eliassen, K.A. (1993), *Making Policy in Europe*, Sage.

Anholt, S. (1993), 'Adapting Advertising Copy Across Frontiers', *Admap*, Vol.28(10).

Ansoff, H.I. (1957), 'Strategies for Diversification', *Harvard Business Review*, Sept–Oct.

Archer, C. (1994), *Organizing Europe: The Institutions of Integration*, Edward Arnold.

Ash, N. (1990), 'The Privatization Dilemma', *Euromoney*, September.

Aylen, J. (1987), 'Privatization in Developing Countries', *Lloyds Bank Review*, Issue 163.

August, R. (1993), *International Business Law*, Prentice-Hall.

Baalbaki, I.B. and Malhotra, N.K. (1993), 'Marketing Management Bases for International Market Segmentation', *International Marketing Review*, Vol.10(1).

Van Bael, I. (1990), *Anti-Dumping and Other Trade Protection Laws of the EEC*, 2nd edition, CCH Publishing.

Baines, A. (1995), *Handbook of International Direct Marketing*, Kogan Page.

Balling, M. (1993), *Financial Management in the New Europe*, Basil Blackwell.

Barrell, R. (1990), 'European Currency Union and the EMS', *NIESR Review*, May.

Bartels, R. (1968), 'Are Domestic and International Marketing Dissimilar?', *Journal of Marketing*, Vol.32.

Bean, C. (1992), 'Economic and Monetary Union in Europe', *Journal of Economic Perspectives*, 6(4), 31–52.

Belkaoui, A. (1990), *Judgement in International Accounting: A Theory of Cognition, Cultures, Language and Contracts*, Quorum Publishers.

Bennett, R. (1996), 'Doing Business in a Single European Currency', *International Small Business Journal*, 14(2), 1–7.

Black, J.S. and Gregersen, H.B. (1991), 'The Other Half of the Picture. Antecedents of Spouse Cross-Cultural Adjustment', *Journal of International Business Studies*, 15(3), 19–23.

Boatright, J.R. (1993), *Ethics and the Conduct of Business*, Prentice-Hall.

Baddewyn, J. (1983), 'Foreign and Domestic Divestment and Investment Decisions', *Journal of International Business Studies*, 14(3), 23–35.

Bonaccorsi, A. (1992), 'The Relationship Between Firm Size and Export Intensity', *Journal of International Business Studies*, 23(4), 605–635.

Borden, N.H. (1965), 'The Concept of the Marketing Mix', *Science in Marketing*, (ed), G. Schwartz, Wiley.

Boyacigiller, N. (1991), 'The Role of Expatriates in the Management of Interdependence, Complexity and Risk in Multinational Corporations', *Journal of International Business Studies*, October.

Brewster, C. (1991), *Management of Expatriates*, 2nd edition, Kogan Page.

Brewster, C. (1994), 'European Human Resource Management versus the American Concept', in Kirkbride, P.S. (ed), *Human Resource Management in Europe*, Routledge.

Brewster, C. and Bournois, F. (1991), 'Human Resource Management: A European Perspective', *Personnel Review*, 20(6), 4–11.

Brewster, C. and Hegewisch, A. (eds), (1994), 'Policy and Practice in European Human Resource Management', *Price Waterhouse/Cranfield Survey*, Routledge.

Bridgeford, J. and Sterling, S. (1994), *Employee Relations in Europe*, Blackwell.

Britton, A. and Mayes, D. (1992), *Achieving Monetary Union in Europe*, Sage.

Brown, L. (1994), *Competitive Marketing Strategy for Europe: Developing, Maintaining and Defending Competitive Advantage*, Macmillan.

Buckley, P.J. and Casson, M. (1976), *The Future of the Multinational Enterprise*, Macmillan.

Buckley, P.J., Pass, C. and Prescott, K. (1989), 'Measures of International Competitiveness: A Critical Survey', *Journal of Marketing Management*, Vol.4(2).

Burt, S. (1989), *Trends and Management Issues in European Retailing*, MCB University Press.

Calof, J.L. and Bearush, P.W. (1995), 'Adapting to Foreign Markets: Explaining Internationalisation', *International Business Review*, 4(2), 115–132.

Carusgil, T., Yavas, U. and Bykowicz, S. (1992), 'Preparing Executives for Overseas Assignments', *Management Decision*, 30, MCB University Press.

Cheng, J.L. (1993), 'The Management of Multinational R&D: A Neglected Topic in International Business Research', *Journal of International Business Studies*, 24(1), 4–24.

Cho, K.R. (1988), 'Issues of Compensation in International Technology Licensing', *Management International Review*, 28(2), 70–79.

Christou, R. (1990), *International Agency, Distribution and Licensing Agreements*, 2nd edition, Longman.

Cobham, D. (1991), 'European Monetary Integration: A Survey of Recent Literature', *Journal of Common Market Studies*, 29(4), 363–83.

Commission of the European Communities [CEC], (1990a), 'Industrial Policy in an Open and Competitive Environment: Guidelines for a Community Approach', *COM* (90) 556, in *Bulletin of the European Communities: European Industrial Policy for the 1990s*, Supplement 3/91 (Luxembourg).

Commission of the European Communities [CEC], (1990b), 'Enterprise Policy: A New Dimension for Small and Medium-sized Enterprises', *COM* (90) 328.

Commission of the European Communities [CEC], (1991), 'One Market, One Money', *European Economy*, 44, Commission of the European Communities, Brussels.

Commission of the European Communities [CEC], (1992a), *Easier Cross-Border Payment*, Commission of the European Communities, Brussels.

Commission of the European Communities [CEC], (1992b), *Twenty-First Report on Competition Policy*, Office for Official Publications of the European Community, Luxembourg.

Commission of the European Communities [CEC], (1993a), *Accounting Standards Setting in the EC Member States*, Luxembourg: Office for Official Publications of the European Communities.

Commission of the European Communities [CEC], (1993b), 'The European Community as a World Trade Partner', *European Economy*, No.52.

Commission of the European Communities [CEC], (1996), *Panorama of EU Industries 1995/96*, CEC, Luxembourg.

Corbett, R. (1993), *The Treaty of Maastricht From Conception to Ratification*, Longman.

Cordell, V.V. and Wogtada, N. (1991), 'Modelling Determinants of Cross-Boarder Trade in Counterfeit Goods', *Journal of Global Marketing*, Vol.4(3).

Crawford, M. (ed) (1993), *One Money for Europe*, Macmillan.

Crouch, C. (1993), *Industrial Relations and European State Traditions*, Clarendon.

Dany, F. and Torchy, V. (1994), 'Recruitment and Selection in Europe: Policies, Practices and Methods', in Brewster, C. and Hegewisch, A., *Policy and Practice in European Human Resource Management*, The Price Waterhouse/Cranfield Survey, Routledge.

Day, E., Fox, R.J. and Huszagh, S.M. (1988), 'Segmenting the Global Market', *International Marketing Review*, 5(3), 14–27.

Delors, J. (1989), *Report on Economic and Monetary Union in the European Community*, CEC, Committee for the Study of Economic and Monetary Union, Brussels.

Desta, S. (1985), 'Assessing Political Risk in Less Developed Countries', *Journal of Business Strategy*, 5(5), 40–53.

Devereux, M. and Pearson, M. (1989), *Corporate Tax Harmonisation and Economic Efficiency*, Institute of Fiscal Studies.

Dinan, D. (1994), *Ever Closer Union? An Introduction to the European Community*, Macmillan.

Dore, I.I. (1993), *The UNCITRAL Framework for Arbitration in Contemporary Perspective*, Graham and Trotman.

Dunning, J.H. (1981), *International Production and the Multinational Enterprise*, Allen and Unwin.

Dunning, J.H. (1988), 'The Eclectic Paradigm of International Trade: A Restatement and Some Possible Extensions', *Journal of International Business Studies*, Spring.

Dunning, J.H. (1992), 'The Global Economy, Domestic Governance Strategies and Transnational Corporations: Interactions and Policy Implications', *Transnational Corporations*, 1(3), 7–45.

Economist Intelligence Unit (1994), *Predicting European Banking and Capital Markets*, EIU.

Eichengreen, B. (1991), *Is Europe an Optimum Currency Area?*, National Bureau of Economic Research, Cambridge, Mass.

Eichengreen, B. (1993), 'European Monetary Union', *Journal of Economic Literature*, 31(3), 1321–57.

Emerson, M. and Huhne, C. (1991), *The ECU Report*, Pan.

European Industrial Relations Review [EIRR], (1994a), 'Farewell European Works Councils?', *EIRR*, 242, March.

European Industrial Relations Review [EIRR], (1994b), 'European Works Councils – The Action Begins', *EIRR*, 250, November, pp.14–17.

Eurostat (1995), *Data for Short Term Economic Analysis*, Statistical Office of the European Communities, Luxembourg.

Fagan, M.L. (1991), 'A Guide to Global Sourcing', *Journal of Business Strategy*, April 1991, 21–30.

Fagre, N. and Wells, L.T. (1982), 'Bargaining Power of Multinationals and Host Governments', *Journal of International Business Studies*, 8(2), 9–23.

Featherstone, K. and Ginberg, R. (1993), *The United States and the European Community in the 1990s: Partners in Transition*, Macmillan.

Ferner, A. and Hyman, R. (eds), (1992), *Industrial Relations in the New Europe*, Blackwell.

Ferraro, G.P. (1990), *The Cultural Dimension of International Business*, Prentice-Hall.

Fleming, J.M. (1971), 'On Exchange Rate Unification', *Economic Journal*, Vol.81, 467–488.

Francis, J. (1991), 'The Effects of Cultural Adaptation on International Business Negotiations', *Journal of International Business Studies*, 22(3), 421–422.

Frederick, W.C. (1991), 'Moral Authority of Transnational Corporate Codes', *Journal of Business Ethics*, March 1991, 166–176.

Frydman, R. and Rapaczynski, A. (1993), 'Privatisation in Eastern Europe', *Finance and Development*, June 1993, 12–15.

Gammie, M. (1992), *The Ruding Committee Report: An Initial Response*, Institute for Fiscal Studies.

Gates, S.R. and Engelhoff, W.G. (1986), 'Centralisation in Headquarters – Subsidiary Relationships', *Journal of International Business Studies*, Summer, 1986.

Geroski, P. (1989), 'European Industrial Policy and Industrial Policy in Europe', *Oxford Review of Economic Policy*, 5(0.2), 20–36.

Giles, M. (1986), 'Coping with the New Protectionism', *International Management*, 41(9), 20–26.

Gold, M. (1993), *The Social Dimension: Employment Policy in the European Community*, Macmillan.

Goshal, S. and Nohria, N. (1993), 'Organisational Forms for Multinational Corporations', *Sloan Management Review*, Winter, 1993, 23–35.

Grahl, J. and Teague, P. (1991), 'Industrial Relations Trajectories and European Human Resource Management', in Brewster, C. and Tyson, S. (eds), *International Comparisons in Human Resource Management*, Pitman.

Greenwood, J. *et al.* (eds) (1992), *Organized Interests and the European Community*, Sage.

Grilli, E. (1993), *The European Community and the Developing Countries*, Cambridge University Press.

Gros, D. and Thygesen, M. (1992), *European Monetary Integration: From the European Monetary System to European Monetary Union*, Longman.

Grubel, H.G. (1970), 'The Theory of Optimum Currency Areas', *Canadian Journal of Economics*, 53(2), 318–324.

Guild, I. (1985), *Forfaiting: An Alternative Approach to Export Trade Financing*, Woodhead-Faulkner.

Haack, W.G.C.M. (1972), 'The Economic Effects of Britain's Entry into the Common Market', *Journal of Common Market Studies*, 11(2), December.

Hamill, J. (1992), 'Cross-Border Mergers, Acquisitions and Alliances in Europe', in S. Young and J. Hamill (eds), *Europe and the Multinationals: Issue and Responses for the 1990s*, Edward Elgar.

Hamilton, C. and Winter, L.A. (1992), 'Opening Up International Trade in Eastern Europe', *Economic Policy*, 14(1), 77–116.

Harrell, G.D. and Kiefer, R.O. (1993), 'Multinational Market Portfolios in Global Strategy', *International Marketing Review*, 10(1), 60–73.

Harvey, M.G. and Lusch, R.F. (1995), 'A Systematic Assessment of Potential International Strategic Alliance Partners', *International Business Review*, 4(2), 195–212.

Hawk, B. (ed), (1991), *International Mergers and Joint Ventures*, Chancery Law Publishing.

Hawkins, D.T. (1993), *Business of Factoring: A Guide to Factoring and Invoice Discounting*, McGraw-Hill.

Hartmann, F.H. (1983), *The Relations of Nations*, 6th edition, Macmillan.

Hegarty, J. (1993), 'Accounting Integration in Europe – Still on Track?', *Journal of Accountancy*, 175(1), 92–5.

Hegewisch, A. (1993), 'The Decentralisation of Pay Bargaining: European Comparisons', in Hegewisch, A. and Brewster, C. (eds), *European Developments in Human Resource Management*, Kogan Page.

Helm, D. (1993), 'The European Internal Market: The Next Steps', *Oxford Review of Economic Policy*, 9(1), 1–14.

Hofstede, G. (1980), *Culture's Consequences: International Differences in Work Related Values*, Sage.

Hofstede, G. (1991), *Cultures and Organisations*, McGraw-Hill.

Hollinshead, G. and Leat, M. (1995), *Human Resource Management: An International and Comparative Perspective*, Pitman.

Hollis Europe, *The Directory of European Public Relations and PR Networks 1995–96*, 5th edition, Hollis, 1995.

Van Hulle, K. (1993), 'Harmonization of Accounting Standards in the EC. Is it the Beginning or the End?', *European Accounting Review*, 2(3), 387–96.

Hymer, S.H. (1976), *The International Operations of National Firms: A Study of Direct Investment*, MIT Press, Cambridge, Mass.

Incomes Data Services (1995), *Contracts and Terms and Conditions of Employment*, Institute of Personnel and Development.

Jackson, J.H. (1990), *Restructuring the GATT System*, Pinter.

Jacquemin, A. (1993), 'The International Dimension of European Competition Policy', *Journal of Common Market Studies*, 31(1), 91–101.

Jacquemin, A. and Wright, D. (1993), 'Corporate Strategies and European Challenges Post-1992', *Journal of Common Market Studies*, 31(4), 525–37.

James, C.D. (1987), *Tariff and Non-Tariff Barriers to Trade*, Department of Trade and Industry.

Jeffcote, B. (1993), *The Developing European Corporate Tax System*, Macmillan.

Johansson, J.K. and Thorelli, H.B. (1985), 'International Product Positioning', *Journal of International Business Studies*, 16(3), 57–75.

Johnson, H.G. (1963), 'Equilibrium Under Fixed Exchange Rates', *American Economic Review*, Vol.53, 112–116, (Papers and Proceedings).

Julius, D.A. (1990), *Global Companies and Public Policy: The Growing Challenge of Foreign Investment*, Pinter, for The Royal Institute of International Affairs.

Justicia, I. (1994), 'European Late Payments Survey', *Euro-Information*, December 1994, 75/94/EN, Commission of the European Communities.

Kay, N. (1993), 'Mergers, Acquisitions and the Completion of the Internal Market', in K.S. Hughes (ed), *European Competitiveness*, Cambridge University.

O'Keefe, D. and Twomey, P.M. (eds), (1994), *Legal Issues of the Maastricht Treaty*, Chancery.

Khan, M.S. (1988), 'Islamic Interest Free Banking', *IMF Fund Papers*, March 1988.

Kirkbride, P.S. (ed), (1994), *Human Resource Management in Europe: Perspectives for the 1990s*, Routledge.

Kotabe, M. (1989), 'Creating Countertrade Opportunities in Financially Distressed Developing Countries', *International Marketing Review*, 6(5), 36–49.

Kotabe, M. (1993), 'Patterns and Technological Implications of Global Sourcing Strategies', *Journal of International Marketing*, 11(1), 26–43.

Kotler, P. (1984), 'Rethinking the Marketing Concept', in *American Marketing Association News*, Vol.18, 1984.

Krugman, P. (1979), 'A Model of Innovation, Technology Transfer and the World Distribution of Income', *Journal of Political Economy*, 87(1), 253–266.

Kwon, Y.C. and Konopa, L.J. (1993), 'Impact of Host Country Market Characteristics on the Choice of Foreign Market Entry Mode', *International Marketing Review*, Vol.10(2).

Lamming, R. (1993), *Beyond Partnership: Strategies for Innovation and Lean Supply Relationships*, Prentice-Hall.

Lasok, D. and Bridge, J.W. (1991), *Law and Institutions of the European Communities*, 5th edition, Butterworths.

Lawrence, P. (1993), 'Human Resource Management in Germany', in Tyson, S., *et al.*, *Human Resource Management in Europe, Strategic Issues and Cases*, Kogan Page.

Leeds, C., Kirkbride, P.S. and Durcan, J. (1994), 'The Cultural Context of Europe: A Tentative Mapping', in Kirkbride, P.S., *Human Resource Management in Europe: Perspectives of the 1990s*, Routledge.

Lefferink, J.D. (ed), (1993), *European Integration and Environmental Policy*, Belhaven.

Levitt, T. (1983), 'The Globalisation of Markets', *Harvard Business Review*, Vol.61, May/June.

Litka, M. (1991), *International Dimension of the Legal Environment of Business*, PWS Kent, Boston.

Littler, D. and Schlieper, K. (1995), 'The Development of the Eurobrand', *International Marketing Review*, 12(2), 22–37.

Lodge, J. (ed), (1994), *The European Community and the Challenge of the Future*, 2nd edition, Pinter Publishers.

Lorange, P. and Roos, J. (1992), *Strategic Alliances: Formation, Implementation and Evolution*, Blackwell.

McCarthy, E.J. (1981), *Basic Marketing: A Managerial Approach*, Irwin.

McEnery, J. and Desharnais, G. (1990), 'Culture Shock', *Training and Development Journal*, April 1990.

McKinnon, R. (1977), 'The Euro-Currency Markets', *Essays in International Finance*, No.125, Princeton University, December 1977.

Magnifico, G. (1973), *European Monetary Unification*, Macmillan.

Maresceau, M. (ed), (1993), *The European Community's Commercial Policy After 1992*, Dordrecht: Martinus Nijhoff.

Maronick, T.J. (1988), 'European Patent Laws and Decisions: Implications for Multinational Marketing Strategy', *International Marketing Review*, 5(2), 20–30.

Maskers, K.E. (1993), 'Intellectual Property Right and the Uruguay Round', *Economic Review*, Spring 1993, 11–26.

Matsumoto, K. and Finlayson, G. (1990), 'Dumping and Anti-dumping: Growing Problems in World Trade', *Journal of World Trade*, Vol.24(4).

Mayes, D. (ed), (1993), *The External Implications of European Integration*, Harvester-Wheatsheaf.

Mazey, S. and Richardson, J. (1993), *Lobbying in the European Community*, Oxford University Press.

Mendelsohn, M. (1993), *Franchising in Europe*, Cassell.

Mendelsohn, M. and Harris, B. (1991), *Franchising and the Block Exemption Regulation*, Longman.

Millet, T. (1990), *The Court of First Instance of the European Communities*, Butterworths.

Mole, J. (1990), *Mind Your Manners: Managing Culture Clash in the Single European Market*, Industrial Society.

Monnet, J. (1978), *Memoirs*, Collins.

Moynihan, M. (1993), 'How MNCs Ease Expatriates' Return to Home Countries', *Business International*, February 1993.

Mundell, R.A. (1961), 'A Theory of Optimum Currency Areas', *American Economic Review*, 51(4), 657–664.

Murdock, G.P. (1945), 'The Common Denominator of Cultures', in R. Linton (ed), *The Science of Man*, Columbia University Press.

Neven, D. Nuttall, R. and Seabright, P. (1993), *Merger in Daylight: The Economics and Politics of European Merger Control*, Centre for Economic Policy Research.

Nicolaides, P. (1989), 'Economic Aspects of Services: Implications for a GATT Agreement', *Journal of World Trade*, 23(1), 125–136.

Nicoll, W. and Salmon, T.C. (1994), *Understanding the New European Community*, 2nd edition, Harvester-Wheatsheaf.

Nugent, N. (1994), *The Government and Politics of the European Union*, 3rd edition, Macmillan.

Ohlin, B. (1933), *Interregional and International Trade*, Harvard University Press.

Ohmae, K. (1985), *Triad Power, The Coming Shape of Global Competition*, The Free Press.

Ouchi, W.G. (1981), *Theory Z: How American Business Can Meet the Japanese Challenge*, Addison-Wesley.

Page, S. (1991), *The GATT Uruguay Round: Effects on Developing Countries*, Overseas Development Institute.

Papadopoulos, N. and Heslop, L. (eds), (1992), *Product Country Images: Impact and Role in International Marketing*, Irwin.

Peterson, J. (1992), 'Technology Policy in Europe: Explaining the Framework Programme and Eureka in Theory and Practice', *Journal of Common Market Studies*, 24(3), 269–90.

Pitt-Watson, D. and Frazer, S. (1991), 'Eastern Europe: Commercial Opportunity or Illusion?', *Long Range Planning*, 24(5), 19–24.

Poirson, P. (1993), 'Human Resource Management in France', in Tyson, S., *et al.* (eds), *Human Resource Management in Europe*, Kogan Page.

Poorsoltan, K. (1993), 'The US and Mexico Debate Free Trade', *Contemporary Review*, Vol.263, October 1993.

Porter, M. (1980), *Competitive Strategy*, The Free Press.

Porter, M. (1990), *The Competitive Advantages of Nations*, Macmillan.

Pucik, V. (1984), 'The International Management of Human Resources' in Fombrun, C.J., Tichy, N.M. and Devanna, M.A. (eds), *Strategic Human Resources Management*, Wiley.

Randlesome, C., Brierly, W., Burton, K., Gordon, C. and King, P. (1990), *Business Cultures in Europe*, Heinemann.

Rhodes, M. (1991), 'The Social Dimension of the Single European Market', *European Journal of Political Research*, 19(1), 245–80.

Rhodes, M. (1992), 'The Future of the Social Dimension', *Journal of Common Market Studies*, 30(1), 27–35.

Robson, P. and Wooton, I. (1993), 'The Transnational Enterprise and Regional Economic Integration', *Journal of Common Market Studies*, 31(1), 71–90.

Roney, A. (1993), *The European Community Factbook*, 3rd edition, Kogan Page.

Roessler, F. (1985), 'The Scope, Limits and Function of the GATT Legal System', *The World Economy*, 8(4), 287–298.

Rothery, B. (1992), *BS7750: The International Environment Standard*, Gower.

Royal Mail International (1994), *Marketing Without Frontiers*, 2nd edition, RMI.

Ruding, O. (1992), *Ruding Report (Committee on the Taxation of Enterprises Within the EC)*, Luxembourg, Office for Official Publications of the European Communities.

Samiee, S. and Roth, K. (1992), 'The Influence of Global Marketing', *Journal of Marketing*, Vol.56, April 1992.

Sbragia, A. (ed), (1993), *Euro-Politics: Institutions and Policymaking in the New European Community*, The Brookings Institution.

Schwartz, G. and Lopes, P.S. (1993), 'Privatisation: Expectations, Trade-Offs and Results', *Finance and Development*, June 1993, 15–21.

Seringhaus, F.H. (1986), 'The Impact of Government Export Marketing Assistance', *International Marketing Review*, 3(2), 37–56.

Sharp, M. and Pavitt, K. (1993), 'Technology Policy in the 1990s: Old Trends and New Realities', *Journal of Common Market Studies*, 31(2), 129–51.

Simpson, J.R. (1991), 'Rules of Origin in Transition', *Law and Policy in International Business*, 22(4), 665–672.

Singleton, S. (1995), 'Franchising', *Europe Bulletin*, Issue 29, July.

Starr, P. (1989), 'The Meaning of Privatization', in *Privatization and the Welfare State* (eds Kamerman, S.B. and Khan, A.), Princeton University Press.

Stalk, G. (1990), *Competing Against Time: How Time-Based Competition is Reshaping Global Markets*, Collier Macmillan.

Streeton, P. (1992), 'Interdependence and Integration of the World Economy The Rule of States and Firms', *Transnational Corporations*, 1(3), 125–36.

Subhash, C.J. and Tucker, L.R. (1995), 'The Influence of Culture on Strategic Constructs in the Process of Globalisation', *International Business Review*, 4(1), 19–38.

Swamidass, P.M. (1993), 'Import Sourcing Dynamics: An Integrated Perspective', *Journal of International Business Studies*, 24(4), 93–114.

Teague, P. (1993), 'Between Convergence and Divergence: Possibilities for a European Community System of Labour Market Regulation', *International Labour Review*, 123(3), 391–406.

Terpstra, V. (1987), 'The Evolution of International Marketing', *International Marketing Review*, Summer, 1987.

Thorelli, H.B. (1966), 'The Multinational Corporation as a Charge Agent', *Southern Journal of Business*, July, 1966, 5–11.

Tillotson, J. (1993), *European Community law: Text, Cases and Materials*, Cavendish Publishing.

Tixier, M. (1994), 'Management and Communication Styles in Europe: Can They Be Compared and Matched?', *Employee Relations Journal*, 16(1), 8–26.

de la Torre, J. and Neckar, D.H. (1988), 'Forecasting Political Risk for International Operations', *International Journal of Forecasting*, 4(1), 221–230.

Tsoukalis, L. (1993), *The New European Economy: The Politics and Economics of Integration*, Oxford University Press.

US International Trade Commission (1993), *Potential Impact on the US Economy of the North American Free Trade Agreement*, US Congress, 1993.

Usunier, J.C. (1993), *International Marketing: A Cultural Approach*, Prentice-Hall.

Verzariu, P. (1985), *Countertrade, Barter Offsets*, McGraw-Hill.

Walsh, V. (1992), *Winning by Design: Technology, Product Design and International Competitiveness*, Blackwell Business.

Watkins, K. (1992), *Fixing the Rules: North-South Issues in International Trade and the GATT Uruguay Round*, Institute for International Relations, London, 1992.

Weigand, R.E. (1991), 'Parallel Import Channels', *Colombia Journal of World Business*, Spring, 1991.

Weiss, K. and Grippo, L.E. (1992), 'Look Carefully Before you Leap into that Overseas Assignment', *Journal of European Business*, June, 1992.

Welch, L.S. (1992), 'Developments in International Franchising', *Journal of Global Marketing*, 6(2), 81–96.

Welch, L.S. and Pacifico, A. (1990), 'Management Contracts: A Role in Internationalisation', 7(4), 64–74.

Wells, L.T. (ed), (1972), *The Product Life Cycle and International Trade*, Harvard University Press.

Wells, L.T. (1980), 'A Product Lifecycle for International Trade', in *International Marketing Strategy*, eds, H. Thorelli and H. Becker, Pergamon, New York.

Welt, L. (1990), *Trade Without Money: Barter and Countertrade*, Harcourt Brace Jovanovich, New York, 1990.

Whitelock, J.M. (1987), 'Global Marketing and the Case for International Product Standardisation', *European Journal of Marketing*, 23(7), 60–7.

Whittaker, S. and Roney, A. (1993), *Guidance on the Commercial Agents Regulations*, London Chamber of Commerce and Industry.

Wills, J. Jacobs, L. and Palia, A. (1986), 'Countertrade', *International Marketing Review*, Vol.3(2).

Wise, M. and Gibb, R. (1993), *Single Market to Social Europe: The European Community in the 1990s*, Longman.

Wortzel, L.H. (1990), 'Global Strategies: Standardization Versus Flexibility', in *Global Strategic Management: The Essentials*, 2nd edition (eds, Wortzel, H.V. and Wortzel, L.H.), Wiley.

Wyatt, D. and Dashwood, A. (1993), *European Community Law*, Sweet and Maxwell.

Young, S., Hamill, J., Wheeler, C. and Davies, J.R. (1989), *International Market Entry and Development*, Prentice-Hall.

INDEX